6

Communicating in Groups

Applications and Skills

6

Communicating in Groups
Applications and Skills

Katherine Adams
California State University, Fresno

Gloria J. Galanes
Southwest Missouri State University

McGraw Hill

Boston   Burr Ridge, IL   Dubuque, IA   Madison, WI   New York
San Francisco   St. Louis   Bangkok   Bogotá   Caracas   Kuala Lumpur
Lisbon   London   Madrid   Mexico City   Milan   Montreal   New Delhi
Santiago   Seoul   Singapore   Sydney   Taipei   Toronto

The McGraw-Hill Companies

Mc Graw Hill | Higher Education

COMMUNICATING IN GROUPS: APPLICATIONS AND SKILLS
Published by McGraw-Hill, a business unit of The McGraw-Hill Companies, Inc.,
1221 Avenue of the Americas, New York, NY 10020. Copyright © 2006, 2003, 2000,
1997, 1994, 1991 by The McGraw-Hill Companies, Inc. All rights reserved. No part of
this publication may be reproduced or distributed in any form or by any means, or stored
in a database or retrieval system, without the prior written consent of The McGraw-Hill
Companies, Inc., including, but not limited to, in any network or other electronic storage
or transmission, or broadcast for distance learning.

Some ancillaries, including electronic and print components, may not be available to customers
outside the United States.

This book is printed on acid-free paper.

2 3 4 5 6 7 8 9 0 DOC/DOC 0 9 8 7 6

ISBN-13: 978-0-07-304259-6
ISBN-10: 0-07-304259-5

Publisher: *Phillip A. Butcher*
Executive editor: *Nanette Giles*
Senior developmental editor: *Jennie Katsaros*
Senior marketing manager: *Leslie Oberhuber*
Project manager: *Ruth Smith*
Associate production supervisor: *Jason I. Huls*
Associate designer: *Srdjan Savanovic*
Senior media project manager: *Nancy Garcia*
Manager, Photo research: *Brian Pecko*
Art editor: *Katherine McNab*
Interior and Cover design: *Amanda Kavanagh*
Cover image: *Digital Vision; Don Farrall/Getty Images; Photodisk*
Typeface: *10/12 Garamond Regular*
Compositor: *Cenveo, Indianapolis*
Printer: *R.R. Donnelley and Sons Inc.*

Library of Congress Cataloging-in-Publication Data

Adams, Katherine L.
    Communicating in groups : applications and skills / Katherine Adams, Gloria J.
Galanes.—6th ed.
      p.   cm.
    Includes bibliographical references and index.
    ISBN 0-07-304259-5 (alk. paper)
    1. Small groups. 2. Interpersonal relations. I. Galanes, Gloria J. II. Title.
HM736.A33 2006
302.3'4—dc22

                         2004059543

www.mhhe.com

We dedicate this book to our students,
who teach us as much as we teach them.

People can be motivated to be good not by telling them that hell is a place where they will burn, but by telling them it is an unending committee meeting. On judgment day, the Lord will divide people by telling those on His right hand to enter His kingdom and those on His left to break into small groups.

Rev. Robert Kennedy

This quote, given to us by a student, expresses precisely how many people feel about participating in groups. In fact, it describes some of our own experiences! But the quote's sentiment focuses attention on the torture that participating in small groups can produce—and it ignores the uplifting, energizing effect that can also occur through group participation. Group participation *can* feel like torture, but it can also be incredibly rewarding and a lot of fun. Both of us have had the experience of being in a group that so excited us, made us feel alive, gave us a way to express ourselves, helped us connect with others, and so enabled us to accomplish a tremendous amount of work, that we didn't want to see the group end. Yes, that is a rare occurrence. But in this book, we hope to give students tools to help them attain those ideals by providing insight about how groups work and practical suggestions for applying those insights.

This book is designed for the first or second year student who may not have had a prior communication course and who may never take a subsequent course—but who *must* work in groups because that is the nature of corporate, educational, and civic participation in this day and age. Two overarching goals guide our writing. First, being able to work effectively in groups is not a luxury—it's a necessity. Our introductory students want to cut to the chase; they want to know what works *right now.* That is the reason for our distinctly *practical* focus of *Communicating in Groups.* Although this text uses the same research foundation as our more advanced text, *Effective Group Discussion,* we strive here to provide information in a way that is both useful and immediately usable. Second, we want students to recognize that effective group work is, to a great extent, a matter of *communication behavior,* not a matter of personality or fate. Thus, it is to a great extent within their own control. We want students to start thinking about their own communicative choices in groups and to have the tools to make wise choices so they can make the groups they belong to as rewarding and productive as possible.

To meet our goals, we have chosen to use an informal writing style and to provide many examples from our own and others' experiences. We also report research findings in much less detail, with more synthesis and distillation of findings, fewer footnotes, and less evaluation of competing theories than in our other text. This allows readers to focus on what is usually more important to them—the practical application of the research. Finally, we refer to ourselves, Kathy and Gloria, frequently throughout the text. We think of our readers as individuals with whom we are on a first-name basis and we encourage you to think of us the same way, as if we were members of the same small group.

Overview of the Text

With each revision, the hardest thing we have to do is decide what to include and what to leave out. We try to focus on what we believe are the most important concepts, particularly those that will be most useful and practical for students to understand. In this edition, we continue to cover the influence new communication technologies have on small group communication, clarify and expand our discussion of creativity in groups, add material on cultural dynamics in small groups, and refocus our discussion of leader and leadership. We continue to use general systems theory as our structural framework because we believe it provides a framework that is easy to grasp. As before, the chapters are ordered in a way that is logical to us but that does not preclude other methods of organizing a small group course. Each chapter is self-contained and can be taken in an order different from what we provide here.

Part One provides basic information students need to understand how groups function. Chapter 1 introduces some basic terms encountered throughout the book, shows how to classify groups according to their major purpose, and introduces the concept of ethical behavior of group members. Chapter 2 presents general systems theory as a framework for understanding the complexity of group communication. We provide specific illustrations of systems concepts throughout the rest of the book as well.

Part Two provides the foundation for understanding communication in groups. Chapter 3, which may present review material for some readers, discusses basic communication theory, including what communication is, what constitutes effective listening, and how people interpret what they see and hear. Chapter 4 discusses the specifics of verbal and nonverbal messages. Chapter 5 discusses the creative and critical thinking skills necessary for effective group problem solving. We believe creative and critical thinking are at the heart of the group problem-solving process and that students should know something about these processes before understanding problem solving in general. Chapter 6 describes the problem-solving process and introduces the Procedural Model of Problem Solving as a helpful guideline to follow.

Part Three focuses on the group's throughput processes. Chapter 7 explains how a group develops into a team from an initial collection of individuals. Chapter 8 celebrates group diversity, which is group strength but also presents challenges for members who must manage the diversity of member motivation, learning style, personality, culture, gender, generation, and ethnicity. The chapter also offers SYMLOG as a technique for discussing and capitalizing on member diversity. Chapter 9 explains why group conflicts occur and how they can be managed so that the group benefits instead of suffers. Chapter 10 provides a comprehensive picture of leadership and also gives suggestions for applying leadership principles effectively and ethically.

Part Four presents information about oral presentations, the culmination of much group effort. In Chapter 11, students will learn about the types of oral presentations, how to prepare effective presentations, and criteria for evaluating presentations. We wish to acknowledge the contributions of Dr. Hal Bochin (California State University, Fresno) and Robin McGehee (College of the Sequoias—Visalia, California) to this chapter. Dr. Bochin wrote the original version and Robin McGehee continues to revise the chapter for us. Finally, the **appendix** presents information about a number of techniques a member or outside observer can use to gather information about a problem-solving group and help it improve its performance.

New to This Edition

- Stronger integration of text material and tables.
- Content related to leadership is now consolidated and located in Chapter 10, *Applying Leadership Principles.*
- New material on creativity in Chapter 5, *Creative and Critical Thinking in the Small Group.*
- Stronger demonstration of P-MOPS as a flexible procedure for problem solving in Chapter 6, *Group Problem Solving.*
- Chapter 7, *Becoming a Group,* includes new material on punctuated equilibrium as well as new examples of how technology alters traditional roles in groups.
- New material on the role of gender and group processes in Chapter 8, *Celebrating Diversity in the Small Group.*
- Numerous new exercises, case studies, and examples are found throughout the text.

Features

Case Studies: Establish the main ideas of the chapter by providing realistic scenarios for student application, and utilizing a variety of group contexts, such as business, health care, social groups, and civic organizations.

Apply Now! Boxes: Make concepts practical to everyday life, throughout the text.

Ethical Dilemma Boxes: Encourage critical evaluation of typical ethical scenarios faced by groups, and stimulate discussion of their causes, controversies, issues and solutions.

Media and Technology Boxes: Look at how media and technology are changing the ways in which small groups can interact. Topics include online support groups, synchronous and asynchronous computer-mediated communication; terrorism, television and groupthink.

Online Learning Center: Icons prompt students to use the book-specific website www.mhhe.com/adamsgalanes6 where they will find a variety of resources and activities for teaching and study.

Resources for Instructors:

Instructor's Manual: This manual provides exercises, sample syllabi, writing assignments, a list of transparency masters, and a test bank to help faculty, from first-time small group instructors to experienced ones, structure the course in ways that correspond with their teaching goals. The manual is on the book's website, www.mhhe.com/adams6, and on the Instructor's Resource CD.

Videos: *Communicating in Groups: Short Takes* provides numerous brief video examples to help students visualize a number of concepts. (0-697-34989-6)

Acknowledgments

We wish to thank the reviewers, all of whom did a conscientious job of reading the manuscript and providing helpful suggestions. We appreciate their thoughtful suggestions and have incorporated many of them in this sixth edition.

James L. Bonstein, Jr., Merced College

Jo Gottschalk, University of Alaska, Anchorage

Debra G. Harroun, Baker College of Clinton Turnpike

Marjorie Milroy, Victor Valley College

Kimme Nuckles, Baker College of Auburn Hills

We continue to appreciate the advice of reviewers from previous editions:

Hank Flick, Mississippi State University

Amy Bowie Fountain, Mississippi State University

Tim Steffensmeier, University of Nebraska, Omaha

Kathryn C. Jones, Northern Virginia Community College

Mary Helen Brown, Auburn University

Hal W. Fulmer, Georgia Southern University

Pamela McWherter, University of Alaska, Fairbanks

Ellen Arden-Ogle, Cosumnes River College

Bohn D. Lattin, University of Portland

Clay Warren, Washington University

Katherine Adams
Gloria J. Galanes

BRIEF CONTENTS

CONTENTS

PART FOUR
Small Group Public Presentations   285

FEATURES

CASES

APPLY NOW

ETHICAL DILEMMAS

MEDIA AND TECHNOLOGY

ONE

Orientation to Small Group Systems

Part One introduces you to the study of small groups. In Chapter 1 we explain why small groups are important to understand, and we define many of the terms you will encounter in your study of small groups. We discuss the types of small groups you are likely to experience, we address the ethics of small group communication, and we explain the participant-observer perspective used throughout the book. Chapter 2 presents you with a framework, general systems theory, to help organize the many concepts important to understanding how groups function.

1 Small Groups as the Heart of Society

CHAPTER OBJECTIVES

After reading this chapter you should be able to:

1. Explain why groups play a vital role in the personal and professional lives of individuals.

2. Describe the two major stages any problem-solving group goes through.

3. List criteria for determining whether a group or an individual should be used to solve a problem.

4. Define a group, a small group, and small group communication.

5. Differentiate between small group communication, public communication, interpersonal communication, and intrapersonal communication.

6. Explain and give examples of primary groups.

7. Explain and give examples of secondary groups.

8. Compare and contrast the different organizational groups.

9. Explain the four ethical standards any member of a group should be held to.

10. Explain and give examples of a member being an effective participant-observer.

The El Cajon Book Club

CASE 1.1

When Estelle Womack, principal of Madison Elementary School in El Cajon, California, retired, she searched for a way to keep in regular contact with her friends and colleagues at the school district.[1] Her solution was to start the El Cajon Book Club. Members, most of them secretaries and teachers, meet once a month to discuss books, talk, and support each other in a kind of self-help group for educators. Members have come and gone—even Ms. Womack no longer attends—but others from the school district have stepped in to take their places. Because of their common interests in education and children, members often find that their book discussions trigger talk about their jobs within the district. For example, Jane Hamilton's book, *A Map of the World,* where a child charges a school nurse with abuse, prompted discussion about how easy it is to make allegations of abuse. Members learn from each other and say participation in the club has helped them do their jobs better. Principals learn to understand teachers' perspectives, media specialists understand some of the problems of principals, and so forth. Started for one purpose—as a way for a retiring principal to keep in touch with people who have similar professional interests—the club continues because it meets a variety of needs of many different individuals.

This story highlights a central premise of this book: Small groups are *essential* to us in every aspect of our lives! Whether we join a group to accomplish something we can't accomplish alone or whether we join a group for the sheer pleasure of getting together with people we like, groups are necessary to our survival and to our enjoyment of life.

The El Cajon Book Club is a voluntary group of members choosing to meet for both social and professional reasons. Many of the groups you belong to, particularly where you work, may not be voluntary. You may be assigned to a group because you have a particular expertise your employer believes is important to the group's task or because small groups are an essential component of a course in which you are enrolled. No matter what the reason, you must be able to work well in teams, task forces, committees, and all kinds of special problem-solving groups if you want to succeed in the organized world of today. Teams of all kinds, especially multidisciplinary teams, are becoming more common in all areas of American life: business, industry, education, health care, the nonprofit sector, and government. For example, some of the biggest companies in the United States, including every Fortune 500 company, has some version of small groups and teams in place.[2] Companies use teams in a number of ways. For instance, Motorola has more than 5,000 teams operating. Eastman Kodak forms process teams to follow a product through the design, manufacture, and marketing processes. Ritz-Carlton Hotels employees can choose to participate in team-based work in addition to their regular jobs, and 5 percent of the Texas Instruments work force participates in self-directed work teams (described later in this chapter).

But there's a dark side to small group work. In one study of 179 teams, only 13 percent were rated highly effective.[3] A *Newsweek* article highlights some of the problems.[4] The article reports that one survey estimates managers spend one to one-and-a-half days in meetings each week—and half of that is wasted time. Some companies, including Nestlé USA and SC Johnson, ban meetings on Fridays. Another study observes that sit-down meetings take 34 percent longer than meetings where members have to stand. One management consultant estimates that the average meeting in a large company costs approximately $15,000. If meeting time isn't used effectively, that expense can be staggering and wasteful.

Your authors take the position that effective small group work—whether in meetings, on teams, on committees, and so forth—cannot be left to chance. When individuals come together, particularly individuals from differing backgrounds, perspectives, and areas of expertise, teamwork doesn't just happen. Training in *how* to be an effective team member is essential. If you want to succeed as a team member, you must learn how small groups function and what you personally can do to help ensure team success. Chapter 1 helps you start this process by asking you to consider how important groups are in your own life and by introducing you to concepts central to understanding small group processes, the variety of groups you will encounter, and the importance of being an ethical participant-observer in groups.

Groups in Your Life

Lawrence Frey, a leading advocate for the study of small groups in their natural settings, believes that the small group is the most important social formation: "From birth to death, small groups are interwoven into the fabric of our lives."[5] Small groups usher us in when we are born and out when we die, and they are present at every phase in between. The first group you encounter is your family, and, in many ways, this group forms the foundation for other groups that follow. Think about your family of origin for a moment and consider how much of your identity—who you think you are—was formed by that initial group. Development and maintenance of identity remain important functions that only groups can provide for us. This is obvious when we consider groups such as fraternities or sororities, spiritually based groups (churches, synagogues, or other religious organizations), gangs, book clubs, poker clubs, and so forth. Groups formed at work also contribute to who we think we are. Are you a member of a union, for example? A management group? A classroom group? A neighborhood coalition trying to prevent a zoning change in your neighborhood? Each one of these groups, though not expressly formed as an identity-supporting group, will affect how you see yourself in relation to other people.

Professionally, the higher you go in any organization (government, service, manufacturing, education, communication, the military, or whatever), the more time you will spend working as a member of small groups. No matter what specific group you are in, you need to know how to behave in ways that are appropriate and helpful to the group and to any larger organization to which the group may be attached. If you don't work well in groups, you are more likely to be laid off or frozen at a low-level job. A survey of 750 leading American companies asked businesspeople to describe characteristics of the ideal MBA (Master of Business Administration) graduate.[6] The top preference was possession of good oral and written communication skills (listed by 83.5 percent of respondents). The fourth-ranked preference, the ability to work in teams, was listed by 71.4 percent. These communication skills far surpassed even cutting-edge knowledge of the company's field (14.8 percent) and previous work experience (31.9 percent) in importance. Clearly, knowing how to work in a small group can be of practical benefit to you.

Even as a student, you may be surprised to discover how many groups you belong to. For most students, the list goes up to 8, 10, 15, or even 20 or more small groups. Why do most of us belong to so many groups? We humans are social beings with powerful genetic needs to belong to small groups. We need to affiliate with others of our kind, just as do many other animals. A human infant is dependent on others for its care for a long time before it develops self-reliance. Plus, one lone adult cannot provide everything a baby needs. This function is provided by different kinds of small groups, sometimes families with father and mother, but also groupings of the "Full House" sort, kibbutzim, extended family groupings that include a grandmother or aunts, or other child care groups. The famous African proverb is right: "It takes a village to raise a child."

GROUPS AS PROBLEM SOLVERS

You are constantly solving problems: how to find a job, where to eat lunch, how to keep your car running on a limited budget, and even how to keep your company on the cutting edge of its industry in a turbulent economic climate. Life can properly be called an unending series of problem-solving episodes. Solving any problem means coming up with a plan (even if it takes only a split second) and executing it. Planning solutions to problems used to be both the privilege and the responsibility of high-status people: generals, monarchs, dictators, managers, directors, and teachers. Carrying out the solutions was usually the work of lower-ranked people: infantrymen, secretaries, workers, students, and other subordinates. But things are changing. As you can see from the information provided earlier about the number of companies using teams and groups, more and more planning is done by groups—you won't be able to escape it, even in your classrooms! Because you are reading this text, the chances are good that you are in a course requiring participation in small groups. All kinds of courses, not just communication courses, use small group participation as a way to learn actively. If you want to participate in planning and not just carry out assignments planned by others, you will need to be able to work effectively in groups.

PARTICIPATING IN GROUPS

We emphasize how groups can become better problem solvers, but that cannot be accomplished by focusing only on the rational side of human behavior. To understand how groups really operate, you must know something about human feelings and behavior. We believe that effective group problem solving depends on how well members understand and manage such things as informational resources, how members feel about each other, how members feel about the task of the group, how skilled they are at expressing themselves and listening to others, and how well they collectively process the information they have to work with.

Group members must make sure they have the materials (information, tangible resources, time, and so forth) to complete the task, but they also must learn to manage their interpersonal relationships effectively enough to complete the task well. Keyton notes that relational communication in groups encompasses the "verbal and nonverbal messages that create the social fabric of a group by promoting relationships between and among members."[7] This function is equally as important as the task-oriented functions of group work.

General Motors recognized this when it organized its Saturn division in the late 1980s.[8] GM had been hammered by Japanese competitors and had seen its market share drop from 46 to 32 percent. In addition, GM's reputation had taken a beating after several fiascoes that revealed poorly designed and defective cars. The company knew it had to do something drastic, with no room for error. In response, the Saturn division was established as a separate company for manufacturing the Saturn automobile to compete directly with Japanese imports. The car uses teamwork at all stages of the design and manufacturing process. In fact, the Saturn division itself is structured as a series of interdependent teams.

GM invests considerable time and money training employees. New workers receive five days' training on how to work in teams and how to build consensus. This is followed by 100 to 175 hours of training in every aspect of the business, including conflict resolution and finance. In addition, the Saturn labor agreement calls for workers to continue their education by spending 12 or 13 days each year in class. The Saturn experiment helped GM become profitable during the 1990s. GM, knowing this experiment *had* to work, took no chances that the teams would malfunction. The company focused on both the task *and* relationship aspects of working in teams. When a major corporation recognizes that both work skills and people skills are essential, you can bet that other companies value those skills as well! We hope our book furthers your understanding and your skill in group participation.

When groups solve complex problems, they usually go through two major stages: planning and implementing. The planning stage involves considerable discussion and interaction. This is the stage at which all group members, with their differing viewpoints and opinions, must come to some overall conclusions if the group is to move successfully to the implementing stage, where the group's solutions are put into effect. To be valued by your group, you must become competent at the type of interaction demanded in the group's planning stage. Later, you must demonstrate loyalty to the group by being willing to carry out what the group has planned. While all problem-solving groups engage in planning, only some of them are also responsible for implementation. For instance, Saturn work teams have both the authority to do what is necessary to carry out their work and the responsibility of implementing their decisions.

Participation in a group always requires trade-offs. You give up the freedom to do what you want when you want for the advantages of affiliating with others to produce the kind of work possible only when several people coordinate their efforts. However, when individuals must coordinate their efforts, tensions always arise. This is true in all small groups, from a classroom work group to a task force of engineers designing a rocket. This is what *Communicating in Groups* is about: knowing what produces tensions in a group (both in the individuals and in the group as a whole), and knowing how to manage the tensions so that the group's decisions are the best that can be made, the members gain from the group, and the organization that gave birth to the group is improved by the group's work.

1.1   The Instinctive Need to Group Together

Go to **www. mhhe.com/ adamsgalanes6** for additional weblink activities.

MEDIA AND TECHNOLOGY

Some scholars have assessed situations in which a collection of individuals begin to group together. Such effort is common in face-to-face interaction where a particular force, problem, or crisis has created the need for individuals to group. Yet, little is known about how and why individuals with nothing apparently in common or mediating force begin to group. A good example is in a computer-mediated environment.

To examine this unique grouping process, Postmes, Spears, and Lea collected data on students who volunteered to complete a computerized statistics course, which offered participants e-mail options for contacting staff. Participants also used the function to send about 1,200 mail messages to fellow students. The messages were later classified into nine categories reflecting both task and relational functions (e.g., requests, complaints, reactions, humor, emotion, personal revelations). The researchers found that 11 groups formed, in which members spent most of their time (74 percent) interacting about socio-personal topics (reactions to contributions of other group members, humorous contributions, showing affection and emotion). Despite having little impact on the successful completion of the course, these students grouped together to fulfill their need for relational interaction with fellow classmates.

SOURCE: T. Postmes, R. Spears, and M. Lea, "The Formation of Group Norms in Computer-Mediated Communication," *Human Communication Research* 26 (2001), pp. 341–71.

Groups versus Individuals as Problem Solvers

If group work is so tricky and has such potential for problems, why not have individuals plan the solutions to all problems? The benefits of having a group tackle a problem *can* (but not necessarily *will*) outweigh the costs in time and tensions.

Research into the effectiveness of solutions developed by small groups, compared to those planned by individuals acting alone, has shown that groups can be far superior for solving many types of problems.[9] Groups tend to do much better than individuals when several alternative solutions are possible, none of which is known to be superior or "correct." They also are better at conjunctive tasks, where no one person has all the information needed to solve a problem, but each member has some needed information.[10] These are the very sorts of problems most groups and organizations face. For example, which of several designs for a car is most likely to sell well? What benefit options should be available to employees? How can the federal government provide citizens a tax cut and still provide sufficient funds for social programs and the homeland defense?

Many college courses require small group activity of some sort. When instructors move from teacher-centered to more student-centered instruction, they use small groups. Collaborative or cooperative learning rests on the consistent use of student groups.[11] Instructional experts Robert Powell and Dana Caseau extend on the notion that groups are better at collaborative tasks.[12] When student groups tackle a variety of collaborative tasks in the classroom, they become active, not passive, learners. Students can improve problem solving, critical and creative thinking, and social skills in small group learning contexts. Powell and Caseau point out that group activity is a preferred way to learn for some (e.g., Latins, Native Americans, African Americans, and females).

The following story illustrates how a group's greater resources can help the problem-solving process. Gloria recently participated on a steering committee to help integrate a public television station into the university where she teaches. (This case introduces Chapter 6.) This large committee also included a lawyer, the general manager of the TV station, the general manager of the university's public radio station, the director of development, the vice president overseeing physical plant matters, the vice president for finance, along with several other administrators. This committee had six months to complete its work. The lawyer drew up the documents for the Federal Communications Commission (FCC) to approve the license transfer to the university. The vice president overseeing physical plant worked with others to determine how space needed to be modified to accommodate the station's master control units, other equipment, and personnel. The finance vice president kept track of the budget. The TV station manager served a liaison function with her employees and met with them to determine what new equipment was needed. The radio station manager helped the TV station manager and others rewrite the job descriptions so they would be compatible with the university's human resources designations. Many, many other tasks had to be completed in the time allotted for the transfer. No one person possessed the necessary expertise (to say nothing of time and energy) to accomplish this highly complex, conjunctive task. Also, an enormous amount of coordination had to occur for this task to be accomplished successfully, and for that, everybody's people skills were needed. To date, the major tasks have been completed, with smaller, more focused committees taking over the remaining tasks.

WHEN A GROUP IS A GOOD CHOICE

For several reasons, groups working on problems with more than one solution typically make higher-quality decisions than do individuals. Groups usually have a much larger number of possible solutions from which to choose. Group members can help each other think critically by correcting one another's misinformation, faulty assumptions, and invalid reasoning. Several people can often think of issues to be handled in the process of solving a problem that might be overlooked by any one member. In addition, several people can conduct more thorough investigative research than one person working alone. Group members often counteract each other's tendencies to engage in self-defeating behavior.[13] A further advantage is that group members who are involved in planning a job or procedure usually understand that procedure and work hard to implement it. In addition, people are more likely to accept a solution that they have had a hand in designing. These principles have resulted in such small group techniques as quality control circles, self-managed work groups, and collaborative learning groups. But no plan for dealing with a problem or performing a task is better than the willingness to make it work on the part of those who must do the work or live with the results. Satisfaction, loyalty, commitment, and learning tend to be higher when people have a voice.

WHEN A GROUP IS NOT A GOOD CHOICE

But not all problems are suitable for groups, nor is group decision making always a wise or productive use of time. When a problem has a best or correct solution (such as in an arithmetic or accounting task), a skilled person working alone often exceeds the output quality of a group of less knowledgeable people, even if the group includes the highly skilled person as a member. Coordinating the work of several persons when conditions are changing rapidly (as in a weather disaster, battle, or ball game) may be done best by one person (a commander, chief, or coach). Likewise, if small groups have certain social, procedural, or personality-mix problems, the output may be inferior, even though members may produce it with pleasure and confidence in the results. Much of this book addresses how to apply small group theory—based as much as possible on scientific research—to make sure that groups work on the kinds of problems for which they are best suited, and to do so in ways likely to produce a high-quality solution (see Table 1.1).

Your experiences in task-oriented groups may have been unpleasant ones. In fact, you may dread hearing a teacher tell you that you'll be working on a group project. Unfortunately, this kind of **grouphate** is common, probably because many groups do not function as well as they should. If this is how you feel about group participation, it is especially important for you to become familiar with group processes, ways to handle problems, and procedures that can help you solve group problems.

GLOSSARY

Grouphate

Hating or dreading participation in groups

TABLE 1.1	Problems Appropriate for Groups versus Individuals

Problems Suitable for a Group	Problems Suitable for an Individual
1. The problem is complex; one person is not likely to have all relevant information.	**1.** There is a best solution and a recognized expert is most qualified to determine that solution.
2. There are several acceptable solutions, and one best solution does not exist.	**2.** Conditions are changing rapidly (such as during a fire, natural disaster, or other crisis), and coordination is best done by one person.
3. Acceptance of the solution by those who are affected is critical.	**3.** Time is short and a decision must be made quickly.
4. Sufficient time exists for a group to meet, discuss, and analyze the problem.	**4.** Group members have personality, procedural, or social problems that make it difficult or impossible for them to work as a team on the solution.

"*You take two of these at the first sign of the onset of boardroom turbulence.*"

Many organization members have come to dread participation in groups. (© The New Yorker Collection; 1985 Donald Reilly from cartoonbank.com. All Rights Reserved.)

1.1 Individual or Group?

APPLY NOW

What would you do if you were president of a university and your governing board approved the acquisition and license transfer to the university of the public television station in your town? As president, you have the power to make this happen by appointing a high-level person to coordinate the many tasks that need to be done, or you can appoint a committee to accomplish the same thing.

1. How would you weigh the factors (time, energy, expertise) in making your decision?

2. What are the advantages and disadvantages of having your appointee placed in charge of this effort compared with having an appointed committee placed in charge?

3. The members of the committee actually in charge of overseeing the project spent untold hours making sure that no important detail was left undone. What benefits do you think they may have gained by working on this time-consuming project?

Thus far, we have seen that small groups are commonly involved in problem solving. We now introduce you to the types of small groups that engage in problem solving and the situations that create them. We will first define terms necessary to understand group communication. We encourage you to use our definitions when you think about, discuss, and complete assignments about small groups as you read this book.

Groups, Small Groups, and Small Group Communication

Before we discuss *small group communication,* you must first understand how we conceptualize the terms *group* and *small group.*

GROUPS

What is a group? On the surface the answer may appear simple. However, scholars from disciplines such as sociology, social psychology, and communication have all tried to pinpoint the essential features of a group. When Ann Margaret Trautlein grappled with this question she devised three metaphors, "rock," "egg," and "chicken," to characterize three common social collectives we often refer to as "groups".[14]

"Rock" groups (no, not the band Match Box 20) describe collections of animate or inanimate objects grouped by one or more common characteristics. These might include keys in your pocket, females on a city bus, dishes in a cabinet, cars in a parking lot, applicants for a college, red roses on a vine, dogs at a pound, and so on. Rock groups are bound together for only one reason—their commonality. Members of rock groups are interchangeable because there is no sense of any collective identity or purpose—there is no perceived relationship between members by the members or perceived attachment to the collective.

"Egg" groups have all the elements to become living, breathing social groups, but for some reason have not done so. Egg groups have the commonality of rock groups such as shared attitudes, backgrounds, gender, ethnicity, needs, purposes, and so forth. They may even share common rules for behavior and interact with each other; however, they do not act toward each other as if they perceive one another as members of the same group. They act independently and seek individual goals, which sometimes coincide with the goals of other members. Egg groups include a collection of people waiting in line to see a movie, sitting in a classroom listening to a presentation, or standing in an elevator going to the next floor. They have the one ingredient necessary for the beginnings of groups as we conceive of them: awareness of their mutual influence and interaction between members. However, as you will see, that is not enough to define a group as we see it. Group members must communicate with each other in such a way as to realize and reinforce their collective interdependence.

"Chicken" groups contain all the characteristics of rock and egg groups: commonality, rules, and interaction. However, in addition to these elements, they identify with their group and demonstrate accountability toward each other. Most importantly, their common purpose is an interdependent one—that is, it cannot be accomplished without the communicative efforts of all members. Individual member identities become tied to a group identity and vice versa. Chicken groupness arises from the relationships among the individual members, a principle we will address in more detail in Chapter 2 when we discuss groups as social systems.

Chicken groups are the very kind of social collectives that we mean by *group*. To us, being in a **group** means that people have *inter*dependent relationships, and these relationships are the essence of being in a group. In a group, members are bound together through an interdependent purpose or function. Marvin Shaw, one of the most important early small group theorists, defines a human group in terms of interaction producing mutual influence: "persons who are interacting with one another in such a manner that each person influences and is influenced by each other person."[15] We add to this that group members are aware that together they are a part of a group and act interdependently toward a group purpose.

The following example illustrates this. At a recent communication convention, one of us stood waiting for a streetcar with several other individuals, some of whom also wore convention badges. It was late at night and the streetcar was late. This collection of individuals was a "rock" group. However, when we began to talk to each other about how late the streetcar was, how concerned we all were about how we'd be able to get to our respective hotels, and whether there might be an alternative solution, we began to form into an "egg" group. Several of us decided to share a cab to our various hotels. Through our interaction, we formed interdependent relationships, developed a common purpose, and became a "chicken" group—even though it was short-lived and relatively unimportant.

Groups can range in size from very small (three) to very large. In this book, we are concerned only with small groups. The principles that pertain to small groups do not necessarily hold true for large ones, and vice versa. Techniques appropriate for groups of from 3 to 7 members may be disastrous if tried in groups of 30, 70, or more. Likewise, communication techniques and procedures appropriate in large group meetings may be harmful to the effective functioning of small groups. For instance, parliamentary procedures developed for large group meetings (e.g., Robert's Rules of Order) are not meant to help small groups accomplish their tasks efficiently.

SMALL GROUPS

Small as used for human groups has usually been defined either by an arbitrary number or in terms of human perception. We prefer to define it in terms of psychological perception: We use the term **small group** to refer to a group in which individual members perceive each other and are aware of each other as individuals when they interact. This definition is precise only for a given point in time. A committee of five new members may be perceptually large until after each member has had a chance to speak repeatedly, but a seminar of 15 people may be perceptually small after several meetings. At that point, each member could name or describe every other, say who was and who was not at a meeting without taking formal attendance, and say something about what each contributed to the discussion and meeting. That is the idea of small group as we use it.

More practically, small groups usually consist of three to seven members, occasionally more. This seems to be the ideal range, with five as an ideal number if members possess sufficient knowledge and skills to do the job facing the group and have a diversity of perspectives and information relevant to the task. The more members, the more likely there will be inequity and communication overload for some members. We intentionally exclude the dyad (two-person group) from our definition of small group because dyads function differently. For example, dyads do not form networks or leadership hierarchies.

GLOSSARY

Group

Three or more individuals who have a common purpose, interact with each other, influence each other, and are interdependent

Small group

A group of at least three people that is small enough for individual members to perceive one another as individuals during interaction

Groups have continuity that dyads do not. If one member leaves a dyad, the dyad disbands, but members often leave small groups, sometimes to be replaced by new members, and the group itself continues. You are most likely to study dyadic communication in a book and/or course about interpersonal or family communication.

1.2 How Small Is Small?

APPLY NOW

The steering committee overseeing the transfer of the public TV station to the university discussed earlier consisted of 15 people, all administrators of some kind.

1. What evidence suggests this group is actually a group and not a collection of individuals?
2. Would you classify this group as "small"? Why or why not?
3. What kinds of problems might a group of this size encounter? What kinds of advantages might it have over a smaller group?
4. Why is this story a good example of small group communication?

We are most concerned with continuing small groups, in which the members "meet more or less regularly in face-to-face interaction, . . . possess a common identity or exclusiveness of purpose, and . . . share a set of standards governing their activity."[16] Task forces, work crews, sport teams, committees, quality circles, and classroom groups are examples of such groups. One-meeting groups in which members have a sense of shared purpose, interact face-to-face, share at least some standards and procedures for governing their interaction, and have a sense of each other as group members also qualify as small groups by our definition.

SMALL GROUP COMMUNICATION

Our definitions of *group* and *small group* have emphasized the process of members communicating with each other to become interdependent. "Chicken" groups cannot exist without communication. More importantly, regardless of why you are in a group or what its purpose, group work mandates communication. Thus, to undertake the study of small group dynamics necessitates tackling the complexities of communication.[17]

Communication refers to the perception, interpretation, and response of people to messages produced by other people. The definition states that group members send verbal and nonverbal messages—words, gestures, facial expressions, and so forth—and that the other group members observe, interpret, and respond to these messages. This implies that members of a group pay attention to each other and coordinate their communication behavior to accomplish the group's assignment. It is the members' communication with each other—their perceiving, interpreting, and responding to one another's signals—that creates the interdependence necessary for individuals to be called a group. We develop this concept in detail in Chapter 3.

Small group communication refers to the part of the field of group dynamics that focuses on the exchange of verbal and nonverbal information among group members. Small group communication requires interacting. As members create, perceive, interpret, and

GLOSSARY

Communication

The perception, interpretation, and response of people to messages produced by others

Small Group Communication

The verbal and nonverbal interaction among members of a small group

respond to messages, they are engaging in small group communication. This is different from public speaking to large groups (audiences), participating in a large assembly (i.e., a legislature or convention), communicating in a more-or-less-intimate dyad, or talking with one other person in assigned roles such as waiter and customer. While basic communication principles are common no matter what the setting, our emphasis in *Communicating in Groups* is communication that occurs within the group.

Small group communication is different from the communication that occurs in other contexts, such as public communication and interpersonal communication. It is more complex than interpersonal communication, which focuses on the communication between individuals as unique persons, as in a dyad. For instance, in a dyad, only one interpersonal relationship is possible, but in a five-person group 10 unique interpersonal relationships exist. In addition, a main reason people form groups is to get something done, to accomplish a task, which is not usually the main reason for forming interpersonal relationships. Small group communication is more informal and spontaneous than public communication such as giving a speech. In a public speaking situation, usually the speaker's role (speaking) is clearly differentiated from the audience's role (listening), but in a small group these roles are interchangeable. In addition, a public speaker usually has planned his or her remarks, whereas a small group member responds relatively spontaneously to the group interaction. Verbal feedback in a small group is immediate but is usually delayed in a public situation, although much nonverbal feedback is instantaneous in both contexts. However, group members may find themselves in various kinds of public presentations, and some of these, such as symposiums, involve group member speeches. These will be discussed in Chapter 11. Finally, intrapersonal communication, the communication that occurs within an individual human being (such as thinking and self-talk) is always present in all communication contexts, including small groups.

When we have talked about communication in groups, we have specified face-to-face communication. Most small group communication research studies small group dynamics when members are present with each other in the same place and time. However, technology is becoming a critical component of how group members communicate and has changed how we define *group*. Some groups blend face-to-face communication with computer-mediated communication, while others never meet face-to-face. Often such groups do have a sense of belonging and identity, have a shared purpose, and do their work through the exchange of signals—both verbal and nonverbal (e.g., in the form of emoticons, which we discuss in Chapter 4). More important, members of computer-mediated groups often perceive themselves to be part of a group. They find ways to work around computers' limitations by conveying *social presence* or the extent to which computer-mediated communication is socially and emotionally similar to face-to-face communication.[18]

John Cragan and David Wright, two small group theorists, call groups that use technology **cyborg decision-making groups.**[19] The machine, or cyborg, part of these groups includes audiovisual equipment, computers, e-mail, and interactive software. Four different meeting environments are possible with technology. The most common meet in the "same time and place" and may use an LCD projector or even interactive software to facilitate discussion dynamics. The second type of meeting is the "different time but same place" meeting. Members of a group work alone with stored group messages and may do things like coordinate work problems across different shifts (e.g., emergency room nurses). The third cyborg meeting occurs when group members communicate with each other at the "same

GLOSSARY

Cyborg Decision-Making Groups

Groups that blend face-to-face communication with technology such as e-mail and interactive software.

time but not face-to-face." A small group from a class may coordinate an assignment outside of class by talking with each other on a conference call or in a chat room. Electronic bulletin boards illustrate the fourth kind of cyborg meeting: "different time and place."

We will address the impact of technology on small group dynamics throughout the book. Thus, we consider many computer-mediated groups in our definition.

Classifying Groups by Their Major Purpose

How a specific small group functions in part reflects the purpose for which the group exists. We have classified small groups according to the reasons they exist.

PRIMARY OR SECONDARY GROUPS

Many small group writers accept the theory proposed by psychologist Will C. Schutz that three major forces motivate human interaction. These are the needs for inclusion, affection, and control. The first two concern needs for belonging and caring from other people. The third, control, refers to the need for power or control over the world in which we exist, including the people we encounter.[20] A group is classified by sociologists as primary or secondary depending upon which of these needs is the major reason it exists.

APPLY NOW	**1.3** **Meeting Member Needs and Handling Membership Changes**

The membership of the El Cajon Book Club changed regularly, as members left and new members were added. The founder of the club left after nearly nine years of participation. Membership changes present unique challenges to a group.

1. Did it surprise you that the El Cajon Book Club's founder is no longer a member? Why might a long-standing member want to leave a group?

2. Why might a new member choose to join?

3. What challenges does member fluctuation present for group members, existing and new?

4. What can current members do to make new members feel welcomed and part of the existing group?

Primary Groups.   **Primary groups** form to meet the first two types of needs, inclusion and affection. They may accomplish work, but that is not their primary objective. Loving, caring, avoiding feelings of loneliness, sharing, feeling cared about—these are the motives for which we willingly give up some freedom as individuals to be members of primary groups. We are all familiar with families, friendship groups (the television show "Friends"), sororities and fraternities, drinking buddies, cliques, gangs, and those many small groups that seem to form spontaneously to meet interpersonal needs for inclusion and affection. As we mentioned earlier, your family is probably your first group and

GLOSSARY

Primary Groups

Groups formed to meet primary needs for inclusion and affection

GLOSSARY

Secondary Groups

Groups formed to meet secondary needs for control and problem-solving

Support Groups

Groups formed for members to help each other understand, address, and cope with personal issues or problems

mirrors, in many ways, the many groups you belong to now. The communication patterns you learned in your first group likely affect the way you communicate in groups now.[21] In addition, many of the needs that were met by your first group are now met by other groups you belong to.

Secondary Groups.   **Secondary groups,** or task groups, exist mainly to meet control needs: solving all sorts of problems. A secondary group may create or implement a plan (solution) to provide control. Control, in this sense, may include supplying physical needs for food and water, preventing or controlling disease, coping with insects and other vermin, or even more mundane matters such as fixing a flat tire or designing a computer program to organize recipes. This book is mostly about secondary groups. Task forces, committees, work crews, quality circles, and learning groups are all secondary.

No group is purely primary or secondary in its functioning. Primary groups encounter and solve problems. Secondary groups supply members with a sense of inclusion and often with affection. In fact, sometimes the most productive and satisfying secondary groups have strong primary components, where members feel included, appreciated, and even cared for. Think of the best group you can ever remember. Chances are that not only was this group productive, but you also formed close friendships with the other members. Most likely, a number of your psychological needs—for inclusion, affection, and control—were met. Our motives for joining groups are often mixed; we may want to participate in solving a problem, but experiencing pleasure in the interaction with others is also a main reason for our involvement.[22]

TYPES OF SECONDARY GROUPS

Secondary groups tackle a range of tasks. They may be formed for one specific job or a variety of related tasks. Included are support groups, learning groups, organizational groups (such as committees, work teams, self-managed work teams, and quality control circles), and activity groups.

Support Groups.   **Support groups** exist to help members understand and address personal issues or problems. Support groups may be called therapy or personal growth groups. Regardless of what they are called, their purpose is not to solve a problem *as a group* but to help individual members address or solve personal issues or cope with personal problems. Groups based on the well-known 12-step process developed by Alcoholics Anonymous are examples of support groups, as are groups such as breast cancer support groups, anger management groups for abusive spouses, and so forth. The premise of these groups is that individuals can understand and better cope with their own problems if they interact with others whose problems are similar.

One of our friends, after completing treatment for ovarian cancer, started a support group—only the second such group in Missouri—for women diagnosed with the same disease. The treatment prognosis for such women is usually not optimistic, so Joy believed it was especially important for such women to support each other. She felt the need to talk with others who had been through the same experience, particularly those women whose treatments had been successful. But more importantly, she was eager to share her experiences and her message of hope to women newly diagnosed. During the aftermath of the World Trade Center attacks on September 11, 2001, police officers, firefighters, and rescue workers assembled in New York City. Although these people came to help rescue efforts and clean up the devastation, they also provided emotional support to each other and to shocked New Yorkers. Primary and secondary functions were equally important.

"O.K., who else has experienced the best-friend
relationship as inadequate?"

The easy availability of computers has made it possible for people to form support groups of members who never meet face-to-face, yet who experience strong support and comfort from their computer contacts. In a recent study comparing online and face-to-face support groups, Wright found that people benefited from both types.[23] Online groups have the advantages of providing 24-hour access, greater participant diversity of experience and information, and freedom to discuss risky topics. The online support networks also tended to be larger, thereby providing members with more resources. Interestingly, the online support groups did not evolve into face-to-face groups.

Learning Groups.   **Learning groups** of many sorts, as we mentioned earlier, exist to help members understand or control events in their lives and the world around them. Your class is a learning group (probably a large one) that may be further organized into several small learning groups. Learning groups of people from preschool to retirement age discuss all sorts of interests. Study groups are types of learning groups. So are cohort groups; many universities group students into cohorts, who enter a particular program together and stay together throughout their course of study. Cohorts are encouraged to study together and to help each other learn. In a study of adult undergraduate learning cohorts, researchers found a significant relationship between the level of group development and the individual achievement, measured by grade point average, of the members.[24] Not all groups achieved equally, which further emphasizes the importance of understanding group communication and development.

Although this book does not specifically focus on support or learning groups, learning is a first step in many problem-solving groups, and personal affirmation and support are crucial by-products of effective group interaction in all kinds of groups.

For more information on finding groups on the Internet, go to the Online Learning Center at **www.mhhe.com/ adamsgalanes6**

GLOSSARY

Learning Groups

Secondary groups of members meeting to understand and learn about a particular topic

Organizational Groups.   Organizations such as corporations, schools, agencies, legislatures, bureaus, large departments, hospitals, and even social clubs create problem-solving groups to serve them. **Organizational groups** include any such problem-solving group formed within the context of a larger organization.

Committees.   Most **committees** are created by larger organizations to perform a service for the organization. The organization commits a problem or duty to the small group (committee) created for that purpose. For example, at Kathy's university, a fact-finding committee was asked to investigate the possibility of establishing an honor code and report its findings to the faculty and president. Occasionally a special committee is empowered both to select a plan and to execute it, though in most cases problem-solving committees do not go beyond recommending. Instead, they are usually advisory, reporting to an executive or a board that has final authority and responsibility for deciding. A different committee is created to carry out the chosen plan, or an individual may be assigned to execute the solution. Committees in organizations may be standing, ad hoc, or conference.

A standing committee is a permanent committee. Often, an organization's bylaws include a procedure for creating it and a description of its purpose and area of freedom to act. For example, a membership committee may be responsible for recruiting new members and for screening the applicants' qualifications. "Standing" implies that a committee continues indefinitely. However, its membership is usually changed by election or appointment on a periodic basis.

Ad hoc committees are created to perform one special assignment, then go out of existence. The end product might be a report of findings or recommended solutions—for example, evaluations of several sites for a new plant or suggestions about how to cut costs. This report is often delivered in writing and orally to the person(s) who created the special committee. A couple of years ago one of us headed a faculty ad hoc committee formed to prevent the loss of a department's graduate program. This committee put together a plan to build the graduate program, which included a newly designed graduate curriculum, a plan for recruitment, and the policy for a newly formed department graduate committee. This plan was presented orally and in writing to the dean of graduate studies. Its work thus completed, the committee disbanded.

Such groups are often called task forces, with members selected because their knowledge and skills are thought necessary to do the group's work. Presidents have created many task forces to investigate and make recommendations on such national concerns as illegal drug traffic, acid rain, the condition of national parks, health care, waste in government expenditures, and disease epidemics.

Conference committees are composed of members who represent other groups that must find common ground to accomplish their work. For example, the U.S. Senate passed the Patient's Bill of Rights. However, that bill did not become law as it stands. The House of Representatives crafted its own version of a Patient's Bill of Rights that differed in key respects from the Senate's bill. A conference committee composed of both representatives and senators formed to reconcile differences in the two bills. The bill is still being debated. We will use the term *conference* to refer only to such groups of representatives, never as a synonym for committee or task force.

Quality Control Circles.   American, foreign, and multinational companies, including Xerox, Procter & Gamble, Westinghouse, Ford, General Motors, Dow Chemical, Paul Revere Insurance Group, and countless others, use **quality control circles.** Quality control circle or quality circle is a generic name for small groups of company employees who volunteer to tackle any issue that may affect job performance. All quality circles are concerned with the quality and quantity of their work output and attempt to improve their competitiveness with other organizations. They can be found in all types of organizations, ranging from manufacturing and service organizations to state governments, to school systems, to voluntary organizations, and sometimes to individual families. They help involve employees in the organization's decision-making loops.

If instituted properly, quality circles can improve company effectiveness by increasing worker productivity, identifying quality control problems and possible solutions, and enhancing worker involvement. For instance, quality circles helped one international hotel chain cut losses on unused fruit baskets by over $5,500 per quarter.[25] However, for quality circles to produce these kinds of benefits, careful planning is required. The organization must prepare before introducing quality circles and train employees in how to participate.

In addition, a number of consistent problems have occurred with quality circles. Sometimes unions see them as a ploy to increase production without improving wages or benefits. Managers can be threatened if they perceive that suggestions from quality circles sabotage their managerial prerogatives. Quality circle programs stagnate if the company fails to act promptly on suggestions provided by the quality circle or explain why a suggestion is not being implemented. Quality circles often work best in conjunction with an overall organizational development program that supports the concept of employee participation.

Self-Managed Work Teams.   Sometimes called autonomous work groups or modules, **self-managed work teams** are groups of peers who manage their own work schedules and procedures within certain prescribed limits. Members are highly trained and cross-trained—each is able to perform several tasks for the team. The process is similar to having a team of people building a house: "When you need more carpenters, the painters can put down their brushes and pick up hammers for a couple of hours. Or the carpenter goes and helps the plumber when he's behind."[26] Not only is this efficient, but it also helps workers develop a variety of skills and reduces boredom and frustration. Self-managed work teams have been used with great success at such companies as Procter & Gamble, Sherwin-Williams, GM, and TRW.

A self-managed work team elects its own leader, who is a co-worker, not a supervisor or manager. The leader acts as a coordinator, not a boss. The organization establishes the work group's area of freedom, but often these groups have a great deal of latitude in how they operate. Some work groups establish their own schedules and annual budgets, prepare their own reports, develop specifications for jobs and procedures, solve technical problems that occur while completing jobs, and even prepare bids in attempting to attract new company business. For example, at one office furniture manufacturer, the custom-orders team has complete authority to bid jobs under $10,000, custom-design the furniture for the client, and schedule its manufacture. For complex jobs, the whole team goes to the client's office to listen and offer suggestions. The team's success has made the custom-order portion of the business extremely profitable.[27]

GLOSSARY

Quality Control Circles

Organizational groups that address issues of job performance and work improvement

Self-Managed Work Teams

Also called autonomous work groups, groups of peers who manage their own work schedules and procedures

1.4   What's In a Name?

The SC Johnson Company has a meeting-intensive culture that has spawned its own vocabulary to describe various kinds of meetings. *Generals* are weekly one-on-one meetings that bosses hold with their subordinates. *Nice to knows* are optional informational meetings that employees often skip, and *huddles* are meetings designed to provide quick updates.

1. What kinds of group meetings do you attend?

2. What nicknames would you give to them?

Companies that have effectively instituted such programs report that self-managing work teams give a 20 to 40 percent edge in productivity over more traditional work systems.[28] They require less supervision and surveillance, produce higher-quality products, have less lost time, and generally produce high morale and job satisfaction.

Being an Ethical Group Member

Throughout this chapter we have emphasized how important it is for you to understand small groups so you can be a valuable participant in them. You want to be the kind of member others can count on, thus making the small group experience a satisfactory and successful one for all members. In most small group communication classes, we have found one or two project groups plagued by irresponsible members who want credit for the work but are unwilling to do their share of the work. They fail to show up for meetings, they miss report deadlines, they disappear with essential information, or they are absent from rehearsals for presentations. These kinds of members seem to be the greatest source of bad feelings among group members and of poor-quality projects. In the business world, such deadwood or loafers are weeded out of work teams and task forces.

We would hope everyone in a group wants to be a member others can count on. "Chicken" groups require collaborative, cohesive behavior from members. Members thus need to know the kind of behavior that is expected of responsible, ethical members. **Ethics** refers to the "rules or standards for right conduct or practice,"[29] that is, what is considered appropriate behavior in certain contexts. This book provides a variety of behaviors that all contribute to small group problem solving. Ethically, however, it is your responsibility to decide whether you *should* enact any of the courses of action. There is a difference between knowing what to do and asking whether you should do it. Communicative actions among members have consequences to ourselves and others, and because of those consequences our communication involves discerning whether our overall actions are ethical.[30] In a small group, standards for members concern their willingness to communicate, treatment of fellow members, treatment of information, and commitment to the group.

First, members must be willing to communicate and share ideas, information, and perspectives within the group. Groups succeed because several heads are better than one. However, this advantage will not be realized if group members are unwilling to speak up or engage

GLOSSARY

Ethics

Standards and rules for appropriate member and leader behavior

in group dialogue. Being silent deprives the group of your voice. Even if you do not feel comfortable talking, there are multiple ways to contribute.

Second, group members should treat their fellow members with respect and consideration. If members are to respect each other they must operate from the belief that all group members have the same rights. Egalitarian attitudes encourage all members to contribute fully to the task at hand and value good ideas no matter who contributes them. To do otherwise undermines the potential effectiveness of the group. If members do not contribute their voices and resources to a group because they fear being attacked or belittled, then the discussion process is derailed. Treating others with respect is a cultural value embedded in our democratic traditions and is the right thing to do. Even when members disagree with each other, they should learn to do so without being disagreeable or personalizing the disagreement.

Third, group members should use their best critical thinking skills when they evaluate information, ideas, and proposals in a group. They should also evaluate information in a thorough and unbiased way. Earlier, we noted that an advantage to group processes is that members can correct each other's misinformation and faulty reasoning. In fact, it is unethical for them *not* to do so because decisions are only as good as the information and reasoning on which they are based. Perhaps the lives of the Columbia space shuttle crew could have been saved had National Aeronautics and Space Administration engineers more thoroughly and with less bias paid attention to safety warnings. Instead, important information about the structural integrity of the shuttle was ignored. Group members must make a conscientious effort to find and present all relevant information and points of view, must not falsify data or information, and must evaluate all the information in an objective manner. This is the heart of effective group problem solving.

Finally, members must demonstrate a commitment to the group. For as long as they are members of the group, they should place the good of the group ahead of their own individual goals. Committed, responsible members are highly involved in the activity of the group. All members are needed and there is no room for freeloaders. If a group you belong to makes a decision you cannot support, then it may be better for you to leave the group. Some people are unable or unwilling to commit to a group, and they make horrible team members. Committed members support the group's actions and decisions, even if they sometimes are not what any one member would do alone.

Remember, groups exist because members' identities are intertwined with a recognized and valued group identity. Thus, group member communication matters because it affects other members as well as the group. Whenever you are faced with choosing how to behave in your small group, following these four principles should help you. Stand back and consider the impact of your communication on others and the group because membership in groups is not only about participation but also about observation. We turn now to the participant-observer perspective.

The Participant-Observer Perspective

Earlier, we asked you to consider all the groups to which you belong. Even as you learn about the principles of communicating in groups from reading this book, you will continue to be a member of these groups. We hope you will want to use the principles and techniques you learn to improve the functioning of your groups. This means that you will

1.1   Would You Falsify Data?

Your five-member class project group has been given the assignment of serving as consultants to another group. You are charged with observing this group, gathering data about it, evaluating the group's communication, and making recommendations to improve the group's functioning. The problem is that each of your project group members is very busy and you're having a hard time agreeing on a time to observe the other group. Two of you are graduating at the end of the semester and one of you, planning to spend the summer working in Europe, is scrambling to get all assignments finished in time to leave. Two members suggest making up data for your final project. The chances of getting caught are slim, and this "solution" would save you all several hours of observation and work. You personally strongly object to this form of cheating. For one thing, you don't want to chance having a plagiarism charge against you. But mainly you object to this form of lying and you don't want to damage your relationship with your professor. What do you do?

1. Do you speak or remain silent?
2. If you speak, what would you say?
3. What would you do if the entire group—except you—was in favor of falsifying data?
4. Would you talk to the teacher? Why or why not?

be in the role of a **participant-observer,** someone who is a regular member of the group and, at the same time, actively observes the group and adapts to its processes and procedures. This is especially important for the group leader or leaders. Because most group members have not been trained to be effective group participants, it is especially important for us who do know something about small group communication to monitor the group's discussions and help our groups perform as well as possible. A skilled participant-observer can help a group by supplying information, procedural suggestions, and interpersonal communication skills needed by the group. This is an important focus of this book—to help you become a more valuable group member as you sharpen your skills in observing small group processes.

We encourage you to become a participant-observer for the groups you are in. As you read this book, try to think of examples from your own group experiences that illustrate the principles described in the text. Start paying attention in a conscious way to the processes of small group communication. In addition, use the case study before each chapter and application boxes to improve your awareness of group dynamics. As you learn more about communicating effectively in groups, you will feel more comfortable making suggestions to serve the groups to which you belong. We provide additional information about the participant-observer and other types of observers in the Appendix.

GLOSSARY

Participant-Observer (Perspective)

A group member who participates but also observes the group and adapts as necessary

RESOURCES FOR REVIEW AND DISCUSSION

SUMMARY

- People in modern society need to be able to function effectively in small groups if they want to succeed and if they want to be full participants in contemporary organizational life.

- Small group members participating in decision making create and consider more issues, correct each other's misinformation, accept solutions more, and are more loyal to the organization than members who don't participate in decisions.

- Perceptual awareness makes a group "small"; the group must be small enough for each member to participate and for each member to be conscious of and aware of each other member.

- Groups can be classified according to their purpose. Groups can satisfy inclusion, affection, and control needs.

- Ethical members are willing to communicate, treat others with respect, evaluate information thoroughly, and demonstrate commitment to the group.

- Participant-observers, members who know something about the small group process, can help a group succeed.

EXERCISES

1. List all the groups to which you belong. Be sure to include family groups, friendship and other social groups, activity groups, committees, work teams, athletic teams, classroom groups, study groups, political action groups, interest groups, and every other type of small group to which you belong. Categorize them into primary or secondary groups (recognizing that no group is solely one or the other). Discuss your list with the class or in small groups.

2. Ask several individuals to define *group*. Bring your definitions to class and together or in small groups share those definitions. Report aspects of the definitions that are similar and that

are not similar. Compare and contrast them to the one presented in your text. Decide, as a class, your working definition of *group*.

3. Break up into small groups. Devise your own list of ethical standards for group members. You can do this for a general class discussion or you can develop a class list of standards that will be used for all future group work in the class. If the class is structured around a major group project, then individual groups can create their lists relevant to the standards of the group members.

 Go to **www.mhhe.com/adamsgalanes6** and **www.mhhe.com/groups** for self-quizzes and weblinks.

KEY TERMS • CONCEPTS

Committee	Grouphate	Quality Control Circles
Communication	Learning Groups	Secondary Groups
Cyborg Decision-Making Group	Organizational Groups	Self-Managed Work Teams
Ethics	Participant-Observer (Perspective)	Small Group
Group	Primary Groups	Small Group Communication
		Support Groups

 www.mhhe.com/adamsgalanes6

Use the flashcards and crossword puzzles on the Online Learning Center to further your knowledge of these key terms.

Groups as Structured Open Systems

CHAPTER OBJECTIVES

After reading this chapter you should be able to:

1. Explain why systems theory is a useful perspective for studying small group communication.

2. Define and give examples of a system.

3. Define inputs, throughput process, and outputs of a group system.

4. Explain why interaction is at the heart of a group's throughput process.

5. Describe the role of the group's environment.

6. Compare and contrast open and closed systems.

7. Describe what interdependence means to the functioning of a small group system.

8. Explain the valuable role of feedback in helping a system adapt to changing circumstances.

9. Explain why all groups, along with other living systems, experience multiple causes and multiple paths.

10. Explain why nonsummativity is a characteristic of groups.

11. Explain how modern organizations are composed of networks of groups.

The Jamaican Winter Olympic Bobsled Team

CASE 2.1

A Jamaican Olympic bobsled team is about as unlikely as a Popsicle stand in the middle of the Mohave Desert—but that is the true story told in the film *Cool Runnings!* With only three months to find equipment, secure financial backing, and qualify for the Winter Olympics in Calgary, Alberta, Canada, four of the most incompatible, untrained Jamaicans come together to compete for an Olympic gold medal. Sanka is the best pushcart driver in all Jamaica; his friend Derice is Jamaica's beloved track sprinter; Yul is a moody, angry sprinter; and Junior is a wealthy sprinter who tripped both Derice and Yul in the Olympic track qualifiers. Junior's mistake cost Derice his chance to follow his dad's legacy and compete for Olympic gold. Not to be denied, Derice searches for another way to try for a medal. He hears about Irving Blitzer, a former Olympian and friend of his dad. Irv, an Olympic medalist in the bobsled, had tried to talk Derice's father into switching sports because he believed track sprinters would make outstanding bobsledders, but Derice's dad would have nothing to do with the idea. Irv was stripped of both his medals and left the sport in disgrace after cheating. Derice finds Irv in Jamaica and pleads with him to coach the first Jamaican bobsled team. Sanka signs on as a favor for his friend, Yul joins to get off the island, and Junior joins to get away from his domineering father.

This unlikely collection of three track sprinters, one pushcart driver, and a disgraced coach begins with no money, no sled, no ice and snow to practice on, no fan support, skeptical and cruel responses from fellow bobsledders, and animosity between them. Any betting person would predict from these initial factors that they would fail. Not even the Jamaican Olympic committee would give them the money to go to Canada for the bobsled trials. Facing one obstacle after another, these athletes slowly emerge as a cohesive team and find themselves in the Olympics. During the last run for gold, this unlikely Jamaican bobsled team crashes before the finish line because of a loose runner on the sled. Injured but not deterred, they pick up their sled, named "Cool Runnings," and walk over the finish line to the cheers of the other bobsledders and all of Jamaica. What does "Cool Runnings" mean? It translates into "peace be the journey."[1]

The story of *Cool Runnings* illustrates several important aspects of systems theory. We will return to the story throughout the chapter to provide examples of what we mean by these various aspects of systems theory and how they apply to the Jamaican bobsled team. First, let's consider an overview of general systems theory and how it furnishes a useful and popular framework for examining small group communication.

Overview of General Systems Theory

General systems theory was developed by a biologist, Ludwig von Bertalanffy, as a way to examine and explain complex living organisms. Because living organisms, including groups, are constantly changing, they are difficult to study. When a biologist describes an organism, the description is out of date as soon as it is written. Only processes and relationships display any constancy. Think for a moment about your own body, one of the most complex of all organisms. Although it appears to operate as a single unit, in reality it is composed of many smaller units that work interdependently to sustain your life. For example, when you walk across the room, your muscular, skeletal, nervous, circulatory, and respiratory systems all cooperate in moving you to your destination. Even if you are sitting still, your body is involved in constant activity—your eyelids are blinking, your heart is beating, you are breathing automatically, and so forth. Your individual cells constantly change as they take in nourishment through the blood, restore themselves, and excrete waste through the cell walls. This complicated, continuous process is hard to study. Fortunately, systems theory provides us with a way of examining and describing how a system's parts are interrelated, even while they are continuously changing. Systems theory reminds us that when we want to understand any living entity we not only study its component parts, but we must also examine the ways in which the parts operate together if we want to understand the organism as a whole.

In Chapter 1 we introduced you to the rock, egg, and chicken metaphors to help explain the notion of a group. When the separate components of egg groups operate together as a whole they become social systems, or chicken groups. Chicken groups are those in which members realize interdependence such that the multiple parts of the group achieve a wholeness distinguishable from other groups. Their shared patterns of communication create and maintain a unique culture that constantly evolves as the group acts to meet its needs.

Systems theory has helped social scientists, family therapists, business professionals, and others by giving them a useful framework for looking at these chicken groups, or complex human groupings. Many individual elements affect the dynamics of a group—the reason the group was formed, the personalities of the group members, the information members have, the type of leadership, how the group handles conflict, and how successful the group has been in accomplishing its assigned task, to name only a few. But no single element functions alone; the elements interact continuously. Systems theory concepts keep us from oversimplifying our description of group interaction. All parts interact to produce the entity called a "small group" we defined in Chapter 1 as chicken groups.

Characterizing a group as a social system was a significant advance in small group communication theory. The assumption that *communication* connects the relevant parts of a system is fundamental to understanding a small group as a system. This moves the role of communication in emergent social systems to the forefront of small group theory.

Systems theory's contribution to small group communication research and to our understanding of the process of small group interaction is obvious. However, the theory is not without its detractors. Any theory is a human construction and therefore limited in scope—it gives *a* particular view of a phenomenon, not *the* view. Some, for instance, have questioned whether system theory research is merely a descriptive framework, but not a useful explanatory one.[2] Still others take issue with the system theory assumption of homeostasis, or dynamic balance—the idea that systems are self-maintaining and work toward keeping on track. This emphasis on balance, some argue, draws attention to system stability rather than change. However, we have chosen systems theory as our theoretical framework because of its centrality in small group research and focuses on patterns and wholes. Even so, we do want you to know that it is but one theory used by theorists to understand small group communication. Let's now take a closer look at some of the underlying principles of this theory.

"I guess we'd be considered a family. We're living together, we love each other, and we haven't eaten the children yet."

Social systems are composed of interrelated parts. (© The New Yorker Collection; 1995 Sam Gross from cartoonbank.com. All Rights Reserved.)

The Small Group as a System

Several concepts and definitions are important to understanding a small group as a system. We will use the Jamaican bobsled case study we presented at the beginning of the chapter to illustrate these terms and concepts.

DEFINITION OF A SYSTEM

A **system** consists of elements that function interdependently. The system, in our case a small group, also functions interdependently with the environment in which it operates as part of a larger system. Not only is a group made up of several elements that influence one

GLOSSARY

System

A set of elements that functions as a whole because of interdependent relationships

another, but the group also both affects and is affected by its surroundings. Without mutual influence, the group is merely an egg group or a collective of parts with no interdependence.

Think back to that unlikely Jamaican bobsled team (see also Figure 2.1). Several elements and their unique interaction affected the team. Consider first the members themselves, with their various abilities. A winning bobsled team needs a driver and three strong runners to push the sled—and this team has them. Sanka is loyal to Derice and is, after all, the best pushcart driver in all of Jamaica. Yul is strong and fast. Junior is also quick and sharp. Derice was born to compete in the Olympics—he is fast and driven.

A second element is the team's game plan. For example, how should the coach match these abilities with the various positions? Should the pushcart driver be the driver of the sled? The team's first conflict involves this very issue. Sanka thinks he should be the driver, yet the coach points out that the driver has to be focused at all times and is responsible not only for the course but also for the lives of the others. So Derice is selected as the driver and Sanka becomes the brakeman. The other two are the middlemen.

FIGURE 2.1   Bobsled Team as a Small Group System

The third element is the leadership within the team. Derice, for instance, has to figure out how to manage the hard feelings between Yul and Junior. In addition, Yul desires to be no one's teammate but instead wants to use the "team" to get off the island.

The fourth element is Irv's ability to assess the team's competency, earn members' trust, and motivate them to find their own style of sledding. Notice also the interaction of the team with its surroundings. The attitudes of the Jamaicans, their families, other Olympic bobsledders and coaches, as well as the media, first thwarted then later inspired the team. In return, the team's success influenced the entire country of Jamaica and the rest of the winter Olympic community.

CONCEPTS VITAL TO UNDERSTANDING SYSTEMS

To understand systems theory, you need to understand concepts true of all systems. Four basic concepts are essential. Our explanations of these are based on scholarly work by Daniel Katz and Robert Kahn.[3]

Inputs.   Elements involved in a group's dynamics can be classified into three broad categories: inputs, throughputs, and outputs. **Inputs,** the first of these categories, consists of all the factors—people, information, energies, and other resources such as computer programs designed to facilitate group problem solving—that are brought into the group from the outside (see Table 2.1). Inputs are the "raw materials" from which the group is initially formed and are used by members to perform their work. For example, the abilities of the bobsled players—whether they are smart or not, whether they are relatively fast or slow, how well they can "read" the subtle nature of the course—are all input characteristics that the players bring with them to the group and that influence how well the team performs during a run. Other inputs include the instructions on how to synchronize the movements of all four bobsledders and their sled, the continuous stream of information that Irv gathers about the strengths and weaknesses of opposing teams, the three-month time limit they have to qualify for the Olympics, and the beliefs and attitudes of the team members toward each other, the sport, and their coach.

TABLE 2.1	**Examples of Small Group Inputs**

Members	**Resources**	**Environmental factors**
Personalities and characteristics (e.g., age, gender)	Information about the task	Physical surroundings
Needs	Knowledge and expertise	Degree of support from parent group or organization
Attitudes	Time available for group work	
Values	Tangible resources (e.g., money, materials)	
Abilities and skills	Group computer software systems	

GLOSSARY

Throughput Processes

Influences on the system that result from actual activities within the group as it goes about its business

Perhaps your class has been divided into groups to complete a group project. Examples of inputs to your project group include the group's purpose (beginning with the assignment your instructor gave you), the members' attitudes toward the project, the abilities and experiences of the members, the information members have or are able to find about the topic, and the physical or social features of the environment that may affect the group, such as classroom noise that makes it hard to hear other members.

Throughput Processes.   The **throughput processes** of the group are the activities within the group as it goes about its work (see Table 2.2). These include such processes as how roles, rules, and leadership develop; how members handle conflict; and how members evaluate the information they receive. Throughput processes are the "how" of the group, including all the verbal and nonverbal messages that occur within the group. In our bobsled team example, the coach's placement of Derice as the driver instead of Sanka, the

---

TABLE 2.2   **Examples of Small Group Throughput Processes**

MEMBERS' BEHAVIORS

Degree of encouragement for presenting ideas

Demonstration of members' willingness to work

Dogmatic or otherwise stifling behaviors

Methods of expressing and resolving disagreements

Degree to which cohesiveness is expressed

GROUP NORMS

Support for using critical thinking skills to test ideas versus uncritical acceptance of ideas

Support for open disagreement versus suppression of conflict

Support for relative equality among members versus a strict hierarchy

COMMUNICATION NETWORKS

Extent to which each member talks to every other member

Extent to which participation is distributed evenly

STATUS RELATIONSHIPS

Type of leadership

Degree to which power and influence are shared

PROCEDURES

Communication

Decision making and problem solving

Method for implementing solutions

obvious choice, is an example of a throughput process. The informal leadership of Sanka, whose enthusiasm motivated the other members, is also part of the team's throughput processes. Significant for this team was how Yul and Junior reconciled their differences and developed a mutual respect across their socioeconomic lines.

In another example, members of your classroom group may have developed the habit of examining critically all the information they bring to meetings and arguing openly before they reach any decision. This style of handling conflict is an example of a throughput process. This will have a different effect on the group's decisions than if the members uncritically accept any and all information.

The heart of the group's throughput process is **interaction.** You may be accustomed to thinking of interaction as just the talk that occurs within a group, but it actually involves more than that. Interaction includes all the verbal and nonverbal behavior in the group. Interaction assumes that members are aware of one another; are simultaneously sending, interpreting, and receiving messages designed to influence; and are affected by one another.

Recall from Chapter 1 that all four ethical principles for group members are anchored in effective communication. Whether you are showing a willingness to communicate, displaying respect for others, critically assessing information, or demonstrating commitment to your group, you are engaging in a variety of communicative behaviors—all four standards are grounded in what and how you communicate to others. Group communication is the exclusive focus of Part Two of our text.

Outputs.   **Outputs** are the "results," the products of the group's throughput processes (see Table 2.3). They include tangible outcomes, such as decisions the group has made and written reports. However, they also include less obvious results, such as cohesiveness, member satisfaction, personal growth of individual members, and changes in the group's structure. In our bobsled example, a clear result of the team's respect for each other was not a gold medal but instead pride in themselves and from their country. Other outputs included the sledders' increased cohesiveness and new skills, Junior's independence from his father, Yul's team pride, and Derice's realization that a gold medal does not make one a whole person.

TABLE 2.3	**Examples of Small Group Outputs**

Tangible Outcomes	**Intangible Outcomes**
Reports	Feelings among members (cohesiveness, trust; disharmony, dislike)
Recommendations	
Solutions and decisions	Personal growth of members
Physical objects (e.g., table decorations, assembled cars)	Personal satisfaction of members
	Modifications in throughput procedures (e.g., alterations in the status relationships, use of different conflict resolution strategies)

GLOSSARY

Environment

*Systems do not
exist in a vacuum
but are embedded
in multiple
surroundings or
contexts*

Although we hope that the outputs of a small group's interaction are positive and helpful, some outputs are destructive to both the group itself and the organization that established the group. Hasty decisions, dissatisfaction of group members, and shoddy products are examples of destructive outputs. Harmful group outputs are like toxic waste, dangerous to everyone involved, including the organization to which the group belongs.

Input, throughput, and output variables are interdependent. Small group systems are evolving or changing all the time. Outputs reenter the group system as inputs affecting throughput variables and thus influencing new outputs. If a group member enters the group unwilling to communicate to other members, this input impacts the overall group communication creating a climate of suspicion (throughput), which leads to low group satisfaction among other members (output). The members' subsequent lack of commitment becomes a new input variable, which continues to destroy the group's climate (throughput), leading to a group report that is never finished (output). This downward pattern will continue unless group members notice the problems and adjust their communication to change the climate of the group. We will take up the issue of group feedback after we discuss the relationship a small group has with its environment.

Environment.   A group does not exist apart from its surroundings, or **environment**, which consists of everything outside the group that affects the group. In our example, the Jamaican fans and the other bobsledders influenced the team's morale and enthusiasm. Notice that the team affected its environment as well. When the other bobsledders discovered the courage of this Jamaican team, their disrespect turned into support, and those who had rejected the coach for his past cheating accepted him back into the bobsled fraternity.

Your classroom group's immediate environment is the classroom. Your group is affected by whether the classroom is pleasant or ugly, noisy or quiet. In addition, what your friends in other classes say or do may cause your group to change a procedure, a topic, an approach, and so forth. These friends and their classes are part of your group's environment, too.

The effect of a group's environment, or the context within which the group operates, is an important but understudied factor in how well a group operates.[4] The small group system is linked to its environment, which in turn affects communication processes within the small group itself. To understand a small group, it's important to consider the group's environment. Linda Putnam and Cynthia Stohl, two leading scholars in the study of group communication, call this a bona fide group perspective.[5] They emphasize that groups not only are influenced by their environments but also help shape those same environments. This interdependence occurs for several reasons. First, members of groups often belong to other groups that simultaneously influence and are influenced by them. Second, groups typically have to coordinate their actions with other groups within the same parent organization or across organizations. Third, there is frequent internal and external communication over interpretation of group goals, the extent of the group's authority, and support for group actions that helps define a group's accountability for its task. Finally, members bring to their groups a variety of interests, ways of speaking, and mental models of effective group problem solving. This in turn affects how members create their sense of "group."

All group interaction directly and indirectly reflects this back-and-forth relationship between the group and its environment. For example, one of our colleagues is a member of the College of Arts and Humanities' general education subcommittee. This subcommittee is composed of members from all of this college's departments. Members are accountable

2.1   Bona Fide Groups: The Jamaican Bobsled Team

APPLY NOW

The Jamaican Olympic bobsled team is not an isolated group, separate from its environment. As a bona fide group it is connected to its environment and vice versa. Four reasons explain the interdependence between this bobsled team and its environment. Using the information from the case study at the beginning of the chapter, surmise possible answers to the following questions:

1. For each member of the team (sledders and coach), what are all the possible groups these individuals may belong to while they are members of the team (e.g., the coach is a banished member of the Olympic bobsled fraternity)?

2. Bona fide groups are faced with coordinating their actions with other groups. Considering the list of groups for each member of the team, what actions will have to be coordinated (e.g., Junior is supposed to leave the country and attend school to be an accountant)?

3. What kind of internal and external communication about team goals, team authority, and support exists for this team (e.g., the governing body of winter sports disqualifies the team after it successfully qualifies)? With each example, discuss how the communication impacts the group.

4. How might this team vary according to interests, ways of speaking, and past experience on athletic teams?

Once you have compiled some of the information from these questions, examine the complicated manner in which this bobsled team is interdependently connected with its environment.

not only to each of the departments in the college but also to the university's general education committee. The college's committee is influenced by the priorities of all those departments as well as by the biases developed within the college committee. The actions of the college's committee are reported to the university's committee and can change how that committee operates. Nowhere is this complexity of interlocked groups and multiple membership seen more clearly than in the modern organization.

Broome and Fulbright asked real-life group members within larger organizations to list which factors hurt their group efforts.[6] They found that organizational factors beyond a group's control often had strong negative effects on a group's performance. For example, three categories emerged: individual (e.g., member motivation and interest), group (e.g., group leadership), and organizational (e.g., assistance from the organization, including continuing informational support as needed). These findings emphasize the complexity of the group process and suggest that outcomes depend on input factors relating to members, on throughput processes such as leadership, and on environmental factors often beyond the group's control. This and other studies of actual organizational groups support the overall utility of the systems framework, which includes a focus on the group's context.[7]

Most groups are part of a larger organizational structure and must interact with individuals and other groups within that structure. Interestingly, for groups dealing with complex tasks in a very uncertain environment, how often members communicate within the group is not as crucial to their performance as is how often they interact with others in the surrounding environment.[8] This demonstrates how important it is for groups to match their internal abilities to process information with the external informational demands of their environment. Even primary groups are also part of an environment. For instance, the environment of a family may be the neighborhood or the general society in which it lives.

Most of the research in small group communication has focused on groups whose members meet face-to-face with easily identifiable environments (e.g., an office space, a small group course). We began to speculate in Chapter 1 about how traditional group processes may change when members do not meet face-to-face and do not communicate with each other in real time. In our global world, many companies are collaborating on tasks with the help of computer technology that allows the members of multiple groups to interact with each other without being on the same site. For instance, the Boeing 767 airplane is the result of collaboration among Boeing engineers, who designed the fuel system and cockpit; Aeritalia SAI engineers, who developed the fins and rudder; and multiple Japanese firms, whose responsibility was the main body of the plane.[9]

Modern organizations are also rapidly changing. More and more they are composed of employees who do not work in the same place or at the same time. Some of these organizations are **virtual groups**—their "location" is a network of members connected by computer and who may never see each other face-to-face. Members of these work groups may contact each other only via electronic mail (e-mail) or videoconferencing. Some of these virtual groups contain members from different organizations who form a temporary alliance to attain a particular purpose.[10] These groups commonly appear in such industries as telecommunication, aerospace, motor vehicle, electronics, and computer. For example, MoveOn.org is a liberal advocacy group with a membership in 2004 of 2.25 million,[11] but this organization does not have an office. A small staff works from home in different cities communicating mostly by e-mail and instant messaging.

Bona fide group theorists have begun to study these virtual groups. They posit that collaboration is primarily a communicative phenomenon. How then do group members manage their roles, multiple contexts, boundaries, and tasks? Traditional small group concepts are thrown into new light. For instance, traditional groups internally manage their knowledge and can more easily find out where to get needed information, compared to the tasks of virtual groups which can be so innovative and multidimensional as to be beyond the knowledge of any member. In addition, members may have no clue whom to contact for information. Commitment in collaborating groups is complicated by the variety of responsibilities participating members have elsewhere. Formal positions of power are often unrecognizable in these groups, which necessitates the continual negotiation of power positions. Decision-making procedures often created internally in traditional groups are, in virtual groups, affected by the norms of parent companies, cultural changes, orders given by external agents, and even decisions made outside the group. For example, UNIX, a computer desktop environment, is the result of collaboration among a variety of computer companies. Any decisions made by one or more of those companies on products unrelated to UNIX could have affected the decisions made during the UNIX collaboration.

GLOSSARY

Virtual Group

A group in which members do not communicate with each other in the same time and place

CHARACTERISTICS OF SYSTEMS

The concepts that follow describe several important characteristics of social systems. These characteristics help explain how a system functions, both internally and within the surrounding environment.

Open and Closed Systems.   Whether a system is relatively open or closed is determined by the amount of interaction the system has with its environment. A **closed system** (we know of no completely closed human system) has little interaction with its environment, whereas an **open system** has a great deal (see Figure 2.2). The fact that the

FIGURE 2.2   Model of a Small Group as an Open System

Environment

Interfaces

Environment	Members	Resources	
Physical	Needs and	Knowledge	**Input variables**
Social	motives	Funds	
• Parent org.	Attitudes	Tools	
charge	Beliefs and values	Time	
• Society and	Skills	etc.	
culture	Number of participants		
• Competing			
groups			

Interfaces

Members' behaviors and roles
Norms
Status and power relationships
Conflict/cooperation/cohesiveness
Communication network
Procedures
• Communication
• Decision making
• Investigating
• Problem solving
• Action

Throughput (process) variables

Interfaces

Solutions
Personal satisfaction
Modifications in throughput (structural and procedural)
Personal growth
Organizational development
Changes in cohesiveness/status/relationships

Output variables

Feedback channels

Environment

United States is an exceptionally open system made it easier for the World Trade Center terrorist pilots to enter the country, train as student pilots, and travel freely from state to state. Groups are open systems, too, experiencing varying levels of interchange with their environment. Our bobsled team had a moderate amount of interaction with its surroundings. The team was affected by the fans' reactions, and the fans and general public were influenced by the team's successes as well. Your classroom groups also experience degrees of openness with their environments. You may not learn what another group has been doing until group presentations because its members had little interaction with other class members and the instructor. Other groups may often interact with each other in class, getting ideas from those outside groups, and may meet regularly with the instructor to clarify requirements for group projects and presentations. These groups choose more open exchanges with their environments.

Degrees of openness have advantages and disadvantages. For example, some American companies, resisting the changes brought by "outsiders," prefer to stay as closed to outside influence as possible. This enables managers to maintain more control over what happens internally, but it also cuts off the company from what could be helpful information that might improve its operation and profits. Classroom groups that remain relatively closed in an effort to control information may miss valuable information and ideas that could have improved their critical thinking. Groups that choose to be more open with their environments may have more information to coordinate, but they can take advantage of that information in their critical thinking and in carrying out their task.

Openness and free interchange with the environment are distinct advantages for most groups. For example, the Ford Motor Company groups that were responsible for the design of Ford's successful Taurus automobile made a point of seeking input (information, ideas, suggestions) from the factory workers who would build the Taurus and many of whom could be expected to buy it. The workers supplied numerous suggestions, which were adopted. If the Taurus engineering group had remained closed to opinions from workers and others outside the immediate group, the Taurus might not have been so well designed and sought after by the car-buying public.

Interdependence.   **Interdependence** refers to the fact that each element of a system simultaneously influences and is influenced by the other elements. Just as the system as a whole is affected by its environment, so are the system's individual components affected by each other. Have you ever set up a row of dominoes, then tipped over the first one and watched the others fall in turn? That's interdependence. Within small groups, one element, idea, behavior, or person can change the functioning of the entire group. In our bobsled story, we saw how the sledders' abilities determined, in part, the coach's strategy, and how the personality of individual players such as Sanka, the eternal optimist, could spur a team to greater effort, which in turn increases the likelihood of team success.

Another characteristic of interdependence among elements of a small group is the interdependent goal toward which all group members work. The members of the group rely on each other as they strive to reach their objective; one member cannot reach the objective alone. As with the bobsled team, group members win and lose as a group. Sports teams cannot have one member win and the rest of the team lose. So it is with most small groups as they work to accomplish a task as a group. If one member is to achieve the goal, then all members must achieve it. For example, if your project group is required to give a presentation to the rest of the class, the goal is reached for all members when the presen-

GLOSSARY

Interdependence

The elements of a system are related interdependently such that all elements mutually influence each other

2.1   The Influence of Computer-Mediated Communication on the System

Go to
**www.mhhe.com/
adamsgalanes6**
for additional
weblink activities.

MEDIA AND TECHNOLOGY

The integration of technology, and the potential for various modes of CMC, has begun to influence the way we view small group systems. Technological advances have increased the potential for group members to interact more freely with the environment by opening the lines of communication between those inside and outside of the group. For instance, an input such as the time a member can allocate to the group has become less restrictive as technology can be used to allow any time or place interaction. The Internet also has increased group access to information about the task (i.e., search engines), increased the flow of information (i.e., e-mail and instant messaging), and allowed for telecommuting opportunities (i.e., netmeeting and group computer software systems). What other group inputs described in this chapter may be enhanced as a result of an increased reliance on technology? What about throughputs and outputs?

Although each of these resources functions to create a more open group system, integration of technology can also produce a variety of drawbacks that may discourage its use. Think about how the types of inputs you bring to the group (personality, abilities, and expertise) are influenced by your physical presence. If you were relegated to working off-site for a group meeting, would it be possible for you to exert the same input? In an examination of telecommuting, Mallia found that individuals using this approach lose status within the group. They also reduce their prospect for upward mobility in an organizational hierarchy chain because of the lack of face-to-face interaction. Can you think of other disadvantages that may result for a group or organization by fostering CMC interaction?

To learn more about the advantages and disadvantages for integration of technology into an organization or group, visit **www.gilgordon.com** for a comprehensive list of available resources on the subject.

GLOSSARY

Computer-Mediated Communication (CMC)

Any interaction via computer technology like chat rooms

Feedback

The return of system outputs as system inputs, which allows the system to monitor its movement toward goals and make necessary changes

---

tation is completed in a manner satisfactory to all. Interdependence is a key characteristic to look for in determining whether a collection of individuals has become a group.

Feedback.   One valuable feature of human systems is that they are able to adapt to changing conditions and circumstances. In part, they can do this through the use of **feedback,** the part of the system's output that is returned to the system as input. Feedback enables the system to monitor its progress toward the goal and make corrections when needed. In our bobsled story, Irv saw that his arrangement of sledders was successful. This feedback indicated that what he was doing was working, so he didn't need to change their positions. In another example, during practice runs and by studying pictures of the course, Derice could make adjustments in the team's movements for more successful runs.

As we pointed out earlier, open systems interact freely with their environments. Feedback is the environment's response to a system's output. It can come in the form of information or tangible resources and helps the system determine whether it needs to make adjustments to reach its goals. For instance, the critical response you receive from your instructor on group assignments provides your group with information on how well you are accomplishing your group task. Your project group can assess this information and decide which changes need to be made and how they should be made. Uncertainty between group members plays a key role in motivating feedback and gives it its value.[12] Do other group members like me? How did a group member take my comment? Are we on the right track? Did we select the best service organization to work with for our project? Is our group report comprehensive enough? Are our meetings getting us anywhere? These and countless other questions reflect our uncertainties in group work and motivate us to search for feedback to help us answer the numerous questions raised during group work.

However, not all feedback is equally useful—feedback varies in how effective it is to the group. Group members evaluate feedback along various dimensions including characteristics of the feedback and the source of the feedback.[13] Is the feedback relevant, clear, and accurate? Information for information's sake is not good enough. The group must judge the information relevant to its task. In addition, clear and accurate feedback is more beneficial to a group than feedback that is ambiguous and false or not grounded in sound reasoning.

Critical feedback, regardless of its clarity and accuracy, is hard to give and receive. However, it is necessary for effective group problem solving. The best way to give it is to sandwich it between favorable feedback and pose it as a *group* issue, not a personal one.[14] For example, Irv notices the bobsled team is not bonding enough to be a championship team. Rather than tell members he is disappointed in them, he can ask them how they can work together to be more cohesive. He might do this by first sharing with them how much their track speed has increased, followed by his observation that when pressed, they seem to fall apart, but that they have become closer than when they first met as a group of individuals interested in going to the Olympics. The critical observation that they seem to fall apart under pressure is sandwiched between two more favorable observations.

Feedback is evaluated by its content as well as its source. Originally, Irv did not have much credibility with his bobsled team because he had left the sport in disgrace. His feedback about who should play what role on the team and how members should work toward the medal was not received well initially. He had to earn their respect for his feedback to have any credibility. Groups receive feedback from a variety of sources and must ascertain how trustworthy it is, how responsive it is to the needs of the group, and what is the status of the person giving the feedback.[15]

Multiple Causes, Multiple Paths. One feature of all living systems, including small groups, is complexity. Usually, many factors combine to produce a single outcome, indicated by the concept of **multiple causes.** As an example of multiple causes, the Jamaican bobsled team had high morale at the end of the Olympics. This occurred for several reasons: They became medal contenders, the country supported them, they had a leader who was well liked and effective, all the members contributed to the team's success, and other factors that are not readily apparent. Too often, individuals try to pinpoint a single cause for a group outcome. For example, you may have heard someone say, "We would have come up with an excellent proposal if our chair had listened to our suggestions. As it

---

was, everybody hated the group." The behavior of the group's chair definitely contributed to the group's low morale, but other factors probably had an impact as well. Perhaps members did not like each other, the task was not an interesting one, or the group did not have sufficient time or information to do its best. All these factors could have interacted to produce the dissatisfaction.

A related principle of groups is that there is usually more than one appropriate way to reach a particular objective. This principle is indicated by the concept of **multiple paths.** For example, there are a number of ways to plan a fun party, and a variety of ways to develop a respectable undergraduate curriculum for communication majors. Which is the "right" way? All the ways are right—the most effective approach depends on the characteristics of all the participants. Also, the concept of multiple paths implies that two or more groups could come up with similar solutions to a problem, even though each group had members with different abilities and areas of expertise, leadership styles, and ways of resolving differences of opinion. Like multiple causes, the concept of multiple paths encourages us to recognize the complexity of small groups.

Nonsummativity.   **Nonsummativity** refers to the concept that a system is not the sum of its parts. Sometimes, as with the Jamaican bobsled team, a small group performs better than the sum of its parts, and sometimes it performs much worse than expected. The Los Angeles Lakers were favored to be the National Basketball Association's 2004 national champions—even at the start of the season. They had arguably the two best players in the league and had acquired two other outstanding players. Yet they lost to the Detroit Pistons, a team whose player roster did not match in talent or salary the Laker roster. How could this be? A small group is an entity of its own and takes on a life of its own, so it performs better—or worse—than anyone can predict.

Small group researchers have long been aware of this phenomenon. Groups often achieve an assembly effect, or a positive synergy, in which the output is superior to the averaging of the outputs of the individual members. For instance, we heard a television story about a Tucson, Arizona, Little League team called the Diamondbacks who won the 1998 championship, 26–0. What is so unusual about this team winning the championship? The team was made up of all the kids who were not picked for the other teams, the "leftovers"! On the other hand, groups can often experience what some have called process loss, or negative synergy. For example, even groups of intelligent, knowledgeable individuals can make an extremely poor decision, such as the scientists and managers who decided to launch both the space shuttles Challenger and Columbia on their fatal trips.

Although no one knows exactly why one group experiences positive synergy and another negative synergy, it may have something to do with the level of ambiguity that faces the group, whether the group encounters obstacles during its problem-solving process, and how it deals with those obstacles.[16] The Jamaican team faced numerous obstacles: a short time in which to train and qualify, little money, finding a sled for less than $5,000, members with no experience, a country with no snow, a coach lacking respect, ridicule from others, being ousted from the Olympics and getting back in, possible loss of one member, and the list goes on. Yet the team members did not quit and worked together to overcome each obstacle, finding new pride in themselves and their own style of sledding. Communication among members is the key to making the most, instead of the least, of group members' abilities. Group members must understand the problem-solving process and be taught how to use communication that facilitates effective discussion and problem solving.

For more information on multiple paths in a tangled web, go to the Online Learning Center at **www.mhhe.com/ adamsgalanes6**

2.2   CNN's Reporting Disaster: What Happened?

APPLY NOW

CNN, during its premiere of "NewsStand: CNN & *Time*," a television news venture with *Time* magazine, reported in the lead story, "Valley of Death," that the United States had used lethal nerve gas in 1970 as part of a Laotian secret mission to kill American defectors. This report was broadcast June 7, 1998, on "NewsStand: CNN & *Time*" and reported in *Time* despite several oral and written complaints from journalists in both news organizations questioning the validity of the story. A military consultant resigned in light of his concerns. On July 3, 1998, the *Fresno* (California) *Bee,* reported CNN's retraction of the story by Tom Johnson, CNN News Group chair, president, and CEO. Mr. Johnson admitted to serious faults with the broadcast and apologized, saying that CNN was not able to confirm the story. *Time's* managing editor admitted it too could not confirm the story.

A group of television producers and print journalists conducted 200 interviews as they worked together for eight months on the story. The group was headed by two successful producers and included an award-winning documentary producer and a Pulitzer Prize–winning journalist. An independent investigation into the validity of the story concluded that the group members had not intentionally made up the story. Instead, the reporting team drew conclusions based on questionable evidence, led sources into thinking that their suspicions could be supported in unseen evidence, and made decisions based on interview responses to a variety of hypothetical questions. The CNN investigation concluded that those involved in putting together the story so firmly believed what they were reporting they ignored information contrary to what they were finding.

How could a team of talented individuals, after an eight-month investigation and in the face of cautionary criticism, produce a report that ended in people being fired, resigning, and facing reprimands—not to mention embarrassing two highly respected news organizations? Using the system concepts open and closed systems, interdependence, feedback, multiple causes/paths, and nonsummativity, develop your own "systems" explanation for this reporting disaster. You can do this in groups or as a class.

[handwritten margin note: why they failed]

Organizations as Systems of Groups

Much of the work of both corporate and nonprofit America is done in and by small groups. Most organizations are interlocking systems of groups (see Figure 2.3). Think for a moment of how automobile companies design, build, and market their cars. Although many individual engineers are involved in the design of specific car parts, an engineering team is typically responsible for seeing that the individual parts come together into a car that works the way it is supposed to. Decades ago a single manager could oversee the production of cars,

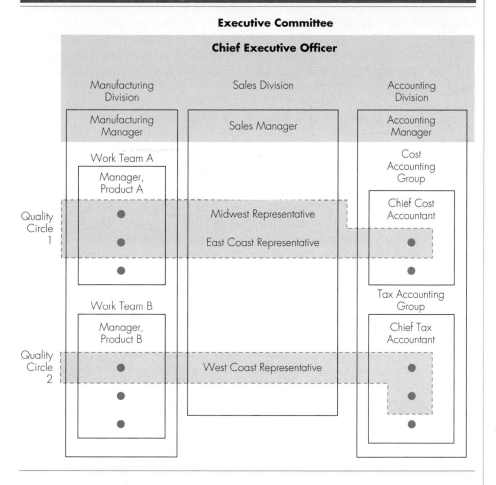

FIGURE 2.3   An Organization as a System of Interlocking Group Subsystems

but today manufacturing teams have that responsibility. Marketing, too, is a complex activity that usually involves a team of researchers, artists, copywriters, photographers, and other specialists.

In a company such as Saturn, for example, self-managed work teams create major components such as engines and transmissions, while other teams assemble the units into completed cars. In addition, quality control circles and special project teams are composed of individuals from numerous departments and divisions. Many other products could not be manufactured and many types of services could not be offered without the functioning of large systems composed of interdependent small groups.

You can see from these examples that complex organizations have small groups as primary components. The principle of larger systems being composed of many subsystems (progressively smaller groups) has many important implications. First, knowing something about how groups function and how to be an effective group member is essential if you hope to survive and prosper in modern society. Second, because there are so many parts to a system, careful coordination and extensive communication among the parts are essential. The individual groups within an organization must find ways of sharing information with each other to avoid duplicating effort or allowing important matters to fall through the cracks. This spotlights the central role of communication, both within each group and among groups, in the effective functioning of modern organizations and society. This extra-group communication has received relatively little attention from researchers, even though it is very important to the long-term survival of the group.[17]

2.3 CNN and *Time* as a System of Groups

APPLY NOW

The previous application example describes the rather complex system of groups that can make up the modern news organization. CNN, or the Cable News Network, together with *Time* produced "NewsStand: CNN & *Time*." Both CNN and *Time* are owned by Time-Warner. Using this information, and the information in the previous application example, construct your own diagram of the system of interlocking group subsystems. Then discuss the role of "extra-group" communication in this example. What went wrong? At which level? What could they have done differently? Is there a way to guarantee a valid, successful story all the time?

The usefulness of the systems perspective should be clear. We can use that perspective to help us identify and describe the individual components of groups, as long as we remember that each part functions in relation to all the other parts of the system; what affects one part affects all the other parts. This is true whether the system being studied is a person, a single group with several members, or a large organization composed of numerous interlocking groups.

RESOURCES FOR REVIEW AND DISCUSSION

SUMMARY

- General systems theory is a useful framework for studying small groups because it reminds us that systems are complex, with all parts of a system being interdependent.

- All systems use inputs to engage in throughput processes and produce outputs. Feedback helps systems monitor their performance, which cannot be predicted by summing the individual performances of the components.

- All systems try to survive by adapting to changing conditions. Open systems freely exchange resources with their environments, but closed systems do not.

- Modern organizations can be pictured as complex systems of interlocking and interdependent small groups.

EXERCISES

1. Bring to class a box of toothpicks and glue. Take out 12 toothpicks and use the glue to create some form out of the toothpicks. After you have finished, display your creation. Discuss all the creations and the concept of nonsummativity. Then move from discussing toothpicks to behaviors and from creations to small groups.

2. Select classmates to form one primary group: a family. Select parents, children, and any other members you want. Then select members of the class to be other individuals who may be involved in the family's life such as a pastor, professor, and boss. With a ball of string, loosely connect all of these individuals to relevant individuals and as you do so create a story about them. For instance, only one spouse may work and so is connected to the boss, the other spouse, and a parent. A child may be connected to only one parent, and so on. Then instruct the various individuals to role-play their parts by periodically pulling on the strings and requesting something of the individual. Use this activity to show the concept of interdependence.

3. Bring a large muffin to class. Use the muffin to discuss inputs, throughputs, and outputs. Make a list of the inputs for making the muffin. Discuss the kinds of throughputs necessary for the creation of the muffin, and then point out the output. Discuss how the environment may influence the muffin. After this discussion, compare the making of a muffin, as a relatively closed system, to the creation of a group, a relatively open system. How are they similar and how are they different?

 Go to **www.mhhe.com/adamsgalanes6** and **www.mhhe.com/groups** for self-quizzes and weblinks.

KEY TERMS ▸ CONCEPTS

Closed System
Computer-Mediated
   Communication
Environment
Feedback
Inputs

Interaction
Interdependence
Multiple Causes
Multiple Paths
Nonsummativity
Open System

Outputs
System
Throughput Processes
Virtual Group

www.mhhe.com/adamsgalanes6

Use the flashcards and crossword puzzles on the Online Learning Center to further your knowledge of these key terms.

Foundations
of Small Group
Communicating

For groups to function effectively, they must create and sustain a solid foundation that supports members' efforts. Part Two focuses on this foundation, the communication process itself. As discussed in Chapters 1 and 2, communication is at the heart of group throughput processes, so your understanding of this process is essential. Chapter 3 presents basic communication principles you should understand to be an effective group member, and Chapter 4 focuses on verbal and nonverbal messages that constitute member interaction.

Communication Principles for Group Members

CHAPTER OBJECTIVES

After reading this chapter you should be able to:

1. Define *communication.*

2. List and explain the five major characteristics of communication.

3. Explain the three major implications derived from the five major characteristics of communication.

4. Describe the difference between listening and hearing.

5. List and explain the seven habits of poor listeners.

6. Explain why listening is active behavior.

7. Describe paraphrasing as a technique for active listening.

Students for Alternative Medicine

CASE 3.1

Students for Alternative Medicine is a group of nursing students interested in alternatives to traditional Western medicine. Each month, the group sponsors a seminar, open to everyone, where the featured speaker is a practitioner of some form of alternative medicine. The group operates with a small budget and usually relies on volunteers to present the seminars; volunteers are given a token gift, such as a T-shirt with the group's logo, but are generally not paid an honorarium. The group's executive committee is responsible for scheduling and publicizing speakers.

At one meeting, member Rhea suggested they invite Chief Robert, a Cherokee medicine man, to address the group. She further suggested that, as compensation for his talk, they buy Chief Robert a piece of equipment he wanted for his work. Members agreed that Chief Robert, a prominent local healer, deserved a substantial gift, but the equipment was expensive ($200) and paying him would set a precedent for future speakers, which the group could not afford. Wade, chair of the executive committee, said, "I don't know how we'll be able to afford something like that, though I agree that he's certainly worth the money." Rhea then said, "OK, that sounds good to me." The group went on to discuss other matters and Chief Robert was forgotten. At their next group meeting, Sonya reported that publicity for Chief Robert's seminar was proceeding well, and the upcoming Sunday paper was planning a feature story on him and the seminar. Rhea noted how pleased she was that they had agreed to buy the chief his equipment and especially how grateful he was for their generosity. At that point, the meeting exploded into cries of "What? What do you mean buy his equipment? We didn't agree to buy that for him!" Members had misunderstood each other, and as a result Rhea had obligated them to a $200 gift that would come close to wiping out their savings. However, at this point, members believed they couldn't back out. It took them several meetings to overcome their anger and begin to trust each other again.

"Frances tells me you're a communications major."

Scenes like this occur every day in small groups and illustrate what can happen
when people fail to understand each other. To function effectively as a team, members must learn to put their thoughts and feelings into messages that other members can interpret and respond to. However, glitches can (and often do) occur in this
creating–sending–receiving–interpreting–responding cycle called *communication*. In our
example, Wade said, "He's certainly worth the money." He meant, "It would be great to
pay him and all of our speakers—they do such a wonderful job—but there's no way our
budget can handle it, so let's stick to T-shirts." Rhea heard his words yet interpreted
them to mean, "We don't have money to pay all our speakers, and it will be hard to
come up with that amount for Chief Robert, but, of all the speakers we've had, he is certainly worth the expense, so we'll figure out some way to pay him." She said, "OK,"
meaning "Great, I'll tell him we'll make an exception in his case." Wade heard her, yet
he *interpreted* her meaning as, "I see what you mean about the expense, and I agree with
you." These collective failures in the messages occurring between group members cost
the group time, money, and energy. Unfortunately, this misunderstanding within a
small group is not unusual. We know you can think of numerous instances you have experienced in your own group experiences!

The primary purpose of Chapter 3 is to help you understand in more detail the communication process so you can think analytically and critically about communication in
your groups. A secondary purpose is to help you improve your own participation in
your group's communication. Communicating effectively takes conscious thought and
hard work. In this chapter and the next, we focus both on the process and on how you
as a group member can communicate more effectively.

Communication: What's That?

The word *communication* has been used in dozens of slightly different ways by different writers. We use **communication** to refer to the *perception, interpretation, and response of people to messages produced by other people.* There are five major characteristics to this seemingly simple definition.

First, *communication is symbolic.* Messages, including gestures, sounds, actions, or words are symbolic.[1] The symbolic nature of communication is central to any definition of communication.[2] A **symbol** is anything (for instance a gesture, sound, action, object, or word) that arbitrarily represents something else with which it has no natural or direct relationship. For instance, there's no natural reason we call something we sit in a *chair* instead of *pig,* or *une chaise.* There is no natural reason why you have the name you do or the student group in Case 3.1 is called Students for Alternative Medicine. In addition, most of our symbols stand for concepts that have no tangible form, such as a relationship, cohesiveness, love, and democracy. Even the concept *communication* holds no tangible form. All words are symbols.

There is no inherent or direct relationship between any word and what it represents. For instance, even within a single language, the same food might be called *dinner, supper,* or the *evening meal* by different people. We noted in Chapter 1 that a collection of people can be called a *collective,* a *group,* a *rock group,* an *egg group,* or a *chicken group.* New symbols are constantly being created to represent new things or ideas: *bioterrorism, interface, surfing the Net,* and *user-friendly.* There is no limit to how many symbols we can invent and use to communicate. Even Homer Simpson, Bart's dad on the popular American cartoon "The Simpsons," can have his expression (symbol) for something gone wrong or doing something really foolish, *d'oh,* selected for official entry into the *Oxford English Dictionary.*

Symbols, due to their arbitrary representations, are convenient for thinking and communicating because we do not need to have the items present to represent them to other people.[3] Groups can discuss their observations about people, places, and things without their presence. In Case 3.1 the members can talk meaningfully about a speaker none of them have met. Symbols free us from the constraints of the here and now. Group members can call up memories of past meetings to reinforce group norms, and they can fantasize about possible new directions to take as a group. Symbol use in communication allows group members to travel simultaneously in the past, present, and future. In addition, symbols allow group members to name individual and group experience. Naming our experiences is the primary way we have of infusing that experience with meaning. The name you give your group carries with it a complex set of meanings. Small groups in our classes often think of names that tell others what topic they are working on, such as Students for Alternative Medicine. Some groups think of names that capture their unique qualities (e.g., The Researchers) and others name their groups for their goals (e.g., The A+s). Symbols allow us to engage in self-reflection because we can use all sorts of labels to describe our self-concepts and feelings. If a group member refers to another as a "leader," that label is associated with a set of assumptions for how to behave, which may come to define what the other group members expect of the labeled "leader."

Symbols can take a variety of forms. Words are the most common, but we also use numbers; pictographs (such as the international signs for cars and restrooms); Morse code; emoticons such as those used in computer e-mail to convey feelings, gestures, or objects; and gestures like those we use for OK.

As convenient and helpful as symbols are, they also have liabilities. Because symbols are arbitrary, *their meaning must be interpreted.* Dangers come from misuse and misunderstanding symbols. Two people can use a symbol to represent different concepts and therefore misinterpret each other without knowing it, as Rhea and Wade did. For example, when you say, "I love you," do you mean the same thing as your boyfriend or girlfriend does? A person may believe that there is a relationship between symbols and tangible events when none really exists. A symbol can evoke different responses than a communicator intended. Liars can manipulate us even more easily with symbols than with signs. In what some called "tortuous linguistic negotiation,"[4] the United States in the spring of 2001 sent a carefully worded letter to China in hopes of securing the release of the crew of the downed U.S. EP-3E surveillance plane from China's Hainan Island. The Americans attempted to offer regrets to China without offering a formal apology for an incident the United States considered an *accident.* Thus, in the letter, U.S. officials used the phrase *feichang wanxi,* or *extreme sympathy,* which the Chinese interpreted as *shenbiao qianti,* or *deep apology.* Misunderstandings and multiple interpretations are likely in small group communication, which makes it necessary to monitor the communication processes in our groups more thoughtfully than we normally do our everyday conversations.

Second, *communication is personal.* Because communication is symbolic, meanings are in people, not in the words themselves. Words can and do have different meanings to different people. Even when two people agree on the dictionary definition of a word, they may disagree vehemently about what that word means to them. For instance, an *excellent* group report to your group may mean one that is free of typographical errors and turned in on time. To your teacher, *excellent* may be reserved for a group report that is not only grammatically perfect but also shows considerable insight and creativity. You both are using the same word, but not meaning the same thing. This fact leads directly to the next principle of communication.

The third characteristic of communication is that *communication is a transactional process, not a thing or state.* First, let's address the notion of process. Communication is an extremely complex process involving human senses, feelings, meanings, and cultural experiences, not just a simple matter of nouns and verbs. During the process with no clearly marked beginning and end, one person experiences a perception or feeling and expresses this experience by putting it, consciously or not, into words and/or nonverbal messages, which others can perceive and respond to. Talking about communication as if it were a simple signal–response event, with nothing likely to go wrong, is naive. It is more complex than any computer circuitry. Messages from a person start as feelings or thoughts, and no one can say when their impact on others ends.

The word we use to capture this kind of complex process is *transactional.* The communication process is often modeled with components that include a source, message, channel, receiver, and response (or feedback). This implies that communication is a one-way or linear process, with feedback similar to a tennis game. The server sends the message, and the receiver lobs a response back. This is misleading because communication is a *multidirectional transactional* process. We try to capture this multidirectional transactional process in Figure 3.1. Pictorial models of communication are gross oversimplifications of a process that is not two dimensional. We use a helix first used by Frank Dance, a noted communication theorist, to depict the irreversible nature of communication.[5] Communication processes are always moving forward while also remaining simultaneously affected

FIGURE 3.1   The Communication Process

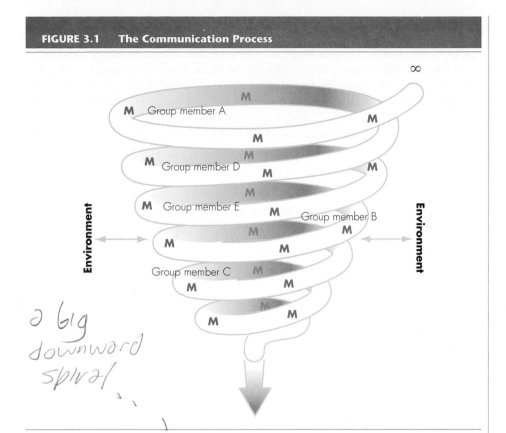

a big downward spiral

by the past, which in turn influences the present as well as the future. We added an arrow at the end of the helix complementing the infinity symbol at the top, to show communication has no distinct beginnings and endings. Group members are not depicted as either sources or receivers because they are simultaneously both. Note also, each group member is both within and outside the helix, which suggests communicators are neither totally separate from their communication nor totally immersed in it. The "Ms" represent the multitude of messages within any communication episode, and once expressed they are a part of the group and cannot be taken back. Note, too, that communication within a group occurs within a larger environment of larger, more complex helixes. The double arrows depict how communication within one group influences and is influenced by the environment(s). Can you think of a better way to depict the transactional process? We have used a pictorial model to name an intangible process explained by another set of verbal symbols all because symbols allow us to do so!

Transactional has two major meanings relevant to face-to-face communication among members of a small group. First, communicating is a simultaneous, multidirectional process. That is, regardless of who is speaking at any given moment, *every* member is simultaneously sending verbal and nonverbal messages that every other member (including the speaker) could potentially receive and interpret. The implication is clear: to be most effective as a group member, you must be aware of actions from all members, even when

GLOSSARY

Transactional

While communicating, all interactants mutually and simultaneously define both themselves and others

you are speaking. For example, a speaker may notice from facial expressions that group members are reacting negatively to her suggestions and thus modify her ideas as she speaks. Communication is not a linear, one-way process but occurs among all members simultaneously. This illustrates the complex, transactional nature of communication.

Second, *transactional* implies that members must work together to create mutual understanding for what words and concepts mean and that members can consciously help each other in this process. For example, consider the following exchange between a friend of ours upgrading his computer system and the computer salesperson "helping" him:

Salesperson:	You'll want to upgrade to Windows so you won't have to go directly through DOS.
Noah:	What's Windows?
Salesperson:	It's a graphic interface that makes computing a lot easier.
Noah:	Graphic—does that mean it works with pictures?
Salesperson:	Right. We call them icons. Windows interfaces between the user and the computer.
Noah:	But why would you want something between you and the computer?
Salesperson:	Well, instead of having to talk to the computer in a difficult language that doesn't seem logical to get it to do what you want, you use pictures to talk to the computer. It's more natural, more like the way people actually think.
Noah:	Oh, I see now. Windows is like a translator between me and the computer and, because it works with icons, it will be easier for me to use.

In this instance, Noah was able to get the computer salesperson to explain the concepts in ways that would make sense to Noah. However, it took some careful listening on his part and a considerable amount of *transacting* for the salesperson's intended meaning to become clear to Noah. Meanings are not so much *re*ceived intact from each person, but instead *con*ceived or created in context between persons.

Fourth, *human communication is both a sender and a receiver phenomenon.* Of course, something must be sent, but if there is no receiver, there is no communication. Talking makes no sense unless listening is understood and vice versa. If you are talking while no one is listening, no communication has occurred. Neither does it occur if you are listening for something that has not been sent. Many people believe that communication means only the sending of messages, so the best way to improve communication is to improve the quality of the messages we send. However, paying attention only to the sending part of communication overlooks the transactional nature of communicating, especially how a person receives and interprets messages. Thus, *both* the sender and receiver are responsible for the effectiveness of any particular communication. The sender is responsible for being as clear as possible, and the receiver is responsible for attending to the sender, trying to understand what the sender means and asking questions to help the sender clarify the message. The communication problems between Wade and Rhea in Case 3.1 resulted from messages that were unclear as sent but were also never clarified by the receivers and thus were interpreted according to what the receivers *wanted* to believe.

3.1 CMC and Communication Richness

MEDIA AND TECHNOLOGY

Go to
**www.mhhe.com/
adamsgalanes6**
for additional
weblink activities.

Businesses and organizations are increasingly relying on computer-mediated communication (CMC). Therefore, it is important to understand how different forms of CMC influence how one's message is received. Daft and Lengel developed the concept of *media richness* to describe the extent to which different media reduce the uncertainty behind different types of messages. From this theoretical perspective, a medium's richness is determined by four factors, including the *personal focus,* or the amount of personal information the medium carries; the *medium's capacity* for immediate feedback; the *number of cues* and senses involved, and the medium's *use of natural language.* A rich medium, such as face-to-face interaction, would possess all four factors to a large extent, whereas a lean medium, such as e-mail, is much more limited in the number of cues, personal information, and immediacy of feedback afforded by the medium. Medium richness directs our attention more to the decision-making processes that individuals go through as they match their communication objectives to the medium that facilitates optimal understanding.

Another factor that influences the effectiveness of a medium is whether the communication is synchronous or asynchronous. With *synchronous communication,* members interact in real time and each participant is simultaneously a sender and a receiver. With *asynchronous communication,* delays occur in the communication interaction, and each participant must take turns being the sender and receiver. E-mail is asynchronous communication because this medium does not allow for interactive, real-time communication between people.

SOURCE: R. Daft, and R. Lengel, "Organizational Information Requirements, Media Richness and Structural Design," *Research in Organizational Behavior* 6 (1984), pp. 191–233.

For more
information on the
relational dimension
of words, go to the
Online Learning
Center at **www.
mhhe.com/
adamsgalanes6**

GLOSSARY

**Content
Dimension**

*The ideas or
"what" of a
message*

**Relational
Dimension**

*The "how" of a
message expressing
the perceived
relationship
between
communicators*

The fifth characteristic of communication is that *all messages involve content and relational dimensions.*[6] The **content dimension** of a message involves the message's ideas or the *what* of the message. When you listen to a teacher's lecture, the content of her or his messages is what you record in your notes. When you listen to a research report from a group member, you often attend to the ideas the member is summarizing for the group. These may be recorded in the group's minutes. The **relational dimension** of a message is *how* the message is expressed and recognizes that content is never expressed in a vacuum. Every time you express a message, you express ideas, and you simultaneously express how you perceive the relationship between yourself and others present. For instance, the teacher's lecture can be given in a variety of ways: boring, passionate, exciting, straightforward, authoritatively, equally, and so forth. Does the teacher talk down to you as if you are a child who must be told what to think, or does the teacher share the information with you as if you are someone with your own valid experiences and knowledge? You usually do not write this dimension in your notes, yet you may talk about it to your friends during and after a lecture: "I really like how Professor Jones treats us like we have something to say, too," or "Man, I am insulted by the way Professor Jones treats us like we are children with no opinions worth listening to!" These same messages are processed in small groups as members offer how it is they see themselves in relation to each other through their messages. We often focus more explicitly on the content of messages; however, the relational aspects of messages are constant and just as integral to the communication dynamics of groups.

Our discussion thus far has focused on communication in traditional, face-to-face groups, but the growing use of computers for small group problem solving continues to change the nature of communication in small groups. We showed in Chapter 1 that with the help of computers, members can get messages to each other during meetings or outside meeting times. Members do not have to hold meetings face-to-face. They can be in different places and "talk" to each other simultaneously or receive their messages at their leisure. Using computers to interact with others inside or outside the group is called *computer-mediated communication,* or CMC. We will explore CMC further in Chapter 4 and other chapters. CMC is a symbolic, personal, and transactional process, yet there is much we still must learn about its nature in comparison to face-to-face communication.

Although skills in both sending and receiving are essential to effective small group communication, most small group members need to pay closer attention to how they *listen* and *interpret* and *how* they express themselves. This is true whether they are communicating face-to-face or doing so through computers. Usually, the *receiving* as well as the *relational* aspects of communication fail to get adequate attention.

Implications for Small Group Communication

The five communication principles just described have several implications that are particularly relevant for small groups. We explain three of the most important ones here.

1. **Making group communication productive is the responsibility of every member.**

   There is a great tendency to blame another person when a statement is ignored, misunderstood, forgotten, or not heard. "If he had just listened to me," or "If she weren't so (boring, arrogant, dominating, nasty, prejudiced, ignorant, etc.) I'd have paid more attention" are typical statements group members use to blame others and disclaim any responsibility for miscommunicating. But communication is a groupwide multidirectional activity. For example, the responsibility for glitches in the Students for Alternative Medicine's meeting was not Wade's or Rhea's alone. If you don't understand, you can (and should) say so. If you can't hear, you can ask the others to talk louder. If you failed to note an assignment for which you are responsible, you have the obligation to ask. Do not expect others to read your mind and supply you with information you are missing. In short, everyone must constantly monitor how the communication process is working and correct problems as needed.

2. **Perfect understanding among group members is impossible.**

   Because of all the communication characteristics we discussed earlier—that it is symbolic, personal, transactional, multidimensional, and so forth—perfect understanding cannot occur. Since we have different words in our vocabularies and different experiences with words, our associations with words and gestures differ.

3.1   **Communication and the Students for Alternative Medicine**

The Students for Alternative Medicine is composed of people with a common interest: alternatives to Western medicine. It is an organized, productive group. However, even groups composed of members with a common interest can encounter communication problems. Perfect understanding is never possible in small groups. Reflecting on the five characteristics of communication in small groups, consider the following:

1. Were any signs mentioned in the case study?

2. Which symbols do you think were the most problematic for the group? Why?

3. What different forms did the symbols take in this case study?

4. Explain how there is no definite beginning and ending to their story.

5. How is the communication among the members transactional?

6. How did the group members work together to create the misunderstanding?

7. Change the script of the meeting and show how the members together could have produced a better outcome.

8. List what you think are the content issues and then list what you believe are the relational issues expressed in how the messages may have been expressed.

9. Was the conflict between Wade and Rhea a breakdown in communication? If so, how might the conflict have looked if it wasn't from a breakdown in communication?

Hence, some degree of difference in meaning always exists between two or more people responding to each other's messages. Fortunately, perfect understanding isn't necessary. In a group, we need only communicate well enough to coordinate our behavior toward a common goal. When we can do this, we are communicating well enough for group success, even though we haven't achieved perfect understanding.

3. **Disagreement and conflict are not necessarily signs of a breakdown in communication.**

People often say that conflicts can be avoided if people would communicate better. Nothing could be further from the truth. Some small group conflicts are due to misunderstandings or lack of information that might be solved through communication, but many conflicts result from group members having different values, goals, beliefs, or personal objectives. (We elaborate on several of these in Chapter 9.) In addition, conflict may occur not over the ideas expressed but rather over *how* they were expressed. Thus, no breakdown or misunderstanding occurs—members are quite clear about what the conflict involves; in this case, matters are made worse if miscommunication is blamed while the gist of the conflict is ignored.

Coordinating the efforts of group members in a functioning system is more dependent on good listening than on good speaking skills, although we often concentrate on speaking. No matter the skill of the speaker, it is the listener who determines whether listening will happen. A beneficial group member must be able to synthesize group sentiments and summarize a discussion cogently. But that is not possible if members were not listening well enough to recall what others said or to think carefully about what they mean. For example, at one time it was estimated that 15 million meetings occurred in the United States every morning. In just one six-person group, 30 minutes of time is wasted every time 5 minutes of information is repeated.[7] Imagine the total waste in all these groups! You can probably see why a national survey of 1,000 personnel managers identified listening as the second most important skill that influences their hiring decisions.[8]

Listening: Receiving, Interpreting, and Responding to Messages from Other Group Members

If a small group is to operate effectively, members must understand each other. Listening is the central component of this process.[9] It is an important skill for both members and leaders of small groups. Members who are perceived as poor listeners are not likely to be chosen as group leaders, but leaders usually are perceived as good listeners.[10] Thus, as a good listener, you will not only be helpful to your group, but you will be influential as well. The following section describes what constitutes good listening.

LISTENING DEFINED

Many people use *hearing* and *listening* as if they were synonyms, but we agree with Steil, Barker, and Watson that **listening** is a four-step process that begins with perceiving a message, then interpreting it, deciding what it means, and finally responding to it.[11] Such listening is not passive; it requires activity. Listening is behavior over which we can exert considerable control.

Most people do not listen well. The majority of participants in half-hour discussions we observed could not list the ideas proposed as possible solutions, the major issues discussed, or the decisions reached. When we ask students to paraphrase previous speakers' ideas, more than half the time they cannot do so (and we expect that college students are not much worse at such listening than are other people). In short, most of the time we listen rather badly. As respondents, we often give the speaker little or no overt feedback. This gives the speaker little opportunity to assess whether we understood the message as intended. This also implies what the speaker said wasn't worth a response.[12]

Effective listening requires that the listener hear what the speaker said, interpret it accurately, and respond appropriately. Usually, hearing what the speaker said presents little problem. Group members are accustomed to asking a member to repeat a statement they weren't able to hear. However, the interpretation and response steps can be tricky because of the nature of symbolic communication we discussed earlier. Different people mean different things with the same words and actions. Major factors that influence what words and

---

GLOSSARY

Listening

A complex process involving perceiving, interpreting, and responding to messages

actions mean to us include our culture, gender, age, sexual orientation, learning style, and personalities. We take a closer look at such diversity in small group interaction in Chapter 8. In addition, the relational dimension of messages in groups gives members all sorts of information about how they see themselves in relationship to each other. This requires that members listen "between the lines" for this information because it often is not directly stated but found in *how* (e.g., tone) the message is expressed. When members of the Students for Alternative Medicine expressed their displeasure with Rhea, they did so with raised voices and harsh tones. How they expressed disappointment in her behavior could send her the message they no longer respect her choices or do not trust what she says.

Steps can be taken to become a more competent listener in small groups. In the next sections, we describe four listening preferences and several of the bad habits of poor listeners, as well as provide suggestions for improving your listening behavior.

LISTENING PREFERENCES

Over time and in a multitude of conversations we all develop listening preferences. When do you enjoy listening? When is listening difficult for you? Who are the people you like listening to? What do you focus on when you listen? Why do you choose to listen? Our preferences can greatly affect the quality of communication in a small group.

There are four general listening preferences: people-, action-, content-, and time-oriented.[13] No one preference is right or wrong; each has its advantages and disadvantages. Being an effective group member means identifying your own preference and those of the other members. It also means shifting your preference to meet the needs of the group.

People-oriented listeners are focused on how their listening behaviors affect relationships. These are members others go to when they want someone to listen. They are attentive and appear nonjudgmental. Their listening behaviors may include the use of *we* more often than *I,* and they incorporate emotional appeals into their discussions. For instance, they might be heard telling a human interest story to calm members who are upset. Showing concern for others is their priority, but people-oriented listeners can attend too much to others' moods and get distracted from the group's task.

The **action-oriented listener** is focused on the job at hand. Such listeners help the group stay on task by paying attention to the details and giving feedback about the goal and how the group may achieve it. They enjoy listening if material is presented in an organized fashion. Sometimes these listeners may appear overly critical, may tune out when the discussion seems aimless, and interrupt too much if the discussion gets off track.

The **content-oriented listener** is drawn to the highly credible source and enjoys analyzing the things she or he hears. These listeners dissect information and can show a group the many sides to an issue. At times, though, they can be seen as overly critical and intimidating. In addition, their listening preference slows the group's problem solving because they like to spend considerable time analyzing information. They also minimize nontechnical information such as anecdotes and devalue information from unknown sources.

The **time-oriented listener** is the member who sets meeting times, reminds members of their time constraints, and discourages wordy discussions. These members value time. They discourage discussion as the time nears for the meeting to end and grow impatient with the more creative, spontaneous activities in groups.

3.2   Students for Alternative Medicine and Listening

Earlier you met three members of the Students for Alternative Medicine's executive committee: Wade, Rhea, and Sonya. Now let's meet two other members: Bob and Eric. Each of these members has his or her own listening preferences, some of which may be seen in the case study. Rhea is a people-oriented listener, Sonya is a content-oriented listener, and Wade is an action- and content-oriented listener. Bob is a time-oriented listener, and Eric avoids listening situations but is required to show up and vote. Wade and Rhea do not get along at most meetings, often arguing over who should be supported by the group. Wade thinks that Rhea gets too upset when others are upset, and Rhea thinks that Wade is overly critical. Sonya is close friends with Eric, who often votes with Sonya. Bob contributes to the group only when he has something worthwhile to say and does so in a very precise fashion. He gets along well with Rhea and Sonya.

Imagine you are a community member who is interested in bringing Dr. Jessica McGehee, a leading practitioner of holistic medicine, to the attention of the group. You would really like the group to sponsor a seminar with Dr. McGehee. You also know the group is low on funds due to the most recent expenditures, but Dr. McGehee will be in town and will be available. You know a generic presentation to the group will not work, so you decide to tailor your presentation to the listening preferences of the group.

1. Whom would you select as the target of your presentation and why?
2. What specific strategies would you use in your presentation to appeal to those you believe you need to convince most?

No preference is the best. Our preferences are influenced by many factors, including the nature of the relationships among group members and time constraints. Each one has positive and negative tendencies that are summarized in Table 3.1. Use them productively and curtail the negative characteristics of each one. Do this by knowing your own and the others' preferences and encouraging the productive use of each preference.

HABITS OF POOR LISTENERS

The irony of being in a small group is that you spend more time listening, yet because you are in a small group, the pressure to listen is not as strongly felt as it is when you are interacting with only one other person.[14] The more people held accountable for the success of the group, the easier it is to get away with poor listening. We all develop poor listening habits, yet effective group discussion is built around recognizing the challenges of good listening. You can do that by recognizing the listening preferences of your group and understanding some common poor listening habits, summarized in Table 3.2.

TABLE 3.1	**Listening Preferences**

PEOPLE-ORIENTED LISTENERS

Advantages:	Focus on relationships.
	Show concern for others.
	Inclusive and nonjudgmental.
Disadvantage:	Can become distracted by others' moods.
Example:	"Tell me more about how you would feel if we went ahead with that option."

ACTION-ORIENTED LISTENERS

Advantages:	Focus on the job.
	Help the group stay on task.
	Help the group stay organized.
Disadvantage:	May sacrifice relationships in favor of task.
Example:	"I know you're upset, but we have a lot of work to do so we'd better get down to business."

CONTENT-ORIENTED LISTENERS

Advantages:	Help the group analyze information.
	Look at issues from many sides.
Disadvantages:	Seem overly critical.
	Dismiss anecdotal or nonexpert information.
Example:	"We aren't ready to decide yet because we haven't really heard every side of the issue."

TIME-ORIENTED LISTENER

Advantages:	Help the group stick to schedule.
	Discourage rambling discussions.
Disadvantage:	Impatience with spontaneous discussion may stifle creativity.
Example:	"Let's make up a schedule so we know we can get done by our deadline."

Pseudolistening occurs when a listener fakes active listening by giving the speaker many of the signs that good listeners give, while actually thinking about something else. The pseudolistener nods, smiles, murmurs, and often looks the speaker in the eye. However, he or she may be daydreaming, thinking up an argument instead of trying to understand the speaker's perspective, or working on a personal problem. It is better to say you are uninterested than to pretend interest.

GLOSSARY

Pseudolistening

A poor listening habit involving pretending to listen to others

TABLE 3.2	**Habits of Poor Listeners**

Pseudolistening: Pretending to listen while thinking about something else or while daydreaming.

Silent arguing: Failing to understand what a speaker is saying, then mentally rehearsing objections to the misunderstood notion of the speaker's idea.

Assuming meaning: Interpreting the speaker's behavior by using the cultural rules appropriate for the listener.

Mind assault: Insistence by poor listeners that they understand better than the speaker what the speaker meant, even though the speaker protests.

Focusing on irrelevancies: Becoming distracted from a speaker's message by unimportant details such as dress, accent, physical appearance, or environmental distractions.

Sidetracking: Changing the topic because you weren't paying attention to the speaker; not connecting remarks to statements of the previous speaker.

Defensive responding: Failing to listen or failing to try to understand what a speaker is saying because poor listeners feel psychologically threatened by something the speaker said or did; responding with "chips on their shoulders."

Silent arguing means the listener forms a quick judgment about the speaker's idea, rejects it without listening to the rest of what the speaker says, and then begins a silent mental search for arguments about what is wrong with the idea. We tend to listen to that which supports our previous beliefs and to ignore or tune out what contradicts them. You cannot listen well while silently arguing.

Assuming meaning occurs when the receiver interprets what the sender said or did through the filter of the receiver's culture, then proceeds to make a judgment about the sender. For example, a Native American may answer a question from a European American without looking the questioner in the eye; the European American concludes that the Native American is hiding something or lying. However, looking down is a sign of respect in many Native American cultures. The European American's conclusion is in error because it is based on what middle-class European Americans do when answering questions. In other words, the Native American's behavior is being interpreted by the wrong set of rules, and a serious misunderstanding has occurred.

Mind assault, a stronger form of assuming meaning, is insisting that a speaker meant what the listener would have meant by a statement and continuing to insist on this meaning despite protests from the speaker.[15] For example, "I know what you really mean. You don't think our professor will object to our topic. You just want to do something else!" assumes that the listener knows better than the speaker what the speaker meant. This behavior attempts to dominate or reject the speaker. Instead, good listeners try to understand another as that person wants to be understood, and only then evaluate the other's ideas and motives.

"I'm sorry—did you say something? I was off creating my own reality."

Focusing on irrelevancies occurs when a listener pays attention to something other than what the speaker is saying. Some people pay so much attention to dress, word choices, grammar, face or body details, accent or dialect, or things in the environment that they have little energy to give to the ideas of a speaker. For example, one of our students mispronounced a word during a group presentation. A faculty member smirked and rolled her eyes. She didn't listen to another word the student said, even though the information was valuable, because she had focused on the speaking mistake the student had made. If you are guilty of this bad habit, constantly remind yourself to concentrate on understanding the speaker and not being distracted.

Sidetracking takes several forms, all of which result in going off on a tangent. The listener makes a statement that is not connected to what was previously said, thus sidetracking the discussion by starting a new topic. In the student discussions David Berg analyzed, the topic was switched on the average of about every minute.[16] The following example illustrates sidetracking by switching issues, thereby giving irrelevant responses to previous remarks:

Pete: We can use our time better if we split up the work. Why don't we each pick the section we want to research?

Jean: Did any of you guys happen to see *Pearl Harbor* last weekend? [a sidetrack]

Defensive responding is likely to occur when a listener perceives a threat from another's remark—someone's "hot button" has been pushed. For example, you may be

Mo-fuckinz

sensitive to attempts of others to control or dominate what you do (shown in how the message is expressed), so, when Tony says, "Get me a Coke while you are at the machine," you reply, "Get your own blankety-blank drink!" People who listen and respond defensively usually quit trying to understand the other's point of view and thus may miss important qualifications or statements that clarify the speaker's meaning. It is especially important to guard against defensive responses when highly emotive words such as *abortion, right to life, gun control, welfare state,* and *liberal* are used. When you feel yourself getting tense and emotionally aroused, sit back, take a deep breath, and try to paraphrase what the other meant before you express either support or opposition. That will keep you from listening or responding defensively.

In all the bad listening habits, the listener is not focusing attention on the ideas of the speaker but on something else—a physical characteristic, a habit of speech, a personal belief, a different topic, a personal definition of a symbol, a private relationship with the speaker, a personally held value, or how the message was expressed. Where and how to focus attention are consistent problems for many, including those who are generally good listeners in other contexts.

LISTENING ACTIVELY

Listening is active, not passive, behavior. When you pay close attention in an effort to understand what another means, your heart speeds up as your metabolism rate rises. In contrast, heart rates of passive listeners who take no personal responsibility for understanding another slow down. Active listening is partly a matter of choosing to focus on the other and of selecting what parts of a message to focus on and try to recall.

A good test for **active listening** is to paraphrase (put in your own words) what you think the other person meant. Merely repeating another's words, like a parrot, does not demonstrate that you understood. An effective paraphrase requires the listener to process the information cognitively. When you paraphrase what you thought the speaker said or the relational message you inferred from how it was expressed, you give the speaker a basis for deciding whether or not you understood the original message adequately or whether you missed or distorted parts of it. The original speaker, after hearing the paraphrase, should accept it if it is accurate or correct the parts that were distorted or omitted, then ask you to try paraphrasing again. Only when the original speaker is completely satisfied that you have understood adequately should you proceed to agree, disagree, elaborate, or change topics. Here is a bit of dialogue that illustrates active listening between two group members discussing medical insurance:

Karla: Medical costs are incredibly high. On the average, it costs about $1,500 per day in the hospital. No wonder 37 percent of our citizens lack hospital insurance! Too many people are making too much money off the illnesses of others. We gotta stop that!

Jeannie: You're saying that the reason so many people lack hospital insurance is that hospital costs are high, and they are so high because a lot of people are paid too much in the health care business. Is that right? [Jeannie attempts to paraphrase Karla's statement to understand what Karla meant, especially to clarify the content of her reasoning.]

Karla: Well, basically, but I really don't mean people don't have insurance because the hospital costs so much, but because they can't afford it.

That may be partly because it costs a lot for the insurance—like $350 a month for a young husband and wife with no kids—and partly because the insurance companies have to pay such high hospital and other medical bills. [Karla corrects the paraphrase and clarifies her own reasoning.]

Jeannie: Now let's see if I understand your thinking: 37 percent of our citizens lack hospital insurance because they feel they can't afford it. Part of the reason they can't afford it is that high medical costs have made premiums very high, like $200 a month for a young person. And a lot of people are making more money than you think they should out of the illnesses of others. [Jeannie's second attempt at paraphrasing Karla's statements.]

Karla: Right. [Karla's confirmation of second paraphrase as accurate.]

Jeannie: I partly agree and partly disagree. I think . . . [The paraphrase accepted, Jeannie now begins to explain her position on the issue about why so many people lack hospital insurance.]

Active listeners confirm their understanding *before* they state evaluations. Then, confident of what the speaker meant, active listeners evaluate what they have understood. They may respond by agreeing or disagreeing, saying that the idea is irrelevant to the issue being discussed, that it is logically unsound, that there is no evidence to support it, and so on. In the above example, the group members are focused on clarifying the content of their messages. They could have also been focused on their interpretations of how the

3.3 Poor Listening Habits and Misunderstandings

APPLY NOW

Reconstruct the Students for Alternative Medicine's meeting. Your agenda item is the discussion of whether or not to sponsor a seminar featuring Chief Robert, a Cherokee medicine man and prominent local leader. Get together with six other members of the class to role-play group members. Before your discussion, hand out envelopes to each member. Four of the envelopes will contain a description of one poor listening habit (pseudolistening, silent arguing, assuming meaning, mind raping, focusing on irrelevancies, and sidetracking). The other three envelopes will instruct the member to practice active, focused listening. Allow yourselves to role-play the meeting for about 25 minutes. Ask your classmates to watch the meeting and take notes on the listening behaviors. After the meeting discuss how the poor habits were displayed and their impact on the discussion.

1. Were any behaviors particularly destructive? Why?

2. How well were the members practicing active, focused listening, and did they reduce the effects of the poor habits? How typical are some of these poor habits?

3. How was the role-play of the meeting different from a real meeting?

ideas were expressed. For instance, if Jeannie expressed herself as someone who felt superior to the others, they may have asked if she was trying to tell them what to think or just thinking aloud with peers.

One effect of active listening is that the discussion slows down. Most of us are our own best listeners—we like to talk and, given half a chance, we will. We may become impatient, not taking time to paraphrase even when we should. You should listen actively all the time but paraphrase only part of the time—when a controversial issue is being discussed, when you can see some possibility that the speaker has a different meaning from what you think, when you are confused by what the speaker has said, and when there has been a lot of topic switching or misunderstanding. Be on guard against pseudolistening. If you realize you didn't really listen, apologize and ask for a restatement.

RESOURCES FOR REVIEW AND DISCUSSION

SUMMARY

- Communication is the process by which we create, receive, interpret, and respond to messages from others; this makes communication an ongoing, transactional, sender-and-receiver-oriented phenomenon for which every group member is responsible.

- Symbols, including words, are arbitrary, which makes perfect understanding between group members impossible and demands that effective communication among group members is the responsibility of all members.

- Listening involves hearing a message, interpreting it, deciding what it means, and responding; group members, who typically display a number of bad listening habits, need to improve this skill the most.

- Active listening, especially paraphrasing, helps members understand others more clearly.

EXERCISES

1. This exercise is designed to help you distinguish between viewing communication as one-way, linear communication or as transactional communication. Divide into two large groups. Turn to the Karla and Jeannie dialogue in the text. One group should examine the dialogue from a linear approach to communication. The other group should examine it from the transactional approach. Each group can focus on the following questions:

   a. When does communication occur in the dialogue?

   b. What is the message in this dialogue? Where does the message come from?

   c. Who is responsible for clarifying the meaning of the message? How is clarity created in this dialogue?

   d. Who is the communicator and who is the listener?

   With your classmates discuss how different the answers are to these questions depending on the approach used to answer the questions. Remember, although the approach changed how the communication/dialogue was understood, the communication/dialogue did not change.

2. Recall three recent conversations you have had. (If you are taking part in a major group project think about three recent conversations in your

group meetings.) For each conversation write down whom the conversation was with, what you talked about, how well you listened (on a scale of 1 [not well at all] to 10 [very well]), and what some of the reasons were for your good or poor listening (e.g., time of day, boring topic, preoccupied with something else). During class discussion, look for factors common to good and poor listening.

(If you apply this exercise to your group project, create a list of steps you will take to improve your listening in your next meetings.)

3. This exercise is designed to help you apply and practice active listening. Divide into groups of five or six members. Select a controversial topic and practice active listening as you discuss the topic. Remember that paraphrasing is not simply restating the previous remarks. Each group should use the following rules:

a. A discussant may not have the floor or add anything to the conversation until she or he paraphrases what the previous speaker has said to that speaker's satisfaction.

b. If the paraphrase is not accepted, the discussant may try again until the speaker accepts the paraphrase.

c. Have one member of the group keep track of the number of times paraphrases were accepted or rejected. Each attempt should be recorded.

After the activity, discuss the difficulties encountered in active listening. Look for the benefits of paraphrasing and the problems that may be encountered. Discuss why it may be so hard for group members to understand others before contributing to the discussion.

 Go to **www.mhhe.com/adamsgalanes6** and **www.mhhe.com/groups** for self-quizzes and weblinks.

KEY TERMS · CONCEPTS

Action-Oriented Listener	Defensive Responding	Relational Dimension
Active Listening	Focusing on Irrelevancies	Sidetracking
Assuming Meaning	Listening	Silent Arguing
Communication	Mind Assault	Symbol
Content Dimension	People-Oriented Listener	Time-Oriented Listener
Content-Oriented Listener	Pseudolistening	Transactional

 www.mhhe.com/adamsgalanes6

Use the flashcards and crossword puzzles on the Online Learning Center to further your knowledge of these key terms.

4

Using Verbal and Nonverbal Messages in Small Group Communication

CHAPTER OBJECTIVES

After reading this chapter you should be able to:

1. Define the concept *message*.

2. Describe structuration theory and explain its relevance to small group communication.

3. List and explain five ways to use language appropriately in small group interaction.

4. Explain how to use abstract words effectively.

5. Describe how group members can organize their remarks.

6. Compare and contrast questions of information, interpretation, value, policy, action, procedure, and relationship.

7. Explain how best to phrase questions in small group interaction.

8. Describe the principles and functions of nonverbal communication.

9. Discuss the significance of the major categories of nonverbal signals to small group communication.

10. Compare some of the advantages of computer-mediated communication and face-to-face communication.

The Search for a New Dean

It was the first meeting of the committee charged with conducting the search for a new Arts and Humanities dean at California State University, Fresno (CSUF). As was customary, a student representative was on this search committee in addition to faculty members and administrators. The committee chair used this organizational meeting to let people talk in an unstructured way about what they wanted in a new dean.

The committee discussed diversity issues and brainstormed ways that qualified minorities and women could be recruited to apply for the dean's position. Several members talked about what they perceived as a general need to increase diversity among administrators because of the large percentage of minority and international students currently at CSUF. Suddenly Raj, the student, said, "I don't think that's a big issue because our campus is already very diverse." Simultaneously, two faculty members and one administrator exclaimed, "What?"

Feeling somewhat attacked, Raj became defensive and the meeting threatened to degenerate into a "Yes, it is/No, it isn't" argument. When one member encouraged Raj to explain what he meant, he said, quite reasonably, that the only other campus he had ever visited was a small, church-related school in Fresno that had an even more homogeneous administration. The committee members readily agreed that, from Raj's perspective, the CSUF campus was more diverse administratively than his comparison school. Raj, in turn, agreed that the CSUF campus was less diverse than the schools, such as UCLA, Ohio State, and the University of Maryland, the other committee members were using for comparison.

This brief episode ended well and set the stage for the rest of the committee's meetings, but it could just as easily have alienated Raj and caused the faculty and administrative members to tune him out.

This story, so typical of many small group discussions, illustrates several important points discussed in this chapter. First, many words can be taken in several different ways. For instance, Raj initially responded defensively to the word *what*. He heard the word *what* as meaning, "What on earth are you saying, calling this a diverse administration?" In fact, that is what two of the members *did* mean when they said *what*. However, the third member, as she explained later, simply hadn't heard Raj, so she said, "What?" as a question, meaning, "Could you please repeat what you said?"

Second, verbal and nonverbal signals together contribute to our interpretation of what words mean. For example, how did Raj correctly interpret that two of the committee members intended to challenge his opinion? Probably because of the sharp, disbelieving tone of voice they used and the fact that they both whipped their heads around to look at him when they said it. Raj felt attacked because, in a way, he *was* attacked. In another example, the popular phrase "waazzzup?" makes sense only in how the phrase "What's up?" is said and its use in the appropriate context. Finally, this dean search committee story illustrates the most basic principle of all—*communication creates a group.* The verbal and nonverbal messages all group members send create the working atmosphere in the group. The type of verbal and nonverbal messages members allow determines whether the group will be cooperative or hostile, will think carefully or rush to judgment. In our story, members' basic goodwill and effective listening skills were able to undo the potential harm done by their reaction to Raj's comment. The group went on to be highly productive, cooperative, and cohesive—and it was the members' communication behaviors that made this happen.

In this chapter, we will focus on messages group members exchange and the verbal and nonverbal components of these messages. This chapter examines the complexities of group messages and thus helps improve your use of messages in a group.

Creating Messages in a Small Group

In Chapter 3 we referred to a **message** as any action, sound, or word used in interaction.[1] More specifically, messages are any actions, sounds, or words in interaction interpreted as a whole by another interactant.[2] Messages can be entirely verbal, nonverbal, or a mixture of verbal and nonverbal. For instance, a nod of the head may be interpreted as agreement or disagreement. When Raj's group members challenged his opinion they did so by questioning his opinion simultaneously by saying "what" and raising their voices, conveying to Raj their disagreement with his viewpoint.

The primary way members exchange information and ideas in small groups is by the words they use. While the use of words is obvious in small group communication, verbal and nonverbal messages operate *together* to create meaning; they are indivisible. All communicative acts are expressed via multiple verbal and nonverbal channels, which together create meaning. Think of an orchestra.[3] No single note conveyed by one instrument constitutes the symphony. Notes played together via a multitude of instruments create a symphony. Meaning is found in particular combinations of notes played within a larger symphony. When you document and analyze your group's communication (symphony) you are in fact scoring *both* the notes (words) *and* how they are played (nonverbals).

In this chapter we will first explain how any group's communication overall structures and maintains the group. We will then look at the impact of verbal messages and nonverbal messages in group interaction, remembering that in practice they are inseparable.

How Communication Structures the Small Group

We said earlier that communication, the verbal and nonverbal messages members exchange, is the essential throughput process within a small group. The way members create and maintain this exchange of messages is called **structuration.** The theory of structuration, applied to small group communication by Marshall Scott Poole, David Siebold, and Robert McPhee, is complex, but the main point is this: verbal and nonverbal communication among members creates the group norms and operating procedures and maintains them once they are established.[4]

The theory contains three important assumptions. First, group members do not come to a group with a clean slate about how to behave. They have been taught what is appropriate by their general culture, by their participation in other groups, and by the organizations they belong to. For example, the faculty and administrative culture at CSUF encourages people to treat each other politely and with respect. Thus, when members of the search committee realized that Raj felt attacked, they were motivated to undo the harm they believe they had created.

Second, although people pick up rules and standards for behavior from the general culture, there is no law that forces them to follow those rules. Individuals may choose to ignore norms and rules for behavior. For instance, even if the search committee members knew Raj felt attacked and that norms of politeness required them to try to heal the breach, they could have decided just as easily that his opinion didn't matter: "Well, he's just a student. He hasn't seen any of the world, so who cares what he thinks."

The third important assumption of structuration theory is that the group is never finally created; instead, it constantly re-creates itself through communication so that it is always in a state of becoming. That suggests that change usually happens incrementally. The search committee's meeting where Raj felt attacked was the committee's first meeting, but what if the meeting had been the 10th meeting, with the norm of attacking members well established? Because group members would have been more set in their communicative ways, it would have been much harder (although not impossible) to move the group to a respectful path. That's what structuration is all about—how communication creates and maintains the group over time.

We especially like the communicative focus of the theory of structuration; it reminds us to look at members' communicative behavior—what they say and do in the group. For instance, Raj didn't feel attacked because he had a paranoid personality. He felt attacked because of the communicative behavior of the other members. Similarly, the other members attempted to rebuild bridges with Raj when they said things such as, "I'm sorry, Raj; I didn't mean to sound so sharp. Why do you think CSUF has a lot of diversity? Tell us about the other campus you visited." Again, it was the communicative behavior that changed a developing norm into a more productive one. We now turn to a discussion of the verbal communication the language group members use.

Using Language to Help the Group Progress

Human language consists of symbols, verbal and nonverbal, and rules for using them. The verbal code is the vocabulary, or the set of words, available to the person who uses the language. In print, nonverbal elements include punctuation marks, underlining, CAPITALIZATION, **boldfacing,** and s p a c i n g. The rules are the spoken and unspoken guidelines for arranging words: what to capitalize, how to space, where to place punctuation marks, and so on. Collectively, these are the rules of syntax and grammar. Both the codes and rules vary according to social contexts; communication rules differ for an online chat group, a formal meeting of a city council, or a Jamaican bobsled team. Small

TABLE 4.1	Use Language Appropriately to Help the Group Progress

FOLLOW THE RULES OF STANDARD ENGLISH

- Use standard sentence structure and vocabulary.
- Use correct grammar.
- Avoid jargon, excess slang, and profanity.

ADJUST TO THE SYMBOLIC NATURE OF LANGUAGE

- Guard against bypassing.
- Be as precise and concrete as possible.
- Give specific examples of what you mean when you have to use an abstract term, or use synonyms.

USE EMOTIVE WORDS CAUTIOUSLY

- Recognize words that are likely to trigger strong emotional responses in others and substitute with neutral words.
- Never use name-calling.

ORGANIZE YOUR REMARKS AND THE GROUP'S DISCUSSION PROCESS

- Relate your statement to the preceding statement.
- Make one point at a time.
- State your case directly and concisely.
- Keep yourself and other members on the topic.

BE SURE THE DISCUSSION QUESTION IS CLEAR AND APPROPRIATE

- Use open-ended questions instead of either–or ones.
- Word questions clearly and concretely.
- Don't give the answer in the question.
- Make sure all group members know what question or issue is being discussed.

groups will use their own rules and codes during group meetings, but must also learn how to adapt them for group presentations to others. These rules are outlined in more detail in Chapter 11. Suggestions for using language effectively are detailed in the following section and summarized in Table 4.1. The suggestions in the table and the discussion that follows are appropriate generally for most task groups in the United States. As we will note in Chapter 8, however, different rules apply in different cultures.

4.1   **When to Code Switch and When Not to?**

We have proposed the necessity of adapting to the different rules for communication, or code switching, when the context of the social system changes. A characteristic of communication competence is being aware that different groups use different rules of communicating and changing to meet the expectations and obligations of those different groups. However, the various ways we use language to communicate is highly personal and often resistant to change.

1. When you move from group to group how easily do you adopt the rules of communicating in that group?

2. Are there times when your personal way of communicating should never be given up?

3. Are there appropriate ways of blending both your own personal style and that of the group?

4. Is adapting to the rules of communicating in a particular group a violation of personal language use?

FOLLOW THE RULES

Because different groups and cultures have different rules for communicating, you will increase your chances of being accepted and understood if you follow the rules for the group. For example, some groups are formal: Members address each other by title (e.g., Dr. Adams or Ms. Galanes) and use many abstract words with a complex sentence structure. However, these rules would be inappropriate in a self-managed work team in an auto factory, where concrete language with a clear and concise sentence structure is more effective. Be aware of and adapt to appropriate standards of behavior *for the particular group.* For example, Rick Ayers' communication arts and sciences class at Berkeley High School in California has created its own slang dictionary.[5] Each entry in the dictionary contains its etymological source, a pronunciation key, and a sentence with the entry—the students have laid out the word or phrase and the rules for its use. "Off the hook" was appropriate for 1999, "off the heazie" for 2000, and now the phrase is "off the hizzle." The purpose of this slang dictionary project was to give students an opportunity to use their own rich home language as a viable avenue for creativity in their classroom.

Even as we advise this, however, we note that many of the secondary groups you participate in will take place in the mainstream of the U.S. business, professional, and educational communities. In such cases, you should conform to the vocabulary and grammar rules of standard English. This will help other people understand you and increase your influence because numerous studies have shown that nonstandard dialects and usage lower the credibility of speakers with a variety of listeners. As teacher Rick Ayers recognized, "I want to make them aware of their brilliance, that the way they speak is not wrong, it's just another form of discourse. . . . The trick is teaching them how to translate it into standard English when they need to."[6]

GLOSSARY

Bypassing

Occurs when group members think they have the same meaning for a word or phrase but in actuality they do not

ADJUST TO THE SYMBOLIC NATURE OF LANGUAGE

People who use language effectively in group discussions are keenly aware of its symbolic, personal nature. They realize that words do not have meanings in and of themselves, so they strive to express their ideas in words likely to evoke similar meanings in listeners.

As listeners, they ask themselves, "What does the speaker mean?" rather than, "What do those words mean?" or "What would I mean if I said that?" They are on guard against **bypassing,** in which two or more people have different meanings for a word but do not realize it. Bypassing can lead either to a false agreement or to the perception that a disagreement exists when it really doesn't. For example, the meaning of *patriotism* in the wake of September 11, 2001, has become increasingly complicated for many Americans. Imagine yourself in a small group class trying to figure out what your group's community service task is going to be for the semester. Members begin to brainstorm ideas about how they can show their patriotism in their local community. Everyone appears excited to show their patriotism so they decide that *patriotism* will be their theme. During a subsequent meeting while the group begins to figure out what to do specifically, Lucinda suggests they organize a peace rally. Other members immediately challenge the idea by claiming it is not right to oppose our country's military actions while we are at war. In addition, they become angry with Lucinda because they thought they had all decided to do a patriotic-theme project. This group bypassed on the meaning of *patriotic,* which led to a false agreement affecting a future meeting.

Words vary from highly concrete to highly abstract. For example, the terms in the following list become more abstract (more vague) as you proceed down the list:

Maria Thomas

Public relations major

California State University, Fresno student

College student

Female

Young person

Human

Efficient communicators know that many words, especially abstract ones, will be interpreted differently by different people. The most concrete forms are those that refer to one and only one thing: *Dr. Galanes' desk, Lora Croft of Tomb Raider,* or *Golden Retriever number PD736251.* However, abstract words and phrases such as *liberal, effective, spiritual, democracy,* and *love* are highly ambiguous and likely to be understood quite differently by different group members.

The level of abstractness matters a lot during discussions. Concrete language helps reduce misunderstanding, but confusion can be rampant when highly abstract words are used. Highly abstract statements (such as "Don't you think this is a matter of historical dialecticism?") consistently disrupt discussions among college students, and the amount of confusion and disarray increases as the statements are made more abstract.[7]

Using abstract words is OK; in fact, having a meaningful discussion without them would be impossible. Many of the ideas group members discuss must include fairly abstract words such as *consensus, criteria, leadership, trust, success,* and *climate.* In addition, we sometimes may choose to be ambiguous in an effort to allow for multiple interpretations while exploring an idea. However, you can take steps to help make your remarks more specific and thus clearer. First, speak as concretely as possible to express what you mean. Don't use jargon to show off. Group members belong to a multitude of co-cultures in addition to their own ethnic cultures (e.g., athletes, musicians, computer gamers, bloggers, business professionals, teachers, etc.), which use their own jargon. In a group of members with mixed computer literacy and experience, everyone may not know that the *sandbox* refers to the research and development departments of software companies and *beani* refers to the Macintosh computer key with the cloverleaf sign.

Second, whenever you use a highly abstract term that may be problematic, use concrete examples of what you mean—for instance, "He was a really aggressive chair [abstract concept]. He decided, by himself, when the group would meet, what would and would not be on the agenda, who could and could not speak at the meetings, and what the committee should recommend to the president of the fraternity" [concrete examples of the abstract idea of *aggressive*].

Third, define highly abstract terms by using synonyms or descriptive terms or by explaining an operation the term refers to. Thus, you might define *drunk driving* as "having a level of .08 percent alcohol in the blood as measured immediately after driving by a machine called a Breathalyzer," which is the DWI definition used in many states. This definition combines both a procedure (i.e., measured by a Breathalyzer) and precise quantification for the term (i.e., .08 percent alcohol in the blood).

Fourth, quantify when possible. Frequently, groups use relative terms for comparisons when precise quantification is possible. For instance, instead of saying, "The chances of developing lung cancer are *higher* [a relative term] if you smoke a pack of cigarettes a day than if you don't smoke," you can state quite precisely what the increase in percentage of people developing lung cancer will be.

Listeners are equally responsible for helping to clarify group messages. As a listener you can ask speakers who use highly abstract language to quantify, give examples, or define their terms with less abstract language. You can paraphrase in more concrete terms, then ask the speaker to accept or revise the paraphrase. This will help you interpret the speaker's meaning more accurately.

For more information on defining words with precision, go to the Online Learning Center at **www.mhhe.com/ adamsgalanes6**

4.2   What Do You Do When Emotive Words Are Offensive?

ETHICAL DILEMMA

Two African-American members of your group refer to each other as "nigga" when they greet each other at the beginning of group meetings.[8] You and one other member find the use of the term highly offensive and do not believe any person, no matter her or his color, should use the term. One other member really does not care and does not see the point in making a big deal out of it.

This racial epithet is a highly emotive trigger word in the American culture, and people weigh in with all sorts of opinions on its use. As a group what do you do? How would you discuss this issue? When do the references in personal member greetings become an issue for a group? What new rules might this group create to allow for emotive words yet avoid the consequences of their use?

"Sorry, Chief, but of course I didn't mean 'bimbo' in the pejorative sense."

Don't use trigger words that may offend others. (© The New Yorker Collection; 1987 Lee Lorenz from cartoonbank.com. All Rights Reserved.

USE EMOTIVE WORDS CAUTIOUSLY

Emotive words are terms that call forth strong feelings. Often these are called *trigger words* because they evoke almost instantaneous emotional responses that could interfere with good listening.

For instance, for some people, *feminist* conjures up a very negative image of a bra-burning woman who hates men and is destroying the American family because of her selfish goals. Among the worst trigger words are sexist terms and racial epithets (such as *wet back, femi-nazi, faggot*). Recall the highly controversial use of *nigger* in the televised O. J. Simpson murder trial. Again, we are calling attention to the importance of monitoring your linguistic choices in group interaction. The nature of your communication is not only reflective of the kind of communicative climate in your group but, as we pointed out earlier, it also re-creates that climate over the course of your group's time together.

You can improve the quality of thinking during group discussions by avoiding such words yourself and suggesting alternatives when someone else uses one of them. Consider the following two lists. The first has negative emotive terms; the second, neutral ones that denote the same things.

Negative	Neutral or positive
broad	woman
jock	athlete
Jew-them-down	negotiate or haggle

Negative	**Neutral or positive**
ree-tard	Down's syndrome
hillbilly	native of the Ozarks
cop	police officer

If someone said to you, "He's just a career politician from a podunk state, where most of the people sign X on their welfare checks; why should I vote for him for president?" you could paraphrase as follows: "So you think he would not be a good president because he has held many elected offices and is from a small state with a high illiteracy rate?" This will defuse the trigger words so that the group can begin a more objective, less emotional evaluation of the person's qualifications.

ORGANIZE REMARKS

Organization of the discussion in general and of your own remarks in particular is affected by what you say and how you say it. Frequently, discussions jump almost aimlessly from topic to topic, with no one responding to prior comments. It is often hard to tell exactly what issue or question a speaker is addressing, or even what the point is of some remarks. Good organization can do a lot to overcome these communication problems.

Consider the following discussion of a group of students planning publicity for an upcoming career day seminar:

Lori: OK, the seminar is planned, so now it's time to start working on the publicity. Any ideas?

Deidre: We forgot to include a session on portfolios.

Tony: One of the things we could do is send a memo to all the people in the dorms. That worked well last time.

Chris: I know someone who would do a great job with portfolios, and I'll be glad to call her.

Kevin: I think a memo is a really tacky idea, and we ought to do something more professional.

Lori: I don't like memos either. I'd be happy if we didn't do one.

It's hard to tell from that discussion who is responding to what question, or even exactly what is meant. Let's help the individuals organize their remarks so the discussion is more organized as a *group* process:

Lori: OK, the seminar has been planned, so now it's time to start working on publicity. What ideas do you have for how we could promote the career day seminar? [Not a big change here, but Lori's question to the group is more focused than before.]

Deidre: Lori, could we postpone our discussion of publicity? I'd like to talk first about something we overlooked in the planning. We forgot to schedule a portfolio session. [First, Deidre responds directly to Lori and Lori's question before suggesting a different initial topic.]

Lori: That's a good idea, Deidre. OK, guys, let's spend time making sure the plans are finalized before we talk about publicity. What did you mean by a portfolio session? [Direct response to Deidre, acknowledgment of the legitimacy of her request to postpone discussion of publicity and request for clarification]

Deidre: That was the session where someone showed us how to put together a public relations portfolio so that when we apply for jobs we'll be able to show people what kinds of assignments we've completed. It's like a résumé with specific examples of your work. [Direct clarification response from Deidre]

Lori: You're right; we need that. Big oversight. Glad you thought of it. [Affirming Deidre's good thinking on behalf of the group's project]

Tony: One thing we could do is send a memo to all the people who live in the dorms to let them know about the seminar. [This remark seems to be about publicity and does not appear to respond directly to the portfolio topic.]

Chris: That might be a good idea, Tony, but I'm not sure we're ready to go on to that yet. Were we finished with the portfolio session planning? [Chris doesn't ignore Tony or put him down, but he does help the group keep focused on the topic, and he makes it a group issue by using we.]

Tony: Sorry! I thought we were ready to move on. What do we need to do yet with portfolios? [Apology and direct acknowledgment of the topic under discussion]

Chris: Well, for one thing, we need to figure out who would be a good person to handle that session. [Direct response to Tony and moves the discussion forward]

Kevin: I know someone at Walker, Beard, and Korma Public Relations. I'll call and see if she's available, and, if she isn't, maybe she can suggest somebody else. [Direct response to Chris]

Lori: OK, Kevin, do I understand you right? You'll take care of getting someone to handle the portfolio session and let us know who that is by next week? [Lori has detected an ambiguity in Kevin's earlier remark ("maybe she can suggest somebody else"), so she helps him clarify.]

Kevin: Yes. [Direct answer clears up the ambiguity.]

Lori: OK, Kevin will find someone to handle the portfolio sessions. Now, are we ready to turn to publicity? [Group members nod.] That's great. What ideas do we have for publicizing career day?

In the second version, each comment begins with confirmation of the prior speaker, often using the other member's name. No one switches topics abruptly. Statements are right to the point. In almost all cases, the speaker stays with one point. The following is a list of guidelines to facilitate coherent, orderly, and clear discussion:

1. **Relate your statement to the preceding statement.** Sometimes this will have to be done explicitly in a statement; sometimes it can be done with a word or phrase (e.g., Lori—"That's a good idea"; Tony—"Sorry.")

2. **State one point, not give a multipoint speech.** If you talk about two or more issues, the discussion is likely to go off track because no one can predict which issue the next speaker will pick up on, even if she responds directly to your remarks. The one major exception to this rule occurs when you present an initial description of a problem or make a planned report that has more than one point. In that case, preparing a handout that includes the main findings, facts, statistics, quotations, formulas, and so on, is a good idea.

3. **State the point as directly, concretely, and concisely as possible.** In the dominant culture of the United States, simple declarative sentences are preferable to flowery language and emotive terms. Phrases such as "My point is that . . . " and "This is the idea: . . . " may help focus listeners.

MAKE SURE THE DISCUSSION QUESTION IS CLEAR AND APPROPRIATE

Verbal exchanges among members are often about an issue or a point that has not yet been settled or decided on by the group. It may be a matter of controversy or just a matter of information still under discussion. In Case 4.1 the search committee was just beginning to share opinions on the topic and had not begun discussion on the question. During effective discussions, all members should be able to state the **discussion question,** the central question a group must answer.

Unfortunately, group members often fail to do this. A careful analysis of remarks will show that different members are attempting to answer different questions at the same time. For example, Mary may be trying to evaluate a suggestion Thuy has proposed—to solve the lack of parking spaces on campus—while Sonya is explaining how student parking fees are being spent and LaShonda is presenting her proposal to solve the parking problem. This is certainly a sign of poor listening and disorganized discussion. The result is the kind of confused topic switching described earlier.

Establishing the most effective question is crucial and can determine whether the group produces a good or poor solution. For example, consider the following two discussion questions: *How can we raise money to build another classroom building?* versus *How can we relieve the overcrowding in classrooms?* The first question focuses on an already-decided solution, which may or may not be the best solution to the problem. The second focuses on the problem (overcrowding) without biasing the solution in advance. Building more classrooms may work, but perhaps the problems are due to poor scheduling of existing facilities. Maybe holding classes at off-campus locations such as shopping centers, factories, and offices throughout the city would be more effective in reducing the overcrowding as well as provide better service to students. However, these options will never be discovered if the group is determined to solve the problem by building more classrooms. Thus, how a group states its discussion question influences the entire progress of the group's discussion. As an input, it has a far-reaching effect on the system's throughput process and its subsequent output.

Anytime you feel confused about what is going on during small group meetings, ask yourself or the group what question is being discussed. Get an answer to that question before you proceed, and help the entire group become oriented toward the same goal at the

GLOSSARY

Discussion Question

The main question or issue that a group must answer

TABLE 4.2	**Types of Discussion Questions**

INFORMATION QUESTIONS

Ask for specific information or facts, but not interpretations or opinions.

Examples

1. Why was this meeting called?

2. How many thefts were reported on campus last year?

3. Where did you learn that?

4. What did Jim say was his reason for missing the meeting?

INTERPRETATION QUESTIONS

Ask for personal opinions, interpretations, judgments; they invite discussion.

Examples

1. What might have caused this increase in the rate of theft?

2. What connection might there be between college grades and whether a student has a computer?

3. Do you think our presentation should emphasize the need to reduce the deficit or the need to keep down inflation?

VALUE QUESTIONS

Ask how good, important, significant, or worthwhile something is in the opinion of the responder. A value question is a type of interpretation question.

Examples

1. How good a president do you think Ronald Reagan was?

2. Is this question important enough to take up the group's time?

3. What are the pros and cons of this alternative?

4. How good a case does the prosecuting attorney have against William Roberts?

5. Which of these suits do you think looks best?

6. How much do you like this painting?

POLICY QUESTIONS

Ask what should be done about an issue; the key word is *should*. Usually, groups have discussed a number of information and interpretation questions before they begin to discuss and decide what policy to take.

Examples

1. What should the U.S. government do to reduce the federal deficit?

2. What should our school's attendance policy be?

3. What kinds of skills should be required of all "med tech" graduates?

4. What should the Washington, D.C., police do to reduce drug-related crimes?

same moment. When you ask a question, be sure the type of answer you seek is clear from the phrasing of the question. Seven types of questions, classified on the basis of the type of response requested, with examples of each type are described in Table 4.2. These examples should help you appreciate the number of different types of questions you have to choose from and their functions or the kind of information they can solicit from other members.

When you reply to a question, be sure you give the kind of response sought by the questioner. The following are a few guidelines to help you phrase questions that focus and facilitate group interaction.

| **TABLE 4.2** | **(concluded)** |

ACTION QUESTIONS

Ask how to implement a decision or policy already decided by the group.

Examples

1. How will we make this recommendation to the student senate?

2. Now that we've decided what food to serve at the banquet, who will see to it that it is prepared and served?

3. How can we guarantee that all pilots know about this policy and follow it?

PROCEDURE QUESTIONS

Ask how the group, or an individual member, does something; what procedure the group will use.

Examples

1. Should we vote or try to come to consensus?

2. What would be the best way to present our proposal to our client?

3. What sequence should we use to organize our discussion of this issue?

4. How can we divide the work of the committee in a way that's fair to everybody?

RELATIONSHIP QUESTIONS

Seek information about how members feel toward each other, the group, their responsibilities to the group, the relative status of members, and sometimes what members expect from each other.

Examples

1. Do we need some introductions, or does everybody know everybody else?

2. How do you all feel about our assignment to select an insurance carrier for our medical programs?

3. How did you get the authority to decide when we meet?

4. Paul, something seems to be bothering you. Is there something that's made you upset?

---

1. **Unless the group has already narrowed a list of alternatives to two, avoid either–or questions.**

   Usually these grossly oversimplify the issue by treating questions as if there were only two legitimate answers instead of a wide range. In the list that follows, the first question of each pair is poorly worded in either–or terms; the second version is worded as an open-ended question:

   Is our university's central administration diverse? (Implied is a yes or no answer.)

   How diverse is our university's central administration?

   Should we all take notes or just elect a recorder? (Provides only two options)

   How should we keep track of all the information in our group meetings?

2. **Word questions as concretely as possible.**

   Double-barreled questions that combine two questions in one are confusing. For example, "Do you think we should increase funding to the public schools by instituting casino gambling in the state?" is a double-barreled question. Listeners may

4.1   What Are Our Questions?

In Case 4.1 we described the events of the first meeting of CSUF's dean search committee. During this meeting members talked freely about what they wanted in a new dean. The search they were about to undertake would be a complicated one that would entail developing a recruitment plan, establishing screening and selection criteria, scheduling on-campus interviews, and so forth. Each phase would require a series of questions. For example, during the recruitment phase, members would have to consider how to recruit a diverse and qualified pool of applicants.

Imagine you are a member of this committee and are helping plan the discussion for subsequent meetings.

1. Think of the phases this committee will experience in the course of its work.

2. Compose a list of discussion questions, including questions of information, value, policy, action, procedure, and relationship, that might be asked to guide the group's discussion in each phase.

You can do this by yourself or you can get together in a group. Once the questions have been written critically, go over the examples looking for any questions that may be either–or questions, may not be worded concretely, or may inadvertently suggest an answer.

want to respond differently to each part. For example, maybe someone wants to increase funding to the schools but doesn't want to allow casino gambling in the state. Perhaps both issues need to be addressed but, if so, each question should be asked separately: First, do you think funding to the public schools should be increased? Second, should we approve a measure to allow casino gambling in our state?

3. **Avoid suggesting the answer in the question.**

A question that suggests an answer is not an honest question but an indirect way to make a point. For instance, "Don't you think we should tell Sol we will expel him from the fraternity if he ever steals from a brother again?" suggests a solution.

4. **Apply critical-thinking skills to questions you ask.**

Guidelines for evaluating information and detecting errors in reasoning are explained in Chapter 5. Use them to evaluate and improve the questions you and others ask during discussions.

Up to now we have been emphasizing the importance of words to the messages processed in small group interaction. However, you will recall from our earlier discussion that nonverbal behaviors also carry a significant communicative load in a group.

Nonverbal Behaviors in Small Group Communication

Nonverbal behavior is anything in a message except the words themselves. However, as we pointed out in our introduction to this chapter, our symphonies (communication) are created when we play our notes *together*. Our symphonies use both verbal and nonverbal behaviors simultaneously. Even the words on this page are surrounded by punctuation, varying degrees of white space, in a chosen typeface and in a particular color, all of which affect how you interpret the words. Likewise head nods, eyebrow flashes, posture, touch, clothes usually occur in a larger conversational episode containing spoken and written words. Two communication scholars, John Stewart and Carol Logan, believe we make sense of this complexity by using a continuum.[9] At one extreme are primarily verbal behaviors such as written words; in the middle are mixed behaviors such as spoken words, vocalics, pauses, and silences; and at the other extreme are primarily nonverbal behaviors that can occur without words such as eye gaze, touch, time, and facial expressions. Verbal and nonverbal behavior are inseparable just as two sides of a paper are inseparable.[10]

For the following discussion we will focus on the mixed and primary nonverbal behaviors. These nonverbal behaviors serve a number of purposes. We will explain several important principles of nonverbal behavior, examine key functions performed by these behaviors, and finally explore briefly some common categories of nonverbal behavior that have an important impact on small group communication.

PRINCIPLES OF NONVERBAL COMMUNICATION

Most of the time in a small group, only one person is speaking, but *all* members are sending **nonverbal behaviors** *all* the time. Understanding something about nonverbal behaviors is crucial to understanding what is happening in your groups. However, interpreting nonverbal behaviors can be trickier than interpreting verbal signals.

1. **Nonverbal behaviors are ambiguous.**

   Do you think that a smile means someone is happy? Well, in many cultures that is usually the case, but in Japan, someone who is feeling quite miserable may smile to avoid upsetting the person to whom he is speaking. Do you think that someone who has her arms folded across her chest is uninterested in hearing what you say? Maybe. But maybe she is merely trying to keep warm. Many factors influence the meaning of nonverbal behaviors, including cultural differences. Nonverbal behaviors should be interpreted in context and in conjunction with the words group members are using.

2. **People cannot stop sending nonverbal behaviors, even when they are not talking.**

   As mentioned earlier, only one person in a group usually speaks at a time, but all members continuously process nonverbal behaviors. Even if you choose to be quiet in a group meeting, you will likely leak your feelings nonverbally. For example, a church board member unhappy with the way the church secretary was handling office business chose not to say anything when personnel matters were discussed.

> **GLOSSARY**
>
> **Nonverbal Behaviors**
>
> *Anything in a message that is not the word itself*

However, after the meeting the board chair asked him what was wrong and why he had seemed uninterested at the meeting. This example points out two features of nonverbal behavior. First, even though the member chose not to say anything, he certainly was sending something nonverbally. Second, nonverbal behaviors are easy to misinterpret. The emotion he was feeling was anger at the church secretary, but the board chair thought he was uninterested in the meeting. Thus, we shouldn't jump to conclusions without first checking them out.

3. **When verbal and nonverbal behaviors clash, most people believe the nonverbal behaviors.**

    In fact, when a person is trying to interpret what someone else means in a face-to-face interaction, the nonverbal part of the message counts almost twice as much as the verbal.[11] When the verbal and nonverbal behaviors don't fit, most people trust the nonverbals because they are less subject to deliberate control. Many nonverbal behaviors, such as sweating, blushing, and shaking, are controlled by primitive structures of the brain over which we have little or no conscious control. You can choose your words, but your nonverbal behavior often gives you away. When you clench your fists, turn red, and scream at another group member "No, I'M NOT Mad!" no one will believe you.

FUNCTIONS OF NONVERBAL BEHAVIORS

Nonverbal behaviors perform a variety of functions, most importantly to express how we feel and to indicate how we perceive our relationships to other people. Nonverbal behaviors modify the verbal component of messages exchanged among group members. They can supplement the words we utter by emphasizing them or in effect repeating them, just as underlined or **boldfaced** words in a text are emphasized. Thus, nonverbals can call special attention to the words they accompany. For instance, a person may say, "Look at the rise in air pollution in the Valley during peak traffic hours" while pointing at a bar graph.

Nonverbal behaviors can *substitute* for spoken or written words. In this case, a gesture becomes a symbol, substituting for the more conventional words. For instance, a circled thumb and index finger can express "OK," or a beckoning finger can indicate you want someone to lean closer to you. Kathy and some of her graduate students bring their two forefingers together when indicating a "shared moment," a gesture they picked up from the movie *Chasing Amy.* Much of the communicating among members must be with unspoken substitutes for spoken words. If you aren't conscious of these behaviors and don't look for them, you will miss many important messages among group members and misinterpret other nonverbal messages. In a sense, you will be only half-listening.

Another major function of nonverbal behaviors is to *regulate* the flow of verbal interaction among members. The coordinator of a discussion group may use nods, eye contact, and hand signals to indicate who should speak next. Direct gaze from listeners indicates "continue," whereas looking away is a nonverbal way of saying, "Shut up!" People who want to speak lean forward, slightly open their mouths, extend a hand or finger, and may even utter a sound such as "um." Speakers who ignore such cues are judged inconsiderate and rude. One of us observed a group that contained a blind person who obviously could not see such regulating cues. Other members began to judge this member as arrogant and self-centered for "talking out of turn." Some discussion of visible regulatory cues increased

4.1   The Symbolic Nature of Avatars

In its infancy, computer-mediated communication was primarily text based (i.e., typed messages on a computer keyboard). Because CMC relies so heavily on the text to create meaning, it is hard to guess at the qualities of the individuals you are interacting with in a CMC environment. To adapt to this drawback, Internet providers have begun to use *avatars*. An avatar is a visual representation of yourself that you construct and display next to the textual dialogue. Most sites that offer the use of avatars allow you to select things such as gender, hair color, clothing style, facial expression, and even pets that you want depicted in your visual representation. Ambiguity still exists with avatars; however, users are able to select stronger nonverbal characteristics and cues to accompany the textual dialogue.

Go to **www.mhhe.com/ adamsgalanes6** for additional weblink activities.

These websites provide an opportunity to experiment with the construction of and implementation of avatars in chat rooms or during instant messaging: **http://avatars.yahoo.com/index.html** and **http://www.121chat.com.** If given an opportunity to create your own avatar to use in a chat room, which types of features would you select and why? What things should you consider about another person based on the way they present themselves visually? How do you think avatars illustrate the notion discussed in the section on principles of nonverbal communication? Does the potential for CMC interaction using these media contradict some of the face-to-face principles described?

the members' sensitivity to the communicative problem experienced by their blind member and helped the group pull together.

Finally, as noted earlier, nonverbal behaviors can *contradict* words we utter. A person who says, "I agree" hesitatingly, with a rising pitch at the end of the words, may be perceived as having reservations, or even as disagreeing. A person who says, "I heard you" but will not attempt a paraphrase has indicated nonverbally that he probably was not really

4.2   What If . . .

Earlier you met a group of students planning publicity for a career day seminar. In their meeting they discussed adding a portfolio session and then how best to publicize the seminar. Recollect the following dialogue:

Lori: You're right; we need that. Big oversight. Glad you thought of it.

Tony: One thing we could do is send a memo to all the people who live in the dorms to let them know about the seminar.

Chris: That might be a good idea, but I'm not sure we're ready to go on to that yet. Were we finished with the portfolio session planning?

Tony: Sorry! I thought we were ready to move on. What do we need to do yet with portfolios?

Chris: Well, for one thing, we need to figure out who would be a good person to handle that session.

The goal of this application is to show you how much the context and nonverbal behavior influence the meaning of what we say. Select four trios. Each trio is to role-play the dialogue but from a different relational context. The first trio is composed of close friends who have worked together on several committees. Members of the second trio have never met before and one member is not sure he or she even wants to be on this committee. The third trio has a highly aggressive member who believes he or she knows how to run this group. The fourth trio is composed of individuals who really dislike each other but are trying to be civil.

During the role-plays, have audience members take notes. Ask them to observe the nonverbal behavior and how it changed the meaning of the conversation. When the trios are through, discuss the principles of nonverbal behavior and the functions of nonverbal behavior. You can even discuss how the trios used such things as gestures, facial expressions, movements, and spacing to create the relational context.

listening. When you observe nonverbal behaviors that seem to contradict what a person has just said, and it matters to you what the person really thinks, try saying, "I heard you say . . . , but the way you said it bothers me." Then explain the apparent contradiction you perceived and ask the person to clarify it for you.

CATEGORIES OF NONVERBAL BEHAVIORS

Several categories of nonverbal behavior are especially important to your understanding of small group communication. Personal appearance, space and seating, facial expression, eye contact, gestures and body movement, voice, and time cues are among the major types of nonverbal behaviors most relevant to small groups.

Appearance.   Members of a group form impressions of each other, accurate or not, long before anyone says anything. Sex, race, height, build, dress, grooming, and other visible cues have been shown to influence responses. Cues such as sex, body shape, and ethnicity particularly affect how group members interact with each other initially.[12] Such personal characteristics as status and wisdom may be associated with a member's age and sex. Members also create impressions of each other's physical characteristics including impressions of member clothing, makeup, and other body "artifacts." These impressions may very well impact whether a group member even interacts with another member and if so the character of that interaction. For instance, violating societal norms about dress, grooming, makeup, and accessories can arouse suspicion or even mistrust. Dressing noticeably differently from other members will almost certainly be interpreted as a sign that you do not identify with them. You may have to prove yourself in other ways to be accepted. To date, no research has examined the impact of the relative physical attractiveness of group members on group throughput and outcome variables.[13] This is surprising given how much attention is placed on physical attractiveness in the American culture at large and in interpersonal communication research specifically.

The appearance of group members matters not only to the other members but also to outsiders. Groups do not operate in a social vacuum; how members appear to others can affect their credibility during group presentations and even their success, as is the case with rock bands. The most famous of them all, The Beatles, used black clothes early in their career to mimic the color of beetles.[14] When John Lennon was asked how much of their success was due to their sound rather than their appearance, he replied, "We could have managed, looking like we look and making worse records, or we could have managed, looking like the average pop singer and making our noise. But the combination makes a better impact. We have always looked different from the rest of the mob."[15]

Space and Seating.   Many scientists have examined how people use space to communicate. The amount of space people prefer between them depends on a variety of factors, including culture and gender. For example, in the United States, most business transactions are conducted at what Hall calls *social distance,* which is between four and eight feet.[16] We are comfortable allowing only our intimate friends within a foot or two. However, four feet is much too far for someone from the Arab world or from Latin America. In these countries, people transact business at what we consider close personal distance, which often makes Americans very uneasy. In the dominant culture of the United States, females tend to sit closer together than males, as do people of the same age and social status and those who know each other well.

The seating arrangements in groups and even the way furniture is arranged is called **group ecology.**[17] In a group, sitting close together, especially if the room is large enough for members to spread out, indicates that members like each other and there is a sense of cohesiveness. A member who sits apart from the others may be signaling that he or she does not feel a part of the group.

The nature of a group's ecology and group processes such as status, leadership, power, and member participation are linked to each other. Dominant people often claim more than their fair share of space, and a group's leader usually is given more space by the other members than they claim. In addition, group leaders generally sit in a central position,

GLOSSARY

Group Ecology

A group's space as created by seating choices and furniture arrangements

such as at the head of a rectangular table, where they can see as many of the other members as possible. Quite simply, the most central place in a group's ecology allows members who occupy that space more influence, participation, domination, and opportunity to foster attributions of leadership.[18] People who sit across from each other respond to each other more than people sitting side by side or on the edges of each other's vision. The ideal table for most small group discussions is a round table, where members have easy eye contact with each other. If that is not possible, group members are advised to position themselves around the table, whatever shape it happens to be, in something close to a circle or oval.

Violating space norms may spell trouble for group members, depending on their status within the group.[19] High-status members can get away with moving closer to others and farther away. These violations in expectation actually increase their status. Group members who are high in status or rewarding to others have credits with their groups and can deviate from group norms with little to no punishment. Low-status members are not so fortunate because their deviations are framed within the context of their negative status. Thus, if they move closer to others they can be seen as pushy, and if they move farther away they can be seen as aloof and their attractiveness and persuasiveness diminishes.

Altering seating arrangements may also appear nonconsequential; however, the seating choices you and your group members make indicate how socially accessible you have made yourselves to each other. Social accessibility is important if members are to promote social contact and enhance the more relational group outcomes such as respect and cohesiveness.[20]

Facial Expressions and Eye Contact.   Sitting where you can see every other member of the group is important because it allows you to make eye contact with other members. Eye contact and facial expressions are among the most important nonverbal behaviors for group members as you can see in the cartoon on the following page. For Americans, making eye contact signals that the channel for communication is open. This is why many students look down at their notebooks when a teacher asks a question—they avoid eye contact so they won't be called on to answer. Prolonged eye contact can signal cooperativeness or competitiveness, depending on the circumstances. Most Americans establish eye contact before speaking and continue it intermittently when talking to someone they like. However, people from other cultures are sometimes offended by Americans' direct gazes, while others prefer to maintain an intense, unbroken stare when conversing, which is uncomfortable for Americans. As with other nonverbals, numerous cultural factors influence what a person considers to be appropriate eye contact. In unified and cohesive groups, members tend to look continuously at each other during a discussion. In hostile or tense groups, members avoid eye contact.

People can accurately determine the type of emotion someone in a photograph is experiencing from looking just at the face and eyes. Anger, sadness, happiness, support, disagreement, interest, liking—all are indicated by facial expressions.[21] Some people have "poker" faces; their facial expressions change very little. They tend to be trusted less than those whose faces express their feelings more openly. Most of us monitor the facial expressions of others because they provide clues about what is going on in the group. Even if a group member isn't saying anything about your proposal, you can tell by her spontaneous frown and grimace that she doesn't think much of it. That gives you information

Judging from their facial expressions, what do you think Washington, Jefferson, Roosevelt, and Lincoln are thinking?

about what your next steps should be—drop the proposal, modify it, ask the other member directly what she thinks, or speak with her privately after the meeting.

Emotional expression is one example of how mixed messages play together to affect group communication. The face, eyes, and voice as well as the actual words work together to create a wide range of emotions in small group communication. Although we emphasize the role of rationality in group problem solving, emotion does impact group dynamics. Group climate, which we discuss in Chapter 7, is another label for the emotional atmosphere of any group. Positive and negative emotional expressions have interesting implications for member collaboration.

Movements.   Movements of the hands, arms, and body signal many feelings and attitudes. For example, people turn directly toward others they like and away from those they dislike. Leaning toward each other indicates a sense of mutual inclusiveness, whereas leaning away signals rejection.[22] When group members feel a sense of unity with each other, they tend to imitate each other's posture and body movements. This takes place automatically, without conscious awareness. Mabry found that body orientation changes significantly from one meeting to another.[23] As group members get to know, like, and trust one another more, they tend to increase their eye contact and angle their bodies more directly toward each other.

Both tension and status can be revealed with movements. Members who are swinging a foot, twisting a lock of hair, or tapping a pencil may be indicating tension. It may be hard for the other members to know whether the movements indicate frustration, impatience, or annoyance with the group's progress. Movement can also indicate who has high status in the group. High-status workers tend to be the most relaxed, so they lean back and look around.[24] Members are more likely to imitate the movements of high-status members than those of low-status members.[25]

Voice.   Vocal cues include such factors as pitch, speed, fluency, loudness, and pauses. We rely on tone of voice to interpret someone's mood. Someone who says, "Yeah, I could live with that" softly in a questioning tone of voice is not likely to be believed. In addition, listeners tend to judge the status, educational level, ethnicity, and attitudes of speakers on the basis of vocal cues.[26] In the United States, people who speak in a monotone have less credibility and are less persuasive than those who speak in a more animated tone of voice. However, those who are extremely animated may appear to be irrational or hysterical.

Those nonverbal signals that regulate interaction express group member involvement, dominance, competition, and cooperativeness.[27] For instance, people make nonverbal backchannel sounds, such as "mm-hmmm" and "uh-huh," to indicate involvement and understanding when listening. Interestingly, cultures vary in the use of the backchannel. Most people from Western European backgrounds use the backchannel less frequently than African Americans, Hispanics, or people with Southern European backgrounds. We discuss backchannel differences between African Americans and European Americans in Chapter 8. Backchannel sounds also may be interpreted differently, seen as either showing interest in or acceptance of what is being said. These differences can cause misunderstandings if group members are not aware of them and thus influence how smoothly members can agree on issues. If, for example, you believe group members agree with your ideas based on their "uh-huhs," only to discover later that they were just trying to show you their interest in your idea, you'll probably be upset!

Dialect refers to regional and social variations in pronunciation, vocabulary, and grammar. The different dialects you hear in your groups can influence perceptions of intelligence, competence, and credibility.[28] Countries such as the United States, Great Britain, and Japan have regional and social class language deviations from the "standard" dialect. Group members who use nonstandard dialects, saying for example *dees* instead of *these,* are often given lower status and credibility ratings. General American dialect is rated higher on pleasantness and socio-intellectual status than the dialect of South Boston or the Bronx. Communities of speakers show their uniqueness by creating, among other things, their own dialect. Be very cautious using stereotypes to judge group members with dialects different from your own.

Timing.   Time cues are both culture-related and relational. In some other cultures and in co-cultures of this country, no one would expect to get right to work in a group meeting; first, one must get the feel of the other people. Most rural people tackle business at a slower pace than their urban counterparts. In the fast-paced U.S. business world, people who come late to meetings are judged inconsiderate and undisciplined. North Americans will allow only about a five-minute leeway before they expect an apology from someone who is late.[29] In the predominant culture of this country, coming late and leaving early indicates to fellow group members that your time is precious but it's OK to waste theirs. In dozens of case studies of student groups, one consistently late member was the subject of bitter complaints by the others.

Time is a vital commodity during meetings. People who talk little and those who talk excessively have little impact. Excessive talkers are considered rude and selfish. Although they did not protest at the time, many students have complained about fellow project group members who waste time by chattering at length about social matters or other topics irrelevant to the group's purpose. On the other hand, those who talk somewhat above average are judged favorably on leadership characteristics.[30] In fact, talkativeness, or speaking time, is considered a strong factor in determining how much power a group member is perceived as possessing.[31] Likewise, people who structure the group's time so that every item on an agenda can be discussed are appreciated. If you are insensitive to time cues in your group, you will have little influence and will not be completely accepted by the others.

No type of nonverbal behavior can be overlooked if you want to understand what is going on in a group. Even small group researchers must broaden their efforts to understand the importance of nonverbal behaviors in small group interaction. Relatively little, for instance, is understood about the influence on group behavior of member touch behavior, artifacts such as clothing, emotion, and different kinds of group contexts (e.g., groups in submarines).[32] Remember also that you cannot state with confidence exactly what someone else is thinking or feeling from nonverbal cues alone. We hope the list of nonverbal behaviors presented here encourages you to increase your awareness and sensitivity, but you should not consider this list exhaustive.

Computer-Mediated Communication (CMC) and Group Messages

So far we have discussed face-to-face communication in small groups meeting in real time. In Chapter 1 we began our discussion of small group communication and the use of technology, particularly computers. We elaborated on cyborg decision-making groups and showed you the various ways technology can be used to allow group members to communicate with each other at different times and in different places. In Chapter 2 we introduced virtual groups whose members may never meet in real time but conduct business totally via computer technology. These discussions beg the question, How does the nature of communication change when it is mediated by computers or other forms of technology (e.g., voice mail)? To explore this question, we will now compare computer-mediated communication (CMC) and face-to-face communication (FtF).

CMC can take on a variety of forms including e-mail, chat room discussions, electronic bulletin boards, list servs, video and teleconferencing, to name a few. New technologies have exploded onto the scene and change at a rapid rate. Nowhere is this more prominent than in the corporate world.[33] Organizations use computer technology for strategic planning, assessment, product evaluation, and project coordination. For example, a survey of 100 business-technology professionals found a preference for online versus face-to-face meetings.[34] These professionals find that online meetings can actually increase contact between engineers, allow them to argue better over details, and decrease product development time. To try to determine why these advantages occur, we will look at one of the many technologies that involve CMC: the net conference.

The term **net conference** is used to describe any conference electronically mediated by *networked* computers.[35] A popular kind of net conference is the *videoconference,* which can involve both audio and video net-mediated communication between group members. An *audio conference* can be as simple as a telephone conference call. These are popular in

GLOSSARY

Net Conference

Any conference connected by networked computers

university job searches when a search committee does not have the funds to transport job candidates to campus. Instead the committee schedules a telephone conference call with the candidate and members of the committee. In *computer conferences,* group members actually meet in the same room but sit at different computer terminals. Groups may do this to use a computer program that helps them to brainstorm ideas electronically. Net conferences vary in expense and usefulness. Companies are becoming very sophisticated in their abilities to use these technologies to save time, overcome meeting location problems, and improve on discussion techniques.

All technologies come with advantages and disadvantages. Depending on the kind of net conference, nonverbal messages such as facial expressions and body language are missing or exaggerated.[36] For example, during a videoconference, group members can see each other but they are only as close to each other as the camera allows. Distance between members is simulated, not duplicated. And although they can see each other, they are not actually in each other's physical presence. Taking turns is easier FtF because a net conference often has a half-second delay, causing more overlap of member remarks than normally occurs FtF. Additionally, group members may be tied to their computer keyboard and monitor, which restricts gestures. Immediate feedback may not happen or it is delayed. This could be harmful to the group's efforts to build a consensus on a decision, yet it may not matter if the group is working on listing ideas. The group's sense of sharing, involvement, and team spirit may also be affected negatively.[37]

This brings up the issue of **social presence** first discussed in Chapter 1. Social presence refers to how much group members perceive the communication medium to be like FtF interaction socially and emotionally. Members' perception depends on the degree to which

4.3   The Public Affairs Web Page Committee

APPLY NOW

At Southwest Missouri State University, where Gloria teaches, a six-member committee has been created to establish policies and review materials for the university's public affairs Web page. Initially, their Webmaster drafted the first version of their report, and committee members commented on the draft from the website. After some discussion the committee has decided it will conduct most of its business over the Web due to difficult schedules. In addition, members need to conduct private discussions, so they each have a password accessing the committee's Web page at their convenience.

Pretend you are the Webmaster for this committee. You are familiar with the different kinds of net conferences. You also have extensive knowledge of the advantages and disadvantages of using computer-mediated communication to conduct business as compared to meeting face-to-face. Given that your committee wants to conduct all business over the Web, what would you recommend? Draw up a description of how the Web is to be used by this committee given your expertise. Your suggestions and guidelines will be given to all the members.

they perceive that other members are actually there during the interaction.[38] Asynchronous communication, or communication with a delay between messages (e.g., e-mail), promotes less social presence than synchronous, more simultaneous communication (e.g., electronic chat rooms).

Social presence is influenced not only by the technology but also by the complexity of the group task. Net conferences work better for routine tasks and information sharing. The harder the task, though, the less adequate some CMC can become. However, group members can become very inventive when it comes to creating the same kind of social presence found in FtF communication.[39] For example, group members can choose to sandwich net conferences in between FtF meetings, thereby enhancing their groupness. Groups can use trained moderators who can help improve the process by doing things like reminding members of the rules for speaking and taking turns. Social presence is important to a group and much more needs to be learned about the impact of technology on the felt social presence of group members.[40] Table 4.3 compares the strengths of FtF and net conferences.

TABLE 4.3	**Comparison of Strengths**
Net conferences	**Face-to-face meetings**
• They can be useful for information sharing, routine meetings.	• Face-to-face meetings are better when group cohesiveness and interpersonal relationships are important.
• Quantity and quality of ideas are equal to face-to-face meetings.	• Group organization is easier to maintain.
• In negotiations, evidence is more persuasive than personality.	• Participants can exchange more messages more quickly.
• Participants may pay more attention to what is said.	• Important nonverbal information (facial expressions, uses of space) is available.
• In conflict, more opinion change may occur than in face-to-face meetings.	• People generally prefer face-to-face meetings.
• Audio conferences/computer conferences are cost effective.	• Participants are more confident of their perceptions in face-to-face meetings.

SOURCE: Adapted from Gene D. Fowler and Marilyn E. Wackerbarth, "Audio Teleconferencing versus Face-to-Face Conferencing: A Synthesis of the Literature," *Western Journal of Speech Communication* 44 (Summer 1980), pp. 236–52.

RESOURCES FOR REVIEW AND DISCUSSION

- Group members communicate via messages, verbal and nonverbal signals they send and interpret; these messages, as noted by the theory of structuration, both create and maintain the group.

- More accurate interpretation of verbal signals occurs when members use standard English, clarify abstract language, organize their remarks, and use clear and appropriate discussion questions.

- Nonverbal behaviors, more believable because they are harder to control, are especially hard to interpret accurately; they supplement or substitute for verbal communication, regulate the flow, and express feelings.

- Nonverbal categories especially important to understanding small group communication include appearance, use of space, facial expression, eye contact, movements, vocal cues, and timing.

- Group members increasingly use computers to communicate, and computer use dramatically influences the nature of verbal and nonverbal messages exchanged by members.

1. Browse through several magazines for interesting advertisements. Cut out a variety of advertisements and bring them to class. Discuss with your group or with your class each of the advertisements. Identify the audience for each ad and how the language of the ad is designed to appeal to its audience.

2. Generate a list of words with a positive connotation and a list of words with a negative connotation. Look around at the lists of your classmates and see if any words appear on the same list or different lists. Compile two lists on the board and discuss why some words are on each list and why some words may be on both lists. Where do these connotations come from?

What kinds of experiences contribute to these connotations?

3. Tape-record a group meeting. Watch the tape and note the group's seating arrangements and the space between members. Examine the facial expressions and eye contact. Note their voice qualities and timing. When you are finished, discuss your observations. How do you think these nonverbal behaviors contributed to the overall communicative character of this group?

 Go to **www.mhhe.com/adamsgalanes6** and **www.mhhe.com/groups** for self-quizzes and weblinks.

Bypassing	Group Ecology	Nonverbal Behaviors
Discussion Question	Message	Social Presence
Emotive Words	Net Conference	Structuration

www.mhhe.com/adamsgalanes6

 Use the flash cards and crossword puzzles on the Online Learning Center to further your knowledge of these key terms.

Creative and Critical Thinking in the Small Group

CHAPTER OBJECTIVES

After reading this chapter you should be able to:

1. Define creative thinking and explain why it is important to small group problem solving.

2. Describe brainstorming, synectics, and mind mapping, and explain how they can be used to help enhance group creativity.

3. Define critical thinking and explain why it is important to small group problem solving.

4. List and describe the attitudes most conducive to critical thinking in a group.

5. Explain how group members should use critical thinking during the information gathering stage of problem solving.

6. Describe and give examples of each of the five steps crucial to evaluating information.

7. Define and give examples of each of the five reasoning errors described in the text: overgeneralizing, attacking a person instead of the argument, confusing causal relationships, either–or thinking, and incomplete comparisons.

8. Give examples of probing questions critical thinkers should ask when they evaluate information.

Ozarks Greenways, Inc.

The "Rails to Trails" movement in the United States has been committed to converting unused railroad tracks to biking and hiking trails and establishing usable greenways for citizens to enjoy. Several years ago, a group of committed citizens in Springfield, Missouri, formed Ozarks Greenways, Inc. (OGI), whose mission is to preserve green space through the creation of linear parks. This long-term project would require the members to raise funds to buy and acquire access rights for the greenway. One spur of the Ozarks Greenway system would connect a park near the center of Springfield to Wilson's Creek Battlefield, a national Civil War battlefield 10 miles to the southwest.

Bikers and hikers prefer trails that allow them to proceed at a steady pace without worrying about traffic and traffic lights. That presented a major challenge for OGI because to connect the park and the battlefield, the greenway would have to cross Kansas Expressway, a busy highway dangerous for bikers and hikers. The most obvious solution was to reroute the greenway to have it cross Kansas Expressway at a traffic light. But this would mean rerouting the trail to run parallel to two major highways—a major hazard for bikers, who travel not on sidewalks but on highways next to speeding cars. In addition, rerouting the greenway would force OGI to acquire additional access rights along commercially developed areas. Even if that could be done, it would be prohibitively expensive and would delay completion of the greenway for years, perhaps decades. OGI's goal was to establish a route that was relatively safe and would allow steady biker and hiker movement by avoiding travel on major highways and stoplights that would entail long waits. The OGI committee decided to stick with the original route.

The problem OGI faced could be stated thus: How can the greenway path cross Kansas Expressway safely and without forcing long waits at traffic lights? OGI needed (and eventually found) a creative solution that met all its main criteria: safety, cost, and ease of use. Read the chapter to find out what OGI did.

This chapter examines two processes essential for problem solving in small groups, creative and critical thinking. Both creativity and critical thinking are necessary for effective discussion groups, but neither one alone is sufficient to ensure effective solutions. Also, creative and critical thinking cannot be done simultaneously; that

GLOSSARY

Creative Thinking

Encouraging use of hunch, intuition, insight, and fantasy to promote creativity

would be like trying to drive a car with one foot on the accelerator and one foot on the brake! Group members must learn when to be creative, when to be critical, and what kinds of procedures help the group do both.

What Is Creative Thinking?

Sometimes a group faces a difficult impasse and must come up with an innovative or unusual solution. Creativity "involves the generation, application, combination, and extension of new ideas."[1] In small groups, **creative thinking** is fostered when members use imagination, intuition, hunches, insight, and fantasy to devise unusual or innovative solutions that probably would not emerge from ordinary group discussion. Contrary to the popular myth of the solitary genius working alone, groups produce many of today's creative ideas and innovations.[2]

American business and industry, in particular, recognize how important creativity and innovation are to their success and have focused on how to enhance creative processes. A recent investigation of more than 2,000 senior managers from around the world found four factors related to an organization's ability to innovate: how much support there is for risk-taking, how much tolerance there is for making mistakes, how effectively members can work together as a team, and how quickly decisions can be implemented.[3] A team's climate is especially important, particularly support for innovation and task-orientation, or the ability to get things done.[4] Creative thinking in groups helps us invent better, less expensive products or services that improve our lives. How to enhance that creativity is important for you to understand.

Group creativity involves both *divergent* and *convergent* thinking; each thinking process requires slightly different communication behaviors to succeed.[5] During divergent thinking, ideas should vary—members must think as differently as possible from one another so the team will have a wide array of options from which to choose. Quantity of ideas and breadth of thinking are important. As you can imagine, members must feel safe with the team to be willing to share new and perhaps crazy ideas. Being overly critical at this point stifles creativity. For example, in one study of an electronic problem-solving group, the group's leader gave members feedback privately via computer; even this feedback, designed to motivate, was interpreted as critical and choked group creativity.[6] However, at some point members must select the best ideas or combine them in ways that will actually work—a more convergent process. During this phase, "constructive debate" among members helps them identify the best ideas and eliminate the less useful ones.[7] Too much emphasis on harmony prevents the group from weeding out unworkable ideas.

For a group to be creative, both *individual* and *group* creativity are needed. Creative individuals tolerate ambiguity, have low levels of communication apprehension, and aren't afraid to violate societal norms and rules (think of the student whose hair is dyed purple).[8] They don't fear rejection by others, are open to new ideas, and like to play and have fun. But as important as individual creativity is, *group* processes are just as important. That is the reason Pat, a friend of ours, structures her group meetings so that they will feel like parties—she reasons that people are more creative when they are relaxed and having a good time. She makes sure food is served, people are introduced, and no one feels left out. Ironically, she works hard to help others have fun so that members' potential for creativity isn't derailed by the group's own norms and processes.

Bernard Nijstad and Paul Paulus synthesized considerable research on group creativity and grouped the factors influencing group creativity into four areas.[9] First, creative groups are diverse. Members bring a variety of skills, knowledge, problem-solving approaches, and perspectives to the table. Group diversity doesn't guarantee creative thinking—some groups cannot overcome the challenges that diversity brings (we discuss some of these in Chapter 8). But in general, heterogeneous groups produce more diverse ideas. Second, creative groups structure their discussions so that their creative potential is realized, not lost. Members work to avoid premature consensus and refrain from pressuring others to conform. They allow the group time to develop; it often takes a while for members to understand and appreciate one another's special contributions. They encourage others to share their unique information and points of view. Third, the importance of a group's climate cannot be overemphasized. The ideal climate is one of openness to new ideas, high levels of trust among members, and willingness to disagree. During divergent thinking, members uncritically encourage unusual ideas; during convergent thinking, they encourage constructive debate. Finally, a group's creativity is affected by the environment in which it operates. If a group's parent organization doesn't value creativity or won't allow the group to operate with some autonomy, group creativity will be hurt. Table 5.1 summarizes the individual, group, and environmental characteristics that promote creativity.

TABLE 5.1	**Individual, Group, and Environmental Factors that Promote Creative Thinking**

MEMBERS

Willing to communicate

Willing to be unconventional and violate societal norms

Tolerant of ambiguity

Not afraid of rejection

Open to new ideas

Playful and like to have fun

GROUPS

Have diverse knowledge, skills, perspectives, approaches

Work to overcome norms that interfere with creativity (premature consensus, pressures to conform) and promote norms that foster creativity (take time to learn each other's unique contributions, encourage sharing of diverse ideas)

Develop an appropriate group climate (foster trust, encourage constructive debate)

ENVIRONMENT

Place a high value on creativity

Give the group autonomy and room to breathe

"Never, ever, think outside the box."

Creative thinking is always appropriate, but is especially useful at the beginning of a group's problem-solving process. An ideal time to use creativity-enhancing procedures is when members have learned something about a problem but before they have gotten bogged down in details. Members can create a number of innovative ideas that they later can examine carefully and critically. However, creativity may take extra time, which may not be worthwhile for relatively unimportant decisions.

Enhancing Group Creativity

At some point, you will be asked to help a group discover a creative solution to an interesting problem—an idea for a new product, an eye-catching print advertising campaign, or a novel way to build a safe greenway across a busy expressway. The group may need to be shocked out of its habitual ways of thinking to find a creative idea. You can use brainstorming, synectics, or mind mapping to help a group tap its creative potential.

5.1 Creative Fund-Raising for the College

Several years ago, members of the Advisory Council of the College of Arts and Letters where one of us works met to discuss creative fund-raising ideas to enhance the college's endowment for student scholarships. One council member mentioned a combination lecture/dinner fund-raiser a museum in New York City had initiated, which had become a highly successful event. Members began to talk about ways that event could be modified to work in Springfield, Missouri. They decided to have faculty give presentations or performances based on their expertise, combined with a dinner at one of the council member's homes. For instance, a film professor followed his lecture about a particular film director with a special showing of one of the director's lesser-known films, followed by dinner. Another professor gave a brief piano concert followed by an elaborate dessert. These events, known as the A La Carte Series, have become so successful that the college has a long list of volunteers wanting to host one of the dinners. In addition, the events sell out quickly, sometimes the first day that tickets become available. This is an example of how a group can modify an existing idea to arrive at something unique. Before you read further in this chapter, address the following questions:

1. What communication behaviors and skills would group members have to demonstrate to encourage the kind of creativity demonstrated by the advisory council?

2. What member behaviors would interfere with this kind of creativity?

3. What group rules, norms, and procedures would support this type of creativity?

4. What group norms would interfere?

For more information on using the Internet to brainstorm, go to the Online Learning Center at **www.mhhe.com/ adamsgalanes6**

BRAINSTORMING

Many groups use **brainstorming,** a procedure designed especially to release a group's creativity.[10] Brainstorming is used most often when groups are generating ideas. Brainstorming consciously separates idea creation from idea evaluation by not allowing any criticism to occur while the group is generating ideas. Later, the group evaluates the ideas, combines or modifies them, and selects the best ones. The basic procedure is described below. Figure 5.1 summarizes these brainstorming guidelines.

1. The group is presented with a problem to solve. The problem can range from something specific and concrete ("How can we raise more money for student scholarships?") to something abstract and intangible ("How can we improve the quality of work life for employees?").

2. Members are encouraged to come up with as many solutions as possible to the problem. Quantity is the goal here and several rules must be followed. The first and

FIGURE 5.1   Guidelines for Brainstorming

Group is presented with a problem to solve. → Members generate as many solutions as possible, without any criticism. → All suggestions are recorded for group to see. → Ideas are evaluated at another session.

most important is that no evaluation is permitted during brainstorming. With judgment temporarily suspended, members are encouraged to turn their imaginations loose, to encourage wild and crazy ideas to surface, to build on each other's ideas, to combine ideas, and to strive for more and more suggestions. Second, you do not want to stop generating ideas too soon. Often, the best ideas—the ones a group eventually selects—are listed during the latter part of the brainstorming session.[11]

3. All ideas are recorded so that the whole group can see them. Usually the group's recorder will write ideas on a large pad of paper. As the top sheet is filled, it is posted on the wall so that all ideas are clearly visible at all times. Seeing the previous ideas often triggers new ideas.

4. The ideas are evaluated at another session. Just because brainstorming requires temporarily suspending critical evaluation does not mean the critical thinking function is unimportant. Also, incubation is an important feature of creative thinking. After brainstorming has generated a lot of ideas and the group has had a chance to let the ideas sit for a while, critical thinking is used to evaluate each idea and to modify or combine ideas into workable solutions to the problem.

The basic brainstorming technique has several variations. Often groups have one or two vocal people who are highly creative, share many innovative ideas, and may intimidate others from participating. In this case, it may be more productive for each person to brainstorm silently rather than openly in a group. In this form of brainstorming, called *brainwriting,* each person quietly writes as many new and different solutions as possible on a notepad. Then each person shares one new idea, round-robin fashion, as the facilitator posts it on a chart for all to see. The sharing continues until all ideas have been posted. Members are encouraged to add to the list as new ideas occur to them.

Electronic brainstorming, another variation, takes advantage of the fact that anonymity may remove inhibitions. In this variation, each group member sits at an individual computer terminal (all of which may be in the same room) and types out his or her ideas. The ideas are combined onto a large screen visible to everyone. Because no one knows who contributed what, electronic brainstorming, especially with 8- to 10-member groups, often generates more and better ideas than traditional brainstorming.[12]

SYNECTICS

Synectics is a technique that stimulates thinking in metaphors and analogies.[13] Why is that important to creativity? Consider the example of how the fastener Velcro was created. One day after a walk, Swiss engineer George de Mestral noticed cockleburs stuck to his jacket.[14] Examining one under a microscope, he observed how the hooks latched onto the fabric, and saw its potential as a hook-and-loop fastener. It took him eight years to develop and perfect, but today Velcro turns up everywhere, from shoes to children's clothing to camping equipment. The cockleburs served as the nature-based analogy, or metaphor, for the manufactured fastener.

Serendipity helped de Mestral link burrs from the natural world to this new kind of manufactured fastener. The synectics technique tries to stimulate such chance connections between apparently unrelated elements. First, the group identifies the essence of the problem. For instance, "sticking together" could have been the metaphor that led to Velcro: "How can I create a fastener that sticks together like burrs do to clothing?" Second, the group is asked to create analogies that capture that essence. For instance, group members might ask, "Where in everyday life do we find things that stick together?" Answers could include things like burrs, gooey things from plants, white glue, or zippers. Finally, group members look for metaphors or analogies that use a different sensory perception than the one being observed. For example, if the analogy relates to touch, such as the cocklebur

5.2 Creating Suggestions for Crossing Kansas Expressway

APPLY NOW

Ozarks Greenways, Inc., must come up with a solution to the following problem. Land has been acquired on either side of busy Kansas Expressway for a greenway, a bicycle and hiking path to join Springfield with Wilson's Creek Battlefield. However, there is no traffic light where the land reaches the expressway and the city has no plans to put a light there. Your task is to come up with a solution for the greenway that will keep bikers and hikers moving and that will be safe and inexpensive.

Divide the class into groups of five or six. Appoint a facilitator to record suggestions and make sure the group follows the "no criticism" rule. Ask each group to brainstorm a list of suggestions for the greenway problem. The groups should brainstorm for 10 minutes and should think of as many suggestions as possible. At the end of the period, all the suggestions should be posted at the front of the class so that all can see. The class should then address the following questions:

1. Was it easy or difficult to follow the brainstorming rules? What was the hardest to do?

2. How did members feel during the process?

3. What do members remember thinking during the process?

4. Did anything stand in the way of being imaginative and having fun? If so, how might the process be modified to encourage more imagination and fun?

As an alternative to this exercise, some groups can be instructed to brainstorm in the traditional way while others are instructed to use brainwriting. If this is done, class members can compare the efficacy of each technique. Groups can also use a facilitator to help members stick to the brainstorming rules.

example, members might be asked to think of a visual or hearing metaphor. A visual metaphor could include a fishhook; an auditory metaphor might include the sound of a zipper closing and opening. A different kind of metaphor could be just the thing producing the "aha" insight that leads to a solution. Asking the group to consider the following questions helps trigger such insights.

1. Change your perspective. Sometimes, changing the angle from which you view a problem gives you a different insight. For example, if you are an Ozarks Greenways member, imagine that you are Superman and can view the city's streets from above.

2. Look for a direct comparison, something from another field that is similar to your problem. This is exactly what happened in the Velcro example—the physical attachment of the burrs provided the idea for this new type of fastener.

3. Temporarily suspend reality to use fantasy and imagination. Ignore objective reality for a moment to learn what you can discover. Imagine that your bicycle has wings and can fly over Kansas Expressway to solve the greenway problem.

Synectics may seem strange at first because it forces group members to jump out of their self-imposed conceptual boxes. It feels uncomfortable to group members because it is designed to stimulate rather than reduce ambiguity, but that's exactly why it works. Some corporations, such as General Electric, deliberately send groups of employees away from their normal work settings to jolt them out of possible ruts so they can come up with new ideas.[15] In one such group meeting between GE middle managers and colonels from the Army War College, GE's long-standing rule about having to be number one or two in every business it entered or product it produced was challenged. One of the colonels asked whether that rule perhaps caused the company to miss profitable opportunities. His statement produced an instant "aha" reaction from the GE managers, who recognized that they dismissed good ideas if those ideas wouldn't lead to the top market share. The managers were able to persuade CEO Jack Welch to rethink the "GE must be Number 1 or 2" rule. The limitations of this rule would never have been recognized or questioned from the safety of GE home base—the executives needed to be in a new setting to see things from a different perspective. This is exactly what synectics promotes.

MIND MAPPING

Mind mapping is a technique that tries to jolt a group out of its usual linear way of thinking by encouraging the radiant thinking produced by free association.[16] Radiant thinking sometimes leads to insights that linear thinking misses. Developed as a technique to foster individual creativity, the technique has also been adapted for small groups.[17] In mind mapping, a facilitator places a word or phrase that is the essence of the problem in the center of a large sheet of paper or a white board for all group members to see. That central concept forms the nucleus for the spin-offs that group members will add. Sometimes a facilitator adds the connections as instructed by group members, but often group members themselves use colored markers to print or draw the phrases, ideas, or concepts they associate with the central concept. The final mind map looks like colorful multiple branches of a tree shooting off from the central idea. Because the branches are more like a web than a line, group members often see connections they might otherwise miss.

For instance, assume you belong to the Ozarks Greenways group trying to find a safe way to cross Kansas Expressway without asking bikers to stop for traffic. The facilitator prints the phrase "Crossing Kansas Expressway" in the center of the sheet and draws a circle around it. (As an alternative, a line drawing of a busy highway could be drawn in the center.) Each member then adds his or her mental associations to this central idea. One member connects a bicycle with wings to the central concept. Another draws an arch spanning the busy highway. A third member connects "stop light" to the central idea. Someone else connects the words "annoying" and "interfering with the flow" to the "stop light." The picture of the winged bicycle next to the arch suggests to yet another member the idea of constructing an overpass that would allow bikers to cross without stopping. In fact, construction of an overpass was the solution chosen by Ozarks Greenways, Inc.

Mind mapping can be a lot of fun, particularly if members draw their associations using colored markers. The process taps into members' creativity by encouraging them to make visual connections they otherwise would miss. In addition, drawing is different enough from what groups usually do that members enjoy the process.

As with brainstorming, members should not criticize the associations that appear on the mind map. As the group mind map is being developed, members need to feel mentally and emotionally uninhibited so they can make unusual connections. Fear of being ridiculed or criticized could make them feel self-conscious. However, *after* the mind map has been developed, members should begin to evaluate the ideas on the map.

Creative thinking plays a significant role in group problem solving. Groups trained in creative thinking have been found to show more humor and participation than those not trained to think creatively. Members of such groups support more ideas and criticize less, both of which are important to creative thinking.[18]

Creativity is important, but it is not the only process small groups need. Once a group has come up with creative options for solving problems, its work isn't finished! Now members must carefully and critically examine those options to evaluate which ones are best. Surprisingly, groups have more problems being critical than being creative. In addition, failure to be critical is more dangerous than failure to be creative. Group problem solving can be effective because several heads are potentially better problem solvers than one, but many groups do not achieve this advantage. Members are not as vigilant or critical in their discussion of information because they avoid challenging each other's ideas and developing their own arguments.[19] The implications and consequences can be considerable if a group doesn't think things through carefully, as the following case example will illustrate.

In the remainder of this chapter, we examine how groups can help ensure good decision making and problem solving to complement their creativity.

What Makes Thinking "Critical"?

We have seen that creative thinking is intuitive, unsystematic, and spontaneous. In contrast, **critical thinking** involves using information that is supported by evidence and reasoning and examining both the evidence and the reasoning systematically and logically to ensure that they are sound.

Two principles differentiate critical from creative thinking: (1) the use of **evidence** (facts, data, opinions, and other information backing a claim or conclusion) and (2) the logical **arguments** speakers and writers make with that evidence to support what they believe are valid reasons to accept their claims and assertions. This means that, for critical thinking to occur, a problem must be analyzed thoroughly, using as much relevant information as possible.

GLOSSARY

Critical Thinking

Systematic thinking using evidence, reasoning, and logic to promote soundness

Evidence

Facts, data, opinions, and other information that back a claim or conclusion

Arguments

Claims supported by evidence and reasoning

Problems at NASA

CASE 5.2

On February 1, 2003, many of us watched in horror as the space shuttle *Columbia* disintegrated upon reentry after what had been a successful mission in space. The National Aeronautics and Space Administration's (NASA) investigation into the causes zeroed in on pieces of foam insulation that detached at liftoff, damaging or knocking off some insulation tiles designed to protect the shuttle from the extreme heat of reentry.[20] No longer shielded from the heat, the fuel tank exploded. NASA records disclosed that foam insulation had caused damage to the tiles since the very first shuttle launch! One NASA official lamented, "How were the signals missed?" In early 2004, NASA released the results of an internal survey of its employees, which showed that the culture of NASA contributed to why these signals were missed.[21] The survey, completed by only 45 percent of employees, revealed that many employees are afraid to speak out about safety concerns and are reluctant to "express dissenting views in a large group." One NASA administrator pointed out that in NASA's culture, both managers and peers pressure dissenters to conform, even when they have safety concerns: "We don't have time to listen to everybody moan and groan about every issue out there." NASA concluded that this mind-set contributed to the *Columbia* disaster.

This isn't the first time NASA's culture has been implicated in a disaster. The 1986 explosion of the shuttle *Challenger* shortly after takeoff was caused by malfunctions of the O-ring seals on one of the solid rocket boosters—a particularly distressing event because, like the problems with the foam insulation, NASA knew about potential problems with the O-rings failing to seal in cold weather. In other words, the *Challenger* disaster was predictable. The decision-making procedures *should* have revealed the O-ring safety concern—but did not.

Communication scholars have had time to analyze the decision-making procedures leading to the *Challenger* disaster and have concluded that the procedure was flawed in several ways.[22] NASA officials were biased in favor of the launch because of several previous postponements. The engineers, who showed the most concern about the O-rings, were reluctant to bypass their chain of command to demand that superiors pay attention to their concerns. But the engineers also failed to make their objections clear—they used ambiguous language that minimized the significance of their concerns. Several decision makers discounted the relevance of pertinent technical information that, had it been seriously considered, would have postponed the launch. So even a group of highly trained experts can arrive at a fatally flawed decision that ignores relevant information—in other words, the group doesn't think critically.

Then the solution must be developed on the basis of all that information and the best reasoning and logic you can use.

Although thinking critically is necessary, like creative thinking, it is time consuming. You should be able to determine when you need to take the extra time that critical thinking demands and when you can make a decision that is just "good enough" without analyzing all your choices. For example, suppose your committee is charged with deciding whether to give coffee mugs or comparably priced pens with your organization's logo as souvenirs at your annual banquet. Does it really matter which favor is selected? Will anyone be hurt by your choice? Such a decision probably does not warrant taking the time to agonize over every aspect of the choice. However, with decisions where human lives are at stake, such as whether or not to launch a space shuttle, critical thinking is essential.

Enhancing Critical Thinking in a Group

Critical thinking in a group is not just one thing that members know or do. Critical thinking involves a number of factors, including the attitudes members have toward information, the way they gather information, how careful they are in evaluating information, and how skilled they are in making reasoned judgments on the basis of that information.

ATTITUDES

The most important "technique" to help groups do a good job of critical thinking is not a technique at all—it is the attitude of the members. Ideally, critical thinkers *want* to make the best possible decision, are skeptical when they receive information, and are active in the information gathering and evaluation process.

The most important attitude necessary for critical thinking in groups is the desire to make the best possible decision. You have to want to make a good decision because doing so takes a great deal of time and effort. Your desire is what gives you the energy to engage fully in the critical thinking process. Critical thinkers are **open-minded,** which means they are willing and eager to consider new information and ideas, even if that information contradicts what they previously believed. They go out of their way to look for relevant information and tap a wide variety of sources in their attempt to gather information that supports all sides of an issue. Finally, they pride themselves on being objective and fair about evaluating information. The NASA officials involved in making the original *Challenger* launch decision were apparently prejudiced in favor of the launch. This lack of objectivity biased their search for information, so they did not work as hard to find information that opposed the launch as they did to get information that supported it. They evaluated that information in a biased way—they uncritically accepted pro-launch information but were hypercritical of anti-launch data.

A second important attitude is a "show me" skepticism that indicates members want to think for themselves rather than being told what to think by others. Critical thinkers do not assume that anything they read or hear is true or accept something as true just because a parent, friend, or teacher "said so." They are willing to challenge any information, even information presented to them by experts, high-status individuals, or the group's majority, by raising questions about it.[23] This also means they are willing to hold off making a decision until the facts are in, which suggests they can tolerate ambiguity, at least for a while. They don't latch onto a premature conclusion just to get a tough decision-making process over with. They know that better decisions result from applying the same skeptical approach to all claims, including their own.

Skeptical decision makers try to test information and opinions as well as the sources of such information. To do this, they ask lots of **probing questions** to determine the adequacy and quality of evidence and reasoning supporting a claim or decision. Table 5.2 provides examples of probing questions. Asking the engineers probing questions about the safety of the launch is exactly what officials of the company that manufactured the *Challenger* rockets did not do. Instead, these managers were confident they knew what their subordinates were thinking, so they didn't ask directly.

Finally, critical thinking is an active (rather than passive) process of testing information. It demands hard work to find the information necessary to understand the problem and subject solutions to the most rigorous tests possible. Mentally lazy group members object to this hard work, but critical thinkers look forward to it.

The information just presented describes attitudes essential to critical thinking in a small group. Several attitudes and behaviors make it difficult for group members to engage in critical thinking, and these are worth looking at briefly. It is just as important for you to know what *not* to do as to know what to do, so Table 5.3 summarizes these counterproductive behaviors.

TABLE 5.2	**Probing Questions to Evaluate Evidence and Reasoning**

- What evidence do you have to suggest that statement is true?
- Where did that evidence come from?
- Does anyone have any evidence to contradict the statement we just heard?
- If we make that decision, what will it lead to?
- What might the consequences be if we are wrong?
- How much danger is there that we have reached the wrong conclusion?
- How did you arrive at that conclusion?

TABLE 5.3	**Attitudes and Behaviors Counterproductive to Critical Thinking**

- Oversimplifying the thinking process; evaluating information and ideas in either–or, black–white terms.
- Impulsiveness; jumping to premature conclusions.
- Overdependence on authority figures; waiting for someone else to tell you how to think, what to conclude, or what to do.
- Lack of confidence; withdrawing if someone challenges your ideas.
- Dogmatic, inflexible behavior; closing your mind and being afraid of change.
- Unwillingness to make the effort to think critically; taking the easy way out.

GATHERING INFORMATION

One skill essential to critical thinking is the ability to organize ideas.[24] The first step to organizing your ideas is to assess the information you already have, identify gaps in that information, and then establish and implement a plan for plugging those gaps. In the information gathering stage, you cannot tell what is important and what is not, so you should use "sponge style" thinking—like a sponge, you want to absorb as much information as you can about your topic or issue.[25] You'll evaluate it later.

Assessing Information Needs.   Before group members begin their research, they first need to take stock of the information they possess (see Table 5.4). The quality of an output, such as a plan or policy, cannot be better than the information members have or the way they share and process it. The first step is to make an outline or list of the information you have to help you assess what you need. For example, a university committee was charged with revising the curriculum for communication majors. Members first pooled all the information they had, such as what the current major requirements were, the problems and issues they had observed, and information about what nearby colleges and universities required of communication majors. Committee members soon realized they needed to fill several important information gaps before they could begin any adequate discussion of the problem. For instance, the committee members hadn't assessed the perceptions of current students and alumni about the strengths and weaknesses of the existing program—a major oversight! In addition, prospective employers could provide information about the skills and deficiencies of recent graduates and current student interns. Finally, committee members knew they must have information about current practices in the field of communication, including what communication professionals were saying about the direction of the field.

Information lists help determine not only what information is missing but also where it can be found. The next step in the critical thinking process is the careful gathering of information to fill the gaps.

TABLE 5.4	Gathering Information in the Critical Thinking Process: Assessing Information

1. Take stock of existing information.

2. Identify holes and weaknesses.

3. Make a master list of what information is needed and where it can be found.

4. Collect needed resources by assigning members specific responsibilities for finding needed information from the master list.

5. Use all appropriate information gathering techniques:
   - Direct observation.
   - Reading.
   - Interviews (individual or group).
   - Other sources (radio, television, casual conversation).

Collecting Needed Resources.   Group members should organize their information gathering procedures before proceeding. First, from their master list, members should list all the information they still need. Then they should assign themselves research responsibilities on the basis of their preferences, strengths, and time schedules. Finally, as members proceed with their research, they will discover additional information they need that should be added to the list and assigned to the appropriate group members.

As the committee revising the communication curriculum illustrates, the information a group needs is rarely found in one location. Usually, a variety of information is needed and will have to be gathered in various ways. Some of these are described briefly.

Direct Observation.   Sometimes information you need will come from firsthand observation. For example, if your group is assessing the parking problem at your university, observing the parking lots to count the number of spaces available at different times of day and the number of cars "creating" spaces where there are none is an example of direct observation.

Reading.   A wealth of information can be found in many kinds of printed sources. Published material often can save you considerable time and effort needed to gather information yourself. Useful information may be found in newspapers, books, magazines, scholarly and professional journals, technical and trade publications, government documents, and so forth. The sheer number of sources available can be intimidating. A reference librarian can help save hours of wasted effort by pointing you in helpful directions and steering you away from likely dead ends.

In addition, a number of publications can save you time and effort in locating printed information. Annotated bibliographies and abstracts provide a preview of the type of information in a publication so that you can decide whether it will be worth the search. Encyclopedias summarize vast amounts of information. Specialized indexes and abstracts frequently can help you save time in locating relevant information. For example, the *Business Periodicals Index* summarizes articles from numerous business and trade journals.

The Internet.   An easy and convenient way to access information is through the Internet. Use a browser, such as Netscape or Explorer, to connect to your favorite search engine. (You may want to try more than one search engine, since no one search engine covers the entire Internet.) Use keywords for your search, following the rules of the particular search engine you're using. Although you may have thousands of hits, most search engines give you the most likely hits first, so search those carefully. You may have to try various keyword combinations. For example, if you are seeking information about the effect of riverboat gambling on state economies, you may have to try "riverboat gambling," "gambling," "gaming," and so forth.

Be particularly careful to evaluate information you derive from the Internet. Know that *anyone* can put up *anything* on the Internet; no review procedure evaluates the information for accuracy or truth. Any claim—no matter how outrageous—can be made on the Internet, and websites have been created that contain lies and misinformation. Make sure you use your best critical thinking skills to evaluate information you receive from the Internet.

Electronic Databases.   Electronic databases available at most academic and public libraries provide a very efficient way to find printed information. Many sources formerly available only to those who had physical access to a library can now be accessed at home via the Internet. Electronic databases contain titles, abstracts, and sometimes the full text

"On the Internet, nobody knows you're a dog."

of magazine and journal articles, newspaper articles, and books on thousands of topics. Commonly used databases include InfoTrac, a general-purpose database that accesses nearly 1,000 business and trade journals; ERIC, which holds education-related materials gathered by the U.S. Department of Education; LexisNexis, which accesses legal and business resources; ComAbstracts, which contains information from all communication-related journals; and EBSCOhost, another general-purpose database of nearly 3,000 periodicals, with full text for nearly 1,500. In addition, many newspapers, such as *The New York Times,* can be accessed electronically. As with Internet search engines, electronic databases typically operate using keywords or author names.

Interviews.   Members of your group may need to conduct several interviews. These may be face-to-face individual interviews, group interviews, or those conducted over the phone or via electronic mail. For example, the curriculum committee members interviewed their colleagues in person, phoned or e-mailed colleagues at other schools, and called a sample of alumni to ask for their perceptions and opinions. Examples of the kinds of closed-ended and open-ended questions typically used in interviews are shown in Table 5.5.

Other Sources.   Useful information may come when you least expect it. Radio, television, casual conversation with family or friends, browsing through electronic bulletin boards, stumbling onto relevant information in a magazine while waiting to get your hair cut—all are potential sources. Be prepared to take advantage of these sources by recording the information as soon as possible so you don't forget it. Once you have gathered the information you need, you must decide how useful it is to you.

Go to
**www.mhhe.com/
adamsgalanes6**
for additional
weblink activities.

5.1   Critical Thinking about Internet Sources

MEDIA AND TECHNOLOGY

This chapter has stressed the importance of critical thinking. When using the Internet for information, group members have an ethical responsibility to ensure that evidence and information are accurate and effective. Bourhis, Adams, Titsworth, and Harter recommend using the following criteria to critically evaluate Web sources:

1. *Is the supporting material clear?* Sources should help you add clarity to your ideas rather than confusing the issue with jargon and overly technical explanations.

2. *Is the supporting material verifiable?* You should be able to independently verify facts and details contained on a Web page.

3. *Is the source of supporting material competent?* You should determine the source of the Web material and determine whether or not the source is qualified.

4. *Is the source objective?* All sources—even news reports—have some bias. Your responsibility is to ensure that your sources minimize bias.

5. *Is the supporting material relevant?* Using irrelevant research may make your ideas appear well supported; however, critical listeners will see through this tactic. Only utilize sources that directly address the key points you want to make.

You should also consult the following sources to find more information on evaluating the quality of Web information: **www.virtualsalt. com/evalu8it.htm** and **www.library.cornell.edu/olinuris/ref/ research/webeval.html.**

SOURCE: J. Bourhis, C. Adams, S. Titsworth, and L. Harter, *Style Manual for Communication Studies* (New York: McGraw-Hill, 2002).

EVALUATING INFORMATION

The next step in the critical thinking process is to evaluate the information after you have gathered it. As a sponge, you've absorbed all the information you think you'll need. Now you must "pan for gold" by trying to find the nuggets of information that are valuable to you.[26] If a group bases its decision on inaccurate or outdated information, its decision will be flawed, no matter how systematic the gathering process has been. For example, the curriculum committee described earlier recommended that communication majors take several writing courses offered by the English department. However, even though the recommended courses were listed in the school's current catalog, the English department had revised its curriculum, eliminating several courses and changing several others. This mistake was not a disaster, but it would not have occurred if curriculum committee members had checked with the English department to determine whether any course changes were anticipated.

TABLE 5.5	Open- and Closed-Ended Questions

Open-ended questions	Closed-ended questions
What do you think about the proposal to raise taxes?	Do you agree or disagree that taxes should be raised?
What is your opinion of the performance of the committee chair?	Has the committee chair done a good job?
How might we enhance our presentation audiovisually?	Should we use a skit or a videotape in our presentation?
How can we solve the parking problem on campus?	Where should we put the new parking garage?
How effective are your group's critical thinking skills?	Are your group's critical thinking skills: ____ Very effective? ____ Somewhat effective? ____ Average? ____ Somewhat ineffective? ____ Very ineffective?

How can you tell whether a piece of data is accurate and up-to-date, and whether a source is credible? Evaluation of available information is perhaps the most crucial step in the critical thinking process. Several factors play a role in evaluating information: determining what someone means, distinguishing fact from opinion, clarifying ambiguous terms, assessing the source's credibility, and assessing the information's accuracy and worth. Browne and Keeley's fifth edition of *Asking the Right Questions: A Guide to Critical Thinking* is an excellent summary of how you can assess the value of information.

Determining the Meaning of What Is Being Said.   The first thing you must do is decide exactly what the speaker or writer means. This is not as easy as it may sound. Frequently, people bury the meaning of what they are saying among a jumble of opinions and irrelevant statements. You should identify the author's conclusion, reasons for the conclusion, and evidence to support the reasons. First, ask yourself what conclusion the author is drawing. What does he or she want us to do, think, or believe? Is there an action (such as voting for a particular candidate, writing letters to a television producer, or buying a particular product) that the author wants us to take? Next, determine what main arguments the author provides to support the conclusion or recommended action. For instance, look at the sample letter provided in Apply Now 5.3. What conclusion does the author want you to reach, and why?

Often, keeping track of the arguments and evidence that supports them is easier if you outline the argument on paper. Write the main conclusion at the top; then list each argument beneath it with space after each one. In this space, list every piece of evidence the author or speaker offers in support of the claims. This will simplify your later task of evaluating how good the author's evidence and reasoning are and how valid the conclusions are.

Distinguishing Fact from Opinion and Inference.   You must be able to recognize the difference between a statement of fact and statements of opinion or inference based on that fact. **Facts** are descriptions that can be verified by observations and are not arguable. For example, we can verify that the population of Greene County, Missouri, in 2000 was 240,391 by looking in any of several government publications that record population data. Be careful, though—some statements presented as facts are not facts at all but false statements. For example, the statement "Greene County, Missouri, has 500,000 residents" is not true; therefore, it is not a fact. You will need to determine whether statements presented as facts are actually true and up-to-date.

Opinions and inferences go beyond what was observed directly and imply some degree of probability or uncertainty. **Opinions,** unlike facts, are not all equal, although everyone has an equal right to express an opinion. Some opinions are more valid than others. Einstein's opinion about the way the universe operates should carry more weight than the opinions of the authors of this book because we are not theoretical physicists. The value of an opinion depends on the evidence supporting the opinion and the quality of the reasoning that ties the evidence and opinion together. Determining an opinion's value is part of your job as a critical thinker. For example, someone might say, "Greene County, Missouri, is growing rapidly." That is not a fact; that is an opinion. It is your responsibility to determine the validity of the opinion by asking questions such as the following: What was Greene County's population 10 years ago? What is the average annual rate of growth in the United States? In Missouri? How does Greene County's rate compare with that of other cities in Missouri? If you learn that Greene County's annual rate of growth for the last 10 years has been 2.4 percent, compared to Missouri's .9 percent, you can reasonably conclude that "Greene County is growing quickly." Thus, opinions are arguable and should be evaluated systematically during a group's deliberations. Groups that make poor decisions do so in part because inferential errors impair their critical thinking.[27]

Identifying and Clarifying Ambiguous Terms.   Authors or speakers often make it hard to evaluate information because they use terminology that is **ambiguous,** or unclear. For example, candidate Beasley in Apply Now 5.3 is termed "experienced." What does that mean? What kinds of experiences has she had? Is she experienced as a teacher, a parent, or an administrator? Is she experienced at working in a small group? Each of these experiences is different and paints a slightly different picture of the candidate. Clarification of vague terms is very important in evaluating the worth of your group's information.

Earlier in the chapter, we mentioned the decision made by NASA officials to launch the *Challenger.* In their analysis of the decision-making process, Gouran and his associates discovered that failure to clarify ambiguous terms contributed to that terrible decision. They explain:

> No one went so far as to say, "We recommend that you do not launch." Instead, they claimed making such statements as, "We do not have the data base from which to draw any conclusions for this particular situation"; "We did not have a sufficient data base to absolutely assure that nothing would strike the vehicle."[28]

What do those statements mean? This kind of doublespeak confuses issues because it leaves room for a variety of interpretations by permitting others to read their own favorite interpretations into the message. At NASA, no one asked explicitly for clarification of the ambiguous terms.

Your local parent-teacher organization has received the following letter from one school's site council. The executive committee, of which you are a member, is meeting to decide what to recommend to the entire PTO. Practice evaluating the information and arguments in the letter.

Dear Parent-Teacher Organization Member,

As you know, the vote to elect a new member to the school board will occur on April 5. We want you to know that the Parents' Excellence in Schools Committee supports candidate Mary Alice Beasley for our school board.

Mary Alice Beasley is the best candidate we have running for the Central City school board. We need people like her who care about our kids. She has lived in Central City all her life and now has three children of her own in the school system. She has been an active member of the P.T.O. for the past six years and was chair of the fund-raising committee for Westwood School. Her experience will be invaluable.

In her second term as city councilwoman, she was the chief author of the plan to desegregate the city schools; as we all know, other cities have used this plan as the model for their own desegregation efforts. Mary Alice can represent the entire community well—she taught for nine years before she ran for city council, and she has a master's degree in education. Hers is exactly the kind of caring, experienced leadership we need on the school board. Mary Beasley deserves your endorsement. Remember to vote on April 5.

Either individually or in groups of four to six, answer the following questions and then discuss them as a class:

1. What conclusion are you being asked to reach? Is there an action you are being asked to take in this letter?

2. Like most letters of this type, this letter interchanges fact and inference, or opinion. Make a list of all the facts presented in the letter and a list of all the inferences presented.

3. Ambiguous terms are sometimes difficult to spot because we each think we know what words such as *experienced* mean. Make a list of all the ambiguous terms (terms that can reasonably be understood in more than one way) presented in the letter. Before you assess how the letter's writer interprets each of these terms, what do you mean by each of them? For instance, what does *experienced* mean to you?

4. For each of these terms, what evidence is presented in the letter that supports the author's opinion about Mary Alice Beasley? For example, what facts are presented to support the author's view that Ms. Beasley is "experienced"?

5. Would you vote for Mary Alice Beasley on the basis of this letter? Why or why not? What other information about this candidate would you like to have to help you make your decision? Where would you go for the information you need?

Evaluating Opinions by Determining the Credibility of the Source.   We noted earlier that not all opinions are equal. How can you tell whether an author or a speaker is someone whose opinions are worth your attention? Ask yourself several key questions to help you decide how much trust to place in an opinion.

1. Is there any reason to suspect the person(s) supplying the opinion of bias? For example, if you find a source that debunks the idea that smoking causes lung cancer, you should treat that information with suspicion if it comes from a publication of the American Tobacco Institute. On the other hand, if that statement appears in the scientifically respected *New England Journal of Medicine,* you would have greater reason to expect objectivity.

2. Is the individual, or other source, a recognized expert on the subject? Is this someone whom other experts respect? Would you feel proud or silly quoting this person? We may feel comfortable citing Michael Jordan's opinions about basketball but very uncomfortable citing Aunt Tilly's.

3. Is the opinion consistent with other opinions expressed by the same source? Media sometimes misquote people. Are you reasonably sure the opinion stated is accurate? Is there a later interview or quote that reverses the inconsistent opinion? Sometimes people do change their minds for good reasons. What is the reason given for the change of opinion? Does the evidence offered to explain the change seem reasonable to you? If not, suspect inaccuracy or some unknown bias.

Assessing the Accuracy and Worth of the Information.   Now that you have established a context for evaluating the information by determining exactly what is being said and how credible the source is, you are in a position to evaluate how good that information is (see Table 5.6). After all, it could be misinformation. You should ask yourself a number of questions about the information before using it during group decision making.

1. What types of evidence are offered to support the argument? Is it a personal experience? Statistical support? The combined opinions of a number of recognized experts? Although many people do so, it is unsafe to accept personal experience as the sole basis for supporting an opinion. For example, assume you were once in a successful and productive group led by a dominant leader who decided everything and delegated these tasks to other members. Thus, your personal experience may lead you to believe that groups work best under strong, controlling leaders. But someone else's experience may differ. Assume a fellow group member worked in a democratic group, where there was no one leader but all members contributed to leadership based on their areas of expertise. This member thinks that the only good group is a democratic one. Which of you is right? Each of you is right, for the particular circumstances of your experience, but neither of you is right to try to apply your experience to everyone else.

2. Is the information based on the testimony of a number of experts or authorities in the field? If so, you can place greater trust in it, especially if these experts are widely recognized and accepted by their peers. Be sure to determine if other experts disagree and why. Be especially careful about accepting information from an expert in one field about another field. For example, movie stars frequently express strong opinions about the American political scene. While some may be well informed, others are not.

TABLE 5.6	Evaluating Information in the Critical Thinking Process

DETERMINE WHAT THE SPEAKER OR WRITER IS SAYING

1. What is the conclusion?

2. What does the author want us to do?

3. What are the main arguments in support of the conclusion?

DISTINGUISH FACT FROM OPINION AND INFERENCE

1. What are the facts?

2. What are the opinions?

IDENTIFY AND CLARIFY AMBIGUOUS TERMS

1. What are the ambiguous terms?

2. What do you think the author means by each term?

3. If you can't decide with confidence, what problems does this create?

DETERMINE THE CREDIBILITY OF THE SOURCE

1. Who is the author or speaker? What are his or her credentials on this issue?

2. Is this a recognized expert?

3. Is this a biased source or one with something to gain by expressing this opinion?

4. Is the information consistent with other credible sources?

ASSESS THE ACCURACY AND WORTH OF THE INFORMATION

1. What type of evidence (e.g., personal experience, statistical support, opinions of experts) is being offered in support of the author's arguments?

2. Is the evidence supported by other experts or authorities, or just this author?

3. Is the information based on the scientific method?

4. If the information is based on interviews or questionnaires, was the sample large enough and representative enough? Were the questions clear and not biased or loaded?

3. Is the information based on valid scientific or statistical reasoning? You should ask how the information was gathered, how the questions were worded, whether the data came from a properly designed survey, and so forth. Information must follow strict guidelines before it can legitimately be termed scientific. First, such information must be verifiable by others. Thus, although an experience that happens to someone may be true, it is not scientific unless the event is observed or can be re-created by other people. Second, scientific information must be obtained under controlled conditions by controlled observations. Having an informal conversation with your classmates about the death penalty and concluding that "American college students have the following attitudes toward capital punishment . . ." may be interesting but it is not scientific. But if you surveyed a representative sample of students, asked each of them the same questions, and systematically analyzed their answers, you could reasonably conclude: "Students at my college believe the following about capital punishment . . ." Finally, scientific information must be expressed precisely. Another researcher, after reading an account of a scientifically controlled research study, should be able to carry out a study in exactly the same way, using the same procedures, equipment, and statistical tests.

Information gathered by questionnaires or interviews poses additional questions regarding the individuals who were queried. Were there enough of them, and were they representative of a larger population? In most cases, random sampling is most likely to ensure a representative response. For example, assume your committee is charged with making recommendations regarding parking on your campus and you decide to poll students who drive to campus. If you survey only students who park in one particular lot between 7 and 8 a.m., your results are not likely to reflect the views of the entire student population. Making parking recommendations that will affect thousands of students on the basis of responses from a few students is irresponsible. On the other hand, if you systematically survey students from all campus lots at varying times during the day and evening, your responses are more representative and your conclusions are likely to be more valid.

5.1   What Would You Do?

You and your group have been working on your panel presentation about the death penalty for several weeks, with one week to go before you are responsible for conducting the panel discussion in your class. This project represents a major portion of your grade in the small group class, and you are required to conclude your presentation by taking a position—your group must come out either in favor of or against the death penalty. After hashing this out for weeks, you have sorted through all your evidence and have almost reached consensus that you will come out in favor of the death penalty. This week, while doing library research for another class, you happen upon a new study, based on systematic examination of states with the death penalty, that strongly suggests the death penalty *does not* deter crime. The study seems well done; you don't think you can dismiss it as a piece of biased or poorly done research. But you know if you present it to your group, you'll push your emerging consensus further away, and you hate to do that! You are so close now to agreement, and you know this study will set you back. What do you do?

1. For what reasons would you *present* the article to your group?

2. For what reasons would you *withhold* the article?

3. What would you actually do?

TABLE 5.7	**Checking for Errors in Reasoning**

- Does the author overgeneralize?
- Does the author attack a person instead of the issue?
- Does the author argue that because two events are related, one caused the other?
- Does the author present you with an either–or choice when other alternatives are possible?
- Does the author present you with a comparison that is incomplete or invalid?

GLOSSARY

Fallacies

Mistakes in reasoning and faulty reasoning

Overgeneralization

A conclusion not supported by enough data

CHECKING FOR ERRORS IN REASONING

The final element in the critical thinking process is assessing the quality of the reasoning people provide for their opinions or for supporting one conclusion over another. Unfortunately, most speakers and writers often make a variety of common reasoning errors, called **fallacies,** that makes assessing reasoning challenging. Fallacies tend to divert a listener's attention from the issue or sidetrack the discussion so that members of a group begin to debate something other than evidence and claims. However, critical thinkers working together in a small group should be able to spot each other's fallacies (see Table 5.7). The differing but complementary bases of information that individual members bring to a group discussion can help them compensate for each other's weaknesses to produce, on the whole, a superior group result.[29]

Overgeneralizing.   Generalizations are made when information about one or more instances is said to apply to many or all instances of the same type. In other words, if something is true about a few instances or people, it is assumed to be true about most instances or people in the same category. For example, someone may read in the newspaper that a certain number of college students have defaulted on their government-guaranteed student loans. If that person concludes from this that "college students are irresponsible borrowers," he or she has made a generalization. Even though it isn't stated that way, this implies that *all* college students are irresponsible borrowers, and this is an overgeneralization. An **overgeneralization,** like the loan default example, is a conclusion that is not supported by enough data.

Generalizations by themselves are not automatically wrong. Conclusions based on carefully gathered data that were analyzed with appropriate statistical procedures are often very accurate. Usually such generalizations are qualified and not stated as applying to all cases. Remember, for a generalization to be factual for all cases, someone would have to observe all of these cases.

To decide whether a generalization is a valid conclusion or an overgeneralization, ask yourself a few questions:

- How many cases is the conclusion based on?
- Are there any exceptions to the conclusion?
- What form of evidence is the source asking us to accept: personal or other forms?
- Is the generalization expressed as probability or in "allness" terms?

Attacking a Person Instead of the Argument.   Attacking a person instead of the argument, even if subtly done, is a form of name-calling used to direct attention away from someone's evidence and logic (or lack thereof). Sometimes called *ad hominem* attacks, such arguments take this form: "Because So-and-So is a _____ (woman, Catholic, foreigner, intellectual snob, hillbilly, liberal, and so on), you can't believe his/her opinions about the topic." Such an argument sidetracks the discussion of the opinion into a discussion of the merits of So-and-So. So-and-So may indeed be a crackpot about some things, but his or her views about the topic might be quite accurate. More information is needed before a critical thinker would make that judgment.

Confusing Causal Relationships.   Another common reasoning error occurs when the speaker or writer mistakenly states what caused an event. Two forms of this error are observed frequently. Sometimes people oversimplify by implying or stating that only one cause exists for an event. In other instances, they imply that, because two events are related by subject matter or in sequence, one causes the other. For example, we have heard students say that if a manager implements quality control circles in a company, the company's profits will increase. Such a statement implies that quality circles cause higher profits. In actuality, a variety of factors is likely to contribute to, or cause, increased profits. For example, better employee training, lower costs of raw materials, increased prices for a company's products, improvements in technology, and improved upward communication and morale produced by the quality circle—all of these factors may contribute to the increased profits. It is oversimplifying to assume that quality circles alone are the cause.

Neither can we assume that, just because one event preceded another in time, the first caused the other. It may be that both are caused by a third event or condition. For example, one of us overheard someone mention recent statistics indicating that female graduates of women's colleges are more likely to become members of the U.S. Congress and serve on the boards of Fortune 500 companies than are graduates of coed schools. The person speaking was arguing that attendance at women's colleges *caused* this type of career achievement. However, many women's colleges are academically selective as well as expensive. Women attending such schools are often both exceptionally bright and from families who own or are connected to Fortune 500 companies. It is plausible that these additional factors—ability and family connections—"cause" both the attendance at women's colleges and the career achievement. The relationship between college attendance and later achievement is likely to be a complex one that does not lend itself well to simple causal descriptions.

Either-Or Thinking.   **Either–or thinking** (sometimes called a false dilemma) says that you must choose one thing or another, and no other choices are possible. Seldom is this the case. For example, assume your group is preparing a panel discussion about sex education in the schools and you encounter the following statement: "Sex education is an important element of a young person's education. If the parents won't teach their children about sex, the schools have to." Most people would readily agree with the first sentence. The second, however, reveals either–or thinking. The author is forcing the reader to accept the premise that either the parent will teach the child about sex or the school will. In fact, other alternatives are possible. Perhaps churches, synagogues, or Camp Fire USA leaders could take on the job; or parents and school officials together could design a cooperative program. Just because a writer does not mention other alternatives should not blind you to their existence.

Incomplete Comparisons.   Comparisons, especially **analogies,** help us understand issues more vividly. However, there are limitations to such comparisons. Because one thing bears a resemblance to another does not mean they are identical. At some point the resemblance will break down because no two situations are identical in all characteristics. An incomplete analogy (sometimes called a faulty analogy) asks us to stretch a similarity too far. For example, assume you and other students are discussing how well the public relations major at your school prepares students to be public relations professionals. One student says, "You really can't learn much about public relations from school anyway. It's like trying to ride a bicycle by reading books about it but never getting on an actual bicycle."

5.4   Gun Control

APPLY NOW

Shortly after the school shooting in Springfield, Oregon, many news programs featured point–counterpoint "debates" between people who favored particular solutions to the problem of children killing children. On one morning news show, the first panelist proposed that legislation be passed requiring handguns and semiautomatic weapons to be fitted with lockable triggers. He explained that parents could lock these guards and keep the keys hidden. This would prevent children from accidentally shooting the guns. It would also mean that children who were enraged would not be able to pick up a gun to discharge their rage; they might start a fistfight, but the guns would be out of bounds. The opposing panelist said that requiring locking triggers would simply make it more difficult for homeowners to defend themselves; he favored stiffer penalties and zero tolerance for children violating rules pertaining to weapons. Each panelist argued strongly for his solution and identified all the possible flaws he could with the opposing panelist's solution.

In small groups or as a whole class, discuss the following questions. To get a more vivid idea of the types of arguments made, you may want to simulate the point–counterpoint discussion and ask two class members to role-play each panelist.

1. First, see how many arguments you can create to support each position and put them on the board for all to see.

2. What are the fallacies you are able to identify in the arguments presented?

3. What are the characteristics of that particular television format that encourage these kinds of fallacies to be presented?

4. Assume the two "debaters" are members of a small discussion group charged with identifying a policy to prevent school shootings. What would you say and do if you heard the kinds of fallacies being expressed during the discussion?

At first glance, this remark hits home with many of us who complain that school can't prepare us for the "real world." However, let's look more closely. Yes, there are public relations experiences that cannot be duplicated in school. But there are many activities that *do* prepare students for professional practice. Designing flyers and brochures, writing news releases, taking photographs, planning a mock public relations campaign, and designing a survey are all examples of typical activities that public relations students perform in school and that are also necessary on the job. Thus, whenever you see or hear someone make a comparison, first determine in what ways the two things being compared are similar, but especially look for ways they are different. Ask yourself if the analogy breaks down at any point. If so, where? How does this affect the reasoning you are being asked to accept?

The fallacies previously described are some of the most common ones, but there are many others. Be alert for them by asking the right probing questions about the ideas, opinions, interpretations, and conclusions someone is asking you to accept. Then you need to pay careful attention to the answers you receive (or don't receive).

ASKING PROBING QUESTIONS

We noted earlier that group members with the right "critical thinking" attitude are willing to challenge information and opinions by asking probing questions. This is probably the most important thing you can do if you want to be a critical thinker; it is so important that we are mentioning it again. Do not accept information just because it sounds good, is presented in an entertaining way, comes from someone of high status, supports what you already believe, or is accepted by the majority of group members. Be willing to confront and question the accuracy of the information and the appropriateness of the reasoning you are being asked to accept.

According to Gouran et al., failures to ask probing questions at several steps during the decision-making process and groupthink (discussed in Chapter 9) were prime contributors to the *Challenger* disaster. The problem with the O-ring seals in cold temperatures had been observed for years before the launch, but no one asked the tough questions about what was being done to correct the flaw. The problem just kept being ignored. One engineer who opposed the launch assumed that his objection was passed to superiors, but he did not ask specifically whether this was so. When representatives of North American Rockwell, the manufacturer of the shuttle, relayed their concerns about the launch in vague terms, no one asked specifically whether or not they were recommending postponement. All these isolated incidents, in which no one asked the right questions, together contributed to the *Challenger* disaster. The single most important thing you can do to prevent this kind of disaster is to ask probing questions, even though this is not always easy or pleasant. If other group members call such questioning argumentative or quibbling, reassure them that the purpose of your questioning is not to argue or put anyone down, but to help the group by clearing up any possible misunderstandings, oversights, or fallacies.

A number of group systems support (GSS) tools can help members probe and evaluate information (see next chapter). GSS tools include electronic brainstorming, electronic outliners, idea organizers, and topic commentators. Working with neutral facilitators, groups can lessen the influence of biased information and can be guided in their attempts to track arguments, confront each other's claims, and develop their own lines of reasoning.[30]

RESOURCES FOR REVIEW AND DISCUSSION

SUMMARY

■ To be effective problem solvers, group members must do a good job with both creative and critical thinking. Creative individuals are willing to communicate, to be unconventional, and to play in the group. Creative groups are willing to examine their norms and change those that interfere with creativity.

■ Creativity requires freedom from judgment and can be enhanced through the use of three techniques: brainstorming, synectics, and mind mapping. Brainstorming explicitly suspends criticism, and synectics works by attempting to make the familiar unfamiliar. Mind mapping seeks to avoid linear thinking.

■ Critical thinking involves a concentrated effort to assess the value of ideas and conclusions by gathering relevant information, assessing that information carefully, and judging the reasoning that supports the conclusions and decisions. Critical thinking in small groups involves knowing when to use critical thinking and requires certain attitudes of group members, a methodical search for information, thorough evaluation of the information, and careful assessment of

the reasoning behind opinions and beliefs based on that information.

■ In gathering information, group members first should pool their knowledge and identify any gaps that are apparent. Then, they should fill those gaps by using appropriate research methods, including direct observation; reading; using electronic databases; interviewing individuals or groups; and consulting other sources such as television, the Internet, and radio.

■ When members evaluate information, they first should determine what is being said, which statements are facts and which are inferences or opinions, what terms are ambiguous, how believable the source is, and how accurate and valuable the information is.

■ When they check for errors in reasoning, group members should be especially alert to the common fallacies. Critical thinking consists primarily of asking the right probing questions, which can prevent harmful throughput processes such as groupthink.

EXERCISES

1. Form groups of four to six students. Each of you should be given some ordinary, tangible object, such as a clothespin, an alarm clock, or a ballpoint pen. Find a new use for the item that has nothing to do with the item's ordinary use. To do this, you must perceive the item in entirely new ways. To help you do this, your teacher can lead you in a guided meditation. For instance, imagine that the clothespins are alive and are sending you messages about what they would like to be used for. After you have discussed the problem in your groups for 15 or 20 minutes, present your favorite solution to the class. Then all of you should vote to select

the most creative idea. (Perhaps your teacher will award prizes to the winning group.)

2. The following exercise helps clarify the difference between statements of fact and statements of inference. Place a familiar item (such as a coffee cup, a chair, or a ballpoint pen) in front of the class so everyone can see it easily. Make statements of fact about it. Each statement should be written on the board. After about 15 statements, identify as a class those statements that go beyond what was actually observed. Discuss why these statements are inferences rather than facts.

3. Videotape one of the many television programs that feature panel interviews with public figures (such as "Meet the Press"). Look for errors in reasoning, places where the interviewee seemed to camouflage what she or he was saying, or places where the interviewee was evasive. Dis- cuss the program in class. It will be particularly helpful if you can show your tape in class.

Go to **www.mhhe.com/adamsgalanes6** and **www.mhhe.com/groups** for self-quizzes and weblinks.

KEY TERMS • CONCEPTS

Ambiguous	Either–Or Thinking	Open-minded
Analogies	Evidence	Opinions
Arguments	Facts	Overgeneralization
Brainstorming	Fallacies	Probing questions
Creative Thinking	Mind Mapping	Synectics
Critical Thinking		

www.mhhe.com/adamsgalanes6

Use the flash cards and crossword puzzles on the Online Learning Center to further your knowledge of these key terms.

Group Problem-Solving Procedures

CHAPTER OBJECTIVES

After reading this chapter you should be able to:

1. Explain why using a systematic procedure for group problem solving usually produces better solutions than random or haphazard problem solving.

2. Define key terms such as *problem solving, decision making,* and *area of freedom* with examples.

3. Describe five characteristics of problems.

4. Explain why and how you would adjust the problem-solving process to accommodate any of the characteristics of problems.

5. Describe the Functional Theory of problem solving and decision making.

6. Describe each step of P-MOPS.

7. Explain how you could use techniques such as the *problem census, focus groups, group support systems, RISK,* and *PERT* to help at various stages of P-MOPS.

8. Apply P-MOPS to fit a simple or complex problem.

The Merger

CASE 6.1

In 2000, a crisis loomed for Ozarks Public Television. OPT had oper-ated in Springfield and Joplin, Missouri, for nearly 25 years with a community-owned broadcasting license, using studios rented from a small, private college in Springfield. But in the 1990s, the U.S. gov-ernment mandated that all public TV stations had to switch to digi-tal broadcasting equipment by 2003, a very expensive proposition for OPT. After assessing all their options with the help of a consult-ant, OPT board members decided to seek an educational partner. Eventually the board approached Southwest Missouri State Univer-sity with a proposal for SMSU to take over the broadcasting license and allow OPT to merge with the university. The SMSU board ac-cepted the proposal at its December meeting, and work toward the merger began immediately.

Ideally, the physical move would occur in the summer, when fewer students and faculty would be on campus, but before that could happen, a number of legal items and physical changes had to occur. Most importantly, the Federal Communications Commission (FCC) had to approve the license transfer. Space had to be found on cam-pus to accommodate the OPT staff, equipment, and control room; the decision had to be made about how to finance and when to make the digital conversion; the merger and its benefits to SMSU had to be presented to the faculty, staff, and students; and program planning at a variety of levels had to occur.

Involving every OPT and university employee in each decision would have created chaos! Instead, several groups—each composed of different combinations of SMSU and OPT personnel—were estab-lished to bring about the merger. For example, a facilities subcom-mittee was charged with assessing SMSU space and determining how it needed to be modified. A public relations subcommittee han-dled the delicate process of explaining the merger to the university community and to the many volunteers who had worked for OPT over the years. Several similar groups were established, with their work overseen by the steering committee we introduced to you in Chapter 1. The steering committee established the timeline and kept track of the progress of each of the other groups to ensure that the merger would occur on time and with every detail accounted for.

The OPT–SMSU merger is a typical group problem-solving situation. In this case, two parent organizations—OPT and SMSU—appointed a number of groups to help the larger organizations manage information, make decisions, and complete tasks about a complex problem. A single individual trying to solve the merger problem would have become overwhelmed at the volume of information and the amount of work! Not only that, a single individual would have been unable to think of everything that needed to happen for this merger. Some important piece likely would have fallen through the cracks. On the other hand, involving the entire university community and OPT staff in participating equally to identify and evaluate solutions would have created a chaotic and unmanageable process. In this case, using several smaller groups, with the steering committee in charge, enabled the work to be done on behalf of the two larger organizations.

As we said in Chapter 1, groups can produce solutions to complex problems that are better than solutions produced by individuals; they also produce greater member understanding and more satisfaction.[1] The *assembly effect* is achieved when the group solution is superior both to the choice of the group's most expert member and to an averaging of opinions of all members. That is because group discussion can help members collectively recall information some may have forgotten, correct flawed information, help members understand information so that it is more useful, identify gaps in the information base, and help each other appropriately evaluate and weigh the importance of information.[2] The dark side, however, is that group problem solving is not always better (see Table 6.1). Groups can do a lot, though, to improve the quality of both problem-solving procedures and the solutions they generate. Systematic problem-solving procedures are a key factor in improving the overall quality of their activities. They usually produce better solutions and decisions than unsystematic discussion.[3] This chapter identifies the nature of problems, reports on factors that improve problem solving, and describes procedures for enhancing group problem-solving discussions.

TABLE 6.1	Advantages and Disadvantages of Solving Problems in Groups versus as Individuals

Advantages	Disadvantages
• Solutions for complex problems are usually superior.	• Groups take more time.
• Groups have more resources, including information and methods.	• Participation may be uneven; some members may dominate, others withdraw.
• Members accept the solutions more readily; satisfaction is higher.	• Interpersonal tension, disagreements about the task, and conformity pressures may interfere with critical thinking.
• Members understand the solution more completely.	

A Systematic Procedure as the Basis for Problem Solving

There are a number of ways to solve problems. One way is by turning to an expert or someone you consider to be an authority, the way many people turn to doctors for dealing with illnesses. Or, you may solve problems at an unconscious or preconscious level called *intuition.* This happens when you may be wondering what to do about an assignment and suddenly the answer occurs to you while you're taking a shower.

There's nothing wrong with these methods, particularly for problems that will affect only you. However, intuition can have serious limitations for group problem solving, especially if you use it alone without also using a systematic procedure for checking out the hunch. Careful, critical analysis of information is important as well. What would you say if you went to the doctor because of chest pains and, without doing any tests, she said, "My intuition tells me you need a shot of penicillin"? Ideas derived only through intuition must be examined critically before they are implemented because critical thinking can reveal flaws in the ideas that may not be apparent at first. It's possible the hunch is terrific and may only need to be tweaked to solve your problem, but it's also possible that the hunch may cause more problems than it solves. Systematic problem solving is a way for groups to assess ideas and to manage the mountain of information unearthed by the problem-solving process. For example, the OPT–SMSU merger involved keeping track of dozens of details—far more than any one person could have handled. If the steering committee hadn't met regularly and used a systematic process, some of the information would have been lost, and key options might not have been considered. Any less systematic procedure might have produced a successful merger, but chances are some important element would have been ignored.

Thus, no matter how a group discovers the possible solutions to a problem—through intuition, logic, or authority the group must use a systematic process and the best critical thinking it can muster to check out how well the solutions will work. The rest of this chapter is designed to help you understand what problems are, how certain characteristics of problems affect the problem-solving process you use, what factors promote effective problem solving, and how you can organize group problem solving by using a systematic, yet flexible, procedure called P-MOPS. We also provide a number of specific techniques that help at different stages of the problem-solving process.

What Is a Problem?

Problem refers to the difference between what exists and what you expect or want. For example, you need your entire group to show up for a class presentation, but on the day of the presentation three members are no-shows. You have a problem!

Problem solving and decision making are related concepts and need to be distinguished before we go further. **Problem solving** involves all the things you have to do to move from the existing situation to the goal. It is a multistep process that includes defining the problem, identifying or creating possible solutions, and choosing among the solutions. **Decision making** refers to the act of selecting one or more available options; it does *not* involve creating possible options. Problem solving is a more comprehensive procedure that includes decision making (choosing). The entire process of solving a problem often involves making many decisions, such as how to define the problem, what solutions to consider, which to suggest or act upon, and how to carry out the chosen solution. The steps you take and the order in which you do them can greatly influence the quality of your product. Can you imagine cutting out material for a coat without first having a pattern to guide your scissors?

Every problem situation has three major components. A group needs to understand and articulate these components completely to develop an appropriate solution for a particular problem.

For more information on the digital divide problem, go to the Online Learning Center at **www.mhhe.com/ adamsgalanes6**

1. **An undesirable existing situation.**

   If people believe that something is perfectly satisfactory as it is, there is no problem. For example, when Grupo Latino Americano's meeting place was accessible and affordable, GLA had no problem. But when the landlord suddenly tripled the rent, GLA needed to find a new place to meet. The undesirable present situation in this case was an exorbitant rent GLA couldn't afford.

2. **Desired situation or goal.**

   At the start, a goal may vary from a vague image of a better condition (having a safer neighborhood) to a very precise, detailed objective (starting a neighborhood watch program). Part of effective problem solving involves establishing a precise goal that is achievable, doesn't suggest a solution, and is understandable to all members. Outstanding groups have clear goals that all members support.[4]

3. **Obstacles to change.**

   These are conditions and forces that must be overcome by the chosen solution to achieve the goal. Typical obstacles include insufficient information, the competing interests of other people, lack of tools or skills, insufficient funds, or anything you must overcome in order to reach the goal. For example, when GLA's rent tripled, it had no idea what other facilities were available, what similar facilities rented for, how soon another facility could be located, whether members would be willing to move, what it could afford, and so forth.

AREA OF FREEDOM

The **area of freedom** is the amount of authority and the limitations given to a group charged with solving a problem. Group members must know, at the beginning, what they are and are not supposed to do. A fact-finding group, for instance, may be asked only to investigate a problem, not solve it. Another small group may have authority only to interpret information, as in the case of a jury that can decide guilt or innocence but not the penalty for guilt. Many advisory committees and conferences can recommend a solution but not make it binding. For example, the OPT–SMSU facilities subcommittee charged with identifying available space for OPT was not empowered to start modifying that space until the steering committee had evaluated the options and given the go-ahead.

Committee members must understand the exact charge to the group before they proceed to work on any problem. Otherwise, they will waste time and may become frustrated or angry. A committee one of us observed was charged with making recommendations about the types of student activities on campus. Instead, this committee created a sweeping proposal

6.1 Improving Airport Security

After September 11, 2001, it was clear that the United States had a problem with ensuring security on its airline flights, since terrorists had been able to hijack four different airplanes on the same day. Map this problem according to the problem components described above.

1. An undesirable existing situation: Describe the airplane boarding situation on 9–11 and explain what seems to be undesirable about that situation (e.g., rules permitted box cutter knives to be carried on planes).

2. Desired situation or goal: What would the desired situation look like? For instance, passengers would like to board quickly and efficiently, but they would also like to be protected from other passengers carrying weapons.

3. Obstacles to change: What are obstacles to our achieving these goals? For instance, do we lack information about how terrorists bypass safeguards in our system? Do we lack technology at airports to improve baggage screening?

to fire certain individuals and restructure the student activities department. Even though committee members worked long and conscientiously to develop the plan, it was not accepted because the committee went far beyond its area of freedom.

ADAPTING PROCEDURES TO FIT YOUR PROBLEM

Some problems are complex and others relatively simple. It makes intuitive sense that you would not use exactly the same process for all kinds of problems. Systematic processes for problem solving can and should be modified to fit the particular problem your group faces. To help you do this, you need to understand something about the characteristics of problems and how these can affect group problem solving in order to tailor your procedures to fit your problem. The components described earlier are common to all problems, but specific characteristics vary.

Characteristics of Problems.   You could consider many characteristics of problems when you start to modify the problem-solving process to fit your problem, but the five we discuss here are among the most important.

Task Difficulty.   A complicated task is high in difficulty, but a simple task is low in difficulty. For a difficult task, members should make sure they fully understand the nature of the problem, do a thorough job of unearthing information, carefully coordinate their efforts, and expect to attend many meetings before they finish. Groups are asked to work on difficult tasks because their solutions are beyond what one person alone can do. Extensive problem mapping will be important.

Solution multiplicity.   Are there many possible ways to solve your group's problem, or is there one correct answer? There are many fun and appropriate ways to plan your high school class's 10th reunion, but there may be only one solution to a math problem. When a problem has high solution multiplicity—in other words, has many possible solutions—you will want to make sure that your group identifies as many of those solutions as possible. This focus on generating ideas will be the key to success.

Intrinsic interests.   Are group members really interested and excited about working on this problem (that is, is there high intrinsic interest) or would they rather go to the dentist than have to tackle the problem? When members are excited and interested, they want to talk about the problem or issue, to tell their own stories about it, or to vent their feelings. They don't want to be overcontrolled or overstructured in addressing the problem. But when they are bored and uninterested, they will be happy to have someone—probably the group leader—structure the problem and give them specific assignments to complete.

Member familiarity.   Has the group ever confronted a similar problem? Did it solve the problem successfully? If so, the members have high familiarity with the problem. They may want to focus on establishing criteria for evaluating options. But if they have never undertaken anything similar, or if they have just formed a new group, they will need some time to get to know each other and to familiarize themselves with all aspects of the problem (particularly if it is complex). Detailed problem mapping and using consultants and outside experts will help get the group up to speed.

Acceptance level.   Is acceptance of the solution by people who will be affected by it critical for success? For instance, if a company is considering changing its overtime policies, lack of employee acceptance can derail the "solution" and cause lasting bad feelings. In such a case, the acceptance level needs to be high, making it crucial for the group to solicit the opinions and ideas of those who will be affected. Before committing fully to the solution, the group may want to suggest partially implementing the solution and reevaluating it with those who are affected. But if the solution won't matter much to most people—such as, which party favors to buy for that high school reunion—then members don't need to spend time seeking outside opinions.

You should consider these characteristics when deciding on a problem-solving procedure. Table 6.2 summarizes these factors along with suggestions for modifying the problem-solving procedure.

Sometimes problems are obvious—your landlord triples the rent, your treasurer empties the bank account, you can't get anyone to come to meetings. But most proactive organizations don't wait for a crisis to identify problems. The OPT board didn't wait for the digital equipment conversion deadline to pass before investigating its options. Spotting problems in advance is a good idea.

IDENTIFYING PROBLEMS WITH A PROBLEM CENSUS

The **problem census** is a posting technique for identifying important problems or issues. It can be used to establish agenda items for future meetings of a committee or identify problems on the horizon that a group should work on. Sometimes a group leader wants to encourage participation and make group processes more democratic but doesn't know exactly where to begin. The problem census is ideal for all these purposes because it requires all the members of a group to take responsibility for creating the group's work agenda. Members often become more committed to the group's task because they are enthused about working on items they perceive as important to them. For example, a university department conducts a problem census at the beginning of each semester, generating agenda items for future meetings. As various departmental problems are listed, different

TABLE 6.2	**Problem Characteristics and the Problem Solving Process**

TASK DIFFICULTY

Adaptation for high difficulty

- Plan to meet often

- Detailed problem mapping

- Many subquestions to the problem-solving procedure

- Detailed implementation plan, in writing

SOLUTION MULTIPLICITY

Adaptation for high multiplicity

- Use brainstorming or one of its variations to generate many ideas

- Use synectics or another creativity-enhancing technique to help members relax and be creative

- Leave plenty of time for generating ideas; don't rush the process

INTRINSIC INTEREST

Adaptation for high interest

- Set aside a "ventilation" period early in the problem-solving process for members to express their feelings

- Leave plenty of time for early ventilation

- Don't overcontrol the ventilation process or introduce structured procedures too early

MEMBER FAMILIARITY

Adaptation for high familiarity

- Focus on establishment of clear criteria

- Focus on evaluating the options using the criteria developed

Adaptation for low familiarity

- Detailed problem mapping

- Use consultants and outside experts for help

ACCEPTANCE LEVEL

Adaptation for high acceptance requirements

- Include representatives in your group from groups that must accept the decision

- Use the RISK or similar "last chance" technique to spot potential problems before finally deciding on a solution

- Pretest a solution by partially implementing it and agreeing to pull back if it doesn't seem to work

6.2   Characteristics of OPT's Problem

Assume you are members of the Ozarks Public Television governing board, and it is early 2000. You know that you have a 2003 deadline for converting to digital equipment, a very expensive proposition. You are currently bringing in enough money for OPT to operate both stations in Springfield and Joplin, Missouri, but you aren't making the kind of extra money you'd need—more than $1 million—to make the digital conversion. You have a problem!

1. Identify the elements of this problem: the undesirable existing situation, the goal, and the obstacles to change.

2. Look at the characteristics of the problem-solving process presented in Table 6.2. Evaluate OPT's problem in terms of these characteristics, explaining your evaluation:

   Task difficulty: high or low? Why?

   Solution multiplicity: high or low? Why?

   Intrinsic interest: high or low? Why?

   Member familiarity: high or low? Why?

   Acceptance level: high or low? Why?

faculty members volunteer to investigate the problems and prepare an outline for discussing each problem as it comes up. The following are detailed steps (summarized in Figure 6.1) for conducting a problem census in a face-to-face meeting. Several of these steps are easily handled electronically.

1. **Seat the group in a semicircle facing a chart or board.**

   If you have access to a large computer screen and specialized hardware and software (discussed later), you may also position members at computer terminals facing a large computer screen.

2. **Explain the purpose of the technique, which is to bring out any problems, concerns, questions, or issues any member wants to discuss.**

3. **Ask each participant to present one problem or concern in** round-robin **fashion.**

   After the first person presents one problem, the second presents one, and so forth. Anyone who does not have a problem to list may pass. This continues until all problems are identified. One electronic variation to this is to ask members to brainstorm problems individually and then send them to the centralized computer screen. That way all problems are posted for everyone to see. Another electronic alternative is to ask people to e-mail their list to the group's leader in advance of the meeting; these are easily compiled into a master list that members can be given ahead of time.

4. **Post each problem on a board or chart as it is presented.**

   As each page of the chart is filled, tape it to the wall so that all problems are visible at all times. The group's recorder must never challenge or disagree but may ask for

---

FIGURE 6.1   **Steps for Conducting a Face-to-Face Problem Census**

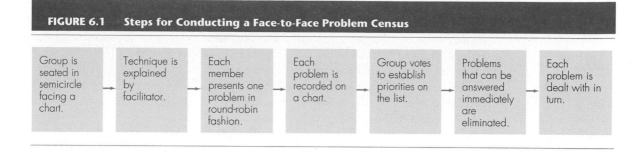

| Group is seated in semicircle facing a chart. | → | Technique is explained by facilitator. | → | Each member presents one problem in round-robin fashion. | → | Each problem is recorded on a chart. | → | Group votes to establish priorities on the list. | → | Problems that can be answered immediately are eliminated. | → | Each problem is dealt with in turn. |

---

clarification or elaboration and may rephrase long problems. The recorder should always ask the speaker whether the rephrasing accurately reflects the speaker's intent.

5. **The group votes to establish priorities on the list.**

   Usually, each member votes individually for three or four top choices. The items are then ranked from most to least votes received. All items remain on the list; voting just prioritizes the agenda. With certain software, this ranking process can be handled electronically as well. Members rank the items individually; the computer automatically tallies and prioritizes the overall list based on member rankings.

6. **Problems that can be answered immediately are eliminated.**

   Sometimes group members can answer questions or solve problems to the satisfaction of the person who initially presented the problem. Such questions or issues are removed from the list.

7. **Each problem is dealt with in turn.**

   Some issues may call for an investigation and report, a lecture, or another informational presentation such as a brochure. Some require the services of outside consultants. However, major problems should be handled by the entire group or a subcommittee, following an appropriate problem-solving procedure.

Once an organization has identified problems to address, it will likely appoint a task force or study group to begin identifying solutions to the problem. Confronting the problem systematically is the best way to ensure that no important information is ignored or overlooked and that group members' time is used wisely. The procedure described below is easily modified so you can take advantage of its flexibility and adapt it to the particular problem your group faces.

Effective Problem Solving and Decision Making

In the early 1900s, American philosopher John Dewey asked his students to think about a problem they had faced and solved, then to recall the sequence they used to solve the problem. From their reports, he created a general sequence of mental steps he called *reflective thinking,* which implied that the students' process was systematic rather than intuitive or haphazard behavior. The individual problem-solving sequence usually goes like this: first we become aware of a difficulty, then define and describe it, think of some possible solutions, evaluate these potential solutions, and make a decision about what to do. If possible, when we implement the solution, we monitor it to see how it's working, then keep it, adjust it, or replace it after testing it.[5] Dewey's model has been adapted for groups to use; group problem-solving procedures based on his model go under such names as the standard agenda, ideal solution, and single-question formats.

As Dewey did with individuals, Gouran, Hirokawa, and their associates have examined problem solving and decision making in groups.[6] Their **Functional Theory** has evolved over the past two decades to describe how communication helps or hinders group problem solving and decision making. It is called "functional" because it focuses attention on the communicative functions that must be performed if a group is to do a good job. Gouran and Hirokawa assume that group members *want* to make a good decision, have all the information and other resources they need to do so, and have the communicative and thinking skills necessary to do a good job. If those conditions are present, whether a group solves problems effectively depends on three factors.

The first factor pertains to the task requirements. According to Functional Theory, five task requirements must be met for a group to succeed. First, members must understand the problem or issue. Second, they must know the minimum requirements of a successful solution, including what criteria it must meet. For instance, is there a budget members cannot exceed or an outside group whose support is essential? Members of effective groups discuss the criteria openly to ensure that everyone understands them. Third, the group must identify the alternatives from which it will make its choice. Many groups stop identifying or creating alternatives too soon; without sufficient realistic alternatives to choose from, the group may miss the best one. Fourth, the alternatives must be thoroughly evaluated, both for strengths and weaknesses, against the agreed-upon criteria. Finally, the best solution—the one that best meets the criteria—should be chosen.

The second major factor in Functional Theory pertains to how well members use their communication skills to overcome natural obstacles to effective problem solving and decision making. For instance, sometimes members fail to discover information pertinent to their problem or fail to share relevant information. Several researchers have found that members tend to share and believe information they have in common (that they all know), but to hold on to unique information that only one or a small number of them know.[7] Sometimes, members consider their relationships with each other more important than finding the best solution; in that case, members will refrain from disagreeing with each other and may try to pressure others to conform. Finally, some members may be more self-interested than interested in helping the group. How the rest of the group deal with such members directly affects the quality of decisions the group makes.

Finally, Functional Theory states that group members must be willing to review their process and reconsider their decisions. If they find flaws, members must be willing to second-guess themselves, even to the point of starting over. They must not remain committed to a solution when it is clear the solution is flawed. Their communication to each other should remind members of the importance of reviewing the process and of being fair in making the ultimate choice.

Many researchers have found that following a planned problem-solving procedure helps groups make better decisions and solve problems more effectively. Such procedures can minimize the bad habits typical of small groups, including getting off track, being pressured by domineering members, prematurely rejecting ideas, and focusing on solutions too early in the process. The procedures help balance participation, improve a group's reflectiveness, coordinate members' thinking, and establish important ground rules for proceeding.[8]

It doesn't seem to matter which problem-solving procedure a group uses; *any* systematic procedure or outline produces better decisions than using no procedure.[9] Step-by-step procedures improve the quality of solutions because they provide logical priorities and steps that must be taken; they remind members of things they might otherwise forget.[10] Evidence suggests that groups arriving at high-quality solutions have made a thorough analysis of the problem, generated a variety of solutions, and conducted a detailed assessment of both the positive and negative aspects of the alternatives being considered by the group.[11] In addition, these groups have focused on a solution's possible problems, and have avoided pitfalls.[12] In other words, using a systematic problem-solving procedure encourages a group to consider the functions (according to Functional Theory) necessary to arrive at an effective solution by helping ensure that an important step doesn't get overlooked.

Group members have said that one of their most urgent needs is for guidance about methods and procedures to use during group work.[13] Group participants have identified the lack of strong procedural guidelines as one of their most troublesome barriers to effective problem solving. In particular, participants want methods that help them generate and organize their ideas about complex problems. One such guideline, the Procedural Model for Problem Solving (P-MOPS for short), has been used with good success.

THE PROCEDURAL MODEL OF PROBLEM SOLVING (P-MOPS)

Several different guidelines can help groups solve problems effectively; we favor P-MOPS for its adaptability and because it focuses a group's attention on the essential tasks outlined by the Functional Theory. The **Procedural Model of Problem Solving** is a flexible framework that can guide each phase of problem solving; it applies to all the principles we have learned about effective problem solving by groups and individuals. Based on Dewey's reflective thinking model, it provides a sequence to guide each phase of the problem-solving process and can be adjusted to suit the special needs of your group.

P-MOPS reminds the group to analyze the problem thoroughly before trying to solve it and to think critically about the positive and negative outcomes likely to occur with each alternative solution. We have shortened its name to P-MOPS to remind you that it will help you "mop up" the details needed for good problem solving. The five steps in this general problem-solving procedure are: (1) describing and analyzing the problem, (2) generating and explaining possible solutions, (3) evaluating all solutions, (4) choosing the best solution, and (5) implementing the chosen solution.

1. DESCRIBING AND ANALYZING THE PROBLEM

During the first stage of problem solving, the group concentrates on thoroughly understanding the problem. Members should consider all three major elements of the problem: what is unsatisfactory, what is desired, and what obstacles exist. This phase of problem solving may require nothing more than sharing the knowledge members now have, illustrated

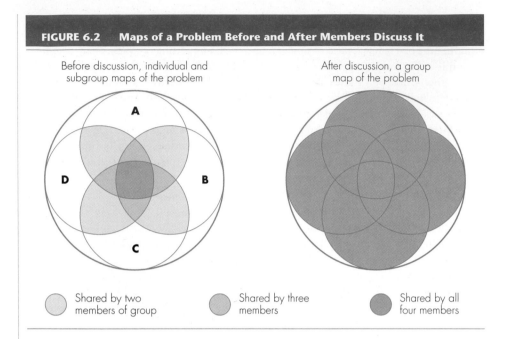

FIGURE 6.2   Maps of a Problem Before and After Members Discuss It

Before discussion, individual and subgroup maps of the problem

After discussion, a group map of the problem

○ Shared by two members of group   ● Shared by three members   ● Shared by all four members

by the mapping procedure depicted in Figure 6.2. That's easier said than done, though. Group members are apt to share freely that information that they already hold in common.[14] Apparently, shared information is more credible and creates common ground among members, who tend to withhold unique information, but this defeats the purpose. For group problem solving to be most effective, *all* information must be shared.[15] Members have to overcome their natural reluctance to share certain kinds of information and be willing to make whatever they know about a problem the property of the group. The description and analysis of a problem should never be rushed—it is crucial to effective problem solving.

Following are several principles to guide your thinking and discussion in step 1 of problem solving.

a. *Be sure you understand the charge precisely.* The **charge** is your assignment of both responsibility and limitations, given by the organization or person who created the group. Getting the charge straight means that you make sure you understand an assignment exactly as intended. Get the charge in writing if possible. A committee should ask for clarification of any unclear terms from the person presenting the charge. For instance, you need to know what form your final product is to take: a recommendation, a research report, a blueprint with perspective drawings, or any other tangible object. You will certainly need to know what limitations are placed on your freedom, such as what information you can obtain from company records, legal restraints, spending limits, and so on. You will want to know when your work must be done; deadlines are part of most charges to groups. Thus, be sure the charge is clear to all members and that it is understood alike by the small group and the parent organization.

b. *State the problem as a single, clear problem question.* A question that suggests the solution biases the group and limits its effectiveness. "How can we convince the administration to put in a new parking lot?" is a *solution question* that assumes the solution to the parking problem is to create a new parking lot. This *problem question* is better: "How can we improve the parking situation on campus?"

c. *Focus on the problem before discussing how to solve it.* One common source of poor solutions is getting solution-centered before the problem has been thoroughly investigated, described, and analyzed. If a group member suggests a solution too early, the discussion leader or another member should then suggest that the group refrain from any talk about what to do until after the group has completed its analysis of the problem.

d. *Describe the problem thoroughly.* Be sure to answer all questions about what is going on, what you hope to accomplish, and possible obstacles to that goal—the way a successful investigative reporter or detective does. A good way to describe the problem is to think of it as an uncharted map with only vague boundaries. Your first job as a group is to make a complete, detailed map of the problem. As we mentioned earlier, this process of information sharing is critical—don't be tempted to shortchange it! Table 6.3 outlines questions you will need to answer.

e. *Make an outline and a schedule based on the Procedural Model of Problem Solving,* especially if it is a major problem requiring extended work over several meetings. This outline and schedule can be modified later, if needed, but at least now the group will reap the benefits of a plan before getting too deeply into the problem analysis.

f. *Summarize the problem as a group.* This ensures that everyone understands it in the same way. In the case of a large problem, this summary may be done in writing by one member and edited by the entire group until all members are satisfied with it.

Sometimes the problem you are addressing will affect a number of people and you may need information about what is important to them. For instance, merging with SMSU was a scary prospect for the OPT employees; they had many concerns about whether their jobs would be retained or changed in major ways. Sometimes, a particular problem may have several aspects, and you may need to know which ones are the main issues or concerns. For example, work on the license transfer to SMSU was a critical step that had to be undertaken first; if the FCC didn't approve the transfer, nothing else mattered. One technique you can use to find out what is important to others is the focus group.

Spotlighting Key Issues with Focus Groups.   The **focus group** technique, which encourages unstructured discussion about a given topic, is often used to analyze people's interests and values. It is a great way for a group or an organization to find out what the important issues are regarding a problem facing the group; however, it is such a flexible procedure that it can be used at several steps in the problem-solving process.

In a focus group discussion, the facilitator introduces a topic to the group and instructs group members to discuss the topic any way they choose. The facilitator gives no further direction to the group but may probe or ask questions. Usually, the group discussion is tape-recorded for later analysis. After the group is finished, the facilitator or representatives of the parent organization listen to the tape for usable ideas.

Although focus groups were created within the advertising industry, many other types of organizations use them in a variety of creative ways. For example, a public relations

GLOSSARY

Focus Group

An unstructured technique in which members freely explore thoughts and feelings about a topic

TABLE 6.3	Questions to Ask as You Analyze the Problem

WHAT ARE ALL THE RELEVANT FACTS?

- Who is involved? When? Where? How?
- What complaints have been made?
- What is the difference between what is expected and what is actually happening?
- What harm has occurred?
- What exceptions have there been?
- What changes have occurred?
- What other information do we need?

WHAT MAY HAVE PRODUCED OR CAUSED THE UNSATISFACTORY CONDITION?

- What events precipitated the problem?
- What other factors may have contributed to the problem?

WHAT DO WE HOPE TO ACHIEVE?

- What form will our solution take?
- What would be a minimum acceptable solution for each person concerned?

officer at a small campus used a focus group to discover more effective ways of scheduling and promoting evening classes. A group of evening students was instructed simply to talk about what it was like to be an evening student. From the discussion it was clear that evening students were often trying to juggle full-time jobs, families, and other responsibilities in addition to school. The school's schedule was forcing them to come to the campus for four nights a week to complete two courses. But the focus group discussion indicated the students would be happy to stay later in the evening if they could take those two courses by coming to the campus only two nights a week. Campus officials found a way to "stack" the evening classes to allow this. In addition, the student comments spurred many imaginative ideas for advertising and promoting the evening offerings.

2. GENERATING AND EXPLAINING POSSIBLE SOLUTIONS

The quality of the solution to a problem will not be better than the quality of the pool of ideas the group considers. Studies of problem solving have shown that the ideas discovered later are more likely to be innovative and of higher quality than the ideas first mentioned.[16] Thus, the major issue of step 2 is not "What *should* be done to solve the problem?" but "What *might* be done to solve the problem?" This subtle change in wording is important.

During step 2, the group should focus on creatively finding and listing possible solutions, not on critically determining their relative merits or on trying to decide what to do. Creative thinking is crucial to this step and was discussed in detail in Chapter 5. The leader may need to remind the group not to argue (yet) the relative merits of proposed solutions.

No criticism should be allowed during step 2, but ideas may be explained and clarified. Someone may ask, "What do you mean?" or "Could you please explain how that would work?" Descriptive explanations help everyone understand the idea and may even stimulate further ideas.

Sometimes, while generating ideas, a member will recognize details of the problem that ought to be explored more fully. The group may then cycle back to the P-MOPS step 1 for further exploration of that issue. For example, faculty on a committee charged with revising the communication major realized, in the middle of evaluating options for the revision, that they had forgotten to solicit feedback from an important group—their alumni. The members conducted a quick telephone survey of selected alumni, thus temporarily setting aside their evaluation to return to analysis of the problem. When they finish the additional analysis for step 1, members return to listing alternatives.

Once a group has completed its list of alternatives, it is ready to proceed with evaluating them.

3. EVALUATING ALL POSSIBLE SOLUTIONS

During the third stage of problem solving, *all* proposed solutions should be evaluated. Critical thinking, as discussed in Chapter 5, is especially crucial during this stage. The options must be tested against the criteria the group has established, and members must be sure the solution is consistent with the facts brought out during discussion, the goals of the group, and the restrictions imposed by the group's area of freedom. It is especially important to consider all possible negative consequences of each solution, or new problems it might create for the group or other people.

Criteria for Evaluating Solutions.   **Criteria** are statements that set standards and limits for comparing and evaluating ideas. For example, search committee members assessing applicants for a library dean's position streamlined their evaluation process by using criteria sheets the members developed. Committee members made a list of the essential qualifications (for example, academic degrees required, years of experience required) and the other desirable characteristics (for example, fund-raising experience, team approach to managing). Then they decided which of the criteria were most important and placed them in a priority listing. This gave each member a set of very specific guidelines to use as he or she read each application.

6.3   **What Could OPT Do?**

APPLY NOW	Assume you are on the OPT governing board and you have to decide what to do about continuing to operate *and* converting to digital equipment. Obviously, "business as usual" isn't going to work. What are your possible options for dealing with this problem? List as many as you can think of, and don't worry right now whether they are realistic.

GLOSSARY

Criteria
Standards and guidelines used to evaluate ideas and solutions

Serious secondary tension (see Chapter 7) may arise as people argue and disagree while they discuss the pros and cons of proposed solutions. Having agreed-upon criteria helps make arguments as constructive as possible and keeps personal defensiveness to a minimum. Establishing criteria is very important—groups that spend time discussing and establishing criteria are more effective than groups that don't.[17] For example, a public utility where one of us lives recently was criticized by the public for its "excessively" generous employee compensation and benefits packages. To determine fair compensation and benefits, the utility's board of directors examined compensation of other public utilities and private companies of similar size and complexity. The directors used this information to develop objective criteria, based on evidence rather than their own hunches, in redesigning the benefits package. Thus, group members should discuss, agree upon, and possibly rank (from most to least important) the criteria for judging their ideas and solutions.

Some criteria are absolute, which means they *must* be met (e.g., "The library dean must have at least a master's degree in library science from an American Library Association-accredited school" is an absolute criterion—the group has no leeway). Other criteria are important but give the group some flexibility (e.g., "A Ph.D. is a preferred qualification for the library dean").

Some criteria are virtually universal in judging among solutions, such as Will the proposed solution actually solve the problem? Can the proposed solution be done? Will the benefits outweigh the costs? Is this solution within our area of freedom? and How acceptable is this idea to the people most likely to be affected by it? Such criteria encourage the group to consider whether or not the ideas proposed are legal, moral, workable, within the competence of the group or organization, within the control of the parent organization, and so on.

These are general, abstract criteria. You will need to express criteria as specifically and clearly as possible to avoid misunderstandings about their meaning. "We must have the OPT staff and equipment moved to SMSU by August 1" is more precise than "We have to move OPT sometime this summer."

Narrowing a Long List of Proposed Solutions.   When a list of ideas has been generated by brainstorming or any other technique, the group will need to reduce this list to a manageable size before it discusses the merits of the ideas. This can be done in a number of ways after the group has established its criteria. Here are three useful techniques:

1. Combine any ideas that are similar or overlapping. For example, "Hold a goodwill party" and "Have a get-acquainted cocktail party" could be combined into "Plan a social event."

2. Allow each member (including the leader) to vote for his or her top three choices. Tally the votes. Any proposed solutions that do not have at least two votes may be removed from the list.

3. Give each member a set of 10 or 15 stickers and ask them to "vote" on their preferred solutions. Members can distribute their stickers any way they want. They can put all their stickers on one item, if they strongly prefer that item, or put each sticker on a different item. The items receiving stickers are easy to spot and list in priority order. The group then discusses the pros and cons of the options that received at least one sticker.

Charting the Pros and Cons.   During the evaluation discussion, a recorder can help greatly by creating a chart of the ideas being discussed, with the pros and cons

TABLE 6.4	**Charting the Pros and Cons of Two Proposed Solutions**

HOW TO REDUCE PASSENGER INJURIES IN AUTOMOBILE ACCIDENTS

Pass federal law to require the use of seat belts	**Require new cars to be equipped with airbags**
PROS • Would reduce or eliminate many injuries. • Would be inexpensive. • Precedent exists in many states. **CONS** • Infringes on individual rights; expect a heated legal fight. • Difficult to enforce. • Some injuries could be worse with seatbelts.	**PROS** • Would be extremely effective. • Technology currently exists. **CONS** • Would increase the cost of cars. • Infringes on individual rights; expect a heated legal battle. • Airbags might inflate incorrectly and cause an accident.

mentioned for each idea, as shown in Table 6.4. Instead of *Pros* and *Cons,* the chart headings might be *Advantages* and *Disadvantages, For* and *Against,* or even + and −. Using such a chart that everyone can see helps the group remember major arguments and think critically about the proposals under consideration. This, too, can be done electronically, either with specialized software or by ordinary e-mail, with someone compiling the comments.

Using Group Support Systems to Evaluate Solutions.   **Group support systems (GSS)** are computer technologies designed to improve the quality and speed of group problem solving. Specifically, GSS exist to help groups with such tasks as idea generation, information organization, evaluation of options, and decision making. Many are designed to allow group members to work collaboratively on a problem even though they may be meeting in different locations at different times. Examples of GSS include e-mail, voice messaging, and computer conferencing. Two of the more well-known support systems for problem solving are GroupSystems and Software Assisted Meeting Management (SAMM). Both include modules created to help groups in every area of problem solving.[18] They are particularly helpful during the evaluation stage because they structure the procedure by which members can honestly react to each other's suggestions and ideas.

Such systems have rapidly increased in number, ease of use, and effectiveness, especially as more and more organizations use local area networks that allow several computers to be connected to each other. People can employ group support systems for either long-term use or for one problem-solving task. For example, workers in geographically dispersed areas can connect via computer to perform group work, even though they may be far apart. Often, however, people meet electronically in the same room, each at his or her own computer

GLOSSARY

Group Support Systems (GSS)

Computer-based systems designed to improve various aspects of group work

6.4   What Is OPT's Best Choice?

APPLY NOW

Again assuming the role of the OPT governing board, look at the choices you established in Apply Now 6.2. Before you evaluate those options, what criteria would you use?

1. Develop the criteria against which you will evaluate your choices about how to handle OPT's problem.

2. Evaluate each choice according to the criteria you just developed. Which option or options seem most likely to succeed?

3. If you were OPT, what would you recommend for the organization?

terminal. This allows several members to "talk" at once by entering their messages into the computer, which compiles them quickly. It also permits anonymity; who submitted a particular comment, idea, criticism, and so forth is not identified. Some group support systems are highly specialized. For example, several are designed to improve the idea-generation step of brainstorming. Others, such as SAMM, are more general and are designed to improve the entire problem-solving and decision-making process, in part by providing structure.

Group decision making using computer support systems seems to be at least as good as traditional group decision making.[19] Members are often more satisfied and like the fact that the computers permit simultaneous talk. Studies conducted in organizations using group support systems suggest that bigger groups are even more satisfied than smaller ones, that group support systems seem to help group members sustain their task focus better, and that less time seems to be spent in meetings. In addition, the anonymity such systems provide is important, more so for groups with individuals of widely varied status than for groups of peers. Group support systems also help improve organizational record-keeping and memory.

Group members should recognize that using GSS is not always beneficial. Problems include some group members' discomfort with using computers, GSS procedures that may structure group interaction too tightly, and managers who may not want group members under their supervision to have full access to information easily obtained via computers.[20]

Be careful with any conclusion drawn about GSS. They are changing daily. They seem to be especially beneficial for certain types of tasks, such as idea generation and decision making.[21] However, face-to-face groups seem to be superior for negotiation and complex, cognitive tasks. Whether group support systems improve performance depends on a variety of factors.[22] Groups using support systems generally make better decisions; such groups generate more alternatives; and participation among members is more even. On the other hand, groups take longer to reach decisions, experience less consensus, and are less satisfied than face-to-face groups. An important key to satisfaction appears to be user familiarity—users' reactions are usually negative at first. Several reviews of GSS have found that group members need time to become familiar with the spirit or intention of GSS. As long as a GSS program is used consistently with its intentions, it can be very effective; however, merely using a GSS program without considering its intent may fail.

6.1   Using Chat Rooms for GSS

Go to
**www.mhhe.com/
adamsgalanes6**
for additional
weblink activities.

MEDIA AND TECHNOLOGY

Group support systems can be as simple as using e-mail to facilitate information exchange between group members or as complex as using specialized group meeting software programs. An important characteristic of effective GSS is anonymity. Group members can feel free to share ideas without fear of reprisal or ridicule if their statements are anonymous. Unfortunately, many e-mail systems make anonymity difficult, and specialized meeting software can be expensive.

One alternative for using GSS is to create a chat room and have group members log on using anonymous nicknames. Chat rooms are special websites that allow any number of users to interact in real time (synchronous communication). Thousands of chat rooms already exist on the Internet. Many online services allow users to create free private chat rooms that could be used for private discussions among friends or for anonymous group discussions. Here are directions for creating a free GSS resource for your group:

1. Got to http://groups.yahoo.com/. This page will display general categories of groups available on Yahoo!.

2. Click the "click here to register" button on the left. You should register using anonymous information. Remember to write down your anonymous user identification and passwords so you can access the group in the future.

3. One group member (or your teacher) can create a new group. As you will discover, groups provide more resources than simply chat rooms including the ability to create polls, share files, and create databases. You should create a public group so that other group members can easily find it. Let other group members know the name of the group and what category (for example, School and Education—Classmates—Our Group) you placed the group in.

4. Each group member should log in using anonymous nicknames and then navigate to the newly created club. Members can chat, create discussion boards (discussion boards are saved whereas chats are not), and even take part in polls created by group members.

Using resources such as the Yahoo! Groups is an easy way to create functional GSS for your group. Using Internet chat rooms is easy once you are familiar with their many features. Group members should familiarize themselves with the chat room or group interface before the group uses this technology to facilitate a group discussion.

GSS do not do the work *for* the group, nor do they work if group members fail to use good communication skills. The same communication skills crucial to traditional face-to-face problem solving are still needed when groups use GSS as tools. The most we can say definitively is that GSS are generally good for groups, although they are not useful in every circumstance.[23]

After all proposals have been thoroughly evaluated, the group has set the stage for the emergence of a final decision on a solution or policy. A favored solution may already have begun to emerge during the discussion.

4. CHOOSING THE BEST SOLUTION

Just as groups experience predictable phases in their overall development, they also go through identifiable decision-making phases. Several well-respected researchers have contributed to our understanding of group decision-making phases.[24] For example, Fisher found that many groups first enter an *orientation* phase, proceed to a *conflict* phase when they argue about their various options, and finally enter the phases of *decision emergence* and *reinforcement*.[25] Decision emergence may begin during step 3, as members gradually move toward a consensus and coalesce around one proposal. The members will usually know when this has happened. Often a discussion leader can hasten this by asking something like, "I think we may have decided on a solution. Is that right?" If members agree aloud or nod their heads, a straw vote by show of hands or simply asking, "Does everyone agree?" or "Does anyone disagree?" can confirm this consensus.

Reinforcement refers to the complimenting and back patting that members give each other after a job well done. They will say things like, "That took a long time, but we really came up with a workable solution," "I really think we did a fine job with that," or "We done good, folks!" Such back patting expresses and reinforces the positive feelings members have toward each other. how about ass paddling? in B-Ball

Not all groups experience exactly the same phases during decision making. That would be too simplistic. Poole, for example, found that many factors influence the types of phases groups experience and the order in which they occur.[26] We present the idea of group phases to help you analyze what may be occurring in groups you belong to, but remember that the subject is more complex than we have described here (see Chapter 7).

Methods of Making Decisions.   A group can make decisions in many different ways, but some methods are likely to produce worse results than others. In some groups, the leader has authority to make decisions and may do so frequently for the group. One person may be perceived as the most expert member on the problem the group is discussing; that person may be asked to make the decision for the group. As a way of avoiding conflict, the group can use a method of chance, such as flipping a coin, drawing straws, or rolling dice. Sometimes numbers can be averaged to produce a decision, such as averaging individual applicant rankings to decide who should be offered a job. Often groups decide by voting, which is mandatory in committees governed by Robert's Rules for Committees.

Three common ways of making group decisions are for the leader or another designated member to decide without consulting the group, for the group leader to consult with other members but then make the final decision, and for the group to make the decision by consensus. A **consensus** decision is one that all members agree is the best one they can make that is acceptable to all; it doesn't necessarily mean that the final choice is anyone's first choice! The first method, decision by leader or designated member, is appropriate for minor

---

GLOSSARY

Consensus

A decision all members agree is the best they can all support but isn't necessarily everyone's first choice

The School Board Breaks a Deadlock

The school board in a city near where one of us lives had been stymied for several meetings over an issue related to a tax increase for schools and what arguments the members should make in the local media to support the tax increase. Most of the members wanted to stress that the tax increase would mean higher salaries for teachers, more teachers in the system, and smaller class sizes. One very vocal member wanted to emphasize the deterioration of the buildings and the necessity for basic facility maintenance. The board was stuck over this and other issues. Members didn't want to alienate the "buildings" member, so, wanting to be polite, they worked hard to find positive things to say about his arguments. However, this just fueled his enthusiasm. The school board president decided to use the university's "Decision Room," a room that had 20 terminals with capacity for full GSS.

Two faculty members assisted the school board; one served as "chauffeur" to run the software while the other served as a neutral facilitator. The school board members typed their ideas into a terminal, where they appeared on a large, overhead screen that all could see. They were able to make anonymous comments about each idea. Finally, they rated each idea on a scale of 1 to 5 and rank-ordered each one as well. The ratings and rankings were instantly tallied and a bar chart was produced that visually reproduced their numerical assessments. It was clear from the ratings and rankings that the "buildings" member was an outlier in the group. His ideas were not supported at all, which became obvious to everyone in the group, including him. This visual representation on the computer screen got through to him when the members' gentle oral comments had not. He dropped his insistence on the building maintenance platform for the tax levy.

1. What do you think are the advantages and disadvantages of using GSS?

2. Why do you think members were direct and clear using GSS where they had not been in face-to-face discussion?

3. What was persuasive about the visual representation that was not persuasive about the oral discussion?

4. For what other kinds of decisions do you think GSS would be helpful?

5. Are there situations where you would not want to use GSS?

decisions, such as where to meet, what refreshments to serve, what color notepads to put in the conference room, or even whom to ask to type the report. It is also appropriate for those decisions for which the leader (or designated decision maker) has all the information needed to make the decision, and support from the group members is guaranteed in advance. The second method, the consultative method, is appropriate when the leader does not have all the needed information, when group members are likely to accept the decision, when members cannot agree but a decision *must* be made, or when time is short. The consensus method is appropriate for major decisions, such as what policy to recommend or how to solve a complex problem, where acceptance is important and the group has the time to deliberate.

Voting, in which a majority decides for the group, merely weighs the power of numbers, not the relative merits of ideas. A majority can be wrong, and a minority of one member may have the best idea. Further, voting may leave a group split, with some who may resent the decision and try to sabotage it. A vote may be required to confirm that a decision has been reached, but whenever possible all members should agree that they have reached the best decision they all can support—a true consensus decision. Even with a large majority, such as five to two, a split vote does not establish such agreement. Scientific research and experience both confirm that you should make a major decision with a majority vote *only* when the group must make a decision without enough time to reach consensus, or the group has exhausted every possible way of achieving consensus. Chapter 9, on conflict, provides suggestions for achieving consensus.

We noted earlier that once a solution has been tentatively adopted, it is a good idea to test that decision among the people who will most be affected. It is especially useful to identify any negative consequences that may occur to others but that the committee has overlooked. The RISK technique helps accomplish this.

Testing a Tentative Solution with the RISK Technique.   The **RISK technique** is designed to help an organization assess how a proposed change or new policy will negatively affect the individuals and groups most involved. Suppose you are responsible for implementing a new employee benefits program at your company. Before you start putting the plan into effect, you want to make sure all problems that could come up have been identified and, if possible, dealt with in advance. RISK will help you do this. The steps for a face-to-face RISK meeting follow and are summarized in Figure 6.3. Like other group techniques, RISK can also be conducted electronically.

A group may have selected an alternative and discovered, with RISK or some other technique, that the solution is acceptable to all concerned. However, its job still isn't finished! Most groups are then responsible for seeing to it that the solution is implemented. Sometimes, that task is given to another group. Nevertheless, the problem-solving process is not complete until the solution has been put into effect.

GLOSSARY

RISK Technique

A technique to help a group assess potential problems or risks with a potential solution

---

FIGURE 6.3   Steps for Conducting the RISK Technique in a Face-to-Face Meeting

| Proposed solution presented in detail; members identify risks or problems with it. | Risks posted without evaluation on a chart in round-robin fashion. | Master list of risks compiled and circulated to participants. | Second meeting held to discuss the list; problems perceived as serious retained. | Retained problems processed into an agenda and handled as in the problem census. |

5. IMPLEMENTING THE CHOSEN SOLUTION

The final step in group problem solving is implementing the solution. Sometimes groups break off their discussion as soon as they have decided on a solution without working out a plan to put their decision into effect. They may feel finished, but they truly are not. Good leaders see that the group works out the details of implementation. During this stage of problem solving, the group answers questions such as the following:

Who will do what, when, and how so that our decision is enacted?

How will we write and present our report?

How will we word our motion to the membership meeting, and who will speak in support of it?

What follow-up should we conduct to monitor how well this solution is working?

Some implementation plans are simple, but others are complicated and detailed, especially if the solution involves many people and numerous assignments. PERT is a procedure designed to help group members track the implementation of a complex solution; however, it is useful for implementing simple solutions as well.

Using PERT to Implement a Solution. PERT (Program Evaluation and Review Technique) is a set of concrete suggestions to help a group keep track of who will do what by when. It can be difficult to follow a complicated implementation plan that involves many people, groups, and tasks. PERT helps do this by asking those responsible for implementation to make a chart showing deadline dates for completion of various tasks and the names of individuals or groups responsible.

Following are the main points:

1. Determine the final step by describing how the solution should appear when it is fully implemented.

2. List all the events that must occur before the final goal is realized.

3. Order these steps chronologically.

4. For complicated solutions, develop a flow diagram of the procedure and all the steps in it.

5. Generate a list of all the activities, materials, and people needed to accomplish each step.

6. Estimate the time needed to accomplish each step; then add all the estimates to find the total time needed for implementation of the plan.

7. Compare the total time estimate with deadlines or expectations and correct as necessary by assigning more or less time and people to complete a given step.

8. Determine which members will be responsible for each step.[27]

Another way to construct a PERT chart is to work backward from a target date. For instance, the students who created the chart in Figure 6.4 worked gradually backward from the due date for their presentation by taking into account how long each major step of the process would take. By doing that, they had a clearer picture of when they'd have to start working on the project to get it completed without undue haste. We recommend PERT to our students whenever they have complex group assignments to complete.

GLOSSARY

PERT

Program Evaluation and Review Technique that helps group members manage and keep track of a complex task

"*You mean no one remembered to bring a rock?*"

Implementation requires careful planning to succeed. (© The New Yorker Collection; 1985 Charles Addams from cartoonbank.com. All Rights Reserved.)

FIGURE 6.4   Sample PERT Chart for a Student Group Project

Date	Aretha	Barney	Candy	Denzil	Entire Group
Tues Apr. 5	Report on prelim observ.		Report on prelim observ.		Decide group to observe; decide variables
Thu Apr. 7		Prelim report, conflict	Prelim report, ldship	Prelim report, roles	Discuss prelim reports; decide methods of analysis
Tues Apr. 12		Complete lib research, Conflict	Complete lib research, Leadership	Complete lib research, Roles	
Thu Apr. 14		Observe group, 8 PM	Observe group, 8 PM	Have observ materials ready: survey, SYMLOG	
Tues Apr. 19		Complete SYMLOG of group	Complete SYMLOG of group		Meet after class, discuss preliminary findings
Thu Apr. 21			Observe group, 8 PM	Observe group, 8 PM Have tape recorder ready	
Tues Apr.26					Discuss overall observations; listen to tape
Thu Apr. 28		Complete first draft, Conflict	Complete first draft, Leadership	Complete first draft, Roles	
Mon May 2	Begin overall editing and typing	Final draft, Conflict; Intro done	Final draft, Leadership; Conclusion done	Final draft, Roles	Look at each other's sections to improve style
Tues May 3					
Wed May 4					
Thu May 5					
Fri May 6	Editing and typing done	Tables and charts to Aretha (conflict)	Tables/Charts to Aretha (leadership)	Tables/Charts to Aretha (roles)	
Sat May 7	Proof: make copies			Proof; make copies	
Sun May 8	Distribute copies to all by 8 PM	Assemble full report by 5 PM	Assemble full report by 5 PM	Make large charts for class presentation	
Mon May 9		Read full paper	Read full paper	Read full paper	Rehearsal at Aretha's, 7 PM
Tues May 10					Final presentation to class

6.5   Moving to New Facilities

Assume you're a member of the committee responsible for moving OPT to SMS facilities. You're working within a four-month time frame, April through July. OPT will need to decide what is staying, what is coming, and what new digital equipment needs to be ordered. Office equipment will be moved, along with 14 staff people. A room on the SMS campus needs to be emptied and rewired for the new equipment, among other things.

Draw up a PERT chart for the move, covering four months:

1. What activities would have to be done and in what order? (For instance, you would want the wiring in the new room ready before you installed the new equipment.)

2. How long do you estimate each activity would take? (For instance, assume it takes two months from the time you order new equipment until the time you receive it.)

3. How many "supervisors" would you put in charge of each activity?

4. Where would you put your PERT chart?

Although groups rarely stick exactly to the P-MOPS (or to any problem-solving guidelines), if you attempt to follow this sequence in the form of an outline of questions written about the problem, you will help guarantee that no important question, issue, or step is overlooked, and thereby create a good solution. The flexibility of the procedure allows you to tailor it to the characteristics of any problem. So that you can understand better how such adaptations are made, we next present examples of outlines written, adapted, and followed by problem-solving groups.

Applications of P-MOPS

Use the information about problem characteristics in Table 6.2 to help you determine how to modify the P-MOPS to suit your particular problem.

The first example of a procedural outline, shown in Table 6.5, was created by a self-appointed advisory committee of students concerned about pedestrian safety on a street just east of campus. The group of students first decided on the general problem they wanted to tackle, then created an outline to guide their investigation over a six-week span. They devised possible solutions, decided on what to recommend, and finally presented their report to both the city council and the president of the university. You will notice that it closely follows P-MOPS. The students' work was tragically timely—shortly after their presentation, a student was killed crossing that very street.

The outline in Table 6.6 is much shorter and simpler; it is designed to be used for a brief class discussion.

TABLE 6.5	**Sample Outline Using P-MOPS for a Complicated Problem**

Problem question: What shall we recommend that city council and university administration do to reduce pedestrian injuries on National Avenue east of campus?

I. What is the nature of our problem involving vehicle–pedestrian accidents on National Avenue east of campus?

   A. How do we understand our charge?

   1. What freedom do we have in this matter?

   2. What limits do we have (such as cost, structure of report, etc.)?

   3. To what does the general problem question refer?

   B. How do we feel about this problem?

   C. What do we find unsatisfactory about the way traffic and pedestrians currently affect each other on National Avenue?

   1. Diagram of present street, buildings, crossing, medians, lights, and so on.

   2. How serious is the problem of injuries to pedestrians?

      a. What kinds of accidents and injuries have occurred?

      b. When do these accidents happen?

      c. Do they tend to occur at any specific times?

      d. What kinds of persons are involved?

      e. How does this compare to accidents and injuries elsewhere?

      f. Are there any other facts we need to learn?

   D. What seems to be causing these accidents:

   1. Characteristics of the location?

   2. Human behavior?

   3. Other factors?

   E. What do we hope to see accomplished:

   1. In reducing the number of accidents and injuries?

   2. In practices of city council and administration?

   3. Any other features of our goal?

(continued)

TABLE 6.5	*Concluded*

F. What obstacles exist to prevent achieving our goal:

   1. Financial?

   2. Priorities of council or administration?

   3. Vested interests, such as businesses?

   4. Other?

II. What might be done to improve the safety of pedestrians crossing National Avenue east of campus?

   A. Brainstorm for ideas.

   B. Do we need explanations or descriptions of any of these proposed solutions?

III. What are the relative merits of our possible solutions to accidents and injuries on National Avenue?

   A. What criteria shall we use to evaluate our list of possible solutions:

      1. Costs?

      2. Acceptability to involved persons?

      3. Probable effectiveness in solving the problem?

      4. Appearance?

      5. Other?

   B. Shall we eliminate or combine any ideas?

   C. How well does each remaining potential solution measure up to our criteria and the facts of the problem?

IV. What recommendation can we all support?

   A. Has a decision emerged?

   B. What can we all support?

V. How shall we prepare and submit our proposal?

   A. In what form shall we communicate with council and administration?

   B. How will we prepare the recommendation?

      1. Who will prepare the recommendation?

      2. How will we edit and approve this report?

   C. How will we make the actual presentation?

   D. Do we want to arrange for any follow-up on responses to our recommended solution?

TABLE 6.6	Sample Outline Using P-MOPS for a Simple Classroom Discussion

I. What sort of final exam would we like for Communication 315?

    A. What is our area of freedom concerning the exam?

    B. What facts and feelings should we consider as we discuss what sort of exam to request?

II. What are our criteria in deciding on the type of exam to recommend:

    A. Learning objectives?

    B. Grades?

    C. Preparation and study required?

    D. Fairness?

    E. Other?

III. What types of exams are possible?

IV. What are the advantages and disadvantages of each type?

V. What will we recommend as the type of final exam?

RESOURCES FOR REVIEW AND DISCUSSION

SUMMARY

- Effective group problem solving uses guidelines to help members think critically rather than relying on their intuition, overrelying on expert authority, or overrelying on personal experience.

- A problem consists of a situation perceived to be unsatisfactory, a desired situation or goal, and obstacles to reaching that goal.

- Five characteristics of problems should be considered by members when they adapt their problem-solving procedures to fit the specific problem: task difficulty, solution multiplicity, intrinsic interest, member familiarity, and acceptance level.

- The Functional Theory of effective problem solving and decision making identifies important functions that must be fulfilled for a group

to solve problems effectively. Members must do a thorough job of meeting the task requirements, use their communication skills well to help the group overcome potential problems, and be willing to review their process, even reconsider their solution if necessary.

- The Procedural Model of Problem Solving (P-MOPS) provides a flexible sequence of steps, based on extensive research, for effective problem solving. These steps include thoroughly describing and analyzing the problem, listing a variety of solutions, carefully and critically evaluating their positive and negative elements, selecting the one that best meets the criteria, and planning how to implement the chosen solution.

■ Several specific techniques can help at each step. For instance, focus groups can help identify key issues pertaining to the problem; group support systems can help, especially with evaluation; the RISK technique can identify problems with a proposed solution the group is seriously considering; and PERT helps a group implement its solution.

■ Group decisions can be made by the leader, by voting, or by consensus.

EXERCISES

1. Think of a current or recent problem you have encountered. Analyze your problem by identifying its component parts (present situation, obstacles, and goal). Pay particular attention to the obstacles you identify. Form into groups of four to six and discuss each of the problems. Ask your team members to help you brainstorm ways of overcoming the obstacles you have identified.

2. As a class, choose two problems, one that is relatively simple and has few options and one that is relatively complex with high solution multiplicity (such as how the university should spend its contingency reserve money of $500,000). Write a leader's outline for structuring a discussion of each of these two issues by adapting P-MOPS to fit the discussion topic.

   After everyone has created an outline, select two leaders, one to guide each of the discussions using his or her outline. After the discussion, talk about what worked and what did not in the outline. How would you modify each outline to improve it?

3. View Part 3 ("An Ineffective Problem-Solving Discussion") of the videotape *Communicating Effectively in Small Groups* that was designed to accompany this text. This segment depicts a group doing a terrible job of problem solving. After viewing the tape, explain what you would do to correct the deficiencies. The following can guide your critique:

   a. Give specific examples of either poor or excellent problem-solving skills demonstrated by the group members.

   b. Examine the behavior of the leader, Alyce. What could she have done to improve the discussion process?

   c. What specific behaviors helped the problem-solving process and what behaviors hurt it? Why did they have such an effect?

    Go to **www.mhhe.com/adamsgalanes6** and **www.mhhe.com/groups** for self-quizzes and weblinks.

KEY TERMS · CONCEPTS

Area of Freedom	Focus Group	Problem Census
Charge	Functional Theory	Problem Solving
Consensus	Group Support Systems (GSS)	Procedural Model of Problem Solving
Criteria	PERT	
Decision Making	Problem	Risk Technique

www.mhhe.com/adamsgalanes6

 Use the flash cards and crossword puzzles on the Online Learning Center to further your knowledge of these key terms.

THREE

Understanding and Improving Group Throughput Processes

The interaction that occurs among group members is the heart of small group communication. Part Three focuses on this interaction and describes in detail several important group throughput processes. Chapter 7 looks at how a group develops from an initial collection of individuals into a team, with roles, norms, and a unique group climate. Chapter 8 explores some of the challenges that occur when members with diverse skills, backgrounds, and approaches to the task must work together. Chapter 9 describes why conflict occurs in a group and how it can be managed to benefit a group. Finally, Chapter 10 explores important leadership principles and provides suggestions for applying them.

Becoming a Group

CHAPTER OBJECTIVES

After reading this chapter you should be able to:

1. Explain why groups have a life cycle.

2. Describe the two main phases groups experience and give examples of the kinds of tasks members must handle during each phase.

3. Define primary, secondary, and tertiary tension; give examples of each.

4. Describe the communicative dynamics of each phase of group socialization.

5. Describe each of the three main categories of roles in groups.

6. Differentiate between formal and behavioral roles and describe how behavioral roles emerge during group interaction.

7. Differentiate between rules and norms and describe the four methods by which norms develop.

8. Explain what you would say and do if you wanted to change a group norm.

9. Describe each of the three main components that contribute to a group's climate.

The *Man of La Mancha* Cast and Crew

Noel, his church's choir director, broke his back in an airplane crash. To make his hospital time pass more quickly, he imagined the choir performing one of his favorite plays, *Man of La Mancha.* When he got out of the hospital, Noel decided to realize his dream by directing the play; he cast all the roles with choir members and performed the lead role of Don Quixote himself. Geoff, an experienced actor, was sidekick Sancho. Geoff couldn't carry a tune, but his acting experience and his unfailing good humor helped the cast mesh into a cohesive team. Gena, in the role of Aldonza, was also an experienced actress but had never before sung solo; however, she had a good sense of rhythm and was able to coach the dancers. Very few of the choir members could sing well, but they had an amazing array of other talents. Davida, who was both shy and clumsy, nevertheless was an outstanding artist and created two fabulous horse heads out of papier-mâché. Her talent created a minimal but effective set that could be positioned and removed quickly from the sanctuary. There were not enough men for all the roles, so Noel cast women in several parts, including the Barber and the horses. Delores had no sense of rhythm and could sing only whatever part the person next to her was singing, but she was a whiz at creating costumes out of Salvation Army thrift shop treasures.

The cast had only three weeks to rehearse, from the play's first read-through to opening night. Given the lack of singing and acting talent, lack of experience, lack of money for costumes and set materials, and time constraints, this play should have been a disaster. Instead, it was a great success. Several experienced theatergoers said that, although they had seen more professionally mounted productions of *Man of La Mancha,* this performance had touched them emotionally more than other performances.

The cast and crew had grown into a cohesive team whose output far exceeded reasonable expectations. Members contributed all their talents (singing and otherwise) to make the performance a success. Why did this small group work, when all "objective" assessments suggested it would fail?

The mutual influence that occurs when group members communicate with each other is at the heart of any group's throughput process. Recall from Chapter 1, "chicken" groups do not just happen because all the ingredients are present. When members interact with each other in such a way as to create an interdependent purpose, and thus succeed or fail together, they have become a chicken group. In Chapter 2, you studied the key principles of these complex social systems and learned that the process of becoming a chicken group is never finished because social systems are always adapting to feedback. This chapter explores more fully some of the throughput processes indicative of an emerging group. You will study in more detail how groups such as the *Man of La Mancha* cast and crew become an effective group. Groups whose individual members emerge into a productive team consistently figure out how to manage their tensions, and create and maintain constructive roles, norms, and a supportive group climate. These groups must also develop and support a stable leadership structure. Leadership is so central to group dynamics that it will be covered more completely in Chapter 10.

The Life Cycle of a Group

Groups as systems have their own **life cycles.** That is, they are always in the process of becoming and are never really finished. In many ways they emerge into and sustain themselves as cultures. A group's culture can be found in the pattern of values, beliefs, norms, and behaviors that are shared by group members and that in turn shape a group's personality. Many factors weave together to create and sustain these minicultures, such as the content and pattern of group communication, and the norms and rules guiding group communication. The cast and crew of the *Man of La Mancha* act in such as way as to become a theater culture with unique ways of speaking about cast and crew roles, of negotiating the desire of the director and actors, of effectively complementing each other's talents and so forth. In their three weeks together they will create a history with each other that will contain cycles of development reflecting all sorts of tensions, norms, and climates unique to them.

The *Man of La Mancha* cast and crew, as a living system, is driven to survive, which may be difficult or even impossible. Even a casual look at nature tells us that the natural life cycle for any system includes conception and birth, growth, maturity, decline, and finally death. But living organisms fight their eventual deaths as long as possible by adapting through feedback to changing conditions. Human groups usually do everything in their power to help ensure their continuation. The cast and crew in Case 7.1 did not abandon their goal of performing *Man of La Mancha* when they faced only three weeks of rehearsal. They did not quit when they assessed their talent and resources. Instead, they emerged into a cohesive unit capable of carrying off a performance that exceeded reasonable expectations.

When members first come together as a new group, they must sort out a variety of factors before they can become a fully functioning group. For instance, they must get to know each other's strengths and weaknesses. A stable leadership structure must emerge, and roles and norms must be established that all members can agree to follow. When these sorts of processes appear, the group can begin to mature and become productive. Individual members may leave and be replaced by new members, but the group can continue indefinitely as a functioning social unit. However, as with any living organism, the small group will eventually decline and disband, perhaps when it no longer has a purpose, when no new members replace those who leave, or when a competing group destroys or absorbs it. At this point, the group has completed its usefulness and is appropriately laid to rest.

Small groups, like all other living organisms, are complex, dynamic, ever-changing systems that conform to the natural order of the universe. Although the complexity of small groups makes them challenging to study, we have learned a great deal about how these systems emerge and function. We will now explore some of those processes that characterize small groups over the course of their existence.

Phases and Social Tensions in the Development of a Group

Groups on their way to maturity go through recognizable phases. Group members often experience a tug-of-war between their task and social demands. When members spend emotional and mental energy on the interpersonal issues, they take away from the energy needed to attend to their work. On the other hand, when members attend to the task at hand, they pay less attention to each other's human needs. Robert F. Bales calls this the equilibrium problem.[1] A group's attention must shift between concentrating on its task and concentrating on the relationships between members. First, the group must develop dependable, harmonious relationships that will give it stability. Bales refers to this as the group's *socioemotional* concern. Second, the group must focus on its charge, or *task* concern. Neither one of these concerns can be ignored if the group is to succeed. Both need to be attended to, in some degree, throughout the life of the group.

Task and socioemotional concerns predominate at predictable periods in the group's life cycle. The first overall phase is the **formation phase,** in which socioemotional concerns predominate. Members work on their relationships with each other. During this structuration process, norms, rules, and roles, including leadership ones, emerge. In Case 7.1, for instance, Geoff could not sing but had valuable acting experience. Davida had not sung solo but had the dancing skills necessary to help coach the dancers. As groups move through their formation period, they begin to mesh into a coordinated, interdependent unit that includes all needed behaviors. The *Man of La Mancha* cast and crew did a particularly good job of working out their relationships effectively and finding a valuable role for everyone.

Primary tension often characterizes a group's interaction during this formation period, especially if members have never met before. During periods of primary tension, interaction is characterized by politeness and long, uncomfortable pauses in the conversation.[2] This kind of social tension can be likened to *stage fright.*[3] Recall how you typically feel the first time you meet with a new group. Like most people, you probably worry whether the others will like you and whether you will belong. You want to be valued by the group, and so does everyone else. This makes members careful not to say or do something that might offend the other members; behavior is very tentative. This stiff, cautious behavior contributes to that overly formal, excessively polite atmosphere often observed in newly formed groups.

The group moves into the **production phase,** or the period in which the group is able to concentrate on its assigned task. Most groups do not have the luxury of getting to know each other well before they have to start working. Instead, members begin resolving their primary tensions at the same time they have to deal with the task concerns of their group. Thus, instead of being separate and sequential, the phases partially overlap and parallel each other in the life cycle of a group. The *Man of La Mancha* cast and crew had to start rehearsing and putting together a show before they had all their interpersonal relationships worked out. As the socioemotional concerns mature, the group can expend more of its

GLOSSARY

Formation Phase

Initial phase of group development where members work out their relationships, roles, rules, and leadership structures

Primary Tension

Anxiety arising early in a group's formation, as members work out their relationships and roles

Production Phase

Second stage of a group's development, during which a group can concentrate more fully on its task

"Before we begin this family meeting, how about we go around and say our names and a little something about ourselves."

energy on task concerns, so the formation phase gradually gives way to the production phase, although the formation phase never completely disappears.

Another kind of social tension, **secondary tension,** occurs later in the group's life cycle.[4] This tension is work related and stems from differing opinions about substantive issues. It is inevitable in task groups because members bring different perspectives to their group's task concerns. Potentially more serious than primary tension, it is often unpredictable and, if not managed well, does not go away with the passage of time.[5] One of the best markers of secondary tension is an abrupt move away from the group's routine. This could happen with a sudden outburst from a member followed by an angry exchange between members and then a rather unpleasant long pause. Poor management of secondary tension potentially threatens the interpersonal health of the group and could evolve into a destructive group climate.

Much of the tension we have observed in groups is not strictly primary or secondary. Instead, groups often become bogged down in arguments that seem to recycle over and over. This inability or even unwillingness to manage issues often represents a power or status struggle between members. This is a modified form of primary tension that can appear on the surface to be secondary tension over content issues. When examined more closely, however, they are struggles over how group members define themselves in relationship to each other. These power struggles produce **tertiary tension** among members. Members struggle over who will decide the rules and procedures for the group. Conflict may occur over how to make decisions, how to resolve conflicts, who has the authority to determine what will happen in the group, who can make assignments, who is an expert at what, what are the rights and privileges of group membership, and so forth. Jury deliberations, for instance, are rife with tertiary tensions.[6] Jurors have been known to pick up their chairs and toss them through windows, engage in fistfights, attempt escapes from heated deliberations, write angry notes to the judge, and shout so loudly they can be heard outside their room. More and more jurors are dismissed for such behavior. These actions have prompted courtrooms to develop booklets for jurors explaining how they can constructively manage diverse opinions during jury deliberation.

One of us observed a classroom group experiencing tertiary tension. The group's class assignment was to observe a task group and gather data about it, either through observation or by talking to the members. Mike insisted that the group use his questionnaire as one method of gathering data. Michelle demanded instead that the group use her questionnaire. This endless argument was a thinly masked power struggle. If this really had been only secondary tension, Mike and Michelle could easily have combined their questionnaires. Instead, each demanded to be in charge of deciding the group's procedures while the others frustrated themselves trying to come up with a compromise that neither would accept. This potentially destructive tension is an example of tertiary tension.

For a group to perform at its best, social tension must be managed appropriately. **First, group members can move through the primary tension stage more quickly if they know each other.** The choir described in the opening case study had an advantage in that members already knew each other fairly well when they began play rehearsals. A get-acquainted period helps members do this—even when members do know each other. Don't hesitate to suggest this, even if your group's designated leader doesn't. The members will be able to accomplish their task much more effectively and quickly if they know the backgrounds of the other members, what they do on the job, and even what hobbies and outside interests they have. Joking, laughing, and having fun together before getting down to work help as well.

Second, members can reduce both primary and secondary tension by sharing what they know about the problem at hand. For instance, if a committee is charged with recommending solutions to a campus parking problem, each member's perception of the scope and seriousness of the problem can be shared so that all will have some common understanding of the problem. This mapping process was described in the previous chapter.

Third, secondary and tertiary tensions can be managed if group members demonstrate tolerance for disagreement. When group members believe that their opinions and ideas are appreciated, even if these opinions are contrary to the ideas of others, then they feel valued by the group. They also are less likely to demand high status if they already believe the group appreciates them. Showing that you appreciate someone else's thoughtful analysis, even if you don't fully agree, can help: "I see what you mean about the hidden costs of that option, Tom, and that's something I hadn't considered" shows Tom that you were listening and that you appreciate the careful thought he gave to the issue. Statements that acknowledge confidence in the group (e.g., "We'll be able to find an answer—we've done a good job so far") help develop solidarity in the group system.

7.1 Managing Tertiary Tensions

A situation arising between Gena and Geoff on the set of *Man of La Mancha* illustrates the type of situation that often leads to tertiary tension. Gena had been in several plays and had studied acting informally. She loved the process of uncovering a character from the inside out and discovering the meaning of a scene or a line through the rehearsal period. Geoff was a more experienced actor with some directing experience as well. He had strong ideas about how certain lines should be read and certain scenes played. When he took it upon himself to advise Gena about how to read certain lines, she felt herself becoming both irritated and confused. She liked Geoff and respected his experience, but she had her own preferred way of developing a character. She knew she had several choices about what to do, and some choices were likely to be more effective than others for the entire enterprise. Consider Gena's situation:

1. What are several options Gena has for handling this situation? For example, she could do nothing or she could quit the cast. (List at least five in addition to these two.)

2. How is Geoff likely to react to each of these choices?

3. What are the likely outcomes to the group as a whole of each of these choices?

4. If you were faced with this choice, what would be more important to you, keeping control of "your" character or keeping harmony among the cast? Are there other things that would be more important to you in this situation than harmony or control? What would those be?

5. What choice would you be likely to make, and why? How effective do you think this choice would be?

Ask two class members to select one of Gena's options and to role-play this situation. After discussion about what worked and what didn't, ask two different class members to role-play a different option. Which communication strategies seem to be more effective? Why?

Humor is also an effective way to handle secondary and tertiary tension in a group. A well-timed, lighthearted comment can move a group past an obstacle that seems insurmountable. Joking and laughing together increase the members' good feelings toward each other. This in turn helps members become more open toward each other, which can lead to resolution of their substantive and status differences. However, NEVER joke to change the topic or to put someone in his or her place because this can destroy the cohesiveness the group has developed.

Tertiary tension is always tricky to handle; indirect methods often don't work. Group members will probably have to address the problem directly by saying something to the offending members. Either a group's designated leader or one of the other members can politely but firmly confront the members involved in the status struggle by pointing out the negative effects the power struggle is having on the rest of the group.

The process of managing the task and socioemotional demands and their accompanying social tensions can be further complicated if a group uses electronic technology as a tool. Many people believe that computer-mediated technology increases a group's task communication while it decreases its socioemotional communication. This occurs because electronic tools keep groups focused on such task-related processes as record-keeping, listing ideas, and structuring the problem-solving process. In addition, GSS tools such as e-mail, which provide limited ways to express nonverbal cues, may encourage members not to think of each other as individual people. However, researchers examining groups using computer-mediated communication have discovered that members find ways to communicate socioemotional information that is the same as the information exchanged in face-to-face groups.[7]

As you can see from our brief discussion of group development, any group's communication displays distinguishable patterns, which change over the life of the group. Phase and stage models attempt to describe the most salient characteristics of each period in the life cycle of a group. In an interesting exploratory study of real-time work teams, Connie Gersick describes a cycle of **punctuated equilibrium**.[8] She found that these work teams moved back and forth between periods of stasis, or inertia, and significant, revolutionary change. These teams in their first meeting defined how they would conceptualize their charge and stayed within that framework until they reached the midpoint of their calendar time frame. Thus, for our *Man of La Mancha* cast and crew this would mean at one and a half weeks. Here the work teams experienced a transition point marked by profound change. At midpoint, teams assessed what they learned and changed how they were working. If constructive changes were not made at this point, they were not likely to be made later because the teams moved into a second period of inertia, solidifying once again how they would work. As the teams approached the end of their time period, they rushed to meet outsider expectations and experienced the consequences of their chosen procedures for accomplishing their goals.

We see this kind of development all the time in small group communication courses. Initially, groups lay out how to proceed, stick to their plans, and then at midterm or midsemester realize they may or may not have understood the assignment well enough to receive a positive final evaluation. They make all sorts of changes. Some groups effectively correct their path while others do not. Then as the time nears for group presentations, many groups spend a concentrated time with each other, sometimes all night, preparing for final presentations. Then they find out their evaluations on their written and oral assignments and experience the consequences of meeting or not meeting outside expectations. Groups can become set in their ways very early in their life cycle, resisting change until midway. Then at midpoint they are most open to assess their progress; however, they must be willing to make constructive changes. At the end, there is another flurry of activity, and the expectations of outsiders become particularly relevant.

The life cycles of groups are complex and do not reveal themselves in clean, discrete stages. However, salient features of development can be found and used by members to assess how well they are proceeding. One factor that can alter a group's development is the change brought on by new members in newly formed groups and existing groups. One common reality is that group membership often changes. We now turn our attention to how both individuals and groups deal with socialization of members.

Group Socialization of Members

When we hear the word *socialization* we generally think about someone who is learning to become part of a group or even society at large. Just as children are socialized into families and society, group members are also socialized into newly formed and established groups. Carolyn Anderson, Bruce Riddle, and Matthew Martin provide a definition of group socialization that supports our belief in the central role of communication in group processes including the socialization of members.[9] **Group socialization** is a

> *reciprocal process of social influence and change in which both newcomers and/or established members and the group adjust and adapt to one another through verbal and nonverbal communication as they create and re-create a unique culture and group structures, engage in relevant processes and activities, and pursue individual and group goals.*[10]

This definition is lengthy so let's take it apart and examine what it implies about the process of group socialization. First, the adapting and adjusting that happen when a new group forms or when new members enter an established group occur through *communication* among group members. Anderson, Riddle, and Martin point out that communication is instrumental in reducing the uncertainty that is often felt during this time.[11] For group socialization to be effective, everyone involved must practice open communication, be accepting of the new member, and exhibit a desire to facilitate the positive change new members can bring. For instance, if the community theater cast members do not talk to each other about Ted (see Apply Now 7.2), welcome him into the troupe, and see his presence as a way to move in new directions, then his willingness to replace Richard will have been a waste.

Second, the definition above highlights the importance of recognizing that effective socialization requires a balance between individual member and group goals as well as comparable positive satisfaction levels between the member and the group. Ted, the community theater director, and the other cast members must have similar goals and levels of comfort if Ted's stepping in for Richard is to be a positive experience.

Finally, the definition rightly focuses on the realization that socialization is an ongoing process that is not only about the new member but also about the group. Our questions about how the community theater group might handle Ted's entry into the group involve thinking about what Ted, the director (or leader), *and* the cast (the group) can do to manage this kind of group change. Understanding the phases of group socialization may help you to further consider how this community theater group and Ted can best manage his entrance into the cast.

PHASES OF GROUP SOCIALIZATION

Anderson, Riddle, and Martin explain group socialization processes as an intricate interplay between five phases: antecedent, anticipatory, encounter, assimilation, and exit.[12] When you study the unique communication demands of each phase, remember several things. This model of group socialization assumes that group members are typically also members of other groups, that socialization involves either newly forming groups or established groups dealing with new members, that groups may move through these phases at different speeds and may revisit one or more of these phases in their acceptance or rejection of new members, and, finally, that behaviors in one phase have a ripple effect through the other phases.

GLOSSARY

Group Socialization

Process by which new and/or established members learn to fit together through communication

For more information on antecedent socialization in online groups, go to the Online Learning Center at **www.mhhe.com/ adamsgalanes6**

7.2 Integrating a New Member

One week before a community theater's opening night of *Hotel Paradiso,* his doctor told leading man Richard, who had been complaining of shortness of breath, that he needed heart bypass surgery—immediately! The cast was devastated. Members were concerned about Richard, of course, but they also were concerned about watching their six weeks of rehearsals go down the drain. The cast and crew had become a tight, cohesive group. Rehearsals had been going well, with the play promising to be the season's top moneymaker. The director debated canceling the run, but prevailed on his talented friend Ted to assume Richard's part. Opening night was delayed for a week to give Ted time to learn the lines and the cast time to integrate a new cast member.

1. If you're the director, what would you do to help the reformulated cast get through its formation phase so members can focus on the play? Is there anything that can speed up the cast's formation phase?

2. If you're Ted, what would you do to help the other cast members feel comfortable with you?

3. If you were the cast members, how would you help Ted feel at ease?

In Chapter 2 we discussed group inputs such as member characteristics and their potential impact on group throughput and outputs. In Chapter 3 we talked about the influence of different listening styles on group interaction and outcomes. In Chapter 8 we will talk about cultural differences and group processes. These individual characteristics play a key role in the **antecedent phase** of group socialization. All members, including Ted in our above example, bring to a group their own attitudes, motives, and communication behaviors, which can profoundly affect how ready and able they are to engage in the socialization process and how willingly they approach group work and building relationships. Let's take, for instance, the attitude commonly referred to as *grouphate*.[13] Many of the ideas and attitudes people bring to new or existing groups are based on previous experiences in groups. If someone has been a member of groups that have struggled to get anything done, she or he may internalize this experience and, in future groups, show a negative bias toward groups and group work. We hear students in small group classes repeatedly verbalize their dislike for anything resembling group work because of horrific experiences in the past. This kind of pessimism would make joining a group difficult. It is very difficult for someone with bad group experiences to join a new group and equally difficult for other group members to welcome such a person to the group.

Another antecedent factor that affects group socialization is our disposition or motive for communication. Recall our discussion of listening styles in Chapter 3. Some of us

GLOSSARY

Antecedent Phase

Phase in group socialization during which members bring previous group experiences, attitudes, beliefs, motives, and communication traits to the process

listen in order to sustain the relationships in the group and others to make sure the work gets done. Others focus their listening on meeting a time schedule and others on information only from trusted sources. These listening preferences are also tied to our motives for communicating and influence effective socialization of members. For instance, those members who communicate to build relationships rather than control others or distance themselves from others report more satisfaction with groups. Those who communicate to facilitate the work talk more in the group. Members highly motivated for both reasons are generally more willing to engage in the socialization process.[14]

Communication apprehension and verbal aggressiveness are two other antecedent factors influencing group socialization. Individuals or group members who are not comfortable talking in groups—that is, who experience communication apprehension—find it hard to participate actively in socialization. If socialization in groups is to be effective, members have to communicate with each other to reduce the uncertainty inherent in the socialization experience. On the other hand, individuals or group members may be quite comfortable talking and may even be verbally aggressive—they attack others when expressing disagreement. This kind of communication typically alienates others and does not promote positive socialization experiences.[15]

The **anticipatory phase** of group socialization involves all the initial expectations members have of each other and the group. These expectations are an aspect of socialization because they are the basis for what the individual and the group anticipate will happen over the life of the group. Have you ever expected to really like someone and to have a successful meeting with them, only to have your expectations crushed? Suppose the director had really talked Ted up to the cast, who were led to anticipate a master actor and great opening night. In turn, suppose Ted had been told about the great cast he was joining. Both parties would anticipate a successful experience. However, if their expectations were not accurate, socialization could be a disaster. In both examples, the more the group members' expectations differ from their actual experience, the more chance there is for anxiety and even anger between members.

Socialization involves both individual expectations (Ted) and group expectations (cast). Individuals enter new or existing groups with all sorts of expectations, including estimating how well they will be received and how much they will be respected as individuals. Ted may predict that he will be well received and, although he is stepping in for Richard, the cast will understand that he brings his own interpretation to the role. If his predictions are not met, he will have a stressful entry into the group and both he and the group may have a negative experience—even perhaps an unsuccessful adjustment. For the cast members (in this case comprising an existing group), their anticipatory phase begins when Ted agrees to take over for Richard. If cast members are open to the adjustment ahead of them, they are more likely to promote Ted's integration into the group.

We asked you to think about what each party could do to help welcome Ted (see Apply Now 7.2). Group socialization is enhanced when groups systematically have in place ways to welcome new members.[16] In the case of the community theater cast, this could include a meeting with Ted in which members introduce each other and talk about their expectations, an informal dinner with Ted, and a tour of the theater, stage, and dressing rooms. Stewart Sigman calls these kinds of activities *audition practices* and they help both the new member and the group draw more realistic expectations and experience less primary tension during socialization.[17]

The third phase of group socialization is the **encounter phase.** The learning that occurs in all forms of socialization begins in earnest during this phase. It begins when the expectations of the anticipatory phase meet the realities of the group and lasts for an indefinite period.[18] During the encounter phase, the individual and the group are adjusting the group's norms, culture, climate, goals, roles, and leadership structure—topics we discuss later in this chapter.

As we mentioned earlier in our discussion of group socialization, it is important to negotiate a balance between individual and group goals. During this phase, members also negotiate their roles in the group. The roles established in a newly forming group can be disrupted later with the addition of a new member. Communication about individual role expectations and careful assessment of what the group needs are necessary if socialization is to be a positive experience. For instance, newcomers who proactively seek information about role expectations are socialized more effectively than those who do not seek this kind of information.[19] We talk more about roles and norms later in the chapter.

The **assimilation phase** is characterized by full integration into the group and its structures.[20] In full integration, new members have become comfortable with the group culture and show an active interest in the group's task and relationships. In turn the existing members demonstrate acceptance of the new member. Members show a productive and supportive blending, enacting communication necessary to sustain the group's culture. If this integration does not occur smoothly, as is often the case, secondary tension could throw the group back into the anticipatory and encounter phases. Do not be surprised if these regressions occur because, over a group's life span, members will often have to negotiate a good fit between themselves and the rest of the group.

The fifth phase of group socialization is the **exit phase.** Earlier we remarked that group socialization is a process that continues over the course of a group's life. This process is experienced at both the individual and the group level and actually ends when the new member leaves or when the group ceases to exist. Exiting a group, whether because an individual leaves or a group breaks up, can be a difficult transition and is one that group members often minimize.[21] If a member leaves, such as Richard in the community theater example, the group must deal with why he left, how he left, how his departure changes their communication, and what comes next. When an entire group disbands, members deal with variations of the same issues.

When an individual leaves a group, the leaving is often complicated because the member may have left psychologically earlier than she or he left physically. Kathy, one of your authors, watched as a colleague and good friend retired. Almost a year before he actually left the department, he mentally pulled out. Kathy watched his interest in department issues fade, which affected what issues he fought for and the votes he cast in faculty meetings. Should you or anyone else leave a group voluntarily, it is a good idea to let others know you are leaving, help the group adjust to your leaving, and try to remain in some sort of contact after you leave. This can help to avert such things as grouphate.

Group turnover is common. How many times have you watched as a member left, and then found yourself dealing with the loss and the adjustment to a new member? This process can be filled with uncertainty and resentment or it can be managed quite well. A group can effectively manage turnover by developing a positive group attitude toward turnover—see it as a way to redefine who you are. When an entire group ends, do not treat it lightly—how you disband affects the kind of experiences you take into the next

GLOSSARY

Role

The part a member plays in a group

group. Joann Keyton recommends that groups give themselves an opportunity to say good-bye and to process their experience.[22]

Group socialization is a complex process spanning the entire life of a group. Recognizing its characteristics adds depth to our understanding of group phases and acknowledges that groups usually do not mature with the same members but do so adapting and adjusting to members coming and going. The encounter phase of group socialization involves several components of group life including roles, rules and norms, and group climate. We turn now to a discussion of group member roles and their importance to group dynamics.

Group Roles

Your **role** is the part you play in a group. The role you perform in any particular group is a function of your personality, your behavior, your expectations, the expectations of other members, and any formal titles or instructions you may have been given regarding that group. Just as an actor has a role in a play, so do we all have a part to play in each group we belong to. And just as an actor has different parts in different plays, so do we have a unique position in each group we join.

TYPES OF ROLES

Member roles are formal or informal. Formal roles are assigned on the basis of a member's formal position or title and are sometimes called positional roles. For example, one member may hold the title of secretary for the group. Secretary is a formal role that carries with it certain requirements and expectations, which the group's rules will state: "The secretary shall write and distribute to all members minutes of all meetings held by the group. At the end of each year the secretary shall provide a written summary of the group's work during that year to the president of the student senate."

Informal roles, sometimes called behavioral roles, are the parts people play that reflect their personality traits, habits, and behaviors in the group. Through trial and error, every member of a group begins to specialize in certain behaviors within the group. For example, one work group included a member who knew how to use databases to find pertinent research reports. She became the group's bibliographer, as well as its prodder by constantly encouraging everyone to finish assignments when promised. Specific roles result from an interplay between the individual's characteristics and other members of the group and emerge from group interaction.

ROLE FUNCTIONS IN A SMALL GROUP

Members' roles in small groups are categorized according to what they do for the group: How does this behavior help or hinder the group in achieving its goal? Small group roles are typically classified into three main behavior categories: task, maintenance, and individual. The first two are helpful to the group; the third is not.

Task Roles.   A task-oriented behavior is one that contributes directly to the accomplishment of the group's task. You probably can think of many task-related behaviors you have seen performed in groups. Recently, one of us served on a church building committee trying to find a new place to meet. One member said, "Let's make a list of all the possibilities in our price range." After the committee completed the list, the member said,

"Now, let's split up the list and each visit one or two before our next meeting. Who will volunteer to look at the two buildings on Glenstone Avenue?" These remarks, which suggested procedure and also helped *coordinate* the work of the group, are examples of task behavior. Some other helpful task roles are:

Initiating and orienting: proposing goals, activities, or plans of action; defining the group's position in relation to the goal. ("Let's get started by assigning ourselves tasks to complete before the next meeting.")

Information giving: offering facts, information, evidence, or personal experience relevant to the group's task. ("Last year, the library spent $50,000 replacing stolen books.")

Information seeking: asking for facts, information, evidence, or relevant personal experience. ("John, how many campus burglaries were reported last year?")

Opinion giving: stating beliefs, values, and judgments; drawing conclusions from evidence. ("I don't think theft of books is the worst problem facing our library.")

Clarifying: making ambiguous statements clearer or interpreting issues. ("I could support that as long as the cost isn't outrageous, meaning that it is less than $10,000.")

Elaborating: expressing judgments about the relative worth of information or ideas; proposing or applying criteria. ("Here are three problems I see with the production.")

"Would you please elaborate on 'then something bad happened'?"

Summarizing: reviewing what has been said previously; reminding the group of items previously mentioned or discussed. ("So by next week, Delores will have the costumes made and Noel will have cast members committed to the play.")

Consensus testing: asking if the group has reached a decision acceptable to all; suggesting that agreement has been reached. ("We seem to all agree that we do not have enough men for the parts and it is OK for me to find women for those parts.")

Recording: keeping group records, preparing reports and minutes; serving as group memory. ("I have a laptop so I can bring it to our meetings to take notes.")

Suggesting procedure: suggesting a method or procedure to follow. ("Why don't we try brainstorming to help us come up with something new and different?")

Maintenance Roles.   Maintenance behaviors are those that help the group maintain harmonious relationships and a cohesive interpersonal climate. One member of a church building committee welcomed another member back from a three-week trip by saying, "It's great to have you back! Here's a summary of everything we did while you were gone. We held off making a decision until you got back because we really wanted to know what you thought." These remarks demonstrate a *gatekeeping* function by allowing the absent member to contribute to the discussion, and they show solidarity and support. Other helpful maintenance roles are:

Establishing norms: suggesting ways to behave; challenging unproductive ways of behaving; calling attention to violations of norms. ("Let's not call each other names because it does not get us anywhere.")

Supporting: agreeing; expressing support for another's idea or belief; following another's lead. ("I think Noel is right. We should examine this more closely.")

Harmonizing: reducing tension by reconciling disagreement; suggesting a compromise or new alternative acceptable to all; combining proposals into a compromise alternative; calming an angry member. ("Gena and Davida, I think there are areas where you are in agreement. Let me suggest a compromise.")

Tension relieving: joking and otherwise relieving tension; making strangers feel at ease; reducing status differences; encouraging informality. ("We're starting to get on each other's nerves, let's take a break.")

Dramatizing: storytelling and fantasizing in a vivid way; evoking fantasies about other people and places. ("You just reminded me about the time . . . ")

Showing solidarity: indicating positive feelings toward one another; reinforcing a sense of group unity; promoting teamwork. ("We've done a great job pulling together. I have no doubt our performance will win rave reviews.")

Individual Roles.   Individual roles consist of self-centered behaviors. A self-centered member places his or her needs ahead of the group's. These roles do not help the group in any way and may be extremely harmful. Self-centered members may end up reducing their ability to influence other members because they generally are less well liked. Members prefer colleagues whose communication is other- rather than self-centered.[23] For example:

Withdrawing: giving no response to others; avoiding important differences; refusing to cope with conflicts; refusing to take a stand. ("Do whatever you want; I don't care.")

Blocking: preventing progress toward group goals by constantly raising objections, repeatedly bringing up the same topic or issue after the group has considered it and rejected it. ("I know we already voted, but I want to talk about this again.")

Status seeking and recognition seeking: stage hogging, boasting, and calling attention to one's experience when it is not necessary; game playing to elicit sympathy. ("I think we should do it the way I did it last year. I won Committee Chair of the Year award, you know.")

Playing: refusing to help the group with the task; excessive joking, dramatizing, and horsing around; making fun of others who are serious about the work. ("Don't be such a stick-in-the-mud; we've still got lots of time to finish. One time I remember . . . ")

Acting helpless: trying to elicit sympathy by constantly needing help to complete tasks; showing inability for independent thought or action; forcing others to complete or redo work turned in. ("I don't know what you want me to do here. I have never used a computer and I don't think I can do it.")

THE EMERGENCE OF ROLES IN A GROUP

Through communication with each other, members gradually structure their unique contributions and roles. Think for a moment about the groups you belong to. Do you act exactly the same way in each one of them? Probably not. There are variations in your behavior because each group brings out different combinations of your skills, abilities, and personality characteristics. Normal people want to contribute their unique talents and abilities so they will be valued by the group. When the other group members appreciate and reward those behaviors, they perform them more often. In that way, roles and a division of labor develop in the group.

Let's look at an example of how this occurs. Jan had a gift for storytelling. Because Jan felt uncomfortable whenever there was a lull in her seminar's discussion, she generally filled the silences with a story. Stories about her extensive travels easily captured the other members' attention and relieved the uneasiness that silence sometimes caused. The rest of the group encouraged her to relate her stories. Because of both Jan's ability to entertain and the other members' desire to listen, she carved out an informal (behavioral) role as the group's storyteller.

The other members of the group must reinforce a member's behavior if a role is to become stable and strong. If the other members had not been eager to set aside their work momentarily to listen to Jan, they would not have encouraged the development of her storyteller role. Instead, they would have discouraged her by paying little attention or reminding her that she was deflecting the group from its task. In that case, Jan would have downplayed her storytelling and searched for another way to contribute. For example, she also was an active listener who clarified and summarized what others said. If she had not won esteem as the group's storyteller, she might have become the group's recorder, or historian. From this example, you can see how a member's role in a group depends not only on that member's characteristics, but also on how the other members respond.

The advent of new communication technologies such as net conferences and group decision support systems can produce unanticipated effects on group dynamics, including role emergence.[24] Some types of net conferencing require a facilitator to coordinate their use, which can change the role dynamics of the group. More routine computer-mediated

7.3   Creating a Space for Yourself in the Group

Everyone needs to feel valued and appreciated by his or her fellow group members. Sometimes, it isn't clear what your contribution—your role—should be. It was especially hard for members of the *Man of La Mancha* extras to know what their contributions should be. Most of them were not actors or dancers; quite a few were not even very good singers! Assume you are Davida, one of the people cast as extras, with limited performing talent. However, you really like the idea of the project, you like your fellow cast members, and you really want the project to succeed. What can you personally do to make this project your own?

1. As Davida, do a brainwriting assignment: list your assets and talents. (In addition to the artistic talent we know you have, list at least five other assets.)

2. How could those assets and talents be used for this project?

3. Of the talents/assets listed in step 1, which one or ones would you prefer to use to help this project?

4. What strategies could you use to help ensure that you get to contribute in this way?

communication such as e-mail offers those group members experienced in computers opportunities to take over leadership roles they might not otherwise be open to. In addition, the anonymity of some communication technologies and their asynchronous nature can alter who in the group typically dominates, horses around, or fills the leadership functions.

Equally important to understanding the role dynamics of your group is to recognize that effective management of group roles requires that members realize they bring to their groups roles from other groups they participate in. The bona fide group perspective we touched on in Chapter 2 supports the reality that group members are often simultaneously members of other groups. These role demands may conflict with the time and commitment expectations of our roles in other groups. These sometimes conflicting demands brought on by membership in multiple groups affects the role negotiation and emergence of our roles in these groups. Just how might the cast and crew of *Man of La Mancha* manage their simultaneous roles in their theater group with their professional and family group demands?

Most of us desire to be a part of volunteer "life enrichment groups" such as our church and community groups.[25] Anyone who has been a member of one or more of these groups knows they can clash with the demands of work and family. The trick is finding a balance between the multiple group demands on our time and commitments. One strategy people use to balance these demands is to express to the members of the volunteer groups how important both kinds of groups are to them while also showing the sacrifice made to the volunteer group. When conflicts between life enrichment groups and family and work occur, members can either segment or integrate their membership. Should these conflicts arise for the cast and crew of *Man of La Mancha*, they can give priority to family and work during the day and then commit evenings to the theater group. They can also be very clear early as to the limits of their commitment. As more and more of us work at home and the boundaries between work, family, and our volunteer groups blur, negotiating these kinds of multiple group membership may get harder and harder.[26]

Roles emerge from the structuration processes of a group as members seek to balance the demands of the task and their interpersonal relationships. Out of this same trial-and-error interaction, groups will find their rules and norms. We turn our focus to a discussion of how rules and norms form and change over a group's life cycle as well as how they affect group dynamics.

Rules and Norms

Fundamental to our understanding of small groups is the premise throughout this text that communication is the essential throughput process within a small group. Structuration theory, introduced in Chapter 4, helps us explain how a group's communicative patterns create and sustain the group's norms and operating procedures. Recall from this earlier discussion that group members do not come to a group void of any assumptions about how to behave. Instead they bring to the group complex understandings of how to behave learned from the general culture and past group experience. These rules and norms do not force members to act in a certain way but act as guides for behavior. Group member behavior can maintain these standards, modify them, or even ignore them and create new ones. Group communication simultaneously reinforces previous standards and creates new ones to be maintained or changed in the future.

The whole process of communication among group members is rule-governed.[27] **Rules** and **norms** are the standards of behavior and procedures by which group members operate. Norms (informal standards) are not written down. In contrast, rules are more formal and usually are written in minutes or bylaws. Norms and rules tell members what they are allowed to do (e.g., "Members may call for a soda break after an hour"), what they are not allowed to do (e.g., "The seat at the head of the table is reserved for the group's chair and no one else may occupy it"), and what they should do (e.g., "The designated leader is responsible for reserving the meeting place"). Both rules and norms belong to the group as a system rather than to any individual and differ from each other only in their degree of formality. Rules are formally stated, but norms are informal. Norms are enforced by peer pressures, whereas rules are usually enforced by the designated leader. Rules must be changed by voting, but members may agree to change norms after an informal discussion.

Rules and norms serve several functions for the group. By letting group members know what is and is not acceptable behavior, rules and norms reduce the uncertainty members feel about how to act. They establish procedures for working as a coordinated team. In the long run, productive rules and norms help the group achieve a high level of efficiency and quality control so that it can accomplish its assigned task well. Can you imagine how hard it would be if, every time you had a meeting, you had to negotiate the procedures by which the group should operate? You would be wasting all your valuable time deciding *how* you should work instead of getting your job done.

Formal rules are constructed in a couple of ways. Sometimes committees and other small groups establish their own formal rules for how they want to operate. At other times, the parent organization that created the group also gives it rules by which to operate. For example, many large organizations use the committee procedures in *Robert's Rules of Order Revised* to govern meetings.

Norms usually are not discussed openly, but they still have a strong effect on the behavior of the group members. A friend of ours serves on the city council of a small town. The council had developed a norm of meeting until all old business had been cleared, which meant that they sometimes met until midnight. Carla, a new member appointed to fill a vacancy for a council member who had been transferred, started to pack up her materials to leave at 9 o'clock. She explained that she assumed the group would end the meeting by 9 whether members had finished or not, and she had not made child care arrangements past that time. The other members looked at her in surprise. Some were sympathetic, but all continued to meet after she had left. At subsequent meetings Carla, who realized her mistaken assumption about meeting norms, changed her child care arrangements so she could stay until the meeting's end.

DEVELOPMENT OF GROUP NORMS

How do you suppose the council members established their norm of working until the old business was cleared business? There are a number of ways norms are set in a small group.[28]

Behaviors that occur early in the group's history often establish norms through primacy. When group members first meet, they feel uncertain and uncomfortable. Anything that reduces the uncertainty is welcomed. Thus, what first occurs in a group can easily become habit because it helps reduce the feeling of uncertainty. For example, you serve on a committee that includes faculty and students. Initially you aren't sure whether to address the faculty members by their first names; if you hear a fellow student member addressing them by titles, chances are you will follow that lead.

Sometimes norms are established by explicit statements that a leader or another member makes. For example, one member might tell a new member, "The boss likes to have proposals in writing. If you want to make a suggestion about work procedures at the staff meeting, you should bring a handout for everyone to use." This statement relays information about the group leader's preferences and also subtly lets the new member know that suggestions are supposed to be well thought out before being presented to the group.

Some norms are established through critical events that occur in a group. For example, one of us once taught a graduate seminar of nine people who came to trust each other, often revealing personal information in the class. Two of the students told nonmembers some of what occurred in the class. When the other members discovered this, they felt angry. At the next class meeting, members expressed their feelings of betrayal. Before the critical incident, some members thought it was all right to reveal in-class information to selected outsiders, but after the meeting it was clear to all members that such behavior was a serious violation of a group confidentiality norm.

Finally, many norms are taken from the general culture in which the group members live. For example, you know a lot about how to behave as a student, no matter what the class. True, some professors are more formal than others, but certain standards of behavior (such as raising your hand when you have a question or a comment and not calling the professor or other students rude names) carry over from one class to another. Thus, many carryover behaviors in a group are ones we have learned as members of a particular culture.

This particular origin of small group norms may become troublesome when we interact with members from different cultures. For example, we have observed students from Asian cultures behave very submissively in groups of American students. These international students are following the norms of their native cultures, just as are the American

7.1   Norm Enforcement in Internet Groups

Go to
**www.mhhe.com/
adamsgalanes6**
for additional
weblink activities.

MEDIA AND TECHNOLOGY

Participants in an Internet chat room sometimes experience *flaming,* or a personal attack (i.e., insults, sarcasm, intense language) on someone for a posting. Flaming has become a distinct characteristic of CMC and has been interpreted by many providers to be unsuitably hostile. These behaviors range from personal attacks to a mild form of teasing, and a number of researchers have found that flaming can serve an unintended purpose in chat rooms. In his examination of Internet mailing lists, Wang found that flaming was one of the only tools users had to enforce the informal rules they believed to exist. Flaming was used as a form of policing or a method to "educate the ignorant" about the rules and norms of the Listserv. Additionally, findings indicated flaming (when handled appropriately) helped to foster effective communication by encouraging participants to write clearly, thereby reducing the potential ambiguity that may produce flaming. Despite the unintended consequences that flaming has to facilitate the norms and rules for Internet groups, most Listservs or chat room providers attempt to hinder this practice by establishing their own explicit norms for the behavior of its members. These sites include examples of explicit guidelines developed by chat room providers: **www.ybrt.org/guidelns. html** and **www.fortnet.org/fapg/posting.htm.**

SOURCE: H. Wang, "Flaming: More than a Necessary Evil for Academic Mailing Lists," *Electronic Journal of Communication* 6 (1996).

students. Likewise, African Americans and Hispanics tend to use the vocal back channel (saying things like mm-hmm and OK while another is speaking) more frequently than European Americans. Lack of understanding of another's cultural norms can cause problems in a group.

ENFORCEMENT OF GROUP NORMS

If norms are not written down, how do group members learn them? Observant group members pay attention to how other members act. From this information, norms can be inferred. In particular, you should pay attention to two types of behaviors: those that occur regularly and those that incur disapproval.

Behaviors that occur consistently from one meeting to the next probably reflect a group norm. For example, if at every meeting each group member sits in the same seat and waits for the leader to start the discussion, you are seeing evidence of two norms.

Behaviors that are punished by peer pressure also indicate norms. The strongest evidence of a group norm is members' negative reaction to a particular behavior. Most peer pressure comes in the form of nonverbal signals, as group members roll their eyes at each other, glare, shake their heads, or turn away from the violator. Sometimes they pointedly ignore the offending member's contributions. Carla, the new council member who left early, received only mild expressions of surprise and even some verbal expressions of sympathy, but

TABLE 7.1	How Groups Deal with Deviant Members

First, members try to persuade the deviant member to conform to the group norms:

- They try reasoning with the deviant: "When you aren't here, Carla, we miss your important input."

- They try to persuade the deviant, first with teasing and then more insistently: "Your husband can survive one evening without you, can't he, Carla?" and "Look, Carla, it really messes up the rest of our schedules when you leave early. Why don't you get a babysitter for one night a week—that wouldn't be so bad, would it?"

- They may attempt to punish or even coerce the deviant: "If you really want to be a part of this council, Carla, you're going to have to put in the same amount of effort as the rest of us. Otherwise, we can't support that ordinance you've been promoting."

Second, solidarity builds among the other members against the deviant:

- "I don't see why we should go out of our way to help Carla pass that ordinance—she doesn't seem to care about any of our schedules!"

Third, members ignore and will eventually isolate the deviant:

- "Carla, we've all agreed that it would be better if you resigned from the council. We need a full-time member."

there was no doubt that she had violated a norm, and she quickly came into compliance with that norm at the next meeting.

Members who consistently violate important group norms are called **deviants,** and they make the other group members very uncomfortable—even angry. To conscientious group members, deviants seem to thumb their noses at the group by implying that their own needs and wishes are more important than the needs of the group. The other members try to force the deviants to fall in line by applying increasing pressure to conform (see Table 7.1).[29] This is what the rest of the city council might have done had the new member not corrected her behavior right away.

Just because groups usually pressure a deviant to conform does not mean the deviant should automatically cave in to such pressure. Sometimes groups consider people deviant if they disagree or won't go along with a group's plans. However, such people can actually be helpful to a group if they cause the other members to examine information and ideas more carefully. Even so, the other members may not recognize that such disagreement, or idea deviance, can be helpful, so they try to force agreement. This pressure can be hard to resist, even when the deviant has a good case. We present more information about the effect of idea-deviant disagreement in Chapter 9.

GLOSSARY

Deviants

Members who consistently violate group norms

7.1 When Is It OK to Be Deviant?

ETHICAL DILEMMA

In the 1980s, Beechnut, the second-largest producer of baby food in the United States, was found knowingly to have sold adulterated apple juice.[30] The company had been losing money, and using concentrate with artificial ingredients saved millions of dollars. Beechnut officials argued that other companies were also selling fake juice, that it was perfectly safe, and that their own research and development laboratories couldn't prove that their suppliers were providing fake concentrate.

Assume you are a Beechnut executive who strongly disagrees with the action the rest of the Beechnut officials seem determined to take. You've mentioned your disagreement a couple of times and have been getting both subtle and not-so-subtle pressure to keep quiet. Members have said things to you like, "We've been over this and over this. You keep bringing this up after we've decided." You're marketing the juice as "100 percent pure," which isn't accurate. But on the other hand, no one is claiming that the impure juice is unsafe. Is that really so bad, when it's saving money and jobs for the company?

Groups can be vicious to members who are deviant, and you are definitely a deviant in this group.

1. What do you say to the other members?
2. How can you withstand the pressure the others are placing on you? Should you withstand it?
3. For what reasons would you go along with the other members?
4. For what reasons would you resist?
5. What would you do?

CHANGING A GROUP NORM

We noted earlier that behaviors occurring at the first few meetings may become norms that can cause problems later. For example, recall that when members first meet, they experience primary tension, which makes them so polite and stiff that they do not confront or disagree with each other. This can easily develop into a norm of "no conflict," which stops members from expressing disagreements or doubts. As you have seen from the previous chapter on critical thinking, this "no conflict" norm can be detrimental to the group's later decision-making abilities.

Although it isn't always easy, groups recognizing and using their own structuration process can change unproductive norms. One effective approach is to focus the group's attention on the norm and the harm it is creating rather than on the person violating the norm. In addition, do not try to force other members to accept your suggestions for changing the norm. They are likely to become defensive, refuse to change, and resent your attempt to control them. Instead, you want the group to think of ways to change the norm so that all the members participate in establishing a more productive group norm, for only the group can make a lasting change in a norm. The guidelines in Table 7.2 will help you.

TABLE 7.2	**Changing a Group Norm**

PREPARE

1. Make sure you are seen as a responsible, loyal member of the group; others won't appreciate your comments if you have been unreliable or act "holier than thou."

2. Ask yourself, "What harm is the norm causing?" Observe the effects of the group norm on the members and the group as a whole; count the offending behaviors and make notes of your observations.

CONFRONT CONSTRUCTIVELY

1. Select an appropriate time to share your information with other members.

2. Share your observations about the effects of the unproductive norm on the group; explain what you have observed the norm to be and the problems it causes.

3. Ask whether others also have observed these effects or share your concerns.

4. Express yourself supportively, not defensively:

    a. Defensive comment: "I'm sick and tired of always being on time while the rest of you wander in any time you please!"

    b. Supportive comment: "For the past four meetings we have started between 15 and 25 minutes late. We seem to have developed a norm that scheduled starting times do not need to be observed. Two of us have had to leave these meetings before they were finished in order to go to class. As a result we have missed several key decisions, and the rest of you have had to bring us up to date on what happened. Does anyone else see this as a problem?"

The elements we have discussed thus far—the way group members manage their tensions; how they work through important tasks in their development and formation; and the roles, rules, and norms they establish—all help create the group's climate. We now examine how the group's climate contributes to the formation of an effective team.

Development of a Group's Climate

Maintaining a pleasant interpersonal climate was the most frequently mentioned communication skill needed, as reported by managers of work groups.[31] Joseph Folger and Marshall Poole, experts in group conflict, define **group climate** as "the relatively enduring quality of the group situation that (*a*) is experienced in common by group members, and (*b*) arises from and influences their interaction and behavior."[32] A few key ideas are important to keep in mind when you consider your group's climate. This general

7.4   Changing a Norm You Believe Is Harmful

Carla, our city councilwoman, chose to accept the group norm of meeting as long as it took to complete the group's work. However, there are pros and cons to that norm. Yes, the work is not permitted to pile up and the group achieves closure at each meeting. But members are visibly fatigued at midnight and there is a noticeable loss of concentration and productivity after 10 p.m. Assume Carla's position for a moment and address the following questions:

As Carla, you genuinely believe the group would be more productive and make better decisions if they had more, but shorter, meetings. List at least three choices you have for dealing with this norm.

1. What are the consequences, both to you and to the group, of each choice?

2. What strategy do you think would be most likely to succeed? Why?

3. If you decide to try to change this group norm, how would you go about trying to change it? In your answer, include any planning you might do for bringing this up to the group. Also, describe exactly what you would say to bring this up.

Select five people, including one to play Carla, to role-play a city council meeting where Carla brings up the question of the meeting length norm. After the role-play, discuss as a class what worked and what did not. Make sure to let the participants in the "meeting" express any feelings they might have experienced during the role-play.

environment, atmosphere, emotional tone or "air" of a group is pervasive, emerges from and impacts the group's communication, and is experienced by all members of the group. Climates, whether positive or negative, are the ongoing consequences of member communication and relationships.

Members who could disagree without being disagreeable, who could admit mistakes, and who could keep emotions on an even keel were particularly valued by the work group managers mentioned above.[33] You probably have attended group meetings where you felt the warmth and affection of the members for each other. The climate was enabling, flexible, and participatory. Conversely, you probably also have observed meetings where you felt tension and distrust. The climate was defensive, rigid, thwarting, hostile, and authoritarian. These are but two examples of types of group climates or atmospheres. There are many dimensions of a group's climate. We explain three we consider most important—trust, cohesiveness, and supportiveness.

TRUST

Trust refers to the general belief that members can rely on each other. When group members trust each other, they do not have to worry that others might be lying to them or may have secret reasons for their behavior. Instead of being suspicious and secretive, members

Trust

General belief that members can rely on each other

7.2 Can You Be Trusted?

This is a particularly busy semester for you and you feel as if you barely have time to breathe. You will graduate at the end of the semester, and you don't know how you'll manage all your coursework, to say nothing of job hunting. One of your courses entails a group project; you have just met with your team members for the first time in class. The others are enthused about the project and have already started to make a schedule of meeting times for the semester. You think they are planning far too many meetings—many more than the project will need. Privately, you think you can get your own work on the project finished and attend perhaps half of the meetings the others have scheduled. But if you say that to your fellow group members, you're afraid that they'll think you don't care about the project. If you just skip meetings without saying anything now, you're afraid they'll think you're a slacker. But then again, you'll probably never see these people again. Either way, though, it seems like you can't win.

1. What other choices do you think you have besides saying no to the meetings now and just not showing up later?
2. Do you stay silent and make a private decision to make the meetings you can and not worry about the rest?
3. Do you say something to the group? If so, what?
4. For each of the options you came up with, what are the consequences to the group of that action?
5. What action is least likely to undermine the group's trust in you?

who trust one another are more likely to create an open climate where people share freely. Two kinds of trust are particularly important to groups: task related and interpersonal.

A member who is trustworthy regarding the task can be counted on to complete assignments and produce top-notch work for the group. The higher the quality of the individual work that members do for the group, the higher will be the quality of the group's outputs. One behavior that can destroy trust quickly is failure to complete assignments for the group. A member who does not come through for the group forces the other members to pick up the slack. This is one of the most common sources of conflict and can poison a group's climate.

Interpersonal trust refers to the belief that the members of the group are operating in the group's best interests and that they value their fellow members. Assume that a member you trust says to you, "I think there are lots of problems with your idea." You are likely to ask that member for reasons and to pay careful attention to the reasons given. On the other hand, if the same statement comes from someone you don't trust, you may wonder what's behind the statement, ignore it, get into a shouting match, or try to find subtle ways of sabotaging that member's suggestions. Members who appear to operate from **hidden agenda** motives, or personal and private motives, are seen as untrustworthy by others. So are "politicians" who always seem to have a personal angle for their behavior that

GLOSSARY

Hidden Agenda

An unstated private goal a member wants to achieve through a group

has nothing to do with the group. In fact, politicians can be so destructive to a group that Larson and LaFasto, who studied excellent groups, recommended that the group leader get rid of them as soon as possible.[34]

COHESIVENESS

Cohesiveness refers to the attachment members feel toward each other, the group, and the task—the bonds that hold the group together. In a highly cohesive group, members feel a strong sense of belonging, speak favorably about the group and the other members, and conform to the norms of the group. In a group that is not cohesive, members do not feel much sense of belonging. They may not attend faithfully or may even leave the group because they find other groups more rewarding.

As with trust, there are two types of cohesiveness, task cohesiveness and social (or interpersonal) cohesiveness.[35] In a group that has high task cohesiveness, members understand and accept the task, are committed to completing it, may be excited about working on it, and experience what has been called group drive, or motivation to accomplish the task.[36] This describes the *La Mancha* cast very well. Interpersonal, or social, cohesiveness means that members like and are attracted to each other as people. They like to spend time together and enjoy each other's company. These two forms of cohesiveness affect group productivity and decision-making quality in different ways.[37] When a group's cohesiveness is due to interpersonal attraction, the task may take a back seat, which can lower the quality of a group's decisions. In particular, members have to be particularly careful to guard against groupthink (see Chapter 9), the tendency to accept information without thinking critically about it. In addition, sometimes groups high in interpersonal cohesiveness develop norms that keep productivity low, or may find themselves getting off track easily. A friend of ours sorted letters for the postal service. His co-workers let him know that he was working too fast and that if he wanted to stay in their good graces, he would not exceed the informal production norm they had developed. In contrast, groups with high task cohesiveness generally are more productive and decision making is enhanced. Thus, the presence of task-focused norms in a group moderates the effect of cohesiveness—groups with strong task norms and high cohesiveness outperform cohesive groups without strong task norms.[38]

Highly cohesive groups are more satisfying to their members. You have no doubt belonged to a cohesive group where you felt the warmth and closeness among the members. Terry, one of our former students, decided to campaign for office in a campus organization because she had so envied the obvious cohesiveness expressed by the previous year's officers—she wanted the experience of being part of such a group. Table 7.3 provides suggestions you can use to increase the cohesiveness of a group.

SUPPORTIVENESS

In a supportive climate, members encourage each other, care about each other, and treat each other with respect. Supportive members uphold ethical principles about how to treat each other. In a supportive climate, members believe their opinions are valued by the group, even when other members disagree with their opinions. Because members feel safe from psychological assault, they are free to direct most of their energy toward helping the group accomplish its task. On the other hand, a defensive climate emerges when members try to control, manipulate, and criticize each other.[39] If members are afraid they will be attacked by other members, they will hesitate to offer their opinions. They will spend so

GLOSSARY

Cohesiveness

The bonds of attachment members have for each other

TABLE 7.3	**Increasing Cohesiveness in a Group**

- Develop a strong group identity.

- Encourage group traditions, such as annual parties, special greetings and handshakes, and rituals.

- Develop in-group insignia, such as T-shirts and sweatshirts, pins, or hats.

- Refer to the group members as *we* and *us*.

- Give credit to the group as a whole when representing the group to outsiders or other groups.

- Give credit to individuals within the group for contributions they make toward the group's goal achievement.

- Support both disagreement and agreement by encouraging openness and freedom of expression.

- Create a climate of supportiveness in which every individual feels appreciated and believes his or her ideas are valued.

- Set clear and attainable goals for the group.

  —Goals should be difficult enough to provide a challenge and produce group pride when they are met.
  —Goals should not be so hard that they are nearly impossible to attain because failure will lower cohesiveness.

much time defending themselves or being on the alert for psychological assault that they will not pay much attention to the task of the group. Table 7.4 provides a list of supportive and contrasting defensive behaviors with sample statements for each.

All the defensive behaviors include an element of negative evaluation. These are judgmental behaviors that hurt interpersonal relationships within a group. Instead of critically evaluating ideas, members are critical of each other as persons. Notice, also, the relationship between cohesiveness and supportiveness. It is hard to feel strongly attached to a group if you don't know from one moment to the next when you are going to be attacked. Perhaps you also can see the relationship to open-mindedness—a supportive group consists of members who are willing to listen actively to each other and who are egalitarian in their approach to others. Open-minded members will not demand that the group perform in a particular way, the one and only right way. Can you begin to see how each element of the group system is related to all the other elements?

All the factors we have discussed in this chapter contribute to the structure that creates a team out of individual members. The way members develop over time, manage their tensions, the roles and norms that develop, and the climate members create all work together to make each team a unique culture.

| TABLE 7.4 | **Defensive and Supportive Communication Behaviors and Statements** |

Defensive behaviors

Evaluation Judging the other person; indicating by words or tone of voice that you disapprove of a person. "That's a pretty dumb idea!"

Control Trying to dominate or change the other person; insisting on having things your way. "I want to do it this way, so that's what we're going to do."

Strategy Trying to manipulate the other person; using deceit to achieve your own goals. "Don't you really think that it would be better if we did it this way?"

Neutrality Not caring about how the other group members feel. "We don't have time to hear about your car accident right now; we have work to do."

Superiority Maximizing status differences; pulling rank on other members with title, wealth, expertise, and so on. "Well, I'm chair of the committee, and I believe I make the final decision about how we do this."

Certainty Being a know-it-all; acting positive that your way or belief is the only correct one. "I know exactly what we ought to do here, so I'll take care of it."

Supportive behaviors

Description Desiring to understand the other's point of view without making the other person wrong. "Tell me more about how your idea would work."

Problem orientation Trying to search honestly for the best solution without having a predetermined idea of what the solution should be. "What ideas do you all have about how we might solve this?"

Spontaneity Reacting honestly, openly, and freely. "I really like that, and here's something else we could do. . . . "

Empathy Showing by your words and actions that you care about the other group members. "You had a car accident on the way here? Are you OK? Is there anything we can do to help?"

Equality Minimizing status differences; treating every member of the group as an equally valued contributor. "I know I'm the chair, but the solution belongs to the whole committee, so don't give my ideas any more weight than anyone else's."

Provisionalism Being tentative in expressing your opinions; being open to considering others' suggestions fairly. "I have an idea I think might work. . . . "

RESOURCES FOR REVIEW AND DISCUSSION

SUMMARY

- Groups normally experience two major phases in their development. During the formation phase they find ways of managing primary tension and the interpersonal relationships among members. In the production phase, they cope with secondary tension by directing most of their attention toward the accomplishment of their goals.

- Group socialization of new and/or established members and the group is a complex process of learning how to fit together. Effective communication between all parties is crucial to successful and positive socialization, which in turn influences other group processes such as leadership, roles, norms, and climate. The process can be described in five phases: antecedent, anticipatory, encounter, assimilation, and exit. Group

socialization continues throughout the life of the group until the new member leaves or the entire group disbands.

- Task, maintenance, and individualistic roles are functions members perform in the group.

- Rules and norms, the standards of behavior for members of the group, differ only in their degree of formality. Group norms, or informal rules, are established through primacy, explicit statements members make, critical events in the group's history, and carryover behaviors from the culture at large.

- The group's climate is the atmosphere in which members work. Three important aspects of a group's climate include trust, cohesiveness, and supportiveness.

EXERCISES

1. Watch a film that shows group formation (classic examples include *The Breakfast Club, The Commitments,* or *Lord of the Flies*) and discuss the following questions:

    a. How did the group manage important issues in its formation phase? Were there any unresolved issues that later hurt the group?

    b. What instances of primary, secondary, or tertiary tensions did you observe?

    c. Who became the emergent leader of the group? Why did this person emerge? What were the sources of this person's power as a leader?

2. Observe an actual group or watch a video of a task-oriented group. (Two videos produced especially for this textbook contain suitable segments for this exercise.) Make a chart based on the task, maintenance, and individual behaviors described in the chapter. List the people's names at the top and the task, maintenance, and individual behaviors along the left side. Whenever

each person speaks, categorize his or her remarks by making a note in the appropriate category. For each person in the group you observe:

    a. What sort of role profile would you draw for that person?

    b. How would you label that person's informal role?

    c. Do you think the person's behaviors were helpful or not? Why?

    d. How would you change the category system to be more useful for you?

3. Think of the most (or least) cohesive group you have ever belonged to and explain why this group was so cohesive (or uncohesive). Which supportive (or defensive) behaviors were most prevalent in the group? What forms of trust did you observe (or not observe) that made the biggest difference in the group's climate?

 Go to **www.mhhe.com/adamsgalanes6** and **www.mhhe.com/groups** for self-quizzes and weblinks.

KEY TERMS • CONCEPTS

Antecedent Phase

Anticipatory Phase

Assimilation Phase

Cohesiveness

Deviants

Encounter Phase

Exit Phase

Formation Phase

Group Climate

Group Socialization

Hidden Agenda

Life Cycle

Norms

Primary Tension

Production Phase

Punctuated Equilibrium

Role

Rules

Secondary Tension

Tertiary Tension

Trust

www.mhhe.com/adamsgalanes6

Use the flash cards and crossword puzzles on the Online Learning Center to further your knowledge of these key terms.

Celebrating Diversity in the Small Group

CHAPTER OBJECTIVES

After reading this chapter you should be able to:

1. Define *diversity* and give several examples of diversity within a group.

2. Explain how diversity benefits a group.

3. Describe the four learning styles identified by Kolb and explain how each can benefit a group.

4. Describe the four dimensions of the Myers-Briggs Type Indicator® personality inventory.

5. Define *culture,* describe three dimensions on which cultures differ, and explain how each can affect group interaction.

6. Explain how gender, generational, race, or ethnic differences are cultural.

7. Explain why symbolic convergence and fantasy can help group members bridge differences by contributing to a group identity.

8. Explain how SYMLOG methodology can be used to help a group identify and overcome differences.

The Misfit

Judy, a gregarious and sociable class member, had the gift of making everyone laugh. When the class formed task groups that would stay together for the entire semester to complete a major project, several groups wanted Judy to join them. She chose to join a group with two other women and two men who, from their participation in class discussions, were bright and conscientious students. This group had a good mix of talent—members who could organize a task, members who could write well, members who had many contacts throughout the university to help them find the resources they needed, and members, like Judy, who could make the task enjoyable. The group appeared to be headed for success. All the elements existed to make this a productive and fun experience.

Several weeks later, the group members were ready to kill each other. Three of them wanted to fire Judy from the group. The fourth member, Misty, liked Judy well enough, but was also frustrated by her behaviors that pulled the group off task. Her constant joking, socializing, and attempts to ensure that everyone was having a good time had backfired. Instead, the others concluded that Judy was an airhead; they were frustrated by her inability to stay on task and what they perceived as her lack of seriousness. The members wanted an A+ for this major project. They had decided to give the finished project to their instructor a week early for feedback about how to revise and polish it. Judy's constant socializing had slowed them down. The others blamed her for missing their original, self-imposed deadline. By the end of the semester, Misty was the only member who would speak directly to Judy and thus served as the only link between Judy and the others, who ignored Judy whenever they could. The project was turned in on time but not early enough to receive instructor feedback; it received a B, for which everyone (but Judy) blamed Judy.

These students' journals revealed that none of them had much insight into their own or other members' behavior during the semester. Misty and the others held Judy responsible for everything that went wrong. But Judy was the most puzzled and frustrated member of all. She never understood why the others were so "cold." She had looked forward to making some new friends during the project, but her group members didn't seem to be interested in her. The harder she tried to take an interest in them, the more she felt rebuffed.

One of us had the chance to observe a meeting of this group. Judy's sociability and humor could have added quite a bit to the process—if she had only recognized that the others' priorities were not social. But the others, with their extreme task-orientation, were unable to see how Judy's personality could potentially have benefited their group. Instead, group members were locked into a struggle for control over their priorities, and no one won the struggle.

This situation is all too typical. Many groups self-destruct because they mismanage members' diverse perspectives and personalities. Most of us think others should share our goals, priorities, communication patterns, and working styles. When they don't, we often blame them for being wrong. Few of us appreciate others who are quite different from us. Ironically, it is our very differences that contribute to making a group potentially more effective than an individual. After all, if you and I think alike, act alike, and process information alike, one of us is unnecessary to the process! Diversity is the heart of effective group problem solving; it is not a problem to be eliminated! Ineffective management of diversity produces the difficulties so many groups experience.

This chapter hopes to show you how you can celebrate and capitalize on diversity to produce a better group outcome. We discuss several types of diversity, including differences in motives for joining a group, in learning styles and personality, and in cultural backgrounds. We conclude by discussing symbolic convergence and fantasy as a way members can naturally bridge their differences and we present a methodology, SYMLOG (System for the Multiple-Level Observation of Groups), designed to help groups identify their differences and develop strategies for capitalizing on them.

What Is Diversity?

Diversity in a group refers to differences among members. There are endless ways in which members can be unlike each other, from differences in how members learn, to personality differences, to differences of opinion. For example, Roger may remember everything someone tells him, but Tia remembers only what she has read or seen. Suzanna may want to get right to business and complete a task; for her, chitchat is a waste of time. Jamal, however, is able to focus on the task better after he's had a chance to connect informally with the other members; when he can't connect via chitchat, he feels at loose ends.

The best teams have a balance of member abilities, with member approaches and skills complementing one another.[1] However, differences among members make communication more challenging because less can be taken for granted. Even so, it's not enough to be satisfied just coping with diversity—instead, we want to celebrate it as the essence of small group problem solving. Taking the extra time to make diversity work *for* rather than *against* the group is a worthwhile goal.

Diversity

Differences among group members, from personality and learning style differences to differences of opinion

"In the interest of cultural diversity, we've hired Jason, here, who owns a number of hip-hop CDs."

Don't expect your fellow group members to change their basic needs, learning styles, personality styles, or cultural backgrounds! Too often, we assume that we are doing things right and someone else needs to conform to our preferences. One reason we, as teachers, think it is necessary to talk about group diversity is that we want our students to know some of the explanations behind others' behaviors. Members who act differently from you aren't setting out to make your life difficult; they are simply behaving consistently with their own needs, styles, and cultures. Understanding, sensitivity, and appreciation of the differences are more likely to produce a willingness on everyone's part to adjust behavior so the differences have a chance to help rather than harm your group.

DIFFERENCES IN MOTIVES FOR JOINING A GROUP

One of the first differences to face group members is that they haven't all joined a group for the same reasons. People join groups in large part to satisfy psychological needs, among which are the needs for inclusion, affection, and control mentioned in Chapter 1. However, members who join for reasons of affection and inclusion are likely to be looking for something very different in a group than members joining to meet control and achievement needs.

Robert Bales, the small group pioneer mentioned in Chapter 7, notes that our behavior stems from our values and our psychological needs.[2] Members who join primarily to meet control or achievement needs will be task-oriented, whereas members whose needs for affection and belonging predominate will be socioemotional, focusing on the interpersonal relationships in the group. These two sets of needs, and their corresponding approaches to the group's work, can often compete with each other in a group, as you saw in the opening story.

Task-oriented individuals, with their focus on control and achievement needs, believe the group's task is the reason for the group's existence. They perceive any digression from the task as a waste of members' time, so they keep chitchat to a minimum. They feel highly frustrated when the group digresses and may give dirty looks to those who pull the group off task; they are likely to be the ones who bring the group back to task when the group has digressed. Task-oriented members value accomplishment and feel a tremendous sense of achievement and relief when the group's task is completed.

Relationally oriented individuals, on the other hand, value human relationships more than they do task accomplishment. These individuals want to get to know the others in the group and want to experience each member as a friend. Their needs for affection and inclusion take precedence over their needs for control. Thus, if a member is having a personal problem, socioemotional individuals will usually perceive that member's needs as being more important than the group's task and will willingly sacrifice the group's task accomplishment to help the member.

Recent investigations by Anderson and Martin suggest that some motives, particularly the needs for control and affection, may be traits that are consistent across situations.[3] This may pose particular challenges for members with control needs, who tend to focus solely on the task and may downplay the importance of camaraderie and chitchat. These authors note that cohesiveness and satisfaction increase when group members help each other meet their needs.[4] Group members may actually do a better job of accomplishing their tasks when their personal needs for affection are met. Thus, it is important for group members to recognize and help *all* members meet their needs in the group. Task-oriented members must recognize the value of social talk.

Both kinds of members are valuable to the group.[5] The most effective and rewarding teams are often those that combine secondary (task-oriented) and primary (relationship-oriented) elements, as we noted in Chapter 1. In addition, most of us participate in groups for several reasons, of which accomplishing the task is only one. We want to experience the pleasure of each other's company and the fun of interaction.[6] Judy's group fell down on one count—understanding the members' social realities. Judy expected the others to change their task orientation, but that's like asking a tiger to change his stripes. Likewise, the others wanted Judy *not* to have strong needs for inclusion and affection—another impossible wish. Appreciation for and open discussion of their differences could have helped members overcome what turned out to be an insurmountable obstacle to group success.

DIVERSITY OF LEARNING STYLES

Group members also differ in their learning styles. Our learning preferences affect how and what we talk about, whether we understand one another, and what aspects of a group's task we feel most comfortable taking on. Our learning style differences can set us up for misunderstandings if we aren't careful. For example, Gloria is a visual learner. In one group meeting, John, another member, tried to explain something to her in several different ways, none of which got through. Then a third group member drew a simple diagram and Gloria instantly "saw" what they were talking about. Had the third member not observed that she needed a different type of explanation and been flexible enough to provide it, both Gloria and the rest of the group would have stayed stuck on one point.

Other group members may be kinesthetic or touch learners, who process information best if they can physically do something with the information. Group members often reveal these preferences in their talk. For instance, Gloria often says, "I see what you mean," when she understands someone. John says, "I hear you," to indicate understanding, while a third member may say, "I've got it!" Each of these metaphors for "I understand" reveals a clue as to the dominant sensory learning style of the speaker. In cohesive groups,

8.1   Handling Different Motives and Orientations toward Work

Judy and her fellow group members were highly frustrated by each other, in part because their needs and corresponding orientations toward the group's work were so different. However, instead of recognizing this as a potential plus, they responded by blaming each other for not doing things "right."

Assume you are Judy, and you're having a hard time understanding why your group members seem constantly to be rebuffing your attempts at friendship.

1. What is your perception of the group's situation? If you were to describe the situation to a friend, what would you say about it?

2. What effect is your perception of the situation having on your behavior in (and outside) the group?

3. What could you do to make the situation better, from your perspective? List at least five possible things you could do.

4. Which of those actions do you think is most likely to improve the situation, and why?

Assume you are one of the other members of the group and you don't understand why Judy isn't getting the message.

5. What is your perception of the group's situation? If you were telling a friend about it, what would you say the problem was?

6. What effect is your perception of the situation having on your behavior in (and outside) the group?

7. What could you do to make the situation better, from your perspective? List at least five possible things you could do.

8. Which of those actions do you think is most likely to improve the situation, and why?

members tend to converge on a single dominant sensory metaphor without even knowing it.[7] For instance, after a while group members will all start to say things like "It fits," "I grasp what you're saying," or "There's a hole big enough to walk through in that argument" if the kinesthetic or touch metaphor has been "chosen."

There are strengths to having all three preferences included in a group. For example, in a proposal created by the group, Gloria will contribute diagrams and visual displays that communicate well to other visual learners. John may be the member best suited for presenting the proposal orally to the parent organization. Sometimes just talking about these preferences is enough to help members appreciate them and work a little harder to communicate well with members whose preferences are different.

David Kolb has developed another model that demonstrates several key differences in learning styles that can affect how group members work together.[8] He suggests that people have one of four basic preferences for learning new information and they enter the learning cycle by way of their preferred style (see Figure 8.1). We present this information

FIGURE 8.1   The Kolb Learning Cycle

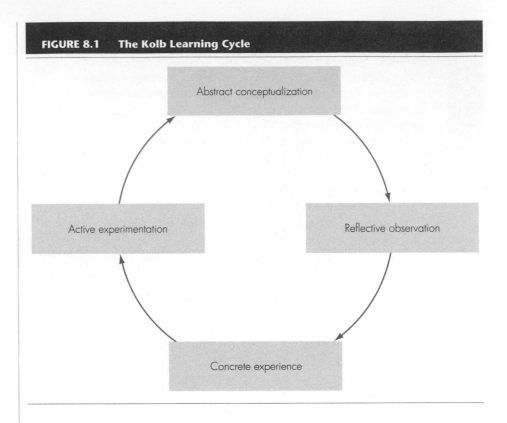

to heighten your awareness of the learning style differences among group members. Each of the styles has strengths to lend a group, which is best served with an overall balance of the styles.

The **concrete experience learning style** describes those individuals who learn well from events they actually observe or activities in which they actually participate. They are concerned with unique, particular experiences rather than theories and generalizations. They trust their feelings and are intuitive. As group members, they are do-ers and may become impatient with theoretical discussions or researching background information. For example, if your group is charged with investigating a parking problem on campus, a concrete experience learner may volunteer to count cars illegally parked or observe how many cars leave a lot without finding a parking place. But such a person may be uncomfortable if asked to synthesize three theoretical articles about traffic flow and facility usage.

The **reflective observation learning style** describes individuals who prefer to get perspective on their direct experience by standing back from it, gaining psychological distance from it, and thinking about it reflectively. They emphasize understanding rather than practical application; they are the group "thinkers." They mull information over in their minds, may talk to others about it, and learn particularly well by writing about the experience. As group members, they are likely to benefit from group discussion about issues. They may help the group think through a group project or show how theoretical concepts are applied, but they may be less comfortable jumping in to help implement a group project.

The **abstract conceptualization learning style** describes learners who process a considerable amount of information by reading and solitary study. They are comfortable working alone, can perceive broad patterns, readily understand theoretical material, and can pull together information from a variety of sources in a way that makes sense. They are logical and emphasize thinking as opposed to feeling. In a group, they are the "synthesizers" and would enjoy pulling together available research for the group's project; however, they may be less enthused about conducting observations or implementing the project.

The **active experimentation learning style** describes individuals who learn by trying different things until they find one that works. Such people are comfortable trying something new. They can apply information in a variety of ways. They like to actively influence others and prefer to do rather than observe. As group members, they will be effective in a crisis because they can think and problem-solve on their feet. Such a member might like to be given responsibility for conducting a pilot test of your group's recommended solution to the parking problem but is likely to have less patience for solitary thinking and writing about the problem.

Generally, our preferences usually lead us to develop strengths in some styles more than others. In a balanced group, though, all styles are represented; the group has members who can research a problem, extract the important information from the research, develop a plan, test the plan and modify what doesn't work, then finally implement the plan. For example, a member who can conceptualize abstractly may be a big asset in step 1 of P-MOPS, when careful analysis of a problem is necessary. On the other hand, a member comfortable with active experimentation may be an asset at step 5, when the group needs to adjust the way a solution is implemented. Members who discover that their group is missing one or more of the styles can make an effort to expand their own abilities, or can invite consultants or trusted outsiders to supply the perspectives they lack.

PERSONALITY DIFFERENCES

Mishandled personality differences create as much havoc in groups as any other factor. As mentioned earlier, it isn't the fact that members have different personal styles that causes the problem—it's the fact that many members don't know how to work with others whose personalities are markedly different. They waste their energy trying to get those with dissimilar personalities to change or are simply unwilling to work with people different from themselves.

Hundreds of personality characteristics have been investigated by social scientists. Instead of making an inventory of characteristics that affect group interaction, we have chosen to look in depth at one classification system, the **Myers-Briggs Type Indicator® (MBTI).**

The MBTI, based on the work of psychologist Carl Jung, is a personality measure developed by Isabel Briggs Myers and Katherine Briggs.[9] The system looks at four dimensions that relate to how individuals interact with the world. Each dimension is a continuum with opposite characteristics at either pole. Each of us leans, a little or a lot, toward one or the other of the poles. The MBTI classifies us into 16 basic personality types based on the particular combination of dimensions toward which we lean. Thus, MBTI assesses our preferences and describes the characteristics we display and the behaviors with which we are most comfortable. However, no one is a "pure" type—we all display some characteristics of all the personality types. In this next section, we will describe the four dimensions that underpin the MBTI® (see Table 8.1).

TABLE 8.1 Strengths and Weaknesses of the Myers-Briggs® Dimensions

	Introvert	Extravert
STRENGTHS	• Can work independently	• Interacts well with others
	• Likes working with ideas	• Is open
	• Is careful before acting	• An active do-er
WEAKNESSES	• Dislikes being interrupted	• Is impulsive and impatient
	• Misses opportunities to act	• Needs change and variety
	• Can be secretive or appear unsociable	• Needs others to work best

	Sensor	Intuitor
STRENGTHS	• Pays attention to details and facts	• Sees possibilities
	• Is patient and systematic	• Likes complicated issues/problems
	• Is practical	• Likes working on novel problems
WEAKNESSES	• Can't see the forest for the trees	• Impatient with tedious work
	• Cannot see possibilities or imagine the future	• Inattentive to detail or practical considerations
	• Is frustrated by complexity	• Jumps to conclusions

	Thinker	Feeler
STRENGTHS	• Logical, analytical, organized	• Considerate of others' feelings
	• Good critical ability	• Understands others' needs/feelings
	• Fair but firm	• Interested in maintaining harmony
WEAKNESSES	• Doesn't notice others' feelings	• Can be disorganized
	• Uninterested in harmony; shows less mercy	• Is overly accepting (of others, of information)
	• Misunderstands others' values	• Not logical or objective

	Perceiver	Judger
STRENGTHS	• Sees all sides of an issue	• Decisive
	• Flexible, spontaneous	• Persistent in staying with a task
	• Is nonjudgmental, accepting	• Makes plans and sticks to them
WEAKNESSES	• Indecisive	• Stubborn and inflexible
	• Easily distracted; does not finish tasks	• Controlled by the plan/tasks rather than in charge of the plan
	• Does not plan	• Decides with insufficient data

SOURCE: Adapted from John N. Gardner and A. Jerome Jewler, *Your College Experience: Strategies for Success,* 2nd ed. (Belmont, CA: Wadsworth, 1995), pp. 83–89.

The **extraversion/introversion dimension** bears on whether your energy is directed toward the outer, observable world or your inner, mental landscape. Extraverts are tuned in to the outer world. They are outgoing, sociable, like variety in their activities, and love being with other people. They may be impatient with slow tasks and don't mind being interrupted. Do you recognize Judy, from our opening story? Introverts, in contrast, like to work alone and dislike being interrupted. They can be patient with details, may be socially reserved, and make decisions relatively independently of what others such as family and friends want. As group members, extraverts usually like and get along well with the other members and are open to others' ideas. Introverts may be uncomfortable working in groups; however, they enjoy working with ideas and can contribute effectively to group problem solving. They may prefer to work independently and bring their work to the group rather than working together with others. Unless extraverts and introverts each know something about the personality characteristics and work styles of the other, their approaches are so different that misunderstandings can easily occur.

The **sensing/intuiting dimension** refers to the type of information you naturally tune in to. Do you prefer to focus on facts in the here and now or are you more likely to dream of possibilities and imagine new connections? Sensing types prefer to deal with facts and information; they mistrust intuitive leaps. They are impatient with abstract theories and are comfortable dealing with details (but they may miss the big picture). Intuitive types become bored easily, especially with details, and relish change. They can see possibilities and like to deal in theories. Imagination and invention are important to them and their conversation may leap from idea to idea (but skip concrete facts). As group members, sensing types are careful and factual; they will be able to provide specific and concrete examples for reports and papers. Intuitive types are creative and imaginative; they may come up with an innovative plan or a novel way to present a project.

The **thinking/feeling dimension** concerns how individuals make decisions, whether by analysis and objective evidence or through empathy for others and subjective feelings. Thinkers use evidence, logic, and careful analysis to arrive at verifiable conclusions and to make decisions. However, they may forget to take others' feelings into account. They are comfortable setting up a single standard and holding everyone to it, regardless of individual circumstances. Feelers, on the other hand, use empathy for others as the standard by which they make decisions. They are comfortable adjusting standards to meet individual circumstances and are more interested in group harmony and interpersonal relationships than on achieving group task goals. As group members, thinkers will be able to evaluate information critically, to spot flaws in arguments, and to produce a logical plan. Feelers will make sure that the group takes people's feelings into account and will help ensure that a decision is acceptable to those who will be affected.

The **perceiving/judging dimension** refers to the way people organize the world around them, whether they are spontaneous and flexible or planned and orderly. Perceivers are like sponges. They tend to gather as much information as they can and to postpone making decisions. They are open and nonjudgmental, welcoming new perspectives and approaches. They are able to see all sides of an issue, but they also have a hard time deciding and reaching closure. When they finish a task, they are constantly second-guessing themselves to see if there was a different or better way they could have done it. Judgers, on the other hand, are decisive and firm in their convictions. They set plans and stick to them. They finish tasks and are ready to go on to the next project. However, they also don't like to have their

GLOSSARY

Extraversion/ Introversion Dimension

The Myers-Briggs® dimension that describes whether someone's energy is directed outward toward observable events or toward an inner, mental landscape

Sensing/Intuiting Dimension

The Myers-Briggs® dimension that describes whether someone focuses on present facts or future possibilities

Thinking/Feeling Dimension

The Myers-Briggs® dimension that describes how people make decisions, by analysis of objective evidence or empathy and subjective feelings

Perceiving/ Judging Dimension

The Myers-Briggs® dimension that describes whether someone is spontaneous and flexible or planned and orderly

8.2   BALANCING THE CHURCH BOARD

APPLY NOW

A friend of ours served on the board of directors of a Unity church. The board and congregation were having problems getting things done. The board made decisions and set policies, but no action took place. For example, the board noticed that, although many new members had joined the church, they often drifted away after a few months. Board members decided to create a program that would help new members integrate themselves quickly into the church community so that they would feel part of the congregation and be motivated to stay. They instituted a volunteer program to help members, especially new ones, identify their talents and find places where they could make their talents available to the church. However, this program never got off the ground, and although new members continued to join, they also continued to leave.

About this time, a representative from the Association of Unity Churches came to conduct a board/congregation seminar based on the Myers-Briggs® classifications. Of the seven board members, six were identified as intuitive feelers and one as an intuitive thinker.

1. What relationship do you see between the classification of board members and the kinds of problems the church was experiencing?

2. What classifications do you think would be most helpful in supplying balance to this board?

3. If you were the board president, what would you do with this information? For instance, would you ask potential board members to construct their profile before endorsing them to run for the board? What ethical problems might this create?

MHHE.com/ groups
For more information on exploring cultural diversity, go to the Online Learning Center at **www.mhhe.com/ adamsgalanes6**

plans changed and may appear rigid and inflexible. In a group, judgers will help ensure that the group's work gets done. They will help the group establish a work plan and encourage fellow members to follow it. They aren't truly comfortable until the group's work is complete. Perceivers, however, can roll with the punches and aren't thrown when circumstances upset the plan. Their flexibility helps members think of options B and C when A falls through. However, they are not so concerned with finishing a plan and are more excited when they start a new project. Judgers and perceivers can drive each other crazy in a group!

The Myers-Briggs® personality types are related to Kolb's learning styles. For example, introversion and reflective observation exhibit similar preferences, as do extraversion and active experimentation. Concrete experience preferences are related both to sensing and feeling; abstract conceptualization preferences are related both to intuiting and thinking.

CULTURAL DIVERSITY

Cultural differences represent a major form of diversity in a group. Groups of the future will continue to be increasingly more diverse, so information about how cultures differ can help you be a more effective group member. **Culture** is the system of beliefs, values, symbols, and rules that underlie communication patterns within a discernible grouping of people. It doesn't necessarily refer to people from another country. A co-culture is a smaller identifiable group contained within a larger cultural grouping. For example, you belong to the co-culture of "college students." In this text, we use the word *culture* to refer also to race, gender, and generational differences, which we'll discuss later.

Unless someone calls our attention to a feature of our culture, we don't think too much about the significant role it plays in shaping our behavior. In addition, we tend to assume that individuals from other cultures share our values, behaviors, and communication patterns, but they don't! Cultures differ along a number of dimensions that affect communication rules and preferences; we discuss three of them here (see Table 8.2).[10] Knowing something about them will help you communicate better in groups made up of individuals from diverse cultures so that you can capitalize on the strengths of these cultures. Moreover, because American business is increasingly becoming global in scope, you likely at some point will belong to a group composed of members from more than one country. In that case, it is especially important for you to be sensitive to cultural differences, not only so you don't offend others but also so you can participate profitably in a global economy.

The first important dimension along which cultures vary is the individualist–collectivist dimension. An **individualistic culture,** such as the predominant culture of the United States, values individual goals more than collective, or group, goals. In a **collectivist culture,** the needs of the group take precedence over the needs of the individual, and conformity to the group is valued. So, for example, a group member from a collectivist culture will willingly abandon personal plans to attend a group meeting, but a member from an individualistic culture will say something like, "I've already got plans, so you'll either have to meet without me or reschedule the meeting at a time that I can make." The underlying value—what's most important—differs. It is easy for group members who value collectivism to become frustrated with a highly individualistic member, whom they will perceive as selfish and uncaring. However, it is also easy for individualistic members to perceive collectivist ones as caring too much about what others think.

Asian, Native American, and Latin American cultures (including the Mexican American co-culture within the United States) tend to be more collectivist than the cultures of the United States or Western Europe.[11] For instance, in Asian cultures, relationships are crucial. If your company sends you to negotiate a contract with a group of executives in Taiwan, you must plan on a perhaps lengthy social engagement before business can be discussed. Americans who rush the process have inadvertently insulted their Taiwanese hosts. Individualistic Americans also tend to be competitive and argumentative, particularly in comparison with collectivist cultures, where allowing group members to "save face" is necessary to preserving group harmony. In conflict situations, they are comfortable forcing their opponents to capitulate. But instead of assuming that someone must win and someone must lose, it may be more productive to find the common ground instead and help your partner save face. We discuss strategies for doing this in Chapter 9.

Individuals from collectivist and individualistic cultures have developed different communication preferences. For instance, individualistic members value clear and direct communication that is unambiguous.[12] In contrast, members from collectivist cultures, which value harmony, prefer ambiguous communication that is more subtle and tentative. For

TABLE 8.2	**Three Important Dimensions of Culture**

Individualism/Collectivism

HIGH INDIVIDUALISM
Values independence, autonomy, and privacy; encourages dissent; encourages people to "do their own thing."

- "I won't be at the meeting tomorrow. I've got a chance to go skiing with a friend and I really need some time off from school."

- "I know you all agree, but I don't, and I won't support that decision."

HIGH COLLECTIVISM
Values harmony, conformity, and loyalty to the group; discourages dissent.
- "I'm taking my mother to the hospital for surgery in the morning, but I'll be at our meeting for sure at noon. I can call from there to see how she's doing."

- "I'll go along with whatever you all want to do."

Power Distance

HIGH POWER DISTANCE
Maximizes status differences between members; values hierarchical structure and strong authoritarian leadership.

- Leader says, "I've decided that we're going to do it this way."

LOW POWER DISTANCE
Minimizes status differences between members; values sharing power, participatory decision making, democratic leadership.

- Leader says, "We've all got to live with the decision we make, so we should all have a say in it. Tell me what you think?"

Context

LOW CONTEXT
The words themselves carry most of the meaning; values direct, unambiguous communication.

- "Your idea is intriguing. Maybe we should explore it in more detail" (said with a smile) means, "I'm interested and I want to explore it in more detail."

- "I love that idea" means "I love that idea."

HIGH CONTEXT
The situation, or context, carries most of the meaning; communication is indirect; nonverbal signals are crucial to understanding a message.

- "Your idea is intriguing. Maybe we should explore it in more detail" (said with a smile) may mean, "I hate it" or "I really like it" or "It might have some possibilities but I can't commit yet."

example, assume both Nguyen and Sam disagree with something contained in a group report being prepared. Nguyen, the collectivist member, says, "I wonder if we should look more closely at Part 2 of the report? Was anyone else confused in that section?" But Sam, the individualist member, says, "I think Part 2 sucks and has to be done over." Nguyen likely thinks Sam is selfish and rude, whereas Sam sees Nguyen as wishy-washy and spineless.

Each way of stating the same opinion has advantages and disadvantages. Nguyen's way is polite and allows the writer of Part 2 to save face; however, we can't tell how strongly Nguyen feels about it, so Part 2's writer can easily misinterpret Nguyen. In contrast, there's no mistaking how Sam feels, but his statement may make the author so angry that nothing in Part 2 gets changed.

The second dimension of culture we discuss is **power distance,** or the extent to which a culture maximizes or minimizes status and power differences among individuals. In a low-power-distance culture (the United States has relatively low power distance), status and power differences among individuals are downplayed. Individuals believe that power should be distributed evenly, that just because someone has a title or money does not entitle them to privileges under the law that others don't have, and so forth. In a group, members from a low-power-distance culture believe that they have as much right to speak up and participate in decisions as the group's leader. In high-power-distance cultures such as Mexico and the Philippines, status differences are magnified and a rigid hierarchy exists. Members of such cultures believe that each person has a preassigned place in the society and should not seek to step out of that niche. In a group, members from high-power-distance cultures expect the leader to control and direct the group and may become frustrated with participatory leadership.

Members from low-power-distance cultures expect to participate in decision making, prefer a democratic leadership style, and assume that everyone else wants to participate in decision making as well. For instance, group leader Sarah says to her group, "What ideas do you all have for solving the parking problem?" Members from high-power-distance cultures value authoritarian leadership and may see a democratic leader as weak and incompetent. They expect low-status members to conform to high-status members. They assume others will accept the leader's control and direction. For example, group leader José says to his group, "I believe the parking problem is due to bad class scheduling. Here's what I want you to do. . . . " You can see the possibility for misunderstanding and hurt feelings here!

The third dimension is that of context. In a **low-context culture,** such as that of the United States, the verbal part of the message carries the meaning—what you say is exactly what you mean. If you say that you like my proposal, I can trust the fact that you really *do* like it. In a **high-context culture,** such as most Asian and Native American cultures, features of a situation or context are more important than the words themselves. So if you tell me you like my proposal, I'd have to take into account the setting, the people, the purpose of our conversation, and other factors to know for sure whether you *really* liked it or you were just being polite to avoid hurting my feelings. High-context cultures tend to be collectivist, with group harmony an important value. Ambiguity and indirectness may help preserve this harmony by allowing disagreement to happen gently in a way that doesn't upset the balance of the group.

GLOSSARY

Power Distance

Whether a culture maximizes or minimizes status and power differences

Low-Context Culture

A culture where the words used convey more meaning than the situation or context

High-Context Culture

A culture where features of the situation or context convey more meaning than the words people use

For example, context differences have caused problems between U.S. managers and their Mexican counterparts at the *maquiladoras*, the assembly plants in Mexico near the U.S. border.[13] Expectations about how managers should express disagreement differ. Mexican managers use an indirect communication style in conflict situations, but U.S. managers expect disagreements to be expressed openly and unambiguously. These differences in expectations can cause problems and misunderstandings.

Group members from low-context cultures sometimes try to force others to be direct and clear. They may perceive members who are not straightforward as manipulative or insincere. On the other hand, members from high-context cultures perceive members who are verbally blunt as rude and aggressive. As the earlier example demonstrates, the advantage of being clear, like Sam, is that your meaning is unmistakable. However, the advantage of being tentative, like Nguyen, is that you allow discussion to occur without polarizing members' opinions or making them lose face.

8.3   Euro-Disney Stumbles

APPLY NOW

According to Carl Hiaasen's book, *Team Rodent: How Disney Devours the World,** Disney's venture in France, Euro-Disney, got off to a slow start when it opened in 1992. Disney executives decided to import the Disney concept intact when they created their European theme park. The Disney parks in the United States have a clean-cut image—at least, as Americans define *clean-cut*. Those who work in the park, mostly young people, abide by strict rules of dress and demeanor. For example, they must not wear bright nail polish, heavy makeup, or facial hair. In addition, the parks do not serve wine or other alcoholic beverages, which contributes to the clean-cut image in the United States.

However, these rules seemed offensive and ridiculous to Europeans, particularly the French. Not serve wine in France? Unthinkable! These factors contributed to Euro-Disney's dismal early performance. However, Disney rethought its rules and relaxed several, in particular the makeup, facial hair, and wine rules. Euro-Disney is beginning to catch on in Europe, the way it has in the United States.

1. Are there any other "rules" or communication patterns observed by North Americans that Europeans might consider silly?
2. Are there any "rules" or communication patterns observed by Europeans that North Americans might consider silly?
3. What does the above story suggest to you about cultural practices, particularly applying in one culture practices that are normal in another?
4. Disney executives are intelligent and experienced. What factors do you think might have contributed to this not-well-thought-out decision by Disney?

*Carl Hiaasen, *Team Rodent: How Disney Devours the World* (New York: Ballantine Publishing Group, 1998).

Appreciation of cultural differences in a group is very important. The United States is a pluralistic culture, to which many different cultures have contributed. This means little can be assumed or taken for granted. It is common now—and will become even more common in years to come—for groups in the United States to be composed of members from different ethnic or racial groups, different generations, and different sexes. Often, open discussion of cultural differences is all that's needed to clear up communication misunderstandings that may occur. Patience helps. So does goodwill and kindness toward others whose communication preferences and practices are different from your own.

Gender Differences as Cultural Differences.   You will never be able to escape one of the most important influences of culture: the effect of gender roles in a group. **Gender** refers to the learned characteristics of masculinity and femininity; **sex** refers to the inherent biological characteristics with which men and women are born. At this point, we don't know which characteristics are inherent and which are learned. However, we do know that the communicative rules we all use have been taught to us by our culture, and that culture strongly influences what kinds of behaviors are appropriate for men and women. There are many more similarities than differences between how men and women behave in groups. Even so, Reich and Wood recently examined research studies about male–female behavior differences. Although men and women both exhibit a range of similar behaviors, there are four areas where men and women have different tendencies; these are not absolute differences but rather are matters of degree.[14]

The first area of difference is between *expressive* and *instrumental* behaviors. Expressive behaviors focus on feelings and relationships. For instance, before the meeting gets under way, Susan may ask Allen how he did on the calculus test he was worried about. Instrumental behaviors focus on accomplishing the group's tasks. Allen may tell Susan he'll talk to her about it after the meeting, but first they have to assess where they are on their group project. Although both men and women exhibit expressive and instrumental behaviors, women engage in more expressive behaviors and men engage in more instrumental behaviors.

A second, related difference is *task* versus *relationship* focus. Women generally place more emphasis on relationships and are more likely to show, by their communication behavior, that they care and want to help. One woman we know, a particularly effective leader, touches base with members between meetings, especially if there has been a disagreement, to make sure everyone is OK and no one's feelings are hurt. She believes that the task goes better when relationships are harmonious. As with expressive and instrumental behavior, men and women both communicate caring as well as interest in the group's task.

Third, there are differences in *forcefulness,* which involves how much someone talks, interrupts others, claims personal space, or otherwise calls attention to him- or herself in the conversation. It also refers to how directly and assertively someone communicates. Men tend to be more forceful than women. They talk more than women, interrupt more, engage more in self-promotion, claim more space, and are more assertive. A man is more likely to say, "OK, here's what I think we should do . . . " but a woman is more likely to say, "This seems like a good idea, but what do the rest of you think?" The first statement is more direct and powerful, but the second is more polite and inviting.

Finally, male–female differences have been observed between *individual* and *group* orientation. Men exhibit more individualistic behavior that calls attention to their own personal status. They tend to seek the spotlight more often and to highlight their own

GLOSSARY

Gender

Learned characteristics of masculinity and femininity

Sex

The inherent biological characteristics of male and female with which people are born

individual accomplishments: "I think I did a great job of researching our topic." In contrast, women show more collectivist behavior that emphasizes the group as a whole: "We have done a wonderful job of gathering all the information we need." They stress building the team rather than increasing their own individual status.

Interestingly, sex itself seems to function as a status characteristic in small groups, with men having higher status. In one study where group members interacted anonymously via computer-mediated communication, men were more likely than women to reveal that they were men.[15] Women hid identifying information or even represented themselves as men. Women believed that their contributions were more readily accepted when they were anonymous than in face-to-face interaction where they could clearly be identified as women. They preferred to remain anonymous during computer-mediated interactions because they believed they had more influence that way.

8.1   Diminishing Implicit Assumptions of Group Diversity

Go to
**www.mhhe.com/
adamsgalanes6**
for additional
weblink activities.

MEDIA AND TECHNOLOGY

Diversity in experience, expertise, and perspective is encouraged in group interaction because of the potential it adds to the quality of group decisions. However, a number of implicit assumptions about diversity (personality, culture, gender, etc.) can sometimes diminish the rewards that would have otherwise been gained by having a group composed of a mixture of personalities and experiences. Think how your group interactions may be different if you had no preconceived assumptions about the members you were about to work with. How would that change the way your group started its meetings? What things would you talk about to develop relationships?

One feature of group support systems discussed in Chapter 6 when describing group support systems is anonymity, a feature that can be used to help circumvent many assumptions members bring to the group (i.e., males are better at working on task, younger group members know more about technology, etc.). Consider some of the stereotypes we have about male and female group members. Do you have different expectations for male group members compared to females? Are there tasks that you feel certain genders are better at? In her examination of gender masking on the Internet, Danet found that, when given the opportunity, individuals (both male and female) enjoyed experimenting with altering their identity because of the freedom that came from gender-free interaction. The anonymous interaction through a CMC environment gives people a chance to understand how social and cultural information about others is used to guide interaction. To learn more about the potential for gender masking, go to **www.newcastle.edu.au/discipline/social-anthrop/staff/ kibbymarj/gender.html** for a comprehensive list of available resources on the subject.

SOURCE: B. Danet, "Text as Mask: Gender, Play, and Performance on the Internet," in *Cybersociety 2.0* ed. S. Jones (Thousand Oaks, CA: Sage, 1998).

Generalizing about male and female behavior is misleading because gender roles continue to change rapidly. Thus, any discussion about gender roles in communication is an overgeneralization and will be out of date in coming years. In addition, the differences we *think* we see capture our attention more than similarities, which are actually much more numerous. We insist on highlighting the differences, partly because they seem to make intuitive sense. The behaviors typically attributed to women and those attributed to men are both valuable and necessary in groups. Gender balance seems like a good idea.

Race and Ethnic Differences as Cultural Differences.

When we talk about diversity, the first thing that comes to most people's minds is ethnic or racial diversity. In the United States, we often don't deal well with ethnic and racial differences. We seem to shout at each other, producing more heat than light, or pretend there are no differences. However, if we don't quickly find a way to celebrate one another's ethnic and racial differences while at the same time finding a way to cooperate in solving common problems, our culture—a grand experiment in democracy—will not succeed. In the 21st century, multiracial and multiethnic groups will be the norm, so we have to do better than we've done in the past.

Major ethnic and racial groups in our country include African Americans, Asian Americans, European Americans, and Hispanic Americans. We know quite a bit about the communication within many cultures, but we don't know very much about interaction between individuals from a variety of cultures. In the next section, we provide information about some of the major differences in communication styles and patterns in these groups, but we focus on differences between African Americans and European Americans because relationships between these two groups are among the most problematic. We offer a very important caution, however. We discuss each culture as if members from that culture display a single consistent pattern of communication, but this is not the case. There are as many communication style differences *within* the African American community as there are between African Americans and Asian Americans. Although we know we are overgeneralizing, if you aren't aware of differing cultural practices, your lack of knowledge may interfere with effective group discussion. If you find yourself uncomfortable in an encounter with someone whose race or ethnicity is different from your own, and your impulse is to blame the other person for your discomfort, stop! Your discomfort may be due to unexamined differences between two cultures; the other person may be just as uncomfortable as you are.

Earlier we presented information about collective and high-context cultures. Asian cultures tend to be both. Asian Americans who are close to their original family cultures may communicate indirectly. Group harmony takes priority, so conflict will be expressed indirectly and ambiguously. Non-Asian Americans may have to pay careful attention to know they've been disagreed with because actions in context are trusted more than words.

Most Hispanic cultures are collective and have a high power distance. This means that individuals are expected to subordinate their wishes to the group and strong, authoritarian leadership is expected. These expectations and values may clash with the individualism and relatively low power distance in the predominant European American culture in the United States.

The relationship between African Americans and European Americans can be particularly touchy. These two cultural groups have traditionally misunderstood each other, often with serious consequences to both. We hope the information we provide about communication

8.1   Different Voices for Making Ethical Decisions

Assume you are on a student judicial committee charged with deciding the punishment of students who have violated your institution's rules and policies. Rob, the student before you, is charged with plagiarism. He submitted a paper very similar to one that another student had turned in the previous semester to another teacher for the same course. Sections of Rob's paper are identical with the earlier paper, but some parts of the paper contain new research and appear to be Rob's own work. Rob has admitted that he plagiarized portions of the paper, but pleads extenuating circumstances and is asking for your committee's mercy. Soon after he started his research for the paper, he learned that his younger sister, still in high school, was diagnosed with leukemia. She is being treated, so far successfully, but for the last few weeks Rob has driven home on weekends to be with her. He and his sister are close; she relies on him for emotional support, which he has been happy to provide. But helping her has drained him of the ability to concentrate and consumed all his time. He took the easy way out, but made sure that he incorporated his original research into the paper he "borrowed." Rob asks you to let him drop the course with no penalty so he can take it again the next semester. However, your institution has an honor code all students sign as freshmen; the code specifies a *minimum* of one semester's suspension for all honor violations, including plagiarism. In practice, though, the student judicial committee's recommendations are accepted. Here are your choices:

- Let him drop the course with no penalty.
- Give him an F in the course.
- Give him an F in the course with a notation that the F is due to plagiarism; this remains on his permanent record.
- Give him an F in the course and suspend him for one semester.
- Give him an F in the course and expel him from school permanently.

1. Before you form groups of five or six, what would you personally recommend for Rob? What is your reasoning for your recommendation?

2. Get together in groups, as if you were the student judicial committee, and come to consensus about what you would recommend. Then discuss what your reasons were for your ultimate recommendation. What considerations were most important to you?

3. How did you balance being fair to Rob, being fair to other students, and upholding your honor code?

8.1   *Concluded*

This example allows for a number of individual differences in ethical reasoning to emerge. Educator Carol Gilligan, in her book *In a Different Voice,** suggests that men and women use different ethical logic systems when making decisions like this. Men are believed to make ethical decisions from so-called objective positions that focus on abstract concepts such as justice, freedom, and truth. Women, Gilligan believes, make ethical decisions based on concerns for people, taking compassion, desire to alleviate suffering, and loyalty into account.

4. Did you observe either of these ethical systems during your discussion? Did any other ethical systems emerge during your discussion?

5. To what extent do you agree with Gilligan's assessment of men's and women's reasoning during ethical dilemmas like this?

6. What implications might the conflict of different ethical systems have for small groups?

*Carol Gilligan, *In a Different Voice: Psychological Theory and Women's Development* (Cambridge, MA: Harvard University Press, 1982).

differences between these groups will prevent you from saying or doing something insensitive that contributes to group self-destruction.

The African American culture values sharing, emotionality, verbal expression, and interactivity.[16] These values express themselves in a variety of ways. African Americans appreciate verbal inventiveness and expression. Verbal play as a type of performance is particularly valued. However, what African Americans intend as a playful display is often interpreted by European Americans as bragging or strutting. African Americans are generally more expressive and interactive. Open expression of feelings is encouraged and seen as an important way to share and connect. However, this too can be misinterpreted. African Americans think European Americans are cold and underreactive because they don't share feelings as readily and are not as expressive. Similarly, European Americans think African Americans are overly emotional and overreactive.

Each group perceives the other negatively.[17] A number of communication patterns may contribute to this. For instance, African Americans stand closer to each other than European Americans, who may interpret that nonverbal behavior as threatening. European Americans make more direct eye contact when they listen than when they talk. For African Americans, the pattern is reversed; they make more direct eye contact when they talk than when they listen. This can seriously affect perceptions of trust, interest, and acceptance.

The African American communication style is much more interactive than the typical European American style. For instance, traditional African American church services often display the call-response style, where congregation members shout "Amen!" and "Tell it like it is, brother!" while the preacher is talking. They also use the back channel more than European Americans. This means that they say things like "Uh-huh" and "Mm-hmm" in everyday conversation to signify interest and attention. However, European

Americans can easily interpret someone talking during another's talk as rudeness. On the other hand, African Americans, who are used to getting such verbal signs of attention, may interpret that lack of back-channel responses from European Americans as lack of interest. African American conversational style is a narrative, storytelling style. European Americans may interpret it as disorganized, rambling, or off-task. To European American teachers, a paper written in traditional African American narrative style can appear disorganized and rambling.

Most African Americans have had more practice in understanding European American culture than vice versa because they have been forced to.[18] Many African Americans consider themselves bicultural because they can negotiate "typical" African American conversational contexts as well as the European American contexts that currently predominate in the business and education arenas. However, it is difficult for minority group members to express themselves fully in groups composed primarily of individuals from other cultures.[19] Unfortunately, this suggests that multicultural groups are not realizing their full potential as groups because they aren't incorporating fully the ideas of the minority group members.

Generational Differences as Cultural Differences.

A few years ago, Gloria served on the board of directors at her church. Gloria is a baby boomer and was the youngest member of the board. As a boomer, she believes all people—women included—have the right to express opinions; she also values frank and open discussion in the course of making decisions. It simply never would occur to her that she *shouldn't* say what she thought. Most of the other members of the seven-member board were a generation older. During their board meetings, they signaled—primarily through their nonverbal behavior—that they were uncomfortable with her high level of participation. It seemed to her that she was violating an unspoken rule of "be seen and not heard until you've paid your dues." Her values and beliefs seemed to clash with the others' values, and she interpreted the clash as stemming from generational differences.

Think, for a moment, about your parents' and their friends' generation. Do you have the same values? Do you live your life in the same way as your parents? What differences do you observe? If you are old enough to have children, what differences do you observe between your own beliefs, behaviors, and values and those of your children?

A number of writers have characterized major generational differences that appear in the U.S. workplace today. Much of this information has been synthesized by Rick and Kathy Hicks, whose work provides the basis for this section.[20] Although the Hickses do not use the term *co-culture,* that is in fact what they describe. Their key assumption is that each generation forms a particular co-culture, with similar values, goals, and outlook on life. The members of each generational co-culture are highly influenced by the major events, people, and activities prominent during their formative years, particularly during the time when they were about 10 years old. At 10 years old, forces outside the family—friends, teachers, the media—begin to assume increased and lasting importance in our lives. To really understand the core values of a particular generational subculture, it is necessary to take a look at those deciding events.

The Hickses describe four broad generations that are found in today's workplace: builders, boomers, generation X, and the net generation. Table 8.3 summarizes this information. As we describe these generations, we recognize that we are again overgeneralizing and oversimplifying. However, you are bound to experience generational clashes in every

TABLE 8.3	**Characteristics, Strengths, and Weaknesses of Four Dominant Generations**

Generation	Characteristics	Strengths	Weaknesses
BUILDERS (1901–1945)	• Major influences: Depression and WWII • Cautious about spending money • Will work hard at a single task until completed • Put own interests aside for common good	• Careful with resources (e.g., money) • Plan ahead • Reliable, dependable • Disciplined	• Too cautious with resources • May lack spontaneity and flexibility
BOOMERS (1946–1964)	• Major influences: TV, Vietnam War, the Pill, assassinations, civil rights movement, size of generation • Major consumers; value "good life" • Self-absorbed; believe they're special • Work as an end in itself; expect to be fulfilled at work • Value education	• Confident • Willing to put in whatever time a task takes • Willing to challenge "old ways" of doing things • Willing to take on big causes	• Think they're right all the time • Expect others to hold similar beliefs/values • May break rules of ethics if they think it's best for them
X-ERS (1965–1976)	• Major influences: rising divorce rate, Watergate, Pentagon Papers, MTV • Distrust institutions, particularly government • Comfortable with diversity • Work is means to an end • Value family (broadly defined) • Comfortable with technology • Endure education	• Independent thinkers • Sensitive to people; value relationships • Tolerant; accept competing points of view • Comfortable with change • Highly computer literate	• Appear pessimistic and negative • Unwilling to put personal life/concerns aside to complete task • May seem alienated and unmotivated

(continued)

TABLE 8.3	*Concluded*

Generation	Characteristics	Strengths	Weaknesses
GENERATION N-GENERS (1977–1997)	• Major influences: AIDS, technology and the Internet; death of Princess Diana • Still young and in process of being formed • Value diversity; highly tolerant • Major consumers • Nonlinear thinkers • Value family	• Open minded and tolerant; welcome different viewpoints • Completely technology and media savvy • Optimistic • Innovative • Comfortable with and like collaborative work, networking	• Seem to lack initiative; seem unmotivated • Unlikely to conform to bureaucracy, hierarchy, organizational "rules"

arena of life—including in small groups you join. Appreciating some of the differences—and perhaps the reasons for them—will help you draw from the strengths of these generational differences instead of being mired in resentment.

The **builders** are a large group of individuals, born from 1901 to 1945, that include many subgenerations. However, there are characteristics that many in this large generational subculture share. These individuals were influenced by the expansiveness following World War I, the bust of the Great Depression, and the horrors of World War II. They learned to work hard, to save their money, and to postpone gratification. Many people who lived through the Depression are uncomfortable about buying goods on credit and prefer to save their money first for things they need. They may be uneasy about spending their money, even when they have enough. Although many builders have retired from the work force, they still are active participants in American governmental and civic life. These people believe in hard work, are patriotic, trust government and other institutions (such as religious institutions), and trust authority. They are comfortable with hierarchy, willingly climbed the corporate ladder, understand responsibility, and will put their own personal interests aside to complete a task. They have learned to postpone gratification and believe strongly in personal discipline and self-sacrifice. They value education, even though many of them were not able to obtain it for themselves. Builders are team players; they do not challenge authority and they will work very hard toward a goal. These values seem old-fashioned and out-of-date to later generations. Because of their own experiences in the Depression and World War II, the builders wanted things to be easier for their own children, the boomers.

The **boomers,** born from 1946 to 1964, were the largest generation for many years. Because of their sheer size, they were the focus of much marketing activity after World War II. Many companies (to say nothing of indulgent parents) paid lots of attention to the

GLOSSARY

Builders

Individuals born from 1901 to 1945; influenced by Great Depression and World War II

Boomers

Individuals born from 1946 to 1964; influenced by TV and social upheaval of 1960s

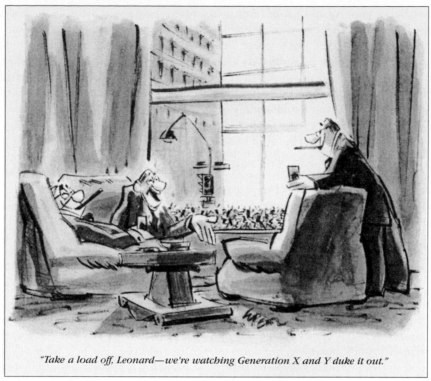

"Take a load off, Leonard—we're watching Generation X and Y duke it out."

needs and wants of the boomers. Consequently, they have a strong belief in their own importance! Boomers were the first television generation, which has helped make them impatient for answers and immediate solutions. They lived through the 1960s, the decade of assassinations, civil rights marches, and general social upheaval. They also were the first generation to have the birth control pill, which dramatically changed the boomers' view of traditional morality. The boomers questioned everything having to do with tradition, although as they age they seem to be moving back to many of the traditions important to their parents. This is an idealistic generation that sought education as a way of addressing societal ills. Although they have a strong belief in hard work, they also believe that work itself should be fulfilling. Many have willingly neglected family life in favor of work. This is also the generation that experienced a massive increase in the divorce rate. The boomers, the first generation able to consume to a great extent, want the good life now and believe they should have it. Others'—and their own—attention was so focused on their wants and needs that the boomers have an ingrained belief that they are right, that whatever they want is good for them and others. Many believe that as long as what they are doing isn't directly harming anyone else, they have the right to do what they want as individuals. The boomers are currently in many leadership positions in industry, education, and government—holding places that gen-Xers would like to have!

Gen-Xers were born between 1965 and 1976. Xers, as they are sometimes called, were the first latchkey generation, often emotionally neglected by their boomer parents. They grew up during Watergate, Nixon's resignation, and the Pentagon Papers, all of which

GLOSSARY

Gen-Xers

Individuals born from 1965 to 1976; influenced by Watergate and general mistrust

heralded a growing mistrust of institutions, particularly government. Because they are small in numbers, they have not received the attention of the boomers and feel somewhat neglected. They would like to prove themselves, but the boomers are hanging onto the jobs Xers believe they are entitled to. This is ironic because the Xers have been described as having relatively fewer job skills and a lower sense of self-confidence than the generations that come before and after. They want the good life and don't want to wait. They value relationships and are not willing to sacrifice them for career, as the boomers were. Work is a means to an end for them, and they don't see themselves climbing the corporate ladder, like the builders. They tend to be cynical and pessimistic, with the highest suicide rate of any of the four generations. They are comfortable with computers, particularly as a mode of entertainment—this was the first generation to experience Atari as children. Xers do not respond well to or respect authority. They don't appear to be team players or want to make long-term commitments. Builders and boomers perceive them as unreliable, ungrateful, and difficult to manage. On the other hand, they have grown up with more diversity than builders or boomers and value it. They have a broad concept of family, which encompasses people they feel emotionally connected to, related or not.

The **net generation** (or N-gen) individuals were born between 1977 and 1997. This group is larger than the boomers and sometimes has been called the echo boom. Because these individuals are still young, they have not had the opportunity to make their influence felt, but like the boomers, this group promises to be a major influence, in part because of its size. N-geners are the first truly wired generation—they have grown up with computers in the home and are completely comfortable using the 'net. Whereas the Xers grew up with computer-based entertainment programs, N-geners use the Internet for everything—information, shopping, and keeping in touch with friends and acquaintances around the world, in addition to entertainment. More hopeful than the Xers, N-geners are even more comfortable with diversity, confident of their skills (particularly their computer skills), and have better relationships with their parents. They are accustomed to collaborative work in school and via the 'net, which makes them value peer relationships and networking, but not hierarchical relationships. They can be good critical thinkers because they have the tools at their disposal to question, seek information, and challenge anything. They tend to judge people by their contributions and don't see any point in "waiting their turn" before they contribute. They are also the most stressed generation—from a young age they have had to keep track of play dates, school activities, lessons, and so forth on their day planners. Personal relationships are more important to this group than institutions, and they have developed a strong live-and-let-live philosophy. They thrive on innovation but, like the Xers, can be seen by boomers and builders as lazy, unmotivated, and rude. Nevertheless, all levels of business, industry, education, and government will have to adjust to this very large and eventually influential group.

The builders are gradually fading from the scene as the boomers assume and hang onto power. The Xers, small in numbers and impaired in terms of job skills and self-esteem, are not a powerful force in the workplace. The N-geners, however, because of their complete mastery of technology and their size, will be a huge force in the workplace and some foresee a major values clash between them and the boomers. In many ways, because the N-geners have used collaborative learning in schools and are used to interacting with people from all over the world, they are well-suited to small group collaboration. But they won't sit quietly and wait to be called on. They want to be respected for their competence and contributions, regardless of their age or position in the company. If you're a boomer, with the expectation that you will command and lead, expect to be challenged!

The previous discussion, as we mentioned earlier, represents overgeneralization and oversimplification. We all can see characteristics of each generation in ourselves. We also know people who display few or none of the characteristics that are supposed to exemplify their generation. However, the point to remember is this: Our early influences from family, friends, and institutions such as the media affect the way we perceive the world around us and the way we communicate, which in turn affects our behavior in small groups. Understanding something about members of generations different from yours—what their hopes and fears are, what pressures operate on them, what the formative events were in their lives—will help you make the most of your differences in small groups instead of bogging you down.

It is easy for a group to get off track or make negative attributions about others whose communication styles and practices differ from ours. We have to learn not to interpret others' actions through the lens of our own culture but to learn to appreciate what other cultures have to offer. If we take the time to do that, our groups and their outputs will benefit. Evidence suggests that, although groups composed of culturally diverse

8.4   Mom's in My Group!

APPLY NOW

In the early 1990s, one of us observed a classroom group of five members who included two men and two women in their early 20s and one woman in her mid-40s. This group had made some progress on its assignment, but tensions were beginning to build between one of the young women, Mindy, and the older woman, Sarah. A single mother with teenagers at home, Sarah had a very full schedule. She tried hard to keep the group task-focused so the project could be completed early, in time for feedback from the instructor. The more she made suggestions about the content of the project, about meeting more often, or about establishing deadlines for the members' individual assignments, the more Mindy resisted: "I can't meet then, I've paid for tickets to a concert and I'm not going to give them up," and "Chill, Sarah, it'll get done" were typical remarks. Mindy, exasperated with Sarah's task focus, complained to one of the other members that Sarah reminded her of her mom—"Always hassling me about something!" This conflict threatened to derail the group's progress.

1. What generations do Mindy and Sarah represent?
2. In what ways does each seem typical of her generation? What communication behaviors seem rooted in generational differences?
3. With whom do you personally have more sympathy? Why?
4. Assume that you are one of the other students in the group. How might you use what you know about generational differences to help the group resolve this problem?

individuals experience more process problems and perhaps lower cohesion initially, over time they can overcome these problems to experience improved performance in certain areas.[21] Groups composed of members from the same nationality and ethnic background demonstrated more effective decision-making processes at first, but over time, the culturally diverse groups caught up. At the conclusion of this study, the diverse groups were outperforming the homogeneous groups in the range of perspectives considered and the number of alternatives generated. Clearly, working in a culturally diverse group is more challenging and requires members to pay greater attention to their communication behaviors, but the payoff can be significant!

We have not intended to teach you everything there is to know about cultural differences. Rather, we have tried to alert you to some common causes of misinterpretations in the listening process. Remember that cultural rules are not automatic; they are taught and constantly evolving. Remember also that cultural differences are not a matter of right or wrong, and that you have absorbed the rules of your culture so completely that they are invisible to you until you start to examine them or to interact with people from a very different culture.

Celebrating Diversity/Bridging Differences

So far in this chapter, we have stressed the value of diversity and provided information and examples to illustrate how diversity can make small group communication more complex. Our ultimate goal, however, is to help group members blend into a well-functioning team that capitalizes on member diversity. How does a group merge into a cohesive, productive team when members are diverse? Naturally occurring fantasy chains can promote a common team identity. SYMLOG can be used to help groups talk about, and eventually bridge, their differences.

CREATING A GROUP IDENTITY THROUGH FANTASY

Diversity is potentially useful, but somehow group members must find common ground if they are to transcend their diverse styles, talents, and perspectives and operate as a team. Developing a symbolic life meaningful to all members can help accomplish this.

Even in the most hardworking, task-oriented groups, members do not stick to business all the time. They often get sidetracked, as if they have made a tacit agreement to "take a work break." Whenever a group is not talking about the here and now of the group, it is engaged in **fantasy.** This technical definition of fantasy does not mean unreal or untrue. It simply means that group members are not discussing the present task of the group but are discussing an apparently unrelated topic.

The study of fantasy stems from the theory of **symbolic convergence.**[22] This theory recognizes that human beings create and share meaning through their talk. For a group to exist, there has to be some shared meaning among the members; otherwise, there would be no group. "Convergence" signifies that members have "come together" on what certain events, ideas, words, and so forth, will mean. Members have developed similar feelings and beliefs about certain things (e.g., "We hate the boss's pep talks because she has no clue whatsoever about our work"). They may have in-jokes, a shared identity, or special meanings for words that only they understand (e.g., "We use 'fish face' as a term of affection because everybody in our group loves to go trout fishing"). They may also have developed

---

GLOSSARY

Fantasy

Group discussion not focused on the present task of the group

Symbolic Convergence

Humans create shared meaning through their talk; the basis of group fantasy

rituals that are meaningful to them (e.g., "We always go out for a pizza on Friday afternoon before everybody goes separate ways on the weekends"). These shared symbols help establish common ground and common bonds that can overcome differences among members.

Fantasy helps such shared symbols come into being. The process works like this. One member introduces a fantasy and other members pick up on it and add to it. This group storytelling, called a fantasy chain, is similar to a party game most of us played as children. One person starts a story, the person to the left adds something, and this continues around the room until each person has contributed to the final story. Group fantasy chains are created in a similar way, and like the party game, they have a central idea, or fantasy theme, that suggests what the fantasy is about.

The following is an example of a fantasy theme that occurred at a student government association executive committee meeting, where members were bemoaning the lack of a day care facility at the campus and were trying to figure out what to do about it. This group includes three men and two women, one of whom (Nan) is a nontraditional student with children.

Char:	I'm not surprised that we don't have a center! We have such a retro-administration. [Char introduces the fantasy, which contains the retro idea.]
Rob:	I know; they're stuck in the 1970s. Next they'll probably let their sideburns grow! [Rob picks up the fantasy and starts the chain.]
Bill:	Can't you just see President Kramer coming to school in a tie-dyed suit? [Bill adds his part in a vivid, colorful way.]
Nan:	Better yet—a tie-dyed leisure suit! That would be about his speed.
Joel:	I can just see a big, tie-dyed sunspot on his chest and peace-sign earrings in his ears! And they ought to change the sign on the administration building to Retro-administration Building! [Joel joins in, embellishing Nan's and Bill's comments.]
Rob:	I feel like we're trying to drag all of them into the 21st century. [Rob's comment hints at what this fantasy might mean to this group.]
Char:	I know they're really behind the times, but we really need to get back to the day care center. How can we get our retro-administration to listen to our ideas about that? [Char ends the fantasy and gets the group back on track.]

What do you think this fantasy is about? Fantasies actually have two themes—the manifest, or obvious, theme and the latent, or underlying, theme. The manifest theme is what the fantasy chain is about at the surface level. The student government committee members were imagining the 70s attire of their retro-administration. The manifest theme is "Wouldn't that kind of clothing be funny?" The underlying meaning, which is actually not very far below the surface, was hinted at by Rob: "I feel like we're trying to drag all of them into the 21st century." In other words, "We, the students, are very forward thinking, but our retro-administration has to be forced to move forward, and we're the ones who have to drag them forward." It's an "Aren't we wonderful, but aren't they a mess" type of self-identity. The operative word here is *we*—these students, different though they may be, have defined themselves as "we" and the retro-administration as "they."

Fantasies—digressions apparently unrelated to the group's task—are introduced by members all the time, but not all fantasies are picked up on by the rest of the members or are meaningful to the group. When a fantasy captures the group's imagination, it usually means that it has some deeper relevance to the members. Thus, although it may appear during a fantasy chain that a group is goofing off, the group may be accomplishing something quite important. First, fantasies can help the group define itself by creating symbols that are meaningful and that help determine its values.[23] For example, the student government committee members who sidetracked into a discussion of tie-dyed clothing were actually using fantasy to help define themselves as forward-thinking representatives of the student body.

Second, fantasies enable a group to discuss indirectly matters that might be too painful, emotionally "heavy," or difficult to bring out into the open.[24] For example, Cassie, one of our students, managed a social service agency. A particular client had become adept at getting what she wanted by manipulating the social workers against one another. The social workers were pointing fingers at each other for the client's problems. Cassie, as the person in charge, dreaded chairing the meeting where the social workers had to come to a decision about what to do with the client. Before the meeting started, one social worker started to talk about the movie *Erin Brockovich* (clearly an off-the-topic fantasy). In particular, she thought the main character exhibited "borderline personality disorder." Others picked up on this idea and added examples from the movie to support the "diagnosis." Soon, one social worker mentioned how Erin Brockovich reminded her of the client they were gathered to discuss. The rest of the social workers started laughing. They had an "aha" reaction when they realized how the client had been able to jerk them around. Cassie reported that they were able to come to a quick, cordial consensus about what to do. Their shared fantasy had allowed them to talk about this potentially difficult topic.

USING SYMLOG TO "PICTURE" DIVERSITY

We have said that diversity in a group is a desirable feature, but we also know that diversity makes group discussion more challenging. Sometimes the very diversity that enhances group problem solving may become difficult or impossible to manage. Something is needed to help members diagnose where their differences are and to know how to make a plan for reconciling those differences so that the group's diversity can help rather than hurt the group. SYMLOG provides a methodology that can "show" a group where its most acute differences are and in what directions members should move to get the group on track.

SYMLOG is an acronym that stands for System for the Multiple-Level Observation of Groups; it is both a comprehensive theory and a methodology that produces a diagram, like a three-dimensional snapshot, of relationships among group members.[25] We present a simplified explanation here so you can understand how SYMLOG can be used to describe and help a group. (Detailed instructions for completing a SYMLOG diagram may be found in *SYMLOG Case Study Kit,* a workbook that explains SYMLOG theory and provides special forms for constructing a diagram.)

SYMLOG theory assumes that behaviors in a group can be classified along three dimensions: dominant versus submissive, friendly versus unfriendly, and task-oriented versus emotionally expressive. An observer uses a 26-item rating scale to categorize each member's behavior; the rating scale is then tallied in a special way so that each member can be placed on the SYMLOG diagram. An example of a SYMLOG diagram, or map, is shown in Figure 8.2. The more a member is task-oriented, the closer he or she is to the top of the diagram; the more emotionally expressive, the closer to the bottom. (The F stands for forward, or task-oriented behavior, and the B stands for backward, or emotionally expressive behavior.) The friendlier a member is toward the other members of the group, the closer he or she is to the right; the more unfriendly, the closer to the left. (The P stands for positive or friendly behavior, the N for negative or unfriendly behavior.) The third dimension, dominance or submissiveness, is shown by the size of the circle; a dominant member has a large circle, while a submissive one has a small circle.

In the SYMLOG diagram in Figure 8.2, Ann is very dominant, task-oriented, and negative toward other members of the group. In contrast, Bob is friendly and emotionally expressive, although he also is dominant. A group with two such strong, but opposite, individuals is likely to experience conflict during meetings. Charlie is moderately dominant, positive, and task-oriented. (This is how democratic leaders and members of productive, democratic groups often appear on SYMLOG diagrams.) If you were asked to describe this group, you would probably say it is unproductive, it lacks cohesiveness, and members appear to waste a lot of time during meetings because there's a struggle between the most task-oriented and most emotionally expressive members of the group.

FIGURE 8.2   *SYMLOG* **Diagram of a Noncohesive Group**

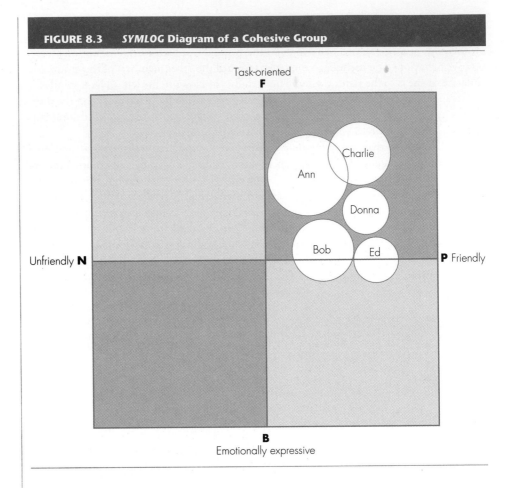

FIGURE 8.3   *SYMLOG* Diagram of a Cohesive Group

The SYMLOG diagram in Figure 8.3 shows a unified, cohesive group. All the members are in or near the upper right-hand quadrant (decision-making quadrant), which shows that they are task-oriented enough to make progress toward the group's goal but friendly enough toward each other that interpersonel relationships are probably harmonious. This group is likely to be productive and efficient.

Thinking in SYMLOG terminology helps you manage the complexity of group interaction as you create a snapshot capturing the essence of a group. Because SYMLOG gives you that visual representation, it is easy to grasp several complex relationships at once. That makes this tool particularly effective in helping you and your fellow group members analyze and diagnose yourselves. It also gives you an idea of what you might do if problems are revealed. A SYMLOG diagram represents the perceptions of the person who constructed it; this provides potentially valuable information to help group members begin discussing their perceptions and preferences. For instance, those members whose SYMLOG diagrams show they perceive Ann as unfriendly may be asked to share specific examples that led them to that conclusion. Likewise, those whose diagrams place Bob in the emotionally expressive area can explain why they see him that way and what they feel about it.

8.5   **Using SYMLOG to Help a Group**

APPLY NOW

Assume you are a consultant who has been brought in to help Judy and her group, described in the opening case. In preparation for meeting with the group, you have asked all the members to rate their own and the others' behaviors with the SYMLOG rating scales and you've constructed five SYMLOG diagrams, one for each member of the group. Judy's diagram is shown on the left below. The other four members' diagrams are almost identical; the diagram on the right is an average of those four diagrams.

Judy's diagram

Average of other members' diagrams

1. Interpret the group from Judy's perspective.

2. Interpret the group from the other members' perspectives.

3. As a consultant, how would you use this information to help the group? What would be the focus of your work with this group?

4. In what ways do you perceive SYMLOG to be helpful to groups such as this?

If it is too threatening or frightening for group members to conduct such discussions on their own, a trusted facilitator can help manage the discussion. Consultants who use SYMLOG often ask members of the group being observed to complete the SYMLOG forms in advance. From these, they create SYMLOG diagrams to distribute to the group. Having the SYMLOG "pictures" prompts members to talk about themselves and their relationships with each other in a relatively nonthreatening way. This can set the stage for tremendous growth and development of the group.

There are a variety of ways to use SYMLOG, and several computer programs have been created to make its use easier.[26] However, it is possible to construct a SYMLOG diagram by hand. If this analysis appeals to you, we recommend that you purchase the *SYMLOG Case Study Kit,* which contains all the instructions and forms you need to produce a diagram by hand.

We have presented two ways in which group members can bridge their differences. However, the most important thing members can do to triumph over and transcend their differences is to *want* to overcome them. Assuming members want to work together productively to celebrate whatever differences they may have, the suggestions in Table 8.4 provide several tips for doing just that.

TABLE 8.4	**Tips for Diversity and Bridging Differences**

- Decide that you want to appreciate the differences among you. Making understanding and appreciation of your diverse talents, approaches, and styles a priority for your group is the single best thing you can do.

- Schedule plenty of "get to know you" time. This can be a purely social gathering with no business conducted or you can set aside a brief "check-in" time before you get started on your business. However, don't rush this process. You will need time to learn about each other.

- Be willing to talk about and praise the differences among you. When people believe their unique approaches or contributions are valued, they relax and are willing to contribute more to the group process.

- Be open to new ways of doing things. Nothing dampens the positive potential of diversity more than rigid adherence to doing things the same way as they've always been done. Be willing to listen and to try new ideas.

- Find ways you can create common experiences for group members. For instance, you may want to schedule a retreat, an outdoor experience, a social outing to a baseball game—anything that gets all members participating in the same activity.

- Create rituals for the group. Meaningful rituals can go a long way toward reminding members that their purpose in coming together is greater than any individual differences they may possess. For example, one church board always begins its routine meetings with a prayer and its annual retreat with a communion service. However, rituals don't have to be serious. Some work groups pass out cookies and bagels at the beginning of the meeting, with members taking turns bringing the bagels.

- Encourage members to create symbols that represent the group. Many groups have T-shirts with a meaningful saying or symbol. Sometimes, members participate in creating symbols or logos for the group.

- Use methods, such as SYMLOG, that provide a vehicle for members to talk about their differences and how they can surmount them. SYMLOG and other methods provide a relatively safe way and a nonjudgmental vocabulary for members to depict and discuss their perceptions of their own and others' behaviors. SYMLOG also gives members a handle on how to establish direction for the future to help the group capitalize on its diversity.

RESOURCES FOR REVIEW AND DISCUSSION

SUMMARY

- Diversity is the essence of group problem solving. The differences by themselves are not a problem, but members often don't know how or don't want to manage their diversity so the group can benefit.

- Diversity comes in many forms. Members may have different motives for joining a group; they may differ in their learning and personality styles.

- Another major way group members differ is in their culture or co-culture. Three main dimensions along which cultures differ were presented: collectivist/individualistic dimension, power distance, and context dimension.

- Gender and race or ethnic differences are, at heart, cultural differences. Men and women consistently differ in four ways; similarly, African, Asian, European, and Hispanic American cultures have developed different communication patterns that can be misunderstood by outsiders.

- Diversity is valuable, and group members can bridge their differences through fantasy and using the SYMLOG methodology.

- Several suggestions were provided for helping group members bridge their differences.

EXERCISES

1. Look at the descriptions of four different work styles below:

   - Task-oriented people, who believe a group's main job is to get down to business as soon as possible.

   - Relational people, who believe group work can be fun and that getting to know each other is part of the fun.

   - Systematic decision makers, who believe in gathering all the facts and weighing them before deciding.

   - Intuitive decision makers, who assess a situation instantly and leap to a conclusion quickly.

     a. Each of the four work styles should be assigned to a different corner of the room. Then, without thinking about it too long or too hard, go to the corner of the room that represents the work style most like yours.

     b. Elect a reporter to record your group's responses and report to the class at the end of the session.

     c. In five to six minutes, write down all the advantages people like you have to offer a group.

     d. In five to six minutes, write down all the disadvantages people like you bring to a group.

     e. Reconvene the class as a whole and ask each group to report, first the advantages and then the disadvantages, while a class member or your teacher writes each one on the board for all to see.

     f. After each group has presented its list, the other groups may add advantages or disadvantages to the list.

     g. Talk as a class about what you learned from this exercise and what you perceive can be the advantages such diversity of approach represented in the group.

2. Your family represents one example of a co-cultural grouping. Form into groups of four to six and ask each person to assume that he or she has invited the rest of your group members home for Thanksgiving dinner with the family.

Each person should describe what the "rules" are for Thanksgiving dinner. For example, where does everyone sit? When do you know you may start to eat? Does the food get passed around or does someone put food on each person's plate and pass the plate down? What are acceptable topics of conversation? Is conversation lively or muted? How did the "rules" become established in the family, and so forth?

When everyone has finished, discuss the differences you discovered among each other's "cultures." What dimensions of culture seem to be most important in each family grouping? Were there any surprises? What does each family do when it encounters a violation of the rules? Are the rules ever discussed openly among family members? Are there rules that prohibit what you can talk about?

3. Class members should divide themselves into groups of four to six along gender, race/ethnicity, or age lines. For example, the class might form several single-sex groups. Each group should first appoint a recorder/spokesperson to take notes. Then each group should discuss the following two questions:

a. How do you see yourselves as group members? What characteristics do you believe you have?

b. How do you see the other group as group members? What characteristics do you believe they have?

Finally, when each group is finished, all should share their results with the class and the class should take this opportunity to talk about the stereotypes they hold and how accurate those stereotypes are (or are not).

 Go to **www.mhhe.com/adamsgalanes6** and **www.mhhe.com/groups** for self-quizzes and weblinks.

Abstract Conceptualization Learning Style

Active Experimentation Learning Style

Boomers

Builders

Collectivist Culture

Concrete Experience Learning Style

Culture

Diversity

Extraversion/Introversion Dimension

Fantasy

Gender

Gen-Xers

High-Context Culture

Individualistic Culture

Low-Context Culture

Myers-Briggs Type Indicator®

Net Generation

Perceiving/Judging Dimension

Power Distance

Reflective Observation Learning Style

Sensing/Intuiting Dimension

Sex

Symbolic Convergence

SYMLOG

Thinking/Feeling Dimension

 www.mhhe.com/adamsgalanes6

Use the flash cards and crossword puzzles on the Online Learning Center to further your knowledge of these key terms.

Managing Conflicts Productively

CHAPTER OBJECTIVES

After reading this chapter you should be able to:

1. Define conflict.

2. Discuss the three prevailing myths about conflict in small groups.

3. Define groupthink and explain its relevance to small group problem solving.

4. Explain the three symptoms of groupthink.

5. Discuss ways to prevent groupthink in small group interaction.

6. Compare and contrast the five major conflict styles.

7. Explain how group members can disagree productively.

8. Discuss how members can maximize their chances to influence the group.

9. List and explain the steps of the nominal group technique.

10. Describe the four steps in principled negotiation and explain how to use them to help resolve a conflict.

The Cask and Cleaver Work Crew

CASE 9.1

The Cask and Cleaver is a local restaurant in California's central valley. Its servers (usually students) meet semiannually to select their shifts. At these meetings, about eight servers take turns, in round-robin fashion, picking a shift. The server with the most seniority picks first, and so on, until all shifts are covered. The servers want to choose shifts that make the most money in the least time so that they can survive financially and still have enough time to study and play. The stakes are higher for those with greater financial needs because they must live with the schedule for six months.

One recent meeting has become legendary as the most contentious meeting in the restaurant's 20-year history. Mark, the senior server, took charge and chose first. At his fourth turn, he realized an earlier turn had been skipped and servers with less seniority had taken one more turn than he had. Mark suggested that they start over again. Some supported his idea, but Tom and Paul did not. They were pleased with their shifts after having lived with very poor schedules during the previous six months. After discussing it, the group decided to start over. During the second round it became apparent that the members were choosing differently; furthermore, the new schedule heavily favored Mark and Beth (Mark's wife), whereas Tom and Paul were not faring well at all. Opposition to starting over was voiced again with greater emphasis. Mark and Beth became defensive, arguing that it was not their fault Tom and Paul had two night classes. Tom and Paul perceived this reaction as callous and reminded Mark and Beth that they had no alternative class sections to choose from. Mark replied, "That's not my problem." Another server, Nathan, sided with Paul and Tom, forming a clique that characterized Mark and Beth as self-centered and unsympathetic to the financial needs of others. Mark, Beth, and another server, Maria, all believed that the others' school schedules were not their concern and shift scheduling was a hit and miss process anyway: Sometimes you do well and sometimes you don't. To them, Tom and Paul were "crybabies" who wanted special treatment because they were university students. Tracey and Jeremy, two other servers, remained neutral, moving between the two cliques, listening to both sides, and conferring between themselves without ever sharing their views of the conflict.

To make the best decision about something, group members must use their collective thinking skills. When group members think critically, disagreement almost always occurs. Conflict, expressed and managed appropriately, can help members sharpen their thinking and decide wisely. In contrast, unexpressed disagreement contributes to *groupthink,* the term popularized by Irving Janis in his classic 1972 analysis of the faulty decision-making process used by President Kennedy's advisers resulting in the Bay of Pigs disaster. We discuss conflict in this chapter—what causes it, how it affects a group, what its relationship to groupthink is, and how it can be managed effectively.

What Is Conflict?

Conflict can range from simple disagreement to war. Hocker and Wilmot's definition describes conflict as "an expressed struggle between at least two interdependent parties who perceive incompatible goals, scarce resources, and interference from the other party in achieving their goals."[1] This definition emphasizes the central role of communication. Conflict can be experienced without being expressed; group members can be acutely uncomfortable without saying a word.[2] But how conflict is expressed and how it is handled are communicative acts, which we explore in this chapter.

You have probably observed conflict in a small group when two or more people express incompatible ideas. Marsha suggests that her group present a skit for its class presentation, but Silvio believes skits are childish. For this group to achieve its goal of a successful presentation, Marsha, Silvio, and the other members must manage this disagreement effectively. Most conflicts you experience in a group will be disagreements similar to this. Like the Cask and Cleaver conflict, they can become heated. But if they are handled well, they can help improve a group's performance.

Myths about Conflict

We would like to dispel a number of commonly believed myths about conflict. These are summarized in Table 9.1.

1. **Conflict is harmful to a group and should be avoided.**

   We all have seen examples of how conflict can hurt a group. Minor misunderstandings can lead to hurt feelings, and a group may dissolve over a conflict. Clearly, conflict can harm a group. However, many students see only the harm and don't realize that conflict can be beneficial to the group *if it is expressed and managed properly.*

   Conflict can help members understand the issues surrounding a decision or problem more completely. One of us served on an advisory board for a nonprofit organization. The administrative officer of the organization wanted to fire an employee immediately, without issuing a warning or giving the employee a chance to correct the offending behavior. One member, experienced with personnel laws, disagreed strongly with what appeared to her to be a lack of due process in the proposed dismissal. When the other members understood the legal and ethical problems with discharging employees before giving them a chance to improve their performance, they agreed to give the employee a clear set of guidelines and expectations to be followed.

TABLE 9.1	**Myths about Conflict and the Reality**

Myth 1 **Conflict is harmful and should be avoided**	**Myth 2** **Conflict represents a misunderstanding or breakdown in communication**	**Myth 3** **Conflicts can be resolved if parties are willing to discuss the issues**
• Conflict can help members understand an issue more clearly. • Conflict can improve group decisions. • Conflict can increase member involvement. • Conflict can increase cohesiveness.	• Some conflicts occur over differences in values, goals, methods of achieving goals, limited resources.	• Conflicts over basic values and goals may not be resolvable. • Conflicts over limited resources and methods of achieving goals may be resolvable through communication if the basic values and goals of the parties are compatible.

One group member's willingness to disagree enabled the others to understand the issue more completely. This type of disagreement illustrates *idea deviance,* mentioned in Chapter 7.

Conflict also can improve a group's decision. Improved decision making is a logical outcome of members understanding an issue more clearly. In the previous example, the dismissed employee could have sued the organization and the board for arbitrarily firing him. Clarifying his job duties and the board's expectations gave him the best possible chance to perform effectively. The disagreement helped members understand these possible consequences. Only after they had argued, over the course of several meetings, did they truly appreciate that giving him a chance to improve was both fair to him and protected them in case of legal challenge.

Conflict also tends to increase member involvement and participation. Group discussions can become boring, but when a controversy occurs, members perk up and voice their opinions. In the previous advisory board example, members who had begun to miss meetings started to come regularly again. Usually, members become more interested when they believe their opinions can make a difference in the group's outcomes.

Finally, conflict can increase cohesiveness. Have you ever had an argument with your dating partner, spouse, or friend, then observed how close you both felt after you had made up? If so, you know how conflict can increase your positive feelings toward one another. During the advisory board's discussion about firing the employee, members expressed strong feelings on several sides of the issue. After all members aired their views, the group eventually came to a consensus decision. As consensus emerged, members became closer than ever. Several members expressed their appreciation to the member who initially spoke up against the firing. They believed that her comments forced the group to anticipate possible problems and to create a better solution, although at the time they did not see her disagreement as helpful. Members realized that they could disagree, express themselves in forceful terms, and emerge more united than before the conflict; cohesiveness increased. After the Cask and Cleaver crew managed to deal with their issues constructively, lighthearted banter about this meeting being the "ugliest scheduling meeting of all time" followed, as well as a promise never to let such contention happen again.

So, although conflict can be harmful to a group, it doesn't have to be. Whether a conflict helps or harms a group depends on a number of other factors, including whether the conflict is resolvable in the first place.

2. Conflicts stem from misunderstandings and breakdowns in communication.

Certainly some conflicts occur due to misunderstandings and communication failures, but others do not. Often conflicts occur when individuals understand each other perfectly well, but disagree on basic values or the distribution of rewards. For example, a classroom group trying to agree on whether to recommend the repeal of the *Roe v. Wade* court decision making abortions legal in the United States was unable to arrive at an answer acceptable to everyone. Several members believed that life begins at conception and that abortion is murder. Other members believed that a woman's life should take precedence over the fetus, at least until the fetus reaches a certain stage of development. Each subgroup understood accurately the position of the other subgroup. Misunderstanding and communication breakdown did not occur. However, the subgroups' differing values and assumptions made agreement impossible.

Other conflicts occur over what goals the group will set, how to achieve them, or how the group will distribute limited resources such as bonus money or access to computer time. Although misunderstandings may contribute to these conflicts, the underlying reason for them is much more basic than a communication breakdown. Such conflicts often reflect a struggle over power or wealth. The underlying resources at issue for our Cask and Cleaver crew were money and time.

3. All conflicts can be resolved if parties are willing to discuss the issues.

MHHE.com/ groups
For more information on conflict resolution, go to the Online Learning Center at **www.mhhe.com/ adamsgalanes6**

As you can see from the previous example, not all conflicts are resolvable. Whether or not a conflict can be resolved depends in part on the underlying reason for the conflict. The conflict over basic values on the abortion question is not resolvable at the present time because it is based on differences in assumptions and values. The two assumptions represented—a fetus is a person from conception and has rights equal to those of the mother versus a fetus becomes a person sometime after conception, until which time the woman's rights take precedence—are not reconcilable. Both cannot be true simultaneously. A group experiencing such a conflict will not be able to come to consensus on a policy regarding abortion.

Conflicts over scarce resources are also difficult, if not impossible, to resolve. One of us serves on a library committee with representatives from many areas of the school. Meetings to distribute limited money fairly are usually full of acrimony. Full agreement is rarely possible. Even members who acknowledge that one area deserves more money for books may vote against that proposal if it means their own areas will receive less money. The problem, recognized by everyone, is that funds to support the legitimate requests of all areas are in short supply.

Conflicts over goals can sometimes be difficult to resolve as well. Assume that you want an A on your group project and someone else is satisfied with a C. If you can't convince the other person of the value of striving for excellence and the other person can't persuade you to lighten up, you can't resolve this conflict. If your goal of receiving an A is very important to you, you may end up having to do a lot of extra work on the project—yours and the other person's.

Conflicts over how to reach goals are sometimes easier to resolve than other types, especially if the basic values of the individuals are similar. In the project grade example, if you and the other member both want to get As, but you prefer to show a movie and the other member prefers a skit, you may be able to compromise or find a third alternative that satisfies you both. Because your basic values and goals are the same, you are more likely to see each other as allies, not enemies, which makes it easier to resolve the conflict.

Conflict itself is not the issue. Any social system, due to the interdependence of the system's components, will experience some kind of conflict. How parties manage the conflict is really the issue. Mishandling of disagreement can produce problematic group outcomes such as faulty decision making. Groupthink refers to a certain kind of mishandling of group disagreement, and we now turn our attention to how it emerges in a group and how a group can avoid its negative consequences.

Groupthink

Conflict can help a group perform its best, but as Soshanna found, it is not easy for someone to disagree with fellow group members, especially in highly cohesive groups where a disagreement can be seen as disloyalty or "making waves." **Groupthink** refers to the tendency of highly cohesive groups *not* to examine critically all aspects of a decision or problem under consideration.[3] The term was coined by Irving Janis, who conducted an exhaustive study of the disastrous 1961 decision made by President Kennedy's advisers to invade Cuba at the Bay of Pigs. This now-classic study concluded that their decision-making process was badly flawed. The group members, all well-informed experts, made several miscalculations. In particular, they didn't use all the available information to make their decision, they made it difficult for members who disagreed to come forward, and they assessed information in a biased way. They defined their roles as supporters of a decision the president already seemed to favor. As a result, the invasion failed, and the United States was widely condemned around the world.

Groupthink represents a failure of the group's critical thinking process—the failure to express doubts, disagreements, and conflict within the group. Consequently, the group's decision is flawed because it is made with partial information that has not been examined carefully. This is exactly what happened with our class project group—members simply ignored the professor's stated criteria for the project. During groupthink behavior, some members may privately have doubts about the group's direction. Soshanna had reservations about the project group, as did presidential adviser Arthur Schlesinger. Soshanna didn't want the other members to think of her as a "compulsive," just as Schlesinger did not want to be considered a nuisance during committee meetings. Both kept silent. Thus, both groups were deprived of the full benefit of *all* members' opinions and reasoning.

GLOSSARY

Groupthink

A negative outcome of group decision making characterized by a group's failure to think critically about its decisions

The Class Project

A group of students in a communication course was given two major assignments: a class presentation of material from one of the book chapters and a research project to be presented to the class. As they prepared to present the book chapter, Cary emerged as the group's informal leader. A theater major, he was charismatic, fun, and creative. At his suggestion, the group created a short play dramatizing the chapter content. The members had a blast preparing the presentation. They bonded tightly to become close friends. The presentation received an A, with high praise from the professor. This made them even more cohesive. When time came to plan the research project, they decided, at Cary's urging, to follow the same creative format. They skimmed over the instructions for the research project and concluded that they could rely mostly on material from the text. They focused all their energies on creating a lively, dramatic presentation. But Soshanna, another member, had doubts about their approach. Afraid they were ignoring several criteria their professor required, she timidly expressed her reservation about the direction they were headed. Cary and the rest of the members teased her for being a worrywart: "We got the highest grade in the class last time, and everybody else was envious! The professor loved it! We are the golden group—there's no way we can fail here. Chill, Soshanna—you are *way* too compulsive." Soshanna stifled her doubts and climbed on the bandwagon.

But things didn't turn out so well this time. The group had ignored several key criteria, including the number of outside references they were required to include, the types of references, the length of the research paper, and the format. Their efforts—as much fun as they had been—earned them a low C. This highly cohesive group suffered from groupthink. The members ignored information available to them that would have helped them earn an A, such as the professor's written description of the assignment and her invitation for students to consult with her about the project. Members with reservations, such as Soshanna, kept quiet. The group got overconfident and stumbled badly.

Soshanna's and Schlesinger's behavior is not unusual—few people want to be perceived as nuisances. A study of upper-management teams in 26 American corporations found that 19 percent of members said they best went about company business by not making waves.[4] Nine percent prefer to maintain good relationships with their co-workers at the expense of getting the job done. That suggests a lot of flawed decision making happening at all levels! Let's look at how this kind of group dynamic can happen.

TABLE 9.2	**Symptoms of Groupthink**

The group overestimates its power and morality	**The group becomes closed-minded**	**Group members experience pressure to conform**
• Group believes its cause is right. • Members convince themselves they cannot fail.	• Group is selective in gathering information; chooses only information that supports its predisposition. • Group is biased in evaluating information. • Group excludes or ignores members and outsiders who seem to hold opposing views.	• Members censor their own remarks. • Members who voice contradictory opinions receive pressure from other members to conform. • Members have the illusion that the group opinion is unanimous.

SYMPTOMS OF GROUPTHINK

Groupthink is most likely to occur in highly cohesive groups under pressure to achieve consensus. In particular, cohesiveness based on interpersonal attraction is related to groupthink, but task-related cohesiveness is not.[5] Members of groups that exhibit high degrees of cohesiveness based on their interpersonal attraction to each other tend to be more psychologically connected to each other and so they resist challenging each other.[6] This is a problem because groups *in general* tend to favor discussing what they already know as opposed to discussing new information.[7] Under conditions of groupthink, this tendency is even harder to monitor. In addition, groupthink is more likely to occur in groups with a long history, groups strongly embedded in their larger organizations, and groups that insulate themselves from their outside environments.[8] Spotting groupthink thus becomes crucial if your decision-making groups are to be effective as they critically analyze problems and draw conclusions. Here are three important symptoms to help you spot groupthink, summarized in Table 9.2:

1. **The group overestimates its power and morality.**

   Group members believe their cause is so right that nothing can go wrong with their plans. President Kennedy's advisers believed that the Cuban people wanted liberation from Castro. Several of the invasion plans rested on this assumption, but the advisers neglected to determine whether it was true. In fact, this belief was wrong.

   Government policy groups are not the only groups that overestimate their power and the rightness of their causes. Many business, education, nonprofit, and student groups have fallen into this trap as well. The student group in Case 9.2 became so excited about the creative aspect of their project that members ignored the requirements for the rest of the project. They prepared a dynamic presentation, but left out important information relevant to the topic. However, they had managed to convince themselves that they were giving the professor what she wanted: "She'll love it. No one else has tried anything like it. I just *know* we'll get an A."

2. **The group becomes closed-minded.**

    Closed-minded people are biased when they evaluate information. Instead of looking open-mindedly at all relevant information, members consider only information that supports their beliefs. Group members may also have a preferred course of action and ignore any information that contradicts their preference. In the Bay of Pigs decision, Kennedy's advisers knew he favored invading Cuba, so they allowed themselves to lean in that direction as well. Information that should have served as a warning was ignored because it contradicted their predispositions. In the class project group, Soshanna's fears about ignoring certain criteria were downplayed: "Oh, that won't be a major problem. Even if we do leave something out, the presentation will be so creative it will more than make up for it." Members talked each other into believing that some criteria didn't matter by ignoring information to the contrary.

3. **Group members experience pressure to conform.**

    Group members experience both internal and external pressures to go along with the group, which show up in several ways. First, members censor their own remarks without apparent pressure from other members. When all the other members of a group favor a certain action, most people are hesitant to express their doubts. This is natural—you want the people in your group to like and respect you, and you don't want to appear like someone "popping others' balloons." Thus, self-censorship often prevents conflicting opinions from reaching the group, to the detriment of the group's problem-solving process.

    Second, a member who does voice a contradictory opinion can be seen as a deviant or "making waves" and receive overt pressure from the group. Groups are uncomfortable with deviants (even idea deviants) and pressure them to go along with the group. The initial teasing Soshanna received about being a worrywart served as a subtle form of pressure to conform. It worked—she quit openly disagreeing. If she hadn't, the pressure would have intensified. The teasing and jokes would probably have turned to persuasion and ultimately coercion to force her compliance.

    Finally, because self-censorship and group pressure suppress disagreement and doubt, the group experiences the illusion that members unanimously support the decision or proposal. For instance, Soshanna's decision to keep silent made it seem to the rest of the group members that they had a consensus about the project. Assuming that the group is in accord, members carry out the decision without testing to see whether the consensus is genuine. What appears to be an agreement may actually have little support from some members, as was the case with the class project group.

PREVENTING GROUPTHINK

You can take a number of steps to prevent groupthink from occurring. Following are suggestions for both group leaders and members, also summarized in Table 9.3.

1. **Encourage members to "kick the problem around" before they start focusing on a solution.**

    One group behavior that fosters groupthink is arriving at premature consensus.[9] The group has shortchanged the recommended first step of most structured problem-solving procedures, which is exploring the problem before trying to solve it. In

TABLE 9.3	**Preventing Groupthink**

ENCOURAGE MEMBERS TO "KICK THE PROBLEM AROUND"
- Be alert to prevent premature consensus.
- Explore the problem thoroughly before attempting to develop a solution.
- Encourage freewheeling argument before settling on a solution.

ESTABLISH A NORM OF CRITICAL EVALUATION
- Encourage members to express disagreement.
- Encourage critical thinking rather than the appearance of harmony.
- Assign a devil's advocate to argue against popular proposals.
- The leader must accept criticisms of his or her ideas open-mindedly.

LEADER SHOULD NOT STATE PREFERENCES AT THE BEGINNING OF A GROUP'S SESSION
- Let other members express opinions first.
- Offer an opinion only as another alternative (not the alternative) to be considered.
- Encourage the group to meet without the designated leader present.

PREVENT INSULATION OF THE GROUP
- Invite outside experts to present information.
- Discuss tentative solutions with trusted outsiders to get an unbiased reaction.
- Be alert to information that contradicts the prevailing opinion of the group.

addition, encouraging conflict at this stage can help group members understand the problem better. Recall that one of the benefits of conflict is the increased knowledge and understanding group members receive. Active disagreement at an early stage of problem exploration promotes this benefit.

2. **Establish a norm of critical evaluation.**

The most important thing a group leader and other members can do to prevent groupthink is to establish a group norm to evaluate carefully and critically all information and reasoning. Such a norm can offset the proven human tendency to ignore or reject information that contradicts one's existing beliefs and values.

Especially helpful is a norm promoting members' expressions of all disagreements. If a group emphasizes getting along instead of critical thinking, members will hesitate to disagree. A norm supporting open expression of doubts and disagreements makes it OK for members to be in conflict with each other. One study found that, in a group where everyone seems to hold the same viewpoint, even one member who is willing to share an opposing view can redirect the group's attention

GLOSSARY

Devil's advocate

A group member who formally is expected to challenge ideas to foster critical thinking

so that members examine their decision more thoughtfully.[10] Had Soshanna stuck to her guns, she may have saved the group's grade!

Another way of encouraging honest disagreements is to assign the role of devil's advocate to one or more members of the group. A **devil's advocate** is a person who has been assigned the task of arguing against a popular proposal. Thus, this person serves as an "official" idea deviant because the devil's advocate helps spot potential flaws in a plan or holes in arguments. If Josie agrees to be the devil's advocate for a particular meeting, it is unlikely the other members will take her criticisms personally.

Groups have also used group support systems and computer-mediated communication (CMC) to encourage honest opinions. As we have mentioned in previous chapters, computer use in group problem solving is valued for its anonymity. Users believe that this produces less pressure to conform and thus encourages more honesty. However, a member operating from behind a computer is still aware of expectations from others. Thus, CMC can both enhance and limit the impact of individual members' influence and power.[11] Sometimes the effect of perceived status differences is actually stronger in CMC.

The norm of critical evaluation must be supported by the leader's behavior. One of us worked with a boss who asked staff members to identify any problems we saw with a plan he had devised to improve the working environment. Taking the boss at his word, a couple of staff members began to question various elements of the plan. As they spoke, the boss became defensive, minimized their concerns, defended his proposal, and appeared to view the questioning members as disloyal. Soon the rest of the members became silent without voicing their objections to the plan. The meeting concluded with the boss thinking the staff supported the plan, although it did not. In the future, whenever the boss asked for honest reactions to proposals he favored, no one was willing to go on the "hot seat" by expressing a criticism.

3. **Leaders should not state their preferences at the beginning of a group's decision-making or problem-solving session.**

One important source of groupthink is a strong or charismatic leader's preference. In the Bay of Pigs decision, President Kennedy clearly favored the invasion and told his advisers so. The advisers, who all admired him and wanted his respect, hesitated to speak up against the invasion because they didn't want to appear disloyal. Thus, the presence of a strong, opinionated leader inhibited dissent and contributed to groupthink. Cary may have not had Kennedy's charisma, but his fellow group members really liked him—he had a way of making group work fun. They would have done almost anything *not* to dampen his enthusiasm.

In addition to not stating your preferences early in a group's discussion, ask the group to meet without you, especially if you are the supervisor rather than an elected chair. If you suspect that your presence or personality inhibits the group members from saying what they really feel and think, schedule one or two meetings that you do not attend. This will make it easier for other members to express their opinions freely.

4. **Prevent insulation of the group.**

Groupthink often occurs when group members become so cohesive and so caught up in their own ideas that they become insulated from external opinion and

9.1   Terrorism, TV, and Groupthink

Go to
**www.mhhe.com/
adamsgalanes6**
for additional
weblink activities.

MEDIA AND TECHNOLOGY

On September 11, 2001, people from around the world watched images of violence on their televisions. In the wake of terrorist attacks on the World Trade Center and the Pentagon, TV news organizations documented the new focus on the war on terrorism. Nonstop coverage of the attacks transitioned into the war with Iraq, which presumed to be connected with 9/11 terrorists and weapons of mass destruction (WMD). However, the lack of WMD and concrete evidence connecting terrorists to Saddam Hussein has caused many to question the decision to go to war. Consider your own experiences watching TV reports of the terrorist actions and the subsequent war on terrorism. To what extent do you think mediated reports of these events made the public susceptible to groupthink? Are there ways that our culture can reduce the effects of groupthink on the way we assign meaning to mediated messages?

In the summer of 2004, the U.S. Senate Intelligence Committee report on pre-Iraq war intelligence emphasized that many mistakes were made because of "groupthink." Committee members said their findings were based on a presumption that misled the intelligence community. That presumption was that over the years, Iraq both had and used WMD. Over time, that knowledge led to a belief that Iraq would continue to try to build and obtain WMD. This belief led to groupthink in which the intelligence community interpreted all new data as consistent with that basic presumption, although, the report concluded, that presumption was flawed. Copies of this report and information reflecting the committee's conclusions can be found at the following addresses: **http://a.rocket-city.us/intelligence.gov.html** and **http://intelligence.senate.gov/conclusions.pdf.**

expertise. Cary and Soshanna's professor encouraged her students to consult with her as they formulated their research projects. She even offered to pregrade the projects in advance, so students could take her feedback into account to improve their final projects. But Cary convinced his group members that they didn't need outside help—after all, their first project, completed without outside advice, was wildly successful.

Leaders and members of the group can offset this tendency. They can encourage members to present tentative decisions to trusted associates outside the group, then report back to the group with the feedback. They can hold public hearings, at which any interested person can speak on the issues facing the group, as zoning commissions do regularly. They can also arrange for outside experts to talk to the group. Most important, they can be alert themselves for any relevant information from outside the group instead of protecting the group from outside influence.

9.1   Learning from Our Mistakes

Throughout this chapter you have learned quite a bit about the class project group that managed to derail its final project. You may even have been a member of a similar group. Groups that are prone to groupthink rush to agree, fear conflict and confrontation, and do not practice critical thinking. You have also read about ways groupthink can be prevented.

As a class, divide into groups of five or six members and review the information about the class project group. Pretend you are members of this group, just beginning to talk about what you will do for your final project. You want to do a good job, but you know that you are susceptible to groupthink, in part because you are so cohesive. You want to do what you can to prevent a project disaster! Given what you know about preventing groupthink, what guidelines can you follow to ensure a high-quality project? Don't just repeat the four prevention steps—be specific about what you, as a member of this group, would suggest and how you would act.

When all the groups have finished, each group should report its guidelines to the class. Compile the individual guidelines into one master set; then discuss your results as a class. How realistic are your guidelines? What can you do to help yourself remember them, especially in the heat of an actual group discussion?

Managing Conflict in the Group

Conflict is inevitable when people must reach decisions together. Trying to squelch conflict does not eliminate it—it just sends it underground. If managed inappropriately, conflict can hurt a group. In this section we discuss how to manage conflict productively.

CONFLICT MANAGEMENT STYLES

There are many different ways of describing how people manage conflict. The five styles we discuss here were described by Kenneth Thomas.[12] Whatever style an individual chooses is based on the answers to two questions: (1) How important is it to satisfy your own needs? and (2) How important is it to satisfy the other person's needs? Figure 9.1 shows how these two dimensions intersect to produce the five common conflict management styles of avoidance, accommodation, competition, collaboration, and compromise. Table 9.4 gives examples of statements illustrating each style. *No one conflict style is best to use in all circumstances.* The most appropriate conflict style depends on the situation. Factors to consider include how important the issue is, how serious the consequences are if the group makes a mistake, whether the group is under any time pressure, whether cultural practices limit what can and cannot be done, and how important it is that the positive relationship between the conflicting parties be maintained. In most groups, preserving and enhancing relationships among the members are important. So conflict management styles incorporating the legitimate needs of all parties are preferable to those producing winners and losers.

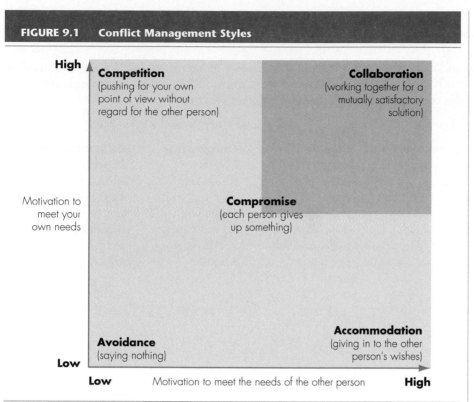

FIGURE 9.1   Conflict Management Styles

SOURCE: Adapted from K. Thomas, "Conflict and Conflict Management," *Handbook of Industrial and Organizational Psychology,* ed. by Marvin D. Dunnette, 1976. Used by permission of Marvin D. Dunnette.

The conflict style that group members use depends largely on how they perceive the situation.[13] The situation is more important, in fact, than what members believe "started" the conflict. Factors such as how often the members have been in conflict in the past and how many negative feelings they harbor against each other, how mutual their goals are, and how ambiguous or structured the solution all affect how a member will approach handling the conflict. Ideally, members recognize that they have a mutual stake in the solution and are motivated to cooperate in resolving the conflict.

Avoidance.   **Avoidance** occurs when any group member chooses not to disagree or to bring up a conflicting point, thus downplaying her or his own needs and the needs of others. When group members fight about other people in the group, group members tend to avoid further conflict with each other. However, if the conflict is about the task, group members tend to be more willing to work together.[14] Avoidance is the basis of groupthink.

We have talked about the dangers of avoiding conflict, but the avoidance style is sometimes appropriate. If the issue is not very important and you are certain that the group's decision will not be hurt by your failure to speak up, avoiding a possible conflict is appropriate. One of us served on a committee planning a banquet. The rest of the members favored a different restaurant from the one your author preferred. Both restaurants were comparable in price, service, and atmosphere. Making an issue over this would have been

GLOSSARY

Avoidance

Conflict style describing a person's unwillingness to confront or engage in conflict

| TABLE 9.4 | **Statements that Illustrate the Five Conflict Management Styles** |

Mary, the college financial director, wants the snack shop to close at 5 p.m. Roger, the evening student counselor, wants it to stay open until 8 p.m. Following are examples of how Roger might respond to Mary, using each of the conflict management styles discussed in the chapter:

Mary: We'll have to close the snack shop at 5. There isn't any money to keep it open later.

Avoidance	Accommodation	Competition	Compromise	Collaboration
Roger: [Says nothing; accepts Mary's statement, even though he disagrees.]	**Roger:** I'd really like to keep it open, but, if there's no money, I guess there's nothing else we can do.	**Roger:** I won't accept that! We can't let the evening students down that way. Cut something else to get the money!	**Roger:** I would accept keeping it open just until 6:30 if you could cut some money from another program.	**Roger:** I understand that it's necessary to contain costs. It's also important to serve evening students. Is there some way we can provide them food service without increasing costs?

This was an actual problem faced by a student services committee. The solution? Provide vending machine service. This maintained constant labor costs but gave students food service after 5 p.m.

silly because there was no risk of making a serious mistake. This was not an important enough issue to argue about.

Accommodation. Accommodation (also called appeasement or giving in) occurs when one person or faction gives in to the other without arguing strongly for a different point of view. This style is similar to avoidance in that a person downplays her or his own needs, but it differs in that the person works harder to meet the needs of others. You should be honest with yourself if you choose to accommodate. Don't give in if the issue really is important to you. We realize this could be hard for those group members who fear talking in front of others.[15] However, if you give in but privately resent it, in the future you are likely to find yourself arguing with the other person for no apparent reason. On the other hand, if the issue is not crucial to you but you know it is important to the other person, then accommodation is appropriate. For example, a faculty/student committee was charged with redecorating a student lounge. The chemistry professor did not like the color scheme recommended by the art professor and said so. But, since the students liked it, the chemistry professor willingly accommodated their preferences. This is an appropriate use of accommodation to resolve conflict.

Competition. Competition, sometimes called the *win–lose* style, occurs when you fight hard to win and you don't care whether the other person is satisfied with the solution or not. The 1994–95 baseball strike is an example of this. Most of the time, highly competitive ways of handling conflict are harmful to a group. If one person tries to impose his or her will on a group, the other members will probably fight back. Competitive tactics

"*The motion has been made and seconded that we stick our heads in the sand.*"

often escalate a conflict, especially when people stop listening to understand each other. Each side tries harder and harder to force the other side to go along. At an advisory board meeting, one member, Sherman, argued strongly for one solution to a particular problem. Two members disagreed with Sherman, who then began to use a variety of tactics to win the argument, starting with persuasion but moving quickly to attempted coercion and intimidation. Sherman's behavior indicated he was more concerned about winning the argument than preserving the group. The visible conflict ended when the rest of the group reacted negatively to the intimidation tactics by voting against Sherman's suggestion.

When a group is doing something you believe is harmful, wrong, or against your values and beliefs, then competition is appropriate. Don't accommodate or avoid conflict if you think your basic values are being compromised or if you think the group is about to make a major mistake. The member opposed to firing the employee, described earlier in this chapter, behaved competitively. She was willing to face the group's disapproval because she genuinely believed they were about to make a big mistake, and she was not willing to compromise. Remember, though, that a conflict where one person wins but others feel like a decision has been forced down their throats will almost certainly erode teamwork. Until the other members came to agree with her position, the member who disagreed about the firing was left out of the group's informal camaraderie and felt very uncomfortable.

Collaboration.   **Collaboration,** the *win–win* style of conflict management, occurs when the people in the conflict want to meet opposing parties' needs along with their own. Like competition, collaboration assumes individuals may argue strongly for their points of view. Unlike competitors, collaborators take care not to attack each other as people or to say or do anything that will harm the relationship. They behave ethically by treating each other as equals. They invest a great deal of energy in searching for a solution that will satisfy everyone. Group members whose communication is collaborative are more satisfied with their group outcomes than members who avoid conflict.[16]

Collaboration can reveal options that other styles miss. For example, the student services committee that served as the model for Table 9.4 initially struggled with two apparently competing goals—making sure that evening students had food available and making sure overhead costs stayed the same. During the discussion, characterized by genuine attempts to help both Mary and Roger achieve their goals, another member suggested the creative option of expanding vending services. This would meet student needs while costing the college nothing, since the vending company would pay for machine costs. But if the committee had voted without discussing the issues, or if either Mary or Roger had kept quiet, this option would never have surfaced.

You may think that collaborative solutions are ideal for groups because they attempt to preserve positive relationships among conflicting parties while members hammer out mutually acceptable solutions. However, collaborative solutions often require much time and energy, which groups don't always have. Not all decisions are important enough for the group to commit the time or energy to create a collaborative solution. If basic values differ or trust is lacking, collaboration may be impossible.

Compromise.   **Compromise** represents a middle-ground conflict management style that can be called a *partial-win/partial-lose* solution for each party. Unlike collaboration, parties using compromise give up something to get something in return. This type of horse-trading is typical of labor–management and government bargaining: "I'll settle for a $1-per-hour raise if you give up the demand for mandatory overtime," or "I'll vote for your bill if you support my amendment." If you know you are going to have to compromise, you will be tempted to inflate your original demands. For instance, if you know you will have to settle for less money than you want, you'll ask at first for a higher figure than you really need.

Although there may be problems with compromising, it is appropriate for many conflicts. When collaboration is impossible due to time pressures or differences in values, compromise may represent the best option available. With compromise, each party does not completely receive what it wanted to begin with. However, if what each party had to give up seems balanced and the solution appears *fair* to all sides, then compromise can work quite well. *We cannot emphasize too strongly the importance of fairness.* A compromise can work only if all parties feel the solution is fair, and that no one has *won.* But parties cannot assume they know what "fair" means. Instead, both parties should explain honestly what they believe is fair, and these individual conceptions of fairness should be included as absolute criteria by which to evaluate the final decision.

There are appropriate times and situations to use each one of the conflict management styles described here. However, approaches that are *integrative*—in other words, that focus on helping participants integrate their goals and needs—generally lead to better group decisions for complex tasks. Kuhn and Poole looked at naturally occurring groups in two major U.S. organizations.[17] Integrative conflict styles—collaboration and sometimes compromise—were more effective than avoiding and confrontational styles. In addition, groups that managed their conflicts productively also did other things that made the groups more satisfying to their members, such as establishing stable roles, relationships, and norms for accomplishing tasks.

GLOSSARY

Compromise

Conflict style showing a preference for giving a little and gaining a little to manage the issue

The groups Kuhn and Poole studied tended to formulate norms for handling conflict early in their development and generally didn't change their patterns much. This makes it especially important to pay attention to a group's emerging norms for handling conflict and to discuss such norms if you believe they are counterproductive to good decision making.

Conflict management styles are based on cultural norms and expectations. The advice we give you here, particularly about openly expressing your disagreement, is consistent with norms for the individualistic cultures of the United States and Western Europe. But we would advise you differently for group work in Asia. A recent analysis of conflict management studies has questioned the view that it is always better to express conflict directly.[18] In Asian cultures, which tend to be collectivist, preserving harmony and helping others save face is paramount in group work. In such cultures, open disagreement is considered rude, in part because it damages relationships. Avoidance, accommodation, and indirect expression of disagreement are considered appropriate responses to conflict. In addition, collectivist co-cultures within the United States will grow in number and influence in the future. This means that you will be involved in groups with members from diverse co-cultures with different views about handling conflict. The best overall advice we can give you is to be aware of cultural differences and sensitive to others' reactions to conflict.

EXPRESSING DISAGREEMENT

When you express disagreement, the *how* is just as important as the *what*. This distinction is significant; no matter how valid your disagreement is, if you express it in a tactless or arrogant way, you hurt your chance of benefiting the group. A legitimate concern (the *what*) can be expressed so insensitively (the *how*) that even a rational group member becomes defensive rather than receptive to what you have to say. The following suggestions, summarized in Table 9.5, will help you disagree without damaging relationships with other group members.

1. **Express your disagreement.**

   A disagreement has no chance of helping a group if it is not expressed. An unexpressed disagreement does not disappear—it goes underground, to resurface in inappropriate ways. Avoiding a conflict is only a temporary "solution." Issues can pile up so that eventually a large blowup occurs when each issue could have been handled individually. Remember that disagreements can help a group arrive at the best possible decision or solution, and that failure to express disagreements can lead to groupthink.

2. **Express your disagreement in a timely way.**

   Research demonstrates that *when* you disagree may be just as important as what you say.[19] When group members approach a deadline, they are less tolerant of a member who introduces a dissenting opinion. This suggests you should express your doubts and disagreements early during the discussion. If you save them for later, when the rest of the members are ready to achieve closure, it will be harder to get them to pay attention.

3. **Express your disagreements with rhetorical sensitivity toward the rest of the group.**

   Disagree with the idea, or parts of the idea, without criticizing the person. Suppose you have just suggested that your campus shut down its snack bar at 5 p.m. to cut

TABLE 9.5	How to Disagree Productively

EXPRESS YOUR DISAGREEMENT
- Failure to express doubts and disagreements deprives the group of potentially valuable information and reasoning.

EXPRESS DISAGREEMENT IN A TIMELY WAY
- Don't wait until the deadline is near to speak.

EXPRESS DISAGREEMENTS WITH SENSITIVITY TOWARD OTHERS
- Disagree with the idea, but do not criticize the person.
- Use neutral, not emotionally charged, language.

REACT TO DISAGREEMENT WITH A SPIRIT OF INQUIRY, NOT DEFENSIVENESS
- Ask for criticism of your ideas and opinions.
- Show you are interested in the other's opinion by listening actively and sincerely.
- Clarify misunderstandings that may have occurred.

costs. Which response would you rather hear: "That's stupid! What are the evening students supposed to do, starve?" or "One problem I see is that your suggestion does not consider evening students' needs for food service." The first response implies that the speaker is stupid, arouses defensiveness, and cuts off further examination of the issue. The second response describes a major problem with the suggestion but leaves room for discussion regarding how to cut food service costs. The second response is helpful; the first is not.

Another way to show your sensitivity is to use neutral instead of emotionally charged language. Name-calling or otherwise pushing people's emotional buttons is never helpful. One of us recently attended a meeting where one member, John, who disagreed with another member, Janos, made a snide play on words using Janos' last name. Naturally, Janos was offended and the atmosphere remained tense until John apologized. Disagreeing by making fun of others does not improve the group's decision-making process. Steer clear of words that you think might be offensive; be rhetorically sensitive.

4. **React to disagreement with a spirit of inquiry, not defensiveness.**

Whether you are the group's leader or just a member, you have a lot of power to determine the atmosphere in your group. When someone disagrees with you, if you show that you are interested in what the other member is saying and his or her reasons for disagreeing, you send the right message to the rest of the group. Even if the disagreement was expressed poorly, you do not have to let someone else's insensitivity control your reaction. Listen actively to the person who disagrees, make sure that person has understood your position accurately, clarify any misunderstandings that

TABLE 9.6	**Maximizing Your Chances to Influence the Group**

- Make sure your arguments are of high quality.

- Make sure your arguments are consistent.

- If you are a member of a subgroup, make sure all the subgroup members publicly agree with each other.

may have occurred, and show that you are willing to work together to find the best possible solution.

Kareema's committee had worked for several months on a proposal to change the criteria for promotion in her department. A new member, appointed to the committee to replace someone who had left the department, questioned the committee's preliminary investigation, saying, "I don't see how that's going to work. Seems to me you'll have more problems than you had before." Although Kareema *felt* defensive, she reacted calmly and asked, "Derek, what problems do you see with the proposal?" Derek explained his concerns, several of which uncovered problems Kareema's committee had overlooked. The committee's revised proposal accommodated Derek's concerns. The final proposal was much stronger and was overwhelmingly approved by the rest of the department. Examples like this show how you can make disagreement and conflict work *for* your group rather than against it.

MAXIMIZING YOUR CHANCES TO INFLUENCE THE GROUP

Expressing your disagreement is the only way to make your ideas and reasoning available to the group. Even so, it is often difficult for people who are perceived as group deviants, even beneficial idea deviants, to influence the other members of the group. Whether you stand alone as an idea deviant or belong to a minority subgroup, the following suggestions will help you maximize your influence when you express your disagreement. Table 9.6 summarizes these suggestions.

1. **Make sure your arguments are of high quality.**

   This is the single most important thing that you can do. Garlick and Mongeau found that, although several factors—including the idea deviant's expertise, attractiveness, and job status—affect that person's status within the group, only the quality of the deviant's argument directly influences the other members' attitude change.[20] That means you must think the problem through carefully and be willing to listen to the objections others may have.

2. **Make sure your arguments are consistent.**

   Lisa Gebhart and Renee Meyers found that subgroups expressing minority opinions are more successful if they generally stick to a consistent message.[21] This is especially important during the latter part of a discussion. These authors recommend, however, that a minority subgroup not be so consistent that it appears rigid and unable to understand others' views.

3. **If you are a member of a subgroup, make sure all the subgroup members publicly agree with each other.**

   Subgroups, or coalitions, are a powerful way group members have of influencing each other in conflict.[22] They occur for a variety of reasons. Some form around popular members, some because members are not sure who has the power and who does not. Often, group members form coalitions because they lack resources or power and hope to increase their influence—"power in numbers." However, coalitions containing members who disagree with each other are less influential than coalitions presenting a united front.[23] The subgroup members should meet privately and hash out any disagreements among themselves before they meet with the rest of the group so that they can agree on a consistent message.

NOMINAL GROUP TECHNIQUE

A major advantage of group over individual problem solving is that several heads can be better than one. But capitalizing on that advantage can be difficult. While the number of ideas increases with additional members, the opportunity for conflict also increases. One technique, the **nominal group technique,** can be used by a group to help members reach a decision on a controversial issue without bitterness from a win–lose conflict.

Nominal means "in name only." The nominal group technique capitalizes on the finding that sometimes people working individually while in the presence of others generate more ideas than while interacting as a group. In addition, sometimes dominant members inhibit the participation of quieter members. The nominal group technique gets around this potential problem by alternating between solitary work and group interaction. One organization used the nominal group technique as part of a detailed decision analysis procedure to decide what type of computer system to buy. This complex organization consisted of many different units and subunits that coordinated work with each other, but it also had unique computing needs that had to be satisfied. The nominal group technique helped all these individual units achieve consensus about the best computer system to buy. Participants were satisfied with both the process and the outcome.[24]

In the nominal group technique, members (usually six to nine) work individually in each other's presence by writing their ideas. Then members record the ideas on a chart, discuss them as a group, and finally evaluate them by a ranking procedure until members reach a decision. The following steps, summarized in Figure 9.2, make up the process.

1. **The problem, situation, or question is stated clearly and concisely.**

   Elements of the problem or question are described, and discrepancies between what is desired and what currently exists are explained, often by a member of top management. Care must be taken not to mention possible solutions. Group members can ask questions to clarify or add information about the problem. If the group is large, it may be subdivided into smaller groups, each with its own facilitator.

2. **The coordinator asks participants to generate a list of the features or characteristics of the problem or question.**

   Steps 1 and 2 may be combined; the facilitator presents the problem and moves the group directly to step 3.

FIGURE 9.2   Steps for Conducting the Nominal Group Technique

3. **The coordinator gives the group 5 to 15 minutes to work silently.**

   Each person brainwrites as many solutions or answers to the original question as possible.

4. **Each suggestion is listed and recorded in round-robin fashion on a chart visible to all members.**

   The first person gives one item from his or her list and the recorder lists it. Then the next person gives one item, and so forth, until the master list is complete. If any additional ideas or items occur to people while the list is being compiled, they should add them to the master list. During this step, no discussion of the merits of the suggestions is permitted.

5. **Members clarify the items but do not yet evaluate them.**

   The group discusses each item on the list, but only to clarify or elaborate on it. Any member may ask what a particular item means, but arguing, criticizing, and disagreeing are not permitted during step 5.

6. **Each person chooses his or her top-ranked items.**

   The easiest way to do this is to give each person a set of stickers to place next to his or her most important items. Sometimes participants are instructed to place one sticker by the five most important items. Other times, participants are told they can distribute their stickers however they want, including placing all five on one item. Then the items with the most stickers become the agenda items for the group's discussion.

but provide vending machines with a variety of sandwiches and snacks. In this way, the legitimate interests of each individual are served. The work crew of Cask and Cleaver all had reasons for their positions. Mark and Beth faced huge doctor bills because Beth has a congenital heart defect. Maria recently started a new business. Paul, Mark's former roommate, felt hurt by Mark's indifference to his schedule. All are legitimate feelings and interests and must be dealt with in the discussion if members are to manage their conflict productively.

3. **Invent new options for mutual gain.**

   Group members should become creative at inventing alternatives. A number of techniques, such as brainstorming, are designed to help groups become more inventive. If Roger and Mary's committee had assumed there were only two available options—keeping the snack shop open past 5 p.m. or closing it—members could never have resolved the issue. The same committee later resolved a similar issue with the bookstore by inventing a solution that was not apparent when the committee first began to discuss the issue. You can probably remember other examples in which a group was able to invent a new option that met everyone's interests.

   In our Cask and Cleaver case, the only options initially presented were to start all over again or keep going and ignore Mark's skipped turn. Another option, one that the crew did not consider, was to go back to the point where Mark was skipped, keep everything the same up until then, and start anew from Mark's skipped turn. In fact, Tracey's option effectively solved the problem. She pointed out that while it was not Mark and Beth's fault that Paul and Tom had night classes, it also was not Paul and Tom's fault that Beth needed surgery. She suggested that Mark give his night shift to Tom so he and Beth, who didn't work that night, could spend some time together. Mark saw the logic in Tracey's solution and gave his valued shift to Tom. All members apologized to those whom they had offended. The crew was able to come up with an option that gave them mutual gain given their reasons for their positions.

4. **Insist on using objective criteria.**

   Much wasted time can be saved if members use criteria they agree are fair and appropriate for evaluating solutions. For example, the *Kelley Blue Book* establishes a price range that helps both used-car buyers and sellers determine the fair price for a car. You may want $10,000 for your 15-year-old Toyota Corolla, but both you and potential buyers know that you won't get it! Using prices supplied by the *Blue Book* as criteria allows the negotiation to take place within narrower, more realistic limits.

   The same use of objective criteria occurs in other situations, too. One of us served on a church finance committee charged with reviewing salaries and recommending adjustments. The salaries for the organist and choir director had not been reviewed in several years. Not knowing whether these salaries were reasonable or not, the committee called the local Council of Churches director, who had data about how much organists and choir directors with comparable responsibilities received at other churches of similar size. When the finance committee presented the recommendations to the full board of directors, the recommendations were easy to defend because of the objective criteria used.

Even with the best of intentions, sometimes a group becomes deadlocked when it tries to resolve a conflict. We recommend that groups try to resolve their own conflicts first,

9.3   Should He Go Back to School?

Sam and Tashie have been married for 12 years. Sam wants to quit his job because he is bored and believes they had an agreement that he would be able to complete his education after they had been married a few years. Tashie owns her own company, which is finally getting off the ground, and she doesn't believe they have the money for Sam to leave his job. Select two students to role-play the discussion between Sam and Tashie in front of the class. After the role-play, use the principled negotiation procedure with the entire class to help Sam and Tashie manage the conflict.

People: Ask the role-players how they feel about the argument, themselves, and the other person. Emphasize the importance of recognizing feelings.

Interests: Distinguish between the irreconcilable positions and the interests behind each position. Have the class and the role-players participate in discovering what each person's interests may be.

Options: Ask the class and the role-players to brainstorm creative options for this couple. Emphasize the point that interests may be met in a variety of ways, one of which is bound to be acceptable to both.

Criteria: Explore whether any objective criteria might apply to this couple's dilemma.

but if that isn't possible, a group can try mediation or arbitration. The principled negotiation procedure can be used by an outside facilitator. This may be necessary if the leader has been actively involved in the conflict. Finally, a group may bring in an outside arbitrator with power to settle the dispute. However, these are last resorts. It is far better if a group can resolve its own conflicts.

RESOURCES FOR REVIEW AND DISCUSSION

- Three common myths about conflict are that conflict is always harmful, it is due to misunderstandings, and it can be resolved by good communication.

- Groupthink is the tendency of highly cohesive groups not to examine critically all aspects of a decision; groups experiencing groupthink overestimate their power, evaluate information in a closed-minded and biased way, and experience pressures to conform to group opinions.

- The five common conflict management styles of avoidance, accommodation, competition, collaboration, and compromise are each appropriate in certain circumstances, but styles that encourage members to look for ways to satisfy all participants are usually preferable.

■ Group members can use the nominal group technique, which balances solitary and group work, to help work through potentially contentious discussions.

■ Group members can also use procedures such as principled negotiation, which focuses on people's interests rather than positions, finding creative options, and using objective criteria to resolve conflicts.

1. Rent either *Twelve Angry Men* or *Lord of the Flies*. Watch the movie and observe types of conflicts, how these conflicts were handled, the effects of the conflicts on the group, how decision making was affected by the various conflicts, and what the group could have done to improve its ability to manage conflict. You can do this yourself or you can discuss your observations with others in class who have also watched the video.

2. Think of a group you currently belong to. Recollect two recent conflicts in the group. Write an essay describing the conflict, labeling the type of conflict, and reporting how it was managed. Draw some conclusions about conflict in group interaction from these observations.

3. Divide yourselves into groups and come to a consensus regarding what you would do about each of the following group problems:

a. Ann has missed the first three meetings of the group. For the first two she said she had to work, but she offered no reason for missing the last one. She also has completed none of the work she agreed to do for the group.

b. Bob is a domineering individual who attempts to control the direction of the group. He evaluates each idea as soon as it is presented. As a result, the rest of the members have stopped volunteering suggestions and ideas.

c. The members of the group have fallen into two subgroups, and competition has arisen between the subgroups. If you didn't have to work together, you would have split apart long ago.

 Go to **www.mhhe.com/adamsgalanes6** and **www.mhhe.com/groups** for self-quizzes and weblinks.

Accommodation

Avoidance

Collaboration

Competition

Compromise

Conflict

Devil's Advocate

Groupthink

Nominal Group Technique

Principled Negotiation

 www.mhhe.com/adamsgalanes6

Use the flash cards and crossword puzzles on the Online Learning Center to further your knowledge of these key terms.

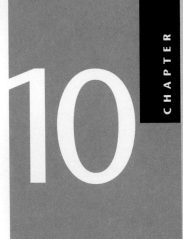

CHAPTER 10

Applying Leadership Principles

CHAPTER OBJECTIVES

After reading this chapter you should be able to:

1. Distinguish between leadership and a leader; differentiate a designated from an emergent leader.

2. Describe the five sources of a leader's power and give an example of each.

3. List and discuss the myths of leadership.

4. Discuss current thinking about leadership.

5. Describe the administrative duties leaders are expected to perform and explain how leaders can perform these effectively.

6. List and explain six tips for leading group discussions.

7. Explain how establishing a climate of trust, developing teamwork, and promoting cooperation can help develop the group.

8. Describe *distributed leadership* and discuss what it means to encourage it.

9. List and explain the ethical guidelines for group leaders.

The College Service Club

TerryAnn was so envious of the close, cohesive executive committee of her service club that she decided to run for office so she could be part of the team. When she was elected president as a junior, she was thrilled. She wanted the club and the executive committee to continue experiencing the same success she had witnessed as a member. Unfortunately, things wouldn't turn out that way. TerryAnn and the rest of the executive committee met soon after the spring election to make plans for the upcoming fall. Although many good ideas surfaced at this meeting, no one wrote them down. TerryAnn was somewhat intimidated by all the seniors on the executive committee, and she was reluctant to assign tasks or even ask the other members to do things. No one else picked up the ball either. Consequently, no one remembered what they had decided or knew who was supposed to do what. Committee members lost valuable summer planning time because they weren't organized. When fall came, they had to scramble to catch up.

TerryAnn's reluctance to guide the process affected both the executive committee and the regular organizational meetings. She made no effort to start the meetings on time, so members got into the habit of coming late. Because there was no agenda, members did not know what they would be discussing or what materials they should bring to the meetings. Discussion was haphazard, jumping from one topic to the next without ever finishing a single subject. No meeting minutes were ever compiled or distributed, so members weren't sure what actions had been decided or who was assigned to what tasks. As a result of the disorganization in the executive committee, service club members became disenchanted with the organization. Membership decreased. As the frustrating year drew to a close, TerryAnn was increasingly depressed because her high hopes for the club had not come close to being realized.

This story could have had a different ending if TerryAnn had known what the other members expected of her. Because she was afraid to be seen as a dictator, she did the exact opposite. But the group members were practically begging for TerryAnn to give them structure and organization so that the club's jobs would get done. TerryAnn's "leadership" did not match what the group needed and expected from her.

In this chapter we will differentiate leadership from leaders, describe the sources of a leader's power, discuss myths about leadership and current thinking about effective leadership, and explain the typical duties of designated small group leaders. In addition, we suggest guidelines to encourage distributed leadership and describe ethical leader behavior.

Leadership and Leaders

Effective leadership is an essential element in successful groups. Most scholars believe that *every* member of a group, not just the leader, can help provide leadership. We now look more closely at how leaders and members actually provide leadership to the group.

LEADERSHIP

What is leadership? Hackman and Johnson define **leadership** as "human (symbolic) communication which modifies the attitudes and behaviors of others in order to meet shared group goals and needs."[1] This definition acknowledges that communication is the central, essential activity of leading, and implies three things. First, leadership is accomplished through communication—what a group member actually says and does in person-to-person interaction. Leadership involves persuasion and discussion, not psychological coercion or physical force. Second, leadership consists of those behaviors that *help* the group achieve shared goals. A rebel—even a popular one others admire—would not be considered a group leader if the rebellious actions interfere with the group's accomplishment of its goals. Finally, the term *modifies* in the definition suggests that group leaders must be adaptable to the changing conditions of the group. Thus, leadership is a dynamic process of exchange, not a fixed quality. To modify others' behaviors in support of group goals, leaders must be aware of the others' needs, beliefs, and attitudes. Leadership does not exist in a vacuum; it is a shared property of the group that is created through communicative interaction.

SOURCES OF POWER AND INFLUENCE

Leadership implies **influence,** which is the use of interpersonal power to modify others' actions—a communicative activity. Where does this ability to influence others come from? Why do some people have an easy time getting others to work with them, but others do not? Raven and French identified five sources of interpersonal power that provide someone with the ability to influence others: legitimate, reward, punishment, expert, and referent power.[2] Table 10.1 summarizes the five.

A member's title or position confers **legitimate power.** For instance, other members expect their president or chair to call meetings, establish an agenda, and coordinate tasks. Just having the title of "chair," whether the individual was appointed or elected to the position, gives that individual the ability and right to influence the others. TerryAnn did not recognize that she had the legitimate power, as president, to do such things as asking another member to take meeting notes or assigning tasks.

Reward power comes from someone's ability to give others what they want and value, and **punishment power** comes from the ability to take those things away. Both rewards and punishments can be tangible or intangible. For instance, Sandra rewards her fellow members with praise and encouragement. These intangible items, along with others such

TABLE 10.1	**Sources of Power and Influence**

Legitimate Power: Leader is elected or appointed; has a title (chair, coordinator, etc.).

Reward or Punishment: Leader can give or take away items of value; may be tangible (money, promotion, titles) or intangible (praise, acceptance).

Expert Power: Leader has information, knowledge, or skills needed and valued by the group.

Referent Power: Leader is admired and respected; other group members try to copy his or her behavior.

as attention and smiling, have great power to influence others. Similarly, frowning, ignoring someone, asking a member to redo an assignment, and so forth are intangible ways of punishing group members. Tangible rewards can include such things as special privileges, monetary bonuses, and promotions. Tangible punishments may include taking away special privileges, giving someone undesirable assignments or work shifts, or even firing a member. **Coercion** is one extreme form of punishment involving threats or force to make a member comply. Such tactics can breed resentment, sabotage, and rebellion. We think coercion is inappropriate to use in small groups.

Another form of power is expertise. An individual with **expert power** is perceived by other members to have knowledge or skill valuable to the group. Becky's group called her the "PowerPoint Queen" because she could do anything with PowerPoint and had a good eye for design. Members took her advice whenever they had to design a public presentation of any kind.

Finally, a person with **referent power** is someone others admire and want to be like. Most of us want the people we like to like us back. That desire gives them tremendous power over us. Since we want them to like us, we will often do what we think they want us to do—even, sometimes, when we know that what they're asking us to do is wrong! In high school, one of us belonged to a social group led by a "cool" informal leader with considerable referent power. Members of her group accepted Sue's opinions about a variety of issues: how to dress, whom to date, what school activities to join. One day, Sue suggested that the group ditch school for the afternoon. Group members did—much to their dismay when they all got caught!

A group leader's influence usually stems from more than just one of these power sources. Sue, for example, had referent power because she was cool. But she also had power to reward and punish—she could invite you to her next party or she could punish you by leaving you out. President Reagan, too, possessed referent power as well as legitimate power, the ability to reward and punish, and expertise about the political process. As you can guess, the more sources of power within a group, the greater a member's ability to influence others.

Thus far, we have equated group leadership with the ability to influence others, and we have examined the sources from which that influence may stem. Now we turn our attention to the specific people who exercise influence—the leaders of a group.

GLOSSARY

Coercion

Using threats of force to make a member comply

Expert Power

Interpersonal influence that stems from someone's perceived knowledge or skill

Referent Power

Influence due to a person's ability to be liked and admired

LEADERS

A **leader** is *any* person who exercises interpersonal influence to help a group attain its goals. That's what makes distributed leadership, discussed in Chapter 1, possible. There are several important implications to this statement. First, this definition of *leader* implies that all individuals in a group can (and should) supply some of the needed leadership services to the group. Second, it does not require that a leader hold a particular title or office. Any member of a group, with or without a title, can at times function as a group's leader. Third, the definition assumes that *communication* is the process through which a person actually leads others. In other words, rather than assuming that leaders are born or must have particular titles, this definition suggests that leaders *perform behaviors* that help a group achieve its goals. We next discuss the two types of leaders found in groups.

Designated Leader.   The **designated leader** is the group's legitimate leader who holds a title (for example, chair, coordinator, moderator, facilitator, president) that identifies him or her as having a specific position in the group. Usually group members expect the designated leader to perform a variety of coordination functions for the group. The designated leader may be elected to the position by group members, or may be appointed by the group's parent organization or supervisor.

Emergent Leader.   An **emergent leader** is a person with the same status as other members in a group of peers, but who gradually emerges as an informal leader. Sue, in our earlier example, was an emergent leader—her group didn't elect her to the post, but by virtue of her personality and influence, she emerged as the group's leader. Most of the groups you belong to will have a designated leader, but understanding how informal leaders emerge will give you insight into what constitutes effective group leadership.

Studies conducted at the University of Minnesota reveal how informal leaders emerge from an initially leaderless group.[3] Researchers observed college students placed in leaderless task groups and found that, at first, all members initially have the potential to be recognized as the leader by the others. However, members who don't speak up or are uninformed are quickly eliminated from consideration. Next to be eliminated are members who, compared to the rest, are overly bossy or dogmatic. Those who remain as potential leaders speak frequently; are well informed on the issues facing the group; and are open-minded, democratic, sensitive, and skilled in expressing ideas for the group. The individual who ultimately emerges as a group's leader is the member who seems able to provide the best blend of task and people skills for that particular group. Especially important is the ability to coordinate the work of other members by communicating effectively with them. Subsequent studies have found that communication relevant to the group's task is the one factor that significantly predicts leadership emergence.[4]

Other behaviors or characteristics related to leadership emergence have been found. They include effective listening,[5] self-monitoring (the ability to pay attention to how others are responding to you and to adjust your own behavior in response),[6] being extraverted and sociable,[7] and intelligence.[8] Although early small group research suggested that men usually emerge as leaders, biological sex now seems irrelevant, although psychological gender is not. Task-oriented women emerge as group leaders as often as task-oriented men. In one study of groups of women, those who emerged as leaders combined intelligence with the personality characteristics of masculinity or androgyny (exhibiting both masculine and feminine characteristics).[9] In mixed-gender groups, regardless of sex, masculine and androgynous members emerged as leaders more often than feminine and undifferentiated members.[10] Groups appear to choose leaders based on performance. Research into gender and leadership shows that men and women lead equally well, and group members are equally satisfied with both male and female leaders.[11]

Although most groups have a designated leader, the process of leadership emergence teaches you two things about being a designated leader. First, emergent leaders influence primarily through referent, expert, and reward power. Without a title, they must rely on communication skills to lead the group. By definition, they have the support of other group members. So even though you may hold the title of leader (or chair, president, co-ordinator, and so forth) in your group, it will benefit you to act like the kind of person who would also emerge as the group's leader. Second, the person who emerges as a leader in one group may not emerge as leader in another. Each group's situation is different, re-quiring a different blend of leader skills. The type of task as well as the personalities and preferences of the members influence what type of leadership is comfortable to a given group. For example, in graduate school, one of us participated in a group where all other members were engineers. They were highly task-oriented and impatient with chitchat, which they saw as irrelevant to the task. In contrast, many groups of communication stu-dents are sociable and would perceive an exclusively task-focused leader as hostile or un-caring. As leader, pay attention to the group's needs so you can adjust your behavior appropriately.

Now that we have talked about leadership and leaders, including how they emerge in a group, we will turn our attention to several misconceptions people have about leadership.

10.1   Informal Leadership in the Group

APPLY NOW

Think of a group you belong to that does not have an official leader. Most such groups will have an informal leader. Picture that person as you answer the questions below. When you are finished, divide into groups of five or six and share your observations with one another. Are there any common characteristics or behaviors that the emergent lead-ers demonstrate?

1. What are the sources of power that give your informal leader the ability to influence? List as many as apply, and provide specific examples of how your leader used his or her power.

2. If you found yourself in a high-stakes project group with this person (for example, in a group that had to complete a project for a major portion of a course grade), would this person emerge as leader in that group? Would this person's leadership skills be a good fit for the project group? Why or why not?

3. Are there other individuals in the group who demonstrate leadership skills? If so, who are they? What sources of power do they possess? Provide examples.

Myths about Leadership

Students usually say that leaders "control the actions of the other members," "give orders," and generally "tell people what to do." In this section we examine several other pervasive myths about leadership.

1. **Leadership is a personality trait that individuals possess in varying degrees.**

   From Plato to the 1950s, the study of leadership consisted of a search for the traits that make people leaders. These traits included intelligence, attractiveness, psychological dominance, and size. However, strict trait approaches to studying leadership possess several flaws. First, there is no trait or set of traits that leaders have but followers do not. No trait differentiates leaders from members.

   A second flaw in the trait approach is the underlying assumption that all leadership situations call for the same trait or set of traits. Think about this for a moment. Does the leader of a classroom discussion group need the same traits as the leader of a military platoon? Do both situations require the same approach? No single set of traits will identify the best leader for any given group or situation.

   A third flaw in the trait approach relates directly to the concept of *trait* as something innate, the belief that leaders are born, not made. If you aren't born with the characteristics of a leader (whatever those may be), you will not become a leader. Instead, leadership consists of *behaving in ways that can be learned* (at least up to a point). Consider, for a moment, Candy Lightner, the woman who developed MADD, Mothers Against Drunk Drivers. Ms. Lightner was an ordinary single parent, not a recognized leader, before a drunken driver killed her daughter. Nothing in her previous background or experience could have predicted that she would become the leader of a national organization. But she cared enough to do the hard work of learning to lead. So can you.

2. **There is an ideal leadership style, no matter what the situation.**

   Since the 1950s, a number of researchers have examined the behaviors associated with leadership, including the styles displayed by various leaders. Several studies indicated that leaders perform both *task-oriented* and *relationship-oriented* behaviors.[12] Leaders could rate high on either one, neither, or both of these dimensions. Many people believed that the ideal style of leadership was one rated high on both task and relationship dimensions, so many organizations instituted training programs to teach their employees how to be simultaneously task- and relationship-oriented.

   Other researchers have examined three general leadership styles: autocratic (authoritarian), democratic (participatory), and laissez-faire (noninvolved). *Autocratic* leaders are primarily task-oriented people who personally make the decisions for the group and control the group's process. They say things like, "Here's what I've decided we'll do." They alone decide the group's agenda, select procedures the group will follow, and decide who will speak when. Highly authoritarian leaders can stifle group members who are expert, creative, and enthusiastic, but their groups can be very productive.

   Democratic leaders want all the group members to participate in decision making, and so are more relationship-oriented than autocratic leaders. They say things like, "What ideas do you have for solving our problem?" Democratic leaders suggest

For more information on analyzing famous leaders, go to the Online Learning Center at **www.mhhe.com/ adamsgalanes6**

but do not coerce. They try to discover the wishes of the group members and help them achieve their common goals. They encourage members to develop the group's agenda as well as to determine what procedures the group will use. Discussants can speak freely within the group. When members propose ideas, they are considered to be the property of the group as a whole. Democratic leaders see their function as helping the group accomplish what the members want, as long as it is part of the group's purpose or charge. Members of groups with democratic leaders tend to be more satisfied, to participate more actively in meetings, to demonstrate more commitment to group decisions, and to be more innovative than members of groups with either autocratic or laissez-faire leaders.[13]

Laissez-faire "leaders," who consider themselves to be no different from the other members, display a hands-off style that really does not provide much leadership. They say things like, "Do what you want; it doesn't matter to me." They create a void that forces the other members to step in or flounder without coordination. This is the mistake TerryAnn made, but the others weren't able or willing to step into the void she created. Occasionally the other members of groups led by laissez-faire leaders blend their efforts to lead the group successfully, but more often such groups end up wasting a lot of time or following the structure provided by an autocratic leader who emerges and takes charge. Only groups of highly motivated experts tend to be more productive and satisfied with laissez-faire leaders than democratic leaders.[14]

Research looking for an ideal leadership style came up with inconsistent findings. While most group members prefer the democratic rather than the autocratic style, some groups composed of authoritarian members actually prefer the more authoritarian style. Plus, autocratic groups sometimes complete more work than democratic groups. About the only consistent finding was that groups prefer either the democratic or the autocratic style to the laissez-faire style.

A recent review of studies of democratic and autocratic leadership suggests that several factors in combination with leadership style influence a group's productivity.[15] Democratic leadership seems to be more productive when it occurs in natural, real-life settings and when the group's task is a complex one. In addition, member satisfaction with democratic leadership is not guaranteed.

The styles approach oversimplifies the complexities of groups as open systems. For example, consider the following two groups: (1) an advertising agency's creative group, in which the members have worked together successfully for two years, and (2) an outdoor survival group of young adolescent boys, strangers to each other, none of whom has ever been camping. Would you recommend the same style of leadership to the coordinator of the creative group and to the adult adviser of the survival group? Everything suggests a democratic approach with the creative group and a more controlling approach with the young boys. Most of us would agree that no one style is right for all situations.

The styles approach also assumes that a particular group will have the same needs over its lifetime. But just as different groups vary in their needs for different leadership services, a single group's needs will change greatly over time as well. Early in a group's history the more inexperienced members may appreciate a take-charge leader, but as group members become more experienced, they may prefer less control.

Most people today discredit the idea that there is an ideal leadership style no matter what the occasion. Rather, a number of factors such as the experience of the members, how long they have been together, how successful they have been in the past, how interesting the job is, and whether or not there is an impending deadline all contribute to determining the most appropriate style.

3. **Leaders get other people to do the work for them.**

When some students are elected or appointed to leadership positions, they assume that their job is to tell other people what to do and often seem surprised that it doesn't work. Recently, the president of a campus organization was disgusted that a colleague failed to complete an assignment for the organization. "I told her what to do, and I told her we needed the information for today's meeting," she said. She didn't understand that just telling someone to do something doesn't ensure that it will happen. If you think your position as leader makes your job easier, think again.

Current Ideas about Leadership

Now that you know that small group leadership isn't a trait, a style, or bossing people around, let's discuss what it *does* involve. Several contemporary ideas about leadership will help you be more effective as a group leader. The ideas we discuss next complement each other.

THE FUNCTIONAL CONCEPT OF GROUP LEADERSHIP

The **functional concept** of leadership contains two premises. First, this concept assumes that certain important functions must be performed for the group to reach its goals: task-related and people-related functions. Task-related functions, such as *initiating* discussion or action, *offering opinions, making suggestions,* and *elaborating* on other members' ideas, are behaviors directly related to getting the group's job done. People-related functions, such as *harmonizing, gatekeeping,* and *relieving tension,* help members work as a team.

Second, the functional concept suggests that performing those functions is the responsibility of *all* the group members, not just the individual designated as the group's leader. One individual cannot give a group everything it needs. We haven't seen anyone with all that knowledge and skills. Also, having only the leader supply everything a group needs deprives the other members of the chance to develop their skills and talents. People want to contribute. Every member of a group needs to know that he or she is valued. When that occurs, members tend to be committed and loyal, and group cohesiveness is high.

For example, one project manager at a Fortune 500 corporation was terrific at motivating and developing her staff. Staff member Tina was a fabulous presenter. Carol could interpret data and incorporate it effectively into the group's reports. Roger was a gifted writer, and Ty was super-organized, with the ability to keep track of where everyone was on a project. Tamika had a quirky sense of humor and could always lighten things up if meetings got tense. These staff members worked as a *team,* with no one member dominating and the leader encouraging them to use all their talents on behalf of the team.

If all members are responsible for providing needed leadership functions, what is your job as a group's leader? In Chapter 1, we suggested that the leader's job is *completing* the

GLOSSARY

Functional Concept

Groups need to have certain functions performed, and all group members can and should perform needed functions

group by supplying any needed functions (services) that other members are not providing or at least seeing that someone supplies them.[16] This gives the designated leader a lot to do. The leader must constantly monitor the group's progress, identify what the group needs at any time, decide whether those functions are currently being performed adequately by other members, and, if not, provide them or encourage someone else to do so. For example, when John notices that Rada has not offered an opinion about an important issue, he deliberately asks Rada her opinion. If the group seems confused, John summarizes and clarifies, or calls on Kim, the group's recorder, to reorient the group. When he sees the group becoming tense, he may joke or suggest a 10-minute break.

The functional approach requires leaders to diagnose what functions are needed as well as to supply them. That means you have to be smart, to figure out what is needed, and flexible, to adapt accordingly. But you can call on your fellow members to help you, because this approach assumes that all members can learn a variety of behaviors and can function as leaders in certain circumstances.

THE CONTINGENCY CONCEPT OF GROUP LEADERSHIP

Related to the functions approach, the **contingency concept** holds that appropriate leadership behavior depends on the situation. As we noted earlier, it doesn't seem reasonable that the same leadership style should be used for a classroom discussion group as for a platoon during a firefight. TerryAnn's laid-back manner of leading did not work in her particular service club, but with a group of experienced pros, it may have proven quite effective. There are several contingency approaches; we will focus on those developed by Hersey and Blanchard.

Contingency approaches suggest that leaders should consider several factors before deciding the specific leadership services appropriate for the group. Among these factors are the type of task, how well the members work together, and how well members work with the leader.[17] A major factor that affects the way a leader should act is the maturity level, or readiness, of the followers.[18] Hersey and Blanchard have provided a model, shown in Figure 10.1, to help match leadership style to the readiness level of the followers. In general, the more experienced, interested, and motivated the members are, the less direction is needed from the leader.

Hersey and Blanchard's model, tempered with your common sense and knowledge of group leadership, helps you know how to adapt. If group members are unable, are unwilling, or don't have enough information to complete the task on their own, they are low in readiness. *Telling* can be an effective leadership style. The leader needs to give them specific instructions and provide close supervision of their work: "Our goal is to increase sales by 15 percent, and here's what I want you to do . . . " The leader tells the members what, how, and when to do something, and the members have little say in the matter. Telling demonstrates high-task and low-relationship behavior.

With low to moderate readiness, group members are usually willing but do not have the skills or experience necessary to perform well. In this case, the leader takes a *selling* approach by providing much of the direction but seeking members' enthusiastic support for this direction: "One of our goals is to increase sales by 15 percent, and I'd really like your input about how we can do that." Two-way communication occurs as the leader encourages members to ask for explanations and additional information. The leader's goal

FIGURE 10.1   Model of Situational Leadership

SOURCE: Based on Paul Hersey/Kenneth Blanchard, *Management of Organizational Behavior: Utilizing Human Resources,* 4th ed. (Englewood Cliffs, NJ: Prentice Hall). Reprinted by permission.

is to promote member enthusiasm while providing the guidance needed to complete the task well. Selling is both high-task and high-relationship oriented.

With members of moderate to high readiness, the leader can pay less attention to the demands of the task and concentrate instead on the relationships among members: "How is the sales campaign going? What can I do to help you?" Here, followers have the skills to perform the job but may feel insecure about taking action or need coordination to work out a set of roles and division of labor. The leader's supportive, democratic style is called *participating* because decision making is shared and the leader's role is mostly one of facilitation and coordination. All members share in leading the group. When members reach this level of readiness, anyone in the group could probably serve as its designated leader.

In a fully ready, mature group, members are both able and willing to perform. They need little task-related supervision or encouragement. In this situation, the *delegating* style is appropriate; the leader turns the responsibility for the group over to the group: "Let me know if you need anything." All members (including the leader) are equal in responsibility. This relatively low-task, low-relationship style is appropriate where a more active leadership style might be perceived as interference. However, even when the group is fully ready, the leader must still monitor the changing conditions of the group and be ready to step in to perform additional services the group may need. This was TerryAnn's style, but her followers were not at this level of readiness.

Most of us have preferred styles of leading. We are not infinitely capable of altering our behavior, and some of us are more flexible than others. Some leadership experts advise us to look for situations that need our preferred styles or to encourage supportive and capable members of the group to assist the leaders.

One theme unites the contingency and functional approaches to leadership: leadership is a property of the *group,* not of the individual who happens to have the title of "leader." This is called **distributed leadership,** which explicitly acknowledges that each group member should perform the communication behaviors needed to move the group toward its goal. Our society's democratic values suggest that participation by everyone is a healthy and desirable goal. Gastil, making a case for democratic leadership, argues that "democratic group leadership amounts to giving group members responsibility, improving the general abilities and leadership skills of the other members, and assisting the group in its decision-making process."[19] This is precisely what the functional approach to leadership suggests: All group members are capable of performing the variety of functions a group needs, even though no *one* person is capable of supplying everything. In one study, overall leadership activity by all members was found to be more related to productivity than activity of the designated leader alone.[20] Distributing the leadership functions is good not only for the members themselves but for the group as well. We talk more about how to encourage distributed leadership later in this chapter.

We have discussed major myths surrounding group leadership, presented current thinking about leadership, and promoted the idea of distributed leadership. It is now time to investigate what members expect from their leaders.

GLOSSARY

Distributed Leadership

Each group member can and should provide leadership services to a group

What Good Leaders Do

A group leader has a lot of work to do, sometimes more than any other member. Recent studies have described what excellent group leaders do to help their teams succeed.[21] **First, excellent leaders establish the group's goal and make sure the group starts in the right direction.** Usually, the goals are put into writing, perhaps as part of a team charter that spells out the charge, area of freedom, and scope of the project. They take the time to ensure that everyone understands and supports the goal, even to the extent of asking a completely unsupportive member to leave the team.

Second, excellent leaders mold the group members into a team with a collaborative climate for working together. They take team building seriously and recognize that to accomplish good group work members must trust one another and feel free to contribute. Excellent leaders constantly monitor the group's interactions to ensure that members are working collaboratively and intervene when they perceive a problem.

Third, excellent leaders never lose sight of the group's task and its progress toward completion of that task. That means they keep track at all times of where the group is in relation to its goals. Along with keeping the group moving forward, they are able to paint the "big picture" so that members know what has been accomplished and what still needs to be done. In that regard, they manage group members' uncertainty about complex tasks. They manage the group's priorities, in part so the group does not get bogged down in unessential

10.2   Which Contingency Style Is Most Appropriate?

You have been asked to conduct a workshop on group leadership for a major corporation in your city. You have selected the contingency approach to leadership as the focus of your workshop. The corporation has asked that your workshop contain several activities to give the participants "hands-on" experience with current thinking about group leadership. You have decided that one of those activities will involve application of the contingency model to several different kinds of groups. Your task now is to construct the activity. To do so, you need the materials to set up the activity and the answers to the activity.

You first will ask the participants to create a matrix that lists the four Hersey and Blanchard leadership styles (participating, selling, delegating, and telling) across the top. Under each style, list the contingencies that make that style appropriate, along with how each contingency is likely to affect the style. Next, you will give participants a list of situations and ask them to determine what style is most appropriate using their matrix. The list of situations includes the following:

1. A group of college students studying together for a final exam.

2. A heart transplant team.

3. A task force of neighbors trying to rid the neighborhood of crack dealers.

4. A group of student senators planning the senate agenda for the following month.

5. A self-managed work group of employees assembling an automobile.

6. A group of four grown children planning their parents' 50th wedding anniversary party.

You will ask participants to use their matrix to determine the appropriate style for each of these. To be prepared to direct discussion after the participants have finished this part of the activity, you must first participate in the activity yourself.

1. Construct the matrix, as you will ask the participants to do.

2. Apply the matrix to the six situations listed.

matters. They also manage the individual members' performance by making sure members are contributing appropriately and by working with them as needed if they are not.

Fourth, consistent with the leadership approaches discussed earlier, excellent leaders develop their members' talents by encouraging them to assume leadership responsibilities for the group. That builds members' confidence in themselves and the team. Excellent leaders also demonstrate appreciation for the work members do on behalf of the team.

Finally, excellent group leaders do not take their leadership for granted. They work at it, think about it, and consciously try to improve their own leadership skills.

TABLE 10.2	**Major Duties Leaders Are Expected to Perform**
PERFORMING ADMINISTRATIVE DUTIES	Planning and preparing for meetings, keeping members informed, following up between meetings, making sure the group keeps complete written records
LEADING GROUP DISCUSSION	Starting discussions and keeping them on track, encouraging participation, stimulating members' creative and critical thinking
DEVELOPING THE GROUP	Fostering a productive and supporting climate; developing teamwork, cooperation, and trust

WHAT GROUP MEMBERS EXPECT LEADERS TO DO

Group members expect that their leaders will be competent, committed, and work for the good of the group. In particular, most group members in the United States assume their designated leaders will provide services in three major categories, described briefly in Table 10.2: performing administrative duties, leading group discussions, and developing the group.[22] The behaviors of excellent leaders presented earlier fall into these three categories. The following information can serve as your concise leader's manual whenever you find yourself elected or appointed designated leader of a group.

PERFORMING ADMINISTRATIVE DUTIES

Leaders should plan for meetings, follow up on members' assignments, and make sure the group's written records are complete. TerryAnn's performance was particularly weak in these areas.

Planning for Meetings.　As leader, you must plan meetings so you don't waste other members' time. Here is a set of guidelines you can follow:

1. **Define the purpose of the meeting and communicate it clearly to the members.**

   Don't have a meeting if there is no reason for it. If a meeting is needed, state the purpose clearly. "To talk about what we're going to do this year" is too vague; "to establish a list of priorities we want to accomplish within the next six months" is clear and specific. Tell the members exactly what outcomes should be produced at the meeting, such as a written report, an oral recommendation, plans for a party, a decision made, and so forth.

2. **Make sure members know the place, starting time, and closing time for the meeting.**

   Let members know this ahead of time and stick to those starting and ending times. In addition, state the meeting place exactly. "At the library" is vague and confusing.

"How about some little pads and pencils?"

It's the leader's responsibility to make sure members have all the supplies they need. (© The New Yorker Collection; 1985 Arnie Levin from cartoonbank.com. All Rights Reserved.)

Some members may go to the lobby, while others to the student lounge. "In room 302 of the library" eliminates confusion.

Although the leader is responsible for communicating this information to members, this task can be delegated to someone else (i.e., a secretary).

3. **If special resource people are needed at the meeting, advise and prepare them.**

Groups often need information and advice from specialists. A personnel committee may need the advice of a psychologist or lawyer; a student group may need to consult with the parking services manager before recommending changes in parking policies. Make sure invited guests know what to prepare and what to expect at the meeting.

4. **Make all necessary physical arrangements.**

Reserve the room, arrange the seats properly, and bring needed materials (e.g., notepads, pencils, microphones, tape recorders).

Following up on Meetings.   Generally two kinds of follow-up are needed: reminding group members of assignments and serving as liaison with other groups.

1. **Keep track of member assignments.**

The leader must make sure that members know what their assignments are and when they are due. Keep written records of assignments, perhaps as part of the group's regular minutes. Keep in touch with members between meetings by telephone or e-mail to monitor their progress. Had TerryAnn done these things throughout the summer following her initial planning meeting as president, her term might have been memorable for positive rather than negative reasons.

2. **Serve as liaison with other groups.**

   The leader is the group's spokesperson. This means the leader represents the group to other groups and the media, answers questions about the group and its work, and keeps the parent organization informed. For example, the chair of each subcommittee working on the Ozarks Public Television merger with the university, described in Chapter 6, was simultaneously a member of the steering committee overseeing the merger. This made liaison and coordination easy.

Managing the Group's Written Communication.   Any group needs written messages to provide continuity from meeting to meeting and to serve as the group's collective memory. As leader, you may delegate these activities to a secretary or ask for a volunteer, but you are still responsible for making sure they get done.

1. **A meeting notice and agenda should be sent to each member before each meeting.**

   Meeting notices are reminders of a meeting's date, starting and ending times, location, and purpose. Often, a meeting notice is mailed or e-mailed along with the meeting's **agenda,** the list of items to be discussed at the meeting in chronological order. The agenda helps members prepare for the meeting—nothing wastes time like having a meeting where members have no clue what will be discussed and no ability to prepare. If a meeting involves consideration of something like a special report, that report should be provided along with the agenda. In this age of computers and faxes, it is easy to help members do a good job by giving them all the relevant information they need ahead of time.

2. **Keep personal notes to keep track of what is going on.**

   Making notes helps you focus your listening so you won't forget what the group is discussing. These should be very brief—just enough to help you keep track of such things as important facts, proposed ideas, major interpretations, assignments you and others have accepted, and anything else important to the discussion.

3. **Keep minutes of each meeting so you will have a record of what you did.**

   Minutes are notes of what occurred at each meeting. They are distributed to members after the meeting and are legally required for some groups, such as governmental committees. Even if not required, keeping minutes is a good idea—otherwise, like TerryAnn's group, members forget important information and neglect to complete assignments. Minutes contain summary information, not details. Records of important actions should be contained in a group's minutes, including all conclusions, decisions, and assignments. However, because members need to express themselves freely, some things should *not* be contained in group minutes. These include such things as confidential information, sensitive information, who proposed a course of action, how anyone voted (unless that is required by law), or who provided what information. Minutes can be presented in a variety of different formats, two of which are shown in Figure 10.2.

FIGURE 10.2   Examples of Group Minutes Using Two Different Formats

---

Minutes of November 16, 2005, Meeting of Committee A (Version 1)

Committee A held a special meeting at 1:30 p.m. on Wednesday, November 16, 2005, in room 14 of the Jones Library.

Attendance: Walter Bradley, Marlynn Jones, George Smith, Barbara Trekheld, Michael Williams

Absent: Jantha Calamus, Peter Shiuoka

1. The minutes of the November 6 meeting were approved as distributed.

2. Two nominations for membership in the graduate faculty were considered. A subcommittee of Bradley and Trekheld reported that their investigation indicates that Dr. Robert Jordan met all criteria for membership. It was moved that Professor Jordan be recommended to Dean Bryant for membership in the graduate faculty. The vote was unanimously in favor.

   The nomination of Professor Andrea Long was discussed; it was concluded that she met all criteria, and that the nomination had been processed properly. It was moved that Professor Long be recommended for appointment to the graduate faculty. The motion passed unanimously.

3. Encouragement of grant activity. Discussion next centered on the question of how to encourage more faculty members to submit proposals for funding grants. Several ideas were discussed. It was moved that we recommend to President Yardley that

   a. A policy be established to grant reduced teaching loads to all professional faculty who submit two or more grant proposals in a semester.

   b. Ten percent of all grant overhead be returned to the department that obtained the grant for use in any appropriate way.

This motion was approved unanimously.

FIGURE 10.2 *Concluded*

Minutes of November 16, 2005, Meeting of Committee A (Version 2)

Attendance: Walter Bradley, Marlynn Jones, George Smith, Barbara Trekheld, Michael Williams (chair)

Members absent: Jantha Calamus, Peter Shiuoka

Topic	Discussion	Actions/ recommendations
Minutes of 11/16/05	None	Approved as distributed
Nominations for graduate faculty membership	Subcommittee of Bradley and Trekheld reported that both Dr. Robert Jordan and Dr. Andrea Long meet all criteria and should be recommended to Dean Bryant for membership.	Recommendation passed unanimously, for Drs. Jordan and Long
Grant activity	Discussion centered on how to encourage faculty members to submit proposals for funding grants. After discussion of several proposals, motion was made to recommend to President Yardley that	Motion to submit the two recommendations to Pres. Yardley passed unanimously
	1. Professional faculty who submit two or more grant proposals in a semester be given reduced teaching loads.	
	2. Ten percent of all grant overhead be returned to the department that obtained the grant, to use in any appropriate way.	

Respectfully submitted,

George Smith, Secretary

4. **Keep in a permanent file copies of any reports, resolutions, or recommendations made by a group.**

As with minutes, these should become part of the group's permanent record. Often, a group's end product is a major written report submitted to the parent organization, with a brief oral presentation by the designated leader. The leader is responsible for submitting the report by a particular deadline, but normally one or two members actually write the report. Usually, a draft is given to all members ahead of time for suggestions and revisions, followed by discussion and agreement on the final version. All committee members sign the final report.

Sometimes a group's final product is a resolution of a motion the leader will make during a meeting of the parent organization. In that case, members of the group often accompany the leader and are available to answer questions, make supporting speeches, and counter objections. A common format for motions and resolutions can be found in any comprehensive parliamentary manual, such as *Robert's Rules of Order Revised,* if the organization does not have its own manual that must be followed.

LEADING GROUP DISCUSSIONS

One of your most important duties as designated leader is coordinating discussions so that they are productive. Plan how you will start the meeting, keep the discussion organized, encourage all members to participate, and stimulate both creative and critical thinking. You also should monitor the group so that what is not accomplished at one meeting can be addressed at the next. This was TerryAnn's most crucial failing.

Initiating Discussions.   Opening remarks set the stage for the meeting and help members begin to focus on the group's task. Here are guidelines for you to follow:

1. **Help reduce primary tensions, especially with new groups.**

Members may need to be introduced to each other. Name tags may be needed. An icebreaker or other social activity may be used to help members get to know one another.

2. **Briefly review the purpose of the meeting, the specific outcomes desired, and the area of freedom of the group.**

Members should have been informed of these before the meeting, but some members may want clarification. Discussing them early helps prevent misunderstandings later. Food helps! It's amazing what coffee and snacks can do to relax people.

3. **Give members informational and organizational handouts.**

These may include informational sheets, an agenda, outlines to guide the discussion, copies of things to be discussed, and so forth.

4. **See that special roles are established as needed.**

Decide what roles are needed and how they will be handled. Most groups appoint a recorder to keep written records of meetings. Decide whether these positions will be rotated or handled by only one individual.

5. **Suggest procedures to follow.**

Members should know whether decisions will be made by consensus or majority vote, and whether the group will follow the small group procedures recommended

10.1   Group Leaders and the Use of Technology

MEDIA AND TECHNOLOGY

This chapter has introduced a number of leadership functions. The leader must facilitate communication before, during, and after meetings; ensure that appropriate materials are provided to group members; and guarantee that a historical record of the meeting, usually in the form of minutes, is kept.

Technology can help group leaders manage information. For example, e-mail can be used to disseminate agendas and other written material before meetings; Web pages can display minutes of previous meetings; and computer networks can store documents and other materials used by the group.

For groups with virtually unlimited access to technology, someone must help coordinate how technology will be used. If you were designing a "wish list" for technology resources for a group you belong to (for example, a study group, a student group, a work team, etc.), what would you want? Your group may already have access to e-mail, for example. How should group members use e-mail? What other technology resources would be useful to your group and how would you suggest using them?

Go to
www.mhhe.com/ adamsgalanes6 for additional weblink activities.

by *Robert's Rules of Order Revised* or another group technique. We recommend that you suggest procedures to the group, then ask the members to accept, modify, or suggest alternative procedures. (If bylaws or other laws impose specific procedures on the group, such as on a jury, you won't have this flexibility.)

6. **Ask a clear question to help members focus on the first substantive issue on the agenda.**

   This helps launch the group into the substantive portion of the meeting. You may want to review the examples of discussion questions in Table 4.2. A group leader might open the group's meeting this way: "At this meeting, we must decide which two of our five job applicants we should interview in person. You all received copies of the résumés prior to the meeting. Unless you'd rather proceed in a different way, I suggest we go in alphabetical order and assess each person's strengths and weaknesses against the criteria we adopted at our last meeting. After we've talked about each one, we can compare them to determine our top two. Does that seem OK? [Wait for feedback.] Fine, then let's look at James Adams's résumé first." Such a statement makes the meeting's goals, procedures, and desired outcomes clear from the beginning.

Structuring Discussions.   Once the group members know each other and are oriented to the task, the leader should organize the discussion. Effective leaders help maintain productive relationships among the members, but their primary focus should be on the group's task. This is what most group members expect.[23] That includes constantly monitoring the group's process and making needed adjustments. Following are some suggestions:

1. **Keep the group goal-oriented; watch for digressions and topic changes.**

    Be sure the members understand and accept the goal. A certain amount of digression is normal and desirable because it can foster team spirit. You don't want to stifle every digression, but if a lengthy digression occurs, help bring the group back on track: "We seem to be losing sight of our objective," or "We're getting off track. What we were talking about was . . ." Topic switches are common, so be on constant watch for them. When you notice one, point it out and suggest that the group finish one topic before going on to another: "We're jumping ahead. Let's finish our parking recommendation before we start talking about scholarships." When a change of issue, irrelevant topic, or premature solution crops up, ask if that person would mind waiting until the group has finished its analysis of the current issue or post it on a flip chart—the "parking lot"—for later consideration.

2. **Put the discussion or problem-solving procedure on the board or in a handout.**

    If the group is using a procedure such as brainstorming, help the group remember the steps by summarizing them briefly in writing. This helps keep comments to the point.

3. **Summarize each major step or decision.**

    It is easy for members to lose track of what the group is doing. Before the group proceeds to the next issue or agenda item, help all members keep track by summarizing and asking members for feedback. In many cases, a secretary can help summarize. This also helps make a clear transition to the next step in the discussion.

4. **Structure the group's time.**

    Nothing is more frustrating than running out of time before you have a chance to discuss an issue important to you. Since members often get caught up in a discussion, it is up to the leader to keep track of time and remind the group of what still needs to be done and how much time is available.

5. **Bring the discussion to a definite close.**

    Do this no later than the scheduled ending time for the meeting, unless all members agree to extend the time. In your conclusion, include a brief summary of progress the group has made, a review of assignments given, a statement of how reports of the meeting will be distributed to members and others, comments about preparation for the next meeting, commendations for a job well done, and, periodically, your evaluation of the meeting to improve the group's future interactions.

Equalizing Opportunity to Participate.   Along with keeping the group's discussion organized, the leader is responsible for seeing to it that everyone has an equal opportunity to speak. This is central to democratic participation discussed earlier in the chapter. You can do several things to produce such equality:

1. **Address your comments to the group rather than to individuals.**

    Unless you are asking someone for specific information or responding directly to what a member has said, speak to the group as a whole. Make eye contact with everyone, especially the less-talkative members. It is natural to pay the most attention to those who talk a lot, but this may further discourage quiet members.

2. **Control dominating or long-winded speakers.**

Occasionally a member monopolizes the discussion so much that others give up. This imbalance can destroy a group. The other members expect you to control domineering members and will thank you for it. Here are several techniques to try. First, avoid direct eye contact. Second, sit where you can overlook them naturally when you ask questions of the group. Third, cut in tactfully and say something like, "How do the *rest* of you feel about that point?" Fourth, help the group establish rules about how long someone may speak; then establish a timekeeper to keep track of members' remarks. Fifth, describe the problem openly to the group and ask the members to deal with it as a group. Sometimes even more drastic measures are needed, such as talking with the offending individual privately or even asking the person to leave the group. This is a last resort; use it only when other measures have failed.

3. **Encourage less-talkative members to participate.**

Quiet members may feel overwhelmed by talkative ones. Encourage less-talkative members: "Roger, finances are your area of expertise. Where do you think the budget could be cut?" or "Maria, you haven't said anything about the proposal. Would you like to share your opinion?" Make a visual survey of members continuously to look for nonverbal signs that a member wants to speak, seems upset, or disagrees with what someone else is saying. Give such members a chance to speak by asking a direct question such as, "Did you want to comment on Navida's suggestion?"

Other techniques for increasing the participation of quiet members include assigning them to investigate needed information and reporting back to the group or inviting them to contribute with their special areas of knowledge or skill. You might say, "Kim, you're a statistical whiz. Will you take charge of the data analysis for the project?" Listen with real interest to what an infrequent participant says and encourage others to do so as well. Nothing kills participation faster than the other members' apparent lack of interest.

4. **Avoid commenting after each member's remark.**

Some discussion leaders comment after each person has spoken. This produces a *wheel* network of verbal interaction. Eventually members start waiting for the leader to comment, which inhibits the free flow of conversation. Listen, speak when you are really needed, but as a rule don't repeat or interpret what others say.

5. **Bounce questions of interpretation back to the group.**

Some groups blindly follow the designated leader's opinions. Especially in a new group, hold back until others have had a chance to express their views. Then, offer yours only as another point of view to be considered. If a member asks, "What do you think we should do?" you can reply, "Let's see what everyone else thinks first. What do the rest of you think . . . ?"

6. **Remain neutral during arguments.**

If you are heavily involved in an argument, you will have a harder time being objective, encouraging others to participate, and seeing that each point of view is represented. If you stay neutral, you can legitimately serve as a mediator for resolving disputes. Of course, feel free to support decisions as they emerge and encourage critical thinking by all members.

Stimulating Creative Thinking.   Many problem-solving groups create mediocre solutions. Sometimes inventive solutions are needed. Chapter 5 discussed the importance of creative thinking. Here we elaborate further on how to encourage group creativity:

1. **Suggest discussion techniques that are designed to tap a group's creativity.**

   Several techniques, such as brainstorming, synectics, and mind mapping, are designed especially to help a group create inventive solutions. Many techniques employ deferred judgment—the group postpones evaluation until all possible solutions are presented. When people know their ideas will not be judged, they feel freer to suggest wild and crazy ideas, many of which may turn out to be useful.

2. **When the flow of ideas has dried up, encourage the group to search for a few more alternatives.**

   Often the best ideas appear late in a period of creative brainstorming. You might use these idea-spurring questions: "What else can we think of to . . . ?" or "I wonder if we can think of any more possible ways to . . . ?"

3. **Discuss the components of a problem one at a time.**

   For instance, ask, "Is there any way to improve the appearance of . . . ?" or ". . . . the durability of . . . ?"

4. **Watch for suggestions that open up new areas of thinking and then pose a general question about them.**

   For example, if someone suggests putting up signs in the library that show the cost of losses to the users, you might capitalize on that idea by asking, "How else could we publicize the cost of losses to the library?"

5. **Force an alternative perspective or switch senses.**

   For example, if you're trying to find a new way to remove plaque from blood vessels, pretend you are a microbe traveling along the blood stream, getting a microscopic view of clogged arteries. Or if your problem is visual ("How can we create an eye-catching graphic for the new store?"), think in sound ("What would an attention-getting ad for the new store *sound* like?")

Stimulating Critical Thinking.   Chapter 5 also covered critical thinking in detail. We remind you here of your responsibility as leader for ensuring that group members carefully evaluate the decisions they make. Here are specific suggestions:

1. **Encourage group members to evaluate information and reasoning.**

   Ask questions to make sure the group evaluates the source of evidence ("Where did that information come from?" "How well respected is Dr. Gray in the field?"), the relevance of the evidence ("How does that apply to our problem?"), the accuracy of the information ("Is that information consistent with other information about the issue?" "Why does this information contradict what others have said?"), and the reasoning ("Are the conclusions logical and based on the information presented?"). Bring in outside experts to challenge the views of the group or to help evaluate information.

10.3   **Red Ribbon Committee and Sober Graduation**

The Red Ribbon Committee is a community group in California's central valley. The committee develops, plans, and presents several community events each year that promote a sober and drug-free lifestyle. Each year the committee debates whether or not the sober graduation party should last all night or end at 2 or 3 a.m. Students, noting that their parents would not approve of an all-night event, have said they'd be willing to go even if it was not all night. Lupe (a 50-year-old Hispanic woman with strong community ties) and Tracy (a divorced Caucasian woman in her late 40s who is quite vocal about how things should be done) argue that it should end early because the students and chaperones get too tired. In addition, they note that the majority of problems usually happen after 2 a.m. They suggest that the main goal of sober graduation is to get as many students as possible to attend and that means guaranteeing their safety. The other four members of the group (a Caucasian female and former school board member; a wealthy female Portuguese dairy owner who is feared in the community; a Portuguese man who is very active in the community; and a young Caucasian man employed by the school district) argue that the goal is to ensure the kids are safe *all* night. Traditionally, they add, these events have been all-night affairs. Lupe and Tracy have become increasingly adamant; they want the others to try their idea at least once to see how it would work.

You are the leader of this group. At this point, how would you stimulate creative and critical thinking in this group?

1. Offer suggestions, relevant to this committee, about how members can stimulate creative thinking.
2. Offer ways the group can critically examine the suggestions generated by creative thinking.

2. **See that all group members understand and accept the standards, criteria, or assumptions used in making judgments.**

   Fair, unbiased judgments are based on criteria that are clear to all members. You might ask, "Is that criterion clear to us all?" "Is this something we want to insist on?" or "Do we all accept this as an assumption?" Criteria were discussed in Chapter 6.

3. **See that all proposed solutions are tested thoroughly before they are accepted as final group decisions.**

   Make sure group members discuss tentative solutions with relevant outsiders, that pros and cons of each solution have been evaluated, and that members have had a chance to play devil's advocate in challenging proposals. For a major problem, propose holding a second-chance meeting, where all doubts, concerns, or untested assumptions can be explored.

4. **Establish a devil's advocate individual or competing subgroups to poke holes in potential solutions.**

   Assigning one or more group members the role of devil's advocate, described in Chapter 9, encourages group members to spot flaws in an argument or problems with a solution. Establishing two subgroups in friendly competition with one another can be a fun way to think critically. Ask each group to find as many problems as possible with the options the group is considering. Whichever group "wins" gets treated to dinner or drinks. This forces the group to consider deficiencies in possible solutions, but does so in an entertaining way.

Fostering Meeting-to-Meeting Improvement. Effective group leaders spend time evaluating each meeting to discover how it could have been improved. Ask the group itself to participate in evaluation. Usually you will privately review your notes to determine whether the major meeting goals were met and how smoothly the meeting went. Then, establish your goals for improving future meetings and adjust your own behavior accordingly to meet the group's goals.

Several studies of effective leaders have shown that good leaders adjust their behavior from one meeting to the next, depending on the specific goals of the meeting. Good leaders monitor their own and the other members' behaviors so they can modify their actions to help the group.

1. **Review personal notes of the meeting.**

   Keep personal notes of important happenings during the meeting. After the meeting, ask yourself, Did we accomplish our purpose? Did everyone have a chance to participate? Did anyone hog the floor? Was the group both creative and critical in its thinking? and, most important of all, What could I personally have done to ensure a better meeting?

2. **Decide how the meeting could have been improved.**

   The answers to the previous questions will guide you. For example, if Sonya believes that the group jumped on an early solution without carefully assessing the problem just to get the meeting over with, then she might decide that the group needs to look at the problem again. If TerryAnn had evaluated her meetings, she would have discovered that the group needed more direction and guidance than she was providing.

3. **Establish specific improvements as goals for the next meeting.**

   After determining where the meeting could have been improved, incorporate this information into planning for the next meeting. Sonya, for example, could place the problem back on the agenda, explain to the group that she perceived a lack of critical thinking, and invite the group to assess the problem again.

4. **Adjust behavior accordingly.**

   Once you, as leader, have diagnosed areas of group communication where improvement could occur and have decided what needs to be done, then you should adjust your behavior to help ensure improvement. For example, TerryAnn needed to be more clear, direct, and concise in her communication. She also needed to keep the group on track instead of letting them digress. Notice that these are *communication* behaviors (not personality characteristics) that TerryAnn should change.

We now consider specific areas in which the designated small group leader can help group members develop, a topic we explored in detail in Chapter 7.

DEVELOPING THE GROUP

One of the most important functions of the leader is to assist in the group's development from a collection of individuals to a productive unit. This involves such things as establishing a climate of trust, promoting teamwork and cooperation, and evaluating the group's progress.

Establishing a Climate of Trust.   Groups perform more effectively when members trust one another. The following suggestions help establish a climate of trust.

1. **Establish norms that build trust.**

   Norms building trust encourage respectful active listening, cooperation, confidentiality, the timely completion of assignments, and the freedom to disagree without being considered deviant. Many leaders are far too slow to speak to members who are manipulative, do poor work, or act out of self-interest harmful to the group.[24]

2. **Function as a coordinator rather than a dictator.**

   Foster a climate of trust by serving the needs of the group, not by ordering people around to serve your personal interests. That way, members feel free to express themselves and to develop skills needed by the group. Ask for volunteers to do jobs for the group rather than ordering: "Cal, could you please get the . . . "

3. **Encourage members to get to know each other.**

   Usually, members trust each other and feel safe in the group if they know one another as individuals. Sometimes an unstructured social period helps create a sense of teamwork. Graduate teaching assistants in one department have a tradition of planning a float trip at the beginning of each fall semester. Social gatherings like this help people get to know each other.

Developing Teamwork and Promoting Cooperation.   Although the leader's principal responsibility is to see that the group accomplishes its task, the development of teamwork can help group members work productively. Here are suggestions you can use:

1. **Speak of *us* and *we*, rather than *I* and *you*.**

   Calling the group members *we* implies commitment to the group and its values. Ask what it means if another member speaks of the group as "you."

2. **Develop a name or another symbol of group identification.**

   Such items as T-shirts, logos, "inside" jokes, and slogans can display shared identification. For example, a successful advertising agency creative group called itself the "Can-Do Team."

3. **Watch for evidence of hidden agenda items that conflict with group goals.**

   If you suspect a hidden agenda item is interfering with the group's agenda, promptly bring it to the attention of the group. Ignoring such problems makes them worse, not better.

6. **Establish clear policies that all group members are expected to follow.**

   Group rules and procedures should be clearly understood. Group members should be encouraged to participate in establishing the group's procedures and policies.

7. **Follow the group rules, just as you expect the others to do.**

   Because of your status as the group leader, you may be given some leeway to violate rules others are expected to follow. Do not abuse this privilege. If others are expected to arrive on time, so should you. If you reprimand members for failing to complete assignments, make sure your own assignments are completed well and on time. As much as possible, be a model member for the group.

As Lao Tse said: "The great leader is he about whom the people say, 'We did it ourselves.'" Will you be that kind of leader?

RESOURCES FOR REVIEW AND DISCUSSION

SUMMARY

- Leadership consists of using communication to modify others' behaviors to meet group goals; a leader is anyone who exerts influence to help a group. Designated leaders are appointed or elected, whereas emergent leaders surface naturally from within a group of peers.

- Leaders derive their ability to influence others from five sources of power: reward, punishment, legitimate, expert, and referent. The more sources of power a leader has, the greater is that leader's ability to influence the other group members.

- Three common myths about leadership are that leaders have special traits that followers don't, that there is an ideal leadership style, and that leaders get other people to do all the work for them.

- The functional approach to leadership encourages all group members to perform whatever

functions a group needs and the contingency approach assumes that the type of leadership a group needs depends on the group's situation.

- Both approaches suggest that the leader serve as a completer, supplying whatever necessary functions the other members are not providing.

- Group members expect leaders to perform four broad types of tasks: providing administrative services for a group, structuring a group's discussions, helping a group develop as a team, and managing a group's written messages.

- Distributed leadership, in which each member takes responsibility for providing leadership services to a group, is an ideal worth striving for.

- Ethical leaders tell the truth, are sensitive to and respectful of others, support the other members, establish clear rules that they expect to follow themselves, and put group concerns ahead of their own personal gain.

1. View Part 1 (Leadership) of the videotape "Communicating Effectively in Small Groups" and discuss the following questions:

   a. What functions did the leader perform?

   b. How effective was each function? How appropriate?

   c. Were there any points during the discussion where the leader failed to supply needed leadership service? Did anyone else step in to provide it? Was the group hurt?

   d. On a scale of 1 to 10, how effective was the leader? Why do you say this?

2. Select five members from your class to act as a problem-solving group. Assign one of the members to be the leader of the group. Ask the group to tackle the following problem:

   The Teacher's Dilemma
   An English teacher in a consolidated, rural school has had extensive dramatic experience. She was chosen by the principal to direct the first play in the new school. The play will be the first major production for the school. Its success may determine whether there will be any future plays produced at the school, and, if well done, it could bring prestige to both the teacher and the school. As a result, the teacher is exhausting every means available to her to make the play an artistic success. She has chosen all the cast except for the leading female part. The principal's daughter wants the part, and the principal told the teacher he really wants his daughter to have it. But she is a poor actress and would jeopardize the success of the show. Tentatively, the teacher has chosen someone who should do an excellent job in the role, but the principal has implied that if his daughter is not selected, he will appoint another director in the future. What should she do?

   Place the group of five in the middle of the class and surround it with the rest of the class members. They are to watch this group's discussion and to evaluate the leader on his or her ability to lead the group discussion. How well did he or she do? On what do you base your evaluation?

3. Form small groups of four to six members. Discuss the "ideal" group leader. Each group is to address not only the specific duties leaders should perform, but also the communicative skills leaders should exhibit and the ethical principles they should both exhibit and uphold. Each group should create a "Guidelines for Group Leaders" manual that could be distributed to student leaders at your school. Discuss each group's guidelines to determine which ones tend to be common to all groups. Why do you think these tend to be the most common?

 Go to **www.mhhe.com/adamsgalanes6** and **www.mhhe.com/groups** for self-quizzes and weblinks.

Agenda	Expert Power	Minutes
Coercion	Functional Concept	Punishment Power
Contingency Concept	Influence	Referent Power
Designated Leader	Leader	Reward Power
Distributed Leadership	Leadership	
Emergent Leader	Legitimate Power	

www.mhhe.com/adamsgalanes6

Use the flash cards and crossword puzzles on the Online Learning Center to further your knowledge of these key terms.

Small Group Public Presentations

Just as it is important to figure out the leadership roles and who will perform them, a group must also assess its strengths and difficulties when it comes to oral presentations. Up to now, we have discussed the complex nature of small group interactions as they occur within group meetings. The successful development of small group interaction helps ensure a more professional and successful oral presentation by individuals and group members. In Part Four, we discuss a three-step process to prepare your group's oral presentation, by focusing on the planning, organizing, and presenting stages of these presentations.

CHAPTER 11

Planning, Organizing, and Presenting Small Group Oral Presentations

CHAPTER OBJECTIVES

After reading this chapter you should be able to:

1. Explain the different choices group members can make in the planning, organizing, and presenting stages.

2. Compare and contrast the three types of public discussions.

3. Discuss the role of the moderator in any type of public discussion.

4. Explain the essential parts of the introduction, the body, and the conclusion of an oral presentation.

5. Compare and contrast the four methods of presenting a speech.

6. Describe and apply relevant criteria to evaluate an oral presentation.

Food for the Homeless

Six students in a small group communication class spent more than half their semester discussing the problems faced by a local homeless shelter. One especially significant problem they noted was the great reduction in contributions, especially of food, during the summer. The shelter seemed to get more than enough donations during the fall and winter holiday seasons, when everyone seemed to be in a giving mood, but contributions dropped significantly during the summer. As part of the solution section of their report, the students recommended a way of getting more edible leftovers from local restaurants to the shelter, a program they had discovered already in operation in a few other communities across the nation.

The students' report earned them an A. Their instructor was so impressed that he showed the report to a close friend, the president of the local restaurant association. She, too, thought the students were on to something and invited them to make a 15-minute presentation about their project at the association's monthly meeting. The students were excited that their work might become something more than a classroom exercise and that they might be able to help the homeless shelter, but they did not know how they should respond to this invitation. Should they let their chair represent them? Should they all go and each say a few words? Should they let their most talkative member make the presentation or the one who seemed to be the best critical thinker? The meeting was coming quickly and they did not know what to do.

The Planning Stage

The moment your group is informed that a presentation will be needed you should immediately schedule a planning meeting to work through important details. Planning to speak to an audience requires advance assessment of the upcoming speaking situation. The most important areas of assessment include: your group's audience, occasion, purpose, topic, member strengths/difficulties, and supplemental logistics. This initial assessment as well as plenty of preparation is essential for a smooth production. In this section, we look at each area of assessment and describe different types of oral presentations that groups often deliver.

GLOSSARY

Audience Analysis

Studying the unique character of who will receive a presentation in order to adapt how a speech will be delivered and what will be presented

YOUR AUDIENCE

Assessing your audience is important for creating a comfortable speaking environment, not only for your audience, but also for your group. Although we often *think* about our audience when giving presentations, too often we do not carefully figure out who this group of listeners is to us.[1] **Audience analysis** is a systematic approach to gathering as much information as possible about the audience for the purpose of tailoring your presentation to the information you uncover in that analysis.[2] Audience members listen to material presented to them through their *own* perspectives, not those of the person presenting the material. This is why it is so important to gather information systematically about the people hearing what you have to say.

How might these perspectives affect how audience members listen to your group presentation? Let's explore audience attitudes toward topics.[3] If you know that your audience is not familiar with your topic, then you should stay with basic facts and provide background information. If your group's topic is new to the audience, such as material on pollution rates during peak traffic hours, then you should show why listeners should care about the topic and demonstrate how these pollution rates are similar to air quality issues they *do* know about. If your audience holds attitudes against your topic, then create a common ground with the audience and relate your group's main points to audience perspectives. For example, your group believes it is necessary to use marijuana for medical purposes; however, you know your audience is against drug use. Show how your group and the audience care about health care for loved ones and then relate your main points to the audience's beliefs about health care for those they love. If your audience is deeply against your group's main points, then consider altering your positions or make sure you build a sound case for your points. All these recommendations are grounded in *knowing* your audience.

You can find out information about your audience in a variety of ways.[4] If you want targeted information about a particular audience, interview them or conduct a survey. This is easy if your audience will be members of your class. Interviews can be composed of open-ended questions and closed-ended questions. We offer examples of these kinds of questions in Chapter 5. You can also answer your questions by giving your audience a written survey. If you want only general information about your audience, you can access published polls, which can give you attitudes on current topics. For example, the Roper Center for Public Opinion holds the largest collection of polls and surveys in the United States (www.ropercenter.uconn.edu). A variety of demographic statistics about the United States can be found on the U.S. Census Bureau's website (www.census.gov).

Once you are aware of *who* your audience is, you can determine the knowledge they may or may not have about the topic you are considering for discussion. As a group, you should answer specific questions about your audience. Will you be speaking only to your class or will your instructor be part of the audience? Will it be the entire membership of your fraternity or just the executive committee? Will it be people you know or will most of them be strangers? Will the audience members be there voluntarily or is someone forcing them to attend? The mood of your audience can depend on whether or not your audience feels required to be there.

A captive or required audience member is going to need a presentation with lots of enthusiasm and reasons why she or he should listen. What can you add to their knowledge or attitude about your topic? You do not want to bore an audience by repeating what they already know, nor do you want to talk over their heads about complex issues they don't quite understand. Don't hesitate to ask if you can observe, interview, or survey your audience before the speaking engagement. Remember, for more opportunities of audience inclusion find out as much as possible about the audience before you start writing your presentation.

YOUR OCCASION

Depending on who has invited your group to speak, you may be able to get much of your information about the audience and the occasion from this lead contact person. Ask if you may visit the facility and room you will be speaking in before the event occurs, check and recheck the time of the event as well as the major purpose and context of this occasion. How many people are expected? Where will you be placed in the speaking lineup and how much control do you have over your setting? Before your group begins serious purpose and topic planning, make sure you clarify why you have been asked to speak to this audience and whether or not there is a specific goal that needs to be met.

YOUR PURPOSE

Typically a speaker wants to have a general purpose of informing, persuading, or entertaining an audience. Knowing clearly what you are trying to accomplish is an essential step in any effective presentation. If your group is unaware of the purpose of your presentation, how can the audience members make sense of what they are supposed to do with the information you have presented? The **informative speech** is used when your group wants to educate, enlighten, or distribute information. For example, if your group is reporting on a new community service group that has just moved into the area and you are offering information that describes who they are, where they come from, and what they offer, your purpose is to inform. If your group wanted the audience to donate time or money to this community service organization, your purpose would be to persuade.

A **persuasive speech** is defined by the call to action. Your purpose, as a group, is to get your audience to do something with the information you have given them. Another example of a persuasive purpose would be trying to influence your fraternity or sorority to try a new fund-raising technique. You want your audience members to agree with you and adopt your suggestion(s).

On occasion, you may be asked to give an **entertainment speech** such as if you are asked to wrap up the year's events or "roast" a colleague at the annual company picnic. You want the audience members to enjoy themselves, to laugh and have a good time. Sometimes it is hard to get an audience to warm up to jokes and different types of humor, so be prepared if you do not get the response you want. Also, be aware that most jokes are directed at or said at the expense of others, so be very careful that your humor is appropriate and tasteful, and does not turn off audience members. What is funny on Comedy Central may not be appropriate for your audience. You're speaking to make a connection with your audience, not to distance them.

Although your purpose may be to entertain, this speech could easily inform or persuade as well. We have heard speeches on many serious issues that were delivered in a thoughtful and entertaining manner.

YOUR SUBJECT OR TOPIC

As soon as you determine the general purpose, establish a specific subject or topic of your presentation. Your instructor or employer often will tell you what to talk about, but

---

GLOSSARY

Informative Speech

A speech given with the primary purpose of teaching something to an audience

Persuasive Speech

A type of speech containing a call to action

Entertainment Speech

A speech with the main purpose of amusing the audience

sometimes, the choice of a specific topic will be left up to you. This step is often one of the most difficult. Where do you start? The best topics come from your own experiences, beliefs, or skills. As a group, sit down and brainstorm different topic ideas from your own individual experiences. What are your interests, hobbies, and subjects you enjoy, read about, and find interesting? Often you are selected to speak because of some expertise you possess. You can also ask whoever asked you to speak which of several topics the audience would find most appealing.

Undoubtedly there will be a time limit for your presentation. You may have 5 minutes, 20 minutes, or you may be told simply to "be brief" or to "fill us in." Keep your time limit in mind when selecting what to say about your subject. Inexperienced speakers often make the mistake of coming to the podium with enough material for two or three speeches. As a result, the audience gets restless or your instructor tells you to stop so that others in the class may have time to speak. Don't try to cover everything you know about a subject; select those matters that are most important to you and of special interest to your audience.

MEMBER STRENGTHS AND DIFFICULTIES

Knowing the strengths and difficulties that your members may have with oral presentations will help in the organizing and presenting stages of presentation development. What information does each individual group member have about the topic that has been chosen for discussion? What contacts or research leads do you have as a group? What is the attitude or feeling of the group about the topic? After assessing the strengths of group members, deciding who will present different points will be easier. Also, if a question-and-answer period is established after your presentation, knowing member's strengths will help in determining who is best qualified to answer the specific questions that are asked.

In addition to looking at the strengths of the group's members, the group also should focus on member difficulties in making oral presentations. Member anxiety can prevent a confident and effective delivery. If your group does an early assessment of this communication apprehension, it will be easier to combat the problem. A group must not rely on the stereotype that "any leader can lead an effective oral presentation." Anxiety is normal and may be experienced in different ways. Just because your group leader or president has no problem speaking to *your* group as a whole doesn't mean she or he will be able to speak to a group that may be larger or unknown to the speaker. Knowing a member's difficulty with public speaking will allow your group to organize different presenting strategies that take the focus off of one person. This knowledge will also be a helpful reminder that your group should practice the delivery to ease tensions.

SUPPLEMENTAL LOGISTICS

Near the end of your planning stage your group should be more knowledgeable about what you need. Will you need supplies to set up your speaking environment? Are you using a visual aid? What will you need to run this visual aid properly (e.g., TV, VCR, laptop computer, projector, audio player, slide machine, etc.)? Speakers often forget a simple item, such as tape, and end up worrying about the poster that will not stand up straight instead of focusing on the words that are just as important as the visual aid. Do not expect a member of your audience, your teacher, or a contact person to provide you with these items. It is your responsibility to plan and remember these essential supplemental tools for your presentation. It never hurts to be overprepared.

Take for example the community service story earlier in the chapter. If your group hasn't gone the extra mile to find pamphlets, booklets, handouts, buttons, balloons, fact sheets, or other items that this homeless shelter has for distribution, then you may be missing out on updated information. Many organizations would be happy to have a volunteer group inform others about their needs and services, and your presentation would look that much more professional because you obtained original, from-the-source, information about your topic.

TYPES OF GROUP ORAL PRESENTATIONS

Once you have completed your presentation assessment, as a group, you must decide which presentation format best fits the purpose and occasion of your presentation. These formats allow for differing viewpoints to be expressed and are often followed by comments and questions from the audience. The three most common group presentation formats are the panel discussion, symposium, and forum (see Table 11.1).

A **panel discussion** is a public interaction between a small number of people, often selected because of their competence and knowledge about a topic and usually holding conflicting viewpoints. The purpose of a panel is to make the audience more aware of a significant topic or to persuade them to act in a certain way (e.g., vote for a specific issue or candidate). For example, your group may be asked by your instructor to serve as a panel and explain your semester project and conclusions to the rest of your class.

The procedure to follow for a panel discussion includes the following:

1. Select a **moderator** to maintain order, see that all the major issues are covered, and ensure that everyone gets to speak. The moderator introduces the members of the panel and keeps the discussion moving by calling on speakers as necessary. The moderator acts as a conversational traffic cop, directing questions to the appropriate panelists and clarifying issues and statements as necessary. The moderator makes appropriate opening and closing remarks and directs any subsequent audience participation.

TABLE 11.1	**Types of Group Presentations**	
Panel: Conversation among experts	**Symposium: Individual uninterrupted presentations**	**Forum: Questions and comments from audience**
Topics outlined in advance	Panelists discuss different aspects of topic	Different viewpoints encouraged
Controversy encouraged	No interaction among panelists	Questions directed at individuals or at entire group
Moderator as traffic cop	Moderator introduces topic and panelists	Moderator selects audience participants

2. Before the discussion, make an outline of all the important points the group wants to cover and decide in what order to cover them. Follow this outline closely during the panel discussion.

3. Make appropriate physical arrangements:

    a. Seat panelists so they can see each other and have eye contact with the audience; a semicircle is appropriate.

    b. Seat panelists at a table or desk so it is easy for them to write notes.

    c. Identify panelists with a name card on the table in front of them or their names on a blackboard behind them. The audience can then address questions to specific panelists easily.

    d. If the discussion is to be held in a large auditorium, place microphones on the table for the panelists to share. If audience participation will follow, strategically locate at least one standup microphone in the auditorium.

    e. Make provisions for panelists to present visual aids. Provide an easel or chalkboard that is easy to reach and will not block the view of the audience or panel.

4. The panelists should not hesitate to disagree with each other, but should do so politely. Even when they are not talking, the audience can see them, so they should refrain from inappropriate nonverbal communication.

A **symposium** is much more structured than a panel discussion. Instead of a relatively free interchange of ideas, the topic is divided into segments and each discussant presents an uninterrupted speech on a portion of the topic. The purpose of a symposium is similar to that of a panel: to enlighten an audience on a subject of importance. For example, on September 11, 2001, after the horrific attacks on the World Trade Center in New York City, Governor George Pataki and Mayor Rudolph Giuliani and other New York dignitaries presented a news conference to disseminate information to the public about the recent terrorist events. After these attacks, New York and the rest of the world wanted and needed information in a quick, controlled manner. This symposium allowed each presenter to deliver information in an uninterrupted format. Most symposiums are usually followed by a forum, which allows the audience to question the panelists and permits the discussants to answer these questions and comment on each other's presentations. In the New York City press conference, reporters asked questions after the concluding remarks, leaving time for each member to comment from his or her own expertise. For example, Mayor Giuliani provided information from a city perspective, working hard to unite his community and disperse information, while Governor Pataki expressed what the state could be providing and how he was working with the president and other authorities to keep events running smoothly. Procedures for a symposium are as follows:

1. Select a moderator to introduce the speakers, introduce the topic, and make concluding remarks.

2. Select a small group of experts to present different aspects of the issue. Because each individual presentation is uninterrupted, make sure there will not be much repetition among the speakers.

3. As with the panel presentation, appropriate physical arrangements should be made.

A **forum discussion** allows members of an audience for a speech, symposium, panel discussion, debate, or other public presentation an opportunity to comment on what they have heard and to ask questions of the speakers. All sides of the question should be given an equal amount of presentation time, and no speaker should be allowed to monopolize the floor. The moderator's role is crucial. Some suggestions for the moderator are:

1. Let audience members know that a forum will follow the panel or symposium so they can prepare their questions or comments.

2. Make sure everyone understands any special rules of the forum segment. How will audience members be recognized? They might raise their hands or step forward to an audience microphone. Will speakers from the audience be allowed to ask a follow-up question? Will someone who has not spoken have preference over someone who has already spoken? If there is a time limit for questions, make sure it is announced and followed.

3. Make sure everyone knows when the forum will end and do not accept questions once that time has been reached. Offer a warning before the last question or two.

4. Try to ensure that a diversity of views is offered. Ask for comments opposed to those that have just been expressed. On a very controversial issue, the moderator might deliberately alternate between a spokesperson from one side and then from the other.

5. Make sure everyone can hear a question or comment. If necessary, repeat it for the audience.

6. Following the last question or comment, offer a brief summary and thank everyone for their participation.

11.1 What Type of Group Presentation Should the Group Make to the Restaurant Association?

APPLY NOW

Form groups of about six people and discuss how you feel about making oral presentations. Next, pretend that you are the members of the discussion group described in Case 11.1 and decide how you would respond to the invitation from the restaurant association.

1. Would you prefer to work together and put on a panel or a symposium? If so, whom would you select to be the moderator? Why?

2. Would you prefer to send a single representative? If so, which of you would you send? Why?

3. Compare your group's answers to these questions with those of the other groups in your class. How do you account for differences and similarities?

The Organizing Stage

The success of the organizing stage depends on how well group members interact and listen to one another. If the group allows one person to take the lead, expecting that this person will plan and organize the presentation, many problems will arise. Not only will only one person know what is going to be discussed, but also resentment on both sides may arise. As with every stage, it is important to have every member present during the organizing stage. In this section on organization, we focus on the importance of delegating member duties, we explain different types of verbal and visual materials that the group can use, and we provide a speaker's blueprint for organizing these materials and the presentation.

DELEGATE DUTIES

Although the delegation of duties may sound like a function of the leader, this is not always the case. After assessing the strengths and difficulties of each member, it is important to determine where each member feels most comfortable and where his or her presentation strength has the best fit. If you don't speak up at this crucial time of organizing, you might be stuck with a job that you don't know how to perform or have no desire to do. When presenting on specific areas, examine the different backgrounds/experiences of your members and analyze where their strength lies. Think about the different majors in a college classroom. If these students had to build a presentation about the parking problem on their campus, which areas of the presentation would be best delegated to whom? For example, math majors could demonstrate, with the use of numbers, car/space ratios, or problems with funding. History majors could give background to this ongoing problem. An art major would be our first choice when deciding on visual aids, and communication majors might have the duty of surveying students and administration on solutions to this problem.

Knowing each group member's responsibilities will help when you plan speaking duties and each member's order in the presentation. After you are aware of who is speaking when and about what, then you want to discuss who will obtain verbal and visual aid materials. Who will be required to set up the TV/VCR, turn the lights off during the slide show, set up a meeting with the American Red Cross? Each duty is extremely important to the success of the group and its presentation and should be planned before the day of the event.

GATHER VERBAL AND VISUAL MATERIALS

Verbal Materials.   Once your group is aware of each member's duties, you can now conduct much more focused research on each person's item for discussion. Often speakers will try to approach the audience with only the information they know, without obtaining supporting material. Listed are three of the most important types of verbal supporting materials: examples, statistics, and statements by authorities (testimony).

- **Examples:** Aristotle said that examples become "witnesses and a witness is everywhere persuasive."[5] Examples are used in inductive reasoning, where a generalization is drawn from looking at a number of specific instances. Examples can range from detailed factual ones (the story of a real victim of rape complete with dialogue, names, and dates) to undeveloped factual examples (a listing of the countries in the world where war is presently occurring) to hypothetical ones (how much a dollar will be worth in 10 years given a certain rate of inflation). You should choose typical examples and offer enough to make your point believable.

■ **Statistics:** Statistics are the use of numbers or quantification to explain or support your position. Audience members can be easily confused by statistics, so make your statistics clear and meaningful. It is hard to imagine how large a country is if the speaker only tells us that it is 200,000 square miles in area. More helpful is a comparison: about the size of California and Oregon combined. To emphasize how large the state budget in California was in 2000 ($61.53 billion), point out that to spend that much, the state had to spend $168.5 million a day, $7 million per hour, or $19,511 per second.

■ **Testimony:** Some people are recognized as authorities on certain issues. To support your position you may want to quote directly or paraphrase what these authorities have said or written about your topic. Obtain this from library research, interviews, or over the Internet. The group mentioned in Case 11.1 got useful materials from interviewing the director of the homeless shelter and from newspaper articles about similar shelters across the country.

Three common types of testimony are: lay, expert, and celebrity. *Lay testimony* is a statement taken from an ordinary individual. Information that is reported by a person who has special training or knowledge about the topic is *expert testimony.* A person who is famous would offer *celebrity testimony.* Let's imagine that your group has decided to give an informative presentation on tips for a long-lasting happy marriage. Who might you interview for lay, expert, and celebrity testimony? Think about the problems that might arise if you chose testimony from someone who is known too well by the audience. For example, picking Britney Spears as your celebrity testimony might cause problems. Although Britney Spears might offer interesting tips for your presentation, the public knowledge of her divorce might taint her message.

The bottom line when assessing verbal supporting material is to be aware of the attitudes that your audience might have around your research— who or what is seen as more credible?

Visual Materials.   Look also for visual materials to keep the audience's interest. Keep in mind what successful attorneys know: a visual aid helps your audience remember your main points. Most lawyers know that juries pay closer attention, understand technical points better, and remember more when oral testimony is coupled with a visual prop. Many will never forget the images of Johnnie Cochran slipping on the leather glove while repeating, "If it doesn't fit, you must acquit" in the courtroom while he was defending O.J. Simpson on trial for murder. If visual images were not important we would not have an obsession with televisions. Imagine listening to your news, sports, and favorite television programming only on the radio. Now that you have a better understanding of the importance of these images, here are a number of possibilities that can enhance your presentation.

■ **Object:** If what you are speaking about is small enough, bring it with you. A small animal is a very effective prop if your talk is about birth control for pets or overcrowding at animal shelters. If your subject is too large or noisy to bring with you, use a model or picture instead.

■ **Model:** A plastic model of the object can allow us to see what you are talking about when the real object is too large. The Concorde will be unable to land on your campus, but a model can easily be displayed on a small table in the front of the classroom.

- **Picture or video:** A photograph, slide, or videotape can focus the audience's attention on your topic. To show the problem of traffic congestion in your city, take a video of rush hour on a busy street, for instance. Slide shows need to be planned and rehearsed well in advance of the performance. Your group does not want to be known as the group with the upside-down slides.

- **Map:** Most Americans' knowledge of geography is weak. Don't assume just because you know where a city is, every one in your audience will, too. Give them a map of the place itself and show it in relation to other familiar points of interest.

- **Transparency:** Putting an outline of your presentation on an overhead projector allows the audience to see your main points and relieves you of having to use the chalkboard. Make sure the projector is centered with your screen and reveal only part of the outline at a time to keep the listeners focused on what you are saying and not looking ahead to what comes next. If too much information is given, in the form of an outline, audience members will wonder why you are reading to them and get quickly bored. Never add every detail of your speech on the outline; include only the main points so the audience has a map to follow.

- **Chart:** Charts are especially useful for showing statistics. Numbers are sometimes hard to grasp in a speech, especially when there are a lot of them. Make it easy for your listeners by putting the figures on a chart. If you are going to compare statistics, consider making a pie chart to demonstrate percentages, a bar graph to exhibit comparisons, and/or a line graph to illustrate increases.

- **Handout:** Many items mentioned earlier can be put on a handout and given to the audience before the presentation begins. If you give an outline, leave some blanks so the listeners can take notes and stay involved with your presentation. Don't forget to look into free handouts that might be provided by local organizations or businesses.

- **Chalkboard:** Use the board only to illustrate something you are saying at the same time. For example, if you use an unfamiliar technical term, write it on the board. But audiences should not have to watch you make a chart on the board of the increase in automobile accidents over the past 30 years. Make a chart of this the night before and have it ready to go when you get to that part of your speech.

- **Multimedia:** Presentation software for your computer, such as Microsoft Power-Point or Adobe Persuasion, can make your presentation polished and professional. You can program everything from charts and slides to video clips with sound for presentation in your speech. You can even create a link to the Internet that the audience can view on your screen. You will need access to a television monitor, a computer-projection table, or an LCD panel that can be placed on a regular overhead projector.

There are a number of do's and don'ts to keep in mind when using visual aids. First, personally make sure that any equipment you are using is in operating order before the presentation. Be prepared to give the speech even if your equipment fails. Second, make sure the visual is large enough for those in the back of the room to see easily. A Polaroid snapshot may picture exactly what you want to show, but unless it is blown up, even the front row may have difficulty seeing it. In addition, hold your visual up or tape it up long enough for everyone to see. Otherwise, someone looking away momentarily may miss the visual. Third, practice with the visual. Know exactly when you are going to use it in your

11.1   **Using Presentation Technology**

Go to
**www.mhhe.com/
adamsgalanes6**
for additional
weblink activities.

MEDIA AND TECHNOLOGY

The availability and simplicity of presentational software such as Power-Point have increased audience expectations for the use of profession-ally created visuals to aid in understanding presentation content. Despite the pervasiveness of this type of technology, many public speaking professionals question whether multimedia visual aids help or hinder speakers. Thus, practitioners recommend using the following guidelines when using PowerPoint:

1. *Don't let technology dictate content.* Determine the most appropriate content and then begin to think how you can use the presentation software to enhance how the material is conveyed to your audience.

2. *Ensure that special effects have a purpose.* Although they may be fun to include (and show off your knowledge of the software) they distract from your content.

3. *Keep wording clear and simple.* Abbreviate your message by outlining thoughts that provide a memory trigger for you and the audience. Use a consistent font size and style with a combination of upper- and lowercase lettering.

4. *Keep a consistent design.* Use color sparingly with backgrounds that allow your text to stand out. A slide is of little use if the audience can't read the material.

Consult the following sources for more information on what to do and what to avoid with PowerPoint presentations:
www.anandnartrajan.com/ FAQs/powerpoint.html and
www.crocker.k12.mo.us/tech/pptrules.htm.

speech. Students have been known to prepare visual aids and in their nervousness and ex-citement, they forget to show their hard work. Fourth, don't pass anything around during your presentation. Your audience's attention will be on the object itself or on the person handing the material to them rather than on you. Pass something out before you begin or tell your listeners that they will receive it after you have concluded. Fifth, use a visual aid only if it pertains to your speech. Although visual aids can make a great contribution to your presentation, this same visual aid will seem "thrown in" or "in the way" if it has no relationship to the topic.

ORGANIZE MATERIALS AND PRESENTATION

The verbal and visual information you have gathered will be a valuable asset as you plan the organization and writing of your presentation. Look at this step of organizing your materials as drawing a road map of how the audience should follow your speech. As with any road map, directions must be clear for the audience to understand how and why you are taking them through your chosen topic. Every speech should have an introduction, a body, and a conclusion (see Table 11.2). Plan to get the audience's attention, explain what you are going to be talking about, talk about it, and then summarize what you have said.

TABLE 11.2	Outline of Options for an Organized Presentation

I. Introduction

   A. Attention Material

      1. Striking statement

      2. Striking quotation

      3. Real question

      4. Rhetorical question

      5. Humor

      6. Story

   B. Need Step

      1. Direct

      2. Indirect

   C. Preview

II. Body

   A. Chronological

   B. Spatial

   C. Cause–Effect

   D. Problem–Solution

   E. Topical

III. Conclusion

   A. Summary

   B. Appeal

GLOSSARY

Introduction

The first of three components of a speech designed to catch the attention of the audience, show a need to listen, and clarify the main point of the speech

---

Introduction.   An **introduction** has three essential elements: an attention step, a need step, and a thesis statement. First, your goal is to motivate your audience to listen. This is called the *attention step,* and you can choose from a number of ways to capture an audience's attention.

1. Use humor.

One way of getting audience members to listen to you is to make them laugh. However, be careful if you use this approach. First, what you say must be funny to others, not just to you. Preview the joke or story to other people before you use it in your presentation. If your friends enjoy it, chances are your audience will also. The humor must be in good taste. You do not want to offend anyone. You want favorable attention, with people wanting to listen to you. Don't risk alienating anyone by telling a story that is going to offend. Finally, your humor should be relevant to your topic or to the audience and occasion. Something that David Letterman said the night before may be humorous, but if it is not related to what you want to talk about, find something more appropriate and relevant.

2. **Ask a question.**

A second way of getting attention is by asking the members of the audience a question. If you are going to talk about parking problems on your campus, ask, "How many of you have been late to a class because you could not find a close place to park?" or "How many of you have gotten a parking ticket from the campus gestapo this semester?" If you want an answer, tell them how to respond: "Please raise your hand." However, don't make your question so personal that you won't get an accurate response. "How many of you use cocaine on a regular basis?" will probably get a laugh, but no hands will go up. Finally, use the information as a transition into the topic of your speech: "That's what I thought. Too many of us are spending too much money on parking tickets when the university should be building more parking structures." You must be able to use any answer as a transition. If no one raised a hand, say something like, "Well, you guys are lucky. In my research I've found too many of us spending. . . "

A rhetorical question is a question that the speaker asks, but does not want the audience to answer aloud. The speaker will answer the question as part of the speech: "Is there any way to stop college students from binge drinking? I think there is and today I am going to offer you three practical solutions to what seems to be a growing problem at our school and at other colleges across the country." The audience will think about the question, but the speaker will provide the answer.

3. **Make a striking statement.**

Say something at the start of your speech to grab the audience's attention and make them want to listen. Saying, "I can guarantee you an A in this course and in every other course you take this semester" will probably gain the attention of every student in your class. Likewise, "Our division has been wasting at least $50,000 a year for the past three years" will gain the attention of your employer. You have to be able to carry out your promise in the rest of your speech, but you can be sure that for the first few minutes, at least, people will be listening to you. Another good example of a striking statement is the tagline used by news programs or talk shows to get you to stay tuned to an upcoming segment. This statement should make your audience feel like they want and need to listen to what your group has to say during the presentation.

4. **Offer a striking quotation.**

Giving a vivid quotation can attract attention. For example, if your group has been doing research on date rape, quoting a victim's own words about how she felt during the attack will attract attention to your topic. Reading a quotation from a song or a poem is another way of attracting favorable attention. Quoting someone

MHHE.com/ groups
Using the Net to find quotations.

familiar and well liked or someone saying something unexpected or out of character can gain attention. For example, a student giving a presentation on myths in student academic performance began, "I've heard it said that 'a theory is a thing of beauty, until it gets run over by a fact.' Nowhere is this more true than in the field of education." Although the quote does not directly relate to education, the speaker makes the connection for the audience while grabbing their attention with vivid word imagery.

5. **Tell a short story.**

   People are interested in other people. Telling a story related to your topic is a great way to gain attention. The story can be true or fictional, but it must help you make your point. If a character in the story is someone audience members can relate to, so much the better.

The second essential part of an introduction is the *need step.* Follow your attention step with a short statement that shows audience members why they need or can benefit from the information you are about to give them. A direct purpose statement shows audience members how the presentation is relevant to their lives and how they can directly benefit by listening. If you are talking about a new medical discovery, tell the audience that your information could help save a life. If your topic is the outrageous prices at the college bookstore, tell them you can save them money. An indirect need step implies that, because the topic is so significant, everyone should know something about it: "What happens to Social Security will affect all of us no matter how young or old we are today."

The third element of a good introduction is the *thesis statement* and *preview.* Here you tell the audience what specifically you will be talking about. Like a road map, it shows your listeners where you are going, making it easier for them to understand your points. Use enumeration (i.e., words like "first, second, third") so listeners know how many main points you will cover. A completed introduction will gain the audience's attention, establish the need to listen, and demonstrate the purpose and main points of your speech.

Body.   The **body** of the speech is the main portion of the presentation in which you actually talk about the ideas you want to cover. Present your ideas in an easily recognized pattern so your audience sees the relationship among them. Remember to use transition statements that help move your speech smoothly from one point to the next. The following are some of the most common patterns of organization.

- **Problem–solution:** The problem–solution pattern is especially important if you are trying to persuade your audience to accept your recommendation. You talk about the problem, its causes and significance, and then present your proposal as a solution for the problem. This pattern is also easy to use if you want to inform, such as by showing how a problem has already been solved. "How New York City dealt with the devastating loss of the World Trade Center" could be discussed using this pattern.

- **Chronological:** A chronological order is a discussion of things as they happen in time. Talking about how something is made, explaining a historical event, or listing the steps one needs to follow when searching for a job naturally calls for a chronological order. The history of your sorority or the development of the motion picture calls for a chronological order.

GLOSSARY

Body

The second of three components of a speech where the main ideas are introduced and developed

"*The main body of this Inaugural Address is great, but he wants a happier ending.*"

- **Spatial:** A spatial order is used to describe things as they exist in space. A presentation describing the best areas to snow ski in California could go from north to south within the state or from east to west.

- **Cause and effect or effect to cause:** Explaining how a particular virus affects millions of people is an example of cause and effect organization. You describe how the virus was discovered and how it works and then discuss the suffering of the people who have contracted it. You can also reverse the process by first talking about the people who are suffering, then describing why this situation exists.

- **Topical:** A topical organization examines the inherent parts of a topic, its essential components. For instance, our American system of government is made up of the executive, legislative, and judicial branches. To cover the entire topic, you have to mention all three parts.

You may discover that pairing some of the organizational styles works more efficiently. No organization style is the best, but using some type of systematic approach is essential to the successful comprehension of your main purpose and ideas. A stream of consciousness is not considered a typical pattern. Members of the audience may not think along the same lines you do. Instead of presenting a topic in exactly the same way the ideas came to you, you are better off choosing a pattern with which audience members are likely to be familiar.

Conclusion

The third of three components of a speech that summarizes the ideas a speaker wishes the audience to remember

Conclusion.   If your purpose was to inform, your **conclusion** should be a summary of the main points you want the audience to remember. What do you hope listeners retain after they leave the room, even if they forget everything else? That should be in your conclusion. Your conclusion is similar to your introduction, but your final summary should be more concrete. Remind the audience of the specific items you covered and, while summarizing your position, explain what you want them to remember.

If your purpose is to persuade, this is your last chance to get the audience emotionally involved in your topic. Use this opportunity to reconnect with your audience, offer a challenge, or help them to see how things could change for better or worse if action is or is not taken.

The Presenting Stage

Surveys show that many Americans fear public speaking more than they fear spiders, snakes, or even death.[6] You may be in a group communication class because you were trying to avoid "the dreaded speech." However, as a group member, you may be faced with this feared endeavor. Many times in your career you may need to speak to a committee or larger audience, so it is wise to work through this fear of making an oral presentation now. We offer advice for checking your language, practicing your speech out loud, and, finally, evaluating your speech or the speeches of others.

CHECK YOUR LANGUAGE

In the English language, we have approximately half a million words to express our ideas. The average college student can recognize 60,000 words and actually uses about 20,000.[7] The more word choices speakers have, the better able they are to make language do their bidding and fulfill their purposes.[8] Speakers often forget that writing the speech is only half the battle; the delivery is just as important. Trying to make your audience feel compelled to listen, participate, and take action requires an effective use of language. Speak to your audience in a conversational style, just as if you are giving the speech to good friends, not in a dry monotone or reading manner. Generally, speakers should strive for a style that is clear, vivid, and appropriate.

Clarity requires language that is concrete rather than abstract. Note the difference between explaining that last night you saw Tom "coming down the street" and saying you saw Tom "staggering" or "crawling" or "stumbling" or "skipping down the street." Clarity also requires that you avoid jargon and use words that your audience will understand.

Vividness attracts our attention. Using figurative language, repetition, and amplification (supporting details that develop or reinforce an idea) will add vividness to your presentation and make it easier for your audience to pay attention. Try to imagine Martin Luther King's famous "I Have a Dream" speech without repetition or figurative language—part of what made his speech memorable.

Make sure your language choices are *appropriate* for the audience and the occasion. A formal classroom presentation probably should not be filled with expletives or street language unless they are being used to illustrate something in the speech.

PRACTICE ALOUD

There are four ways of delivering an oral presentation: manuscript, memorization, impromptu, and extemporaneous. Each method has advantages and disadvantages.

If you write out everything you want to say, word for word in a manuscript, you won't leave anything out when you present the speech. Everything you want to say is right there in front of you. Unfortunately, many speakers become so dependent on their manuscripts that they pay little attention to the audience. They have little eye contact with listeners and may not notice whether listeners understand the material presented. Listeners may feel that the speaker has little interest in them and may find the speech boring. News broadcasters and many political figures avoid this problem by using a TelePrompTer that makes it seem as if they are looking directly at their listener, but such equipment is probably not available to you. If you must use a manuscript, work diligently to make a connection with your audience through eye contact and body language while occasionally looking down to find your next point.

You could also memorize your speech. Thus, you make sure you don't leave anything out and at the same time maintain eye contact with your audience. However, this requires that you have a good memory and do not forget even minor points. No situation is more uncomfortable for a speaker than drawing a blank about what comes next. If you are going to attempt a memorized presentation, make sure it really is committed to memory and that it does not sound memorized. The delivery of a memorized speech often sounds robotic. Because the speaker spends many hours working on the memorization of the material, she or he doesn't have time to work on a natural conversational delivery. Even good eye contact will not fool an audience if you do not sound interested in the subject or in them.

An **impromptu speech** is one delivered off-the-cuff. There are no notes and no specific preparation; you speak from the knowledge that you have gained over a lifetime. Not having to prepare in advance is an advantage, but a disadvantage is that such speeches can sound disorganized or incoherent. The perfect example that might have easily explained your second point may not come to mind until you are well into your third point. The audience is left to put all the little pieces of information together. In a typical group meeting or interaction, the communication that occurs generally consists of members responding impromptu to each other.

An **extemporaneous speech** is a prepared speech, but instead of writing out a manuscript, you write an outline of what you want to cover, using as few or as many notes as you need to present your ideas. Don't prepare too many notes or you might as well read a manuscript. However, make sure that everything is in your note cards: ideas, statistics, quotations, or a final statement. The exact wording of the speech will be different every time you present it, but the main points will always be there. This method permits you to have much eye contact with the audience. It also allows you to react to your audience's feedback without fear of losing your place or forgetting something you want to say. If you realize that some of your listeners do not understand you, you can offer another example or repeat your point in a different way to make the point clear, then return to where you left off in your notes.

Once you have selected the method of delivery you plan to use, practice your speech aloud. Thinking the speech silently to yourself does not take as much time as saying it aloud does, so you may misjudge the length. You also need to hear what the speech sounds like because you may find that something said easily in your head is a real tongue twister when said aloud. A colleague of ours remembers his embarrassment when he wanted to say "needy student" but "nudey student" came out. After a second and then a third

GLOSSARY

Impromptu Speech

A speech delivered without preparation or notes

Extemporaneous Speech

A speech that is prepared and delivered from notes and not read from a manuscript

unsuccessful attempt at "needy" he was forced to switch to "impecunious." If possible, get someone to listen to your speech before you present it to an audience. That person will be able to tell you what you can do to improve the speech.

What Makes a Good Oral Presentation?

Since the time of the ancient Greeks and Romans, a number of criteria have been generally agreed upon as artistic standards to evaluate oral performances. These standards are called the *canons of rhetoric*. Karyn and Donald Rybacki write: "Because rhetorical theory was an outgrowth of observations of the practice of public speaking in classical cultures, the canons are particularly appropriate to the analysis of speeches."[9] The five classical canons were invention, arrangement, style, delivery, and memory. You can use these elements to render an overall evaluation of any presentation, to compare it to other presentations you have heard, or to offer suggestions for improvement. We will concentrate on the first four canons because memory, the use of codes and mnemonic devices the speaker relied on to recall lengthy speeches, has generally been replaced by written notes and the use of TelePrompTers (see Table 11.3).

The canon of **invention** deals with the raw materials of the speech and how they are adapted to a particular audience. Did the speaker choose an appropriate topic? Did the speaker select interesting examples and illustrations to explain an informative thesis? Did

---

11.2   Preparing an Individual Presentation

APPLY NOW

Congratulations. The group mentioned in Case 11.1 has selected you to make the oral presentation to the restaurant association. Although the other members will be present to help answer questions, the primary responsibility for the presentation rests with you.

1. Based on the information you already have, go through the planning stages of preparing an oral presentation. For example, decide whether you are going to try to persuade your listeners to act or to inform them of what your group has discovered. What do you think the audience will be like? How will audience members respond to you? What makes you think so?

2. List the verbal and visual materials you plan to use. Be specific. What types of visual aids would be effective? What kinds of statistics?

3. Assuming that all these materials are available, what pattern of organization would be most effective in presenting them? What type of introduction would best attract the audience's attention?

4. Compare your answers with those of the other members of your class.

GLOSSARY

Invention

A canon of rhetoric identifying the raw materials of the speech and how they are adapted to a particular audience

TABLE 11.3	Criteria for Evaluation (Canons)

1. Invention: raw materials and adaptation to audience

2. Arrangement: organization

3. Style: choice of language

4. Delivery: oral presentation

the speaker use significant and sufficient examples and statistics to support a thesis when attempting to persuade? Did the speaker relate the topic and show its significance to the audience? Did the speaker complete the presentation within any assigned time limits?

In a panel or symposium, did the speakers work together to present varied aspects of the issue? Did the moderator keep the discussion focused? Did the panel cover all the material that would be of interest to the audience?

The canon of **arrangement** is concerned with how the speech is put together or organized. Were the main points clear and easy to follow? Was there an interesting introduction that captured the audience's attention and previewed the body of the speech? Were there effective transitions? Did the conclusion summarize the main points and reinforce the central idea?

11.3   Using the Canons to Evaluate

APPLY NOW

Demosthenes, the great Greek orator of antiquity, is supposed to have claimed that the most important canon was delivery, the second most important was delivery, and the third most important was delivery.

1. Which canon do you think is the most important? How would you divide 100 points among the four canons to show their relative importance?

2. In a small group, discuss which of the canons you feel to be most important, rank them from 1 (most important) to 4 (least important), and figure out the average score for each based on the 100-point scale.

3. Can your group offer any examples of contemporary or historical public speakers who rate high on all the canons? Who rates poorly on all?

4. Compare your responses to those of the other groups in your class.

GLOSSARY

Arrangement

One of the canons of rhetoric specifying how a speech is ordered or put together

In a symposium, did the moderator provide the audience with transitions between the individual presentations? Was there a clear introduction and a conclusion to the discussion? In a panel, did the participants stick to the topic and make clear when they were moving from one aspect to another?

The canon of **style** is concerned with the distinctive manner and appropriateness of the speech's language. Was the language clear and accurate? Was it appropriate to the audience and occasion? Was it free of grammatical errors that make it hard to understand? Was the language vivid and likely to hold the audience's attention?

The canon of **delivery** deals with how the presentation is offered to the audience. Did the speaker maintain eye contact with the audience? Did the speaker avoid any distracting movements and gestures? Did the speaker vary his or her pitch and rate? Was the speaker confident? Were appropriate movements and gestures used?

RESOURCES FOR REVIEW AND DISCUSSION

SUMMARY

- Small groups are often called upon to make oral presentations of their work, so members need to understand how to be effective presenters.

- Public presentation sessions include panels and symposiums, where speakers publicly discuss an issue before an audience; a forum often follows, where the audience can address or question the speakers.

- In preparing a speech, the speaker must first determine whether the purpose is to inform, persuade, or entertain.

- Speakers must analyze the audience to understand how to get their attention; find the most appropriate and interesting ideas, supporting materials, and visuals aids to present; and organize the material so that it is easy for the audience to follow the presentation.

- An effective presentation includes an introduction, body, and conclusion.

- Oral presentations can be evaluated using four criteria, based on the canons of rhetoric, which include invention, arrangement, style, and delivery.

EXERCISES

1. C-SPAN is a nonprofit cooperative of the cable industry. C-SPAN programming covers a variety of political events, including congressional hearings, press conferences, public policy conferences, and so forth. Watch C-SPAN for examples of panels, forums, or symposiums.

   a. Could you distinguish which kind of public presentation was taking place?

   b. Was there a moderator? How effective was the moderator? Why?

   c. What did you find interesting about how the public presentation was conducted? What did you see that was problematic?

   d. Did the public presentation meet with your expectations? Were you surprised? Why?

e. Did you get any ideas about how you might or might not conduct your own public presentation?

2. Take some time to listen to the persuasive speech of a car salesperson and a minister. Compare and contrast the "sales pitch" of both. Both presentations are persuasive in nature, but they are delivered to different audiences. How are their oral presentations the same? How are their oral presentations different?

3. Various videos and CD-ROMs contain the text of famous speeches. You can rent these at your local or school library. Find one with excerpts or the entire speech of someone famous who interests you. Watch the speech and evaluate according to the four canons: invention, style, delivery, and arrangement.

 Go to **www.mhhe.com/adamsgalanes6** and **www.mhhe.com/groups** for self-quizzes and weblinks.

KEY TERMS • CONCEPTS

Arrangement	Extemporaneous Speech	Moderator
Audience Analysis	Forum Discussion	Panel Discussion
Body	Impromptu Speech	Persuasive Speech
Conclusion	Informative Speech	Style
Delivery	Introduction	Symposium
Entertainment Speech	Invention	

www.mhhe.com/adamsgalanes6

Use the flash cards and crossword puzzles on the Online Learning Center to further your knowledge of these key terms.

Techniques for Observing Problem-Solving Groups

Consulting to the Technical College Executive Committee

The technical college's executive committee meetings were boring. Members agreed that communication among the various departments was essential for the college to function effectively, but the weekly staff meetings somehow were not satisfying this need. Real communication about problems, solutions, and goals of the various departments was done outside the meetings. Members didn't complain much, but they showed little enthusiasm for the meetings. The chair of the committee, Basil, was concerned. He asked Gloria to observe the meetings, figure out what was wrong, make recommendations for improvement, and conduct training sessions to help members interact more effectively during the meetings.

For two months, Gloria systematically observed, analyzed, and evaluated the staff meetings. First, she attended meetings, took notes, and completed a content analysis that showed Basil doing most of the talking. He was almost the only member to initiate new ideas during the meetings. Other members contributed only when addressed directly by Basil. Thus, a *wheel* interaction pattern (with Basil at the hub and everyone else as an individual spoke) had become the group's norm. On a questionnaire asking about effectiveness, Basil indicated he believed the meetings were very effective, most other members thought they were moderately effective, and two members rated them completely ineffective. Gloria followed up the questionnaire by interviewing each staff member to determine how the meetings could be improved. She paid particular attention to the comments of the two dissatisfied members.

Gloria concluded that Basil dominated the meetings but that he was unaware he was dominating. Members felt stifled during the meetings but didn't know how to express those feelings to Basil or to change the pattern of their meetings. Members wanted to discuss freely the problems that had come up in their respective departments, and they hoped the staff meetings would provide an open forum for exchanging information and ideas. The two members who were most dissatisfied were quite knowledgeable about college operations and felt particularly ignored. Members were suppressing disagreements for fear of retribution by Basil; although Basil was not a tyrant, he made it clear from his behavior (rolling his eyes, interrupting people, speaking sarcastically) that he did not like it when others disagreed with his ideas. In short, this committee displayed some obvious and some hidden problems, all of which could be overcome with training and desire.

This story highlights the value of having someone observe a group, describe its behavior, evaluate that behavior, and make recommendations to improve the functioning of the group. In this appendix we will present a variety of techniques to help you do that.

The Role of the Observer

The role of group observer can be valuable and helpful if the observer knows how to function. Most group members have not been trained to be effective group participants, so it's especially important for those who do know something about small group communication to monitor the group's discussions and help the group perform as well as possible. Knowledgeable observers function like athletic coaches, helping players improve their performance as a team.

In Chapter 1 we described the participant-observer, a group member who makes available his or her knowledge and skills to help a group perform more effectively. A second type of observer is the **consultant-observer,** an outsider brought in to observe, evaluate, and make recommendations to the group. The consultant-observer may be a member of the organization the group belongs to or an outside consultant trained in small group communication. When executives learn that someone within the organization has small group communication expertise, they often ask that person to apply his or her skills to help the group. That was Gloria's situation when she observed the technical college executive staff, and that may also be your position someday.

Participant- and consultant-observers have unique advantages and disadvantages. The consultant-observer may be able to maintain more objectivity regarding group members and group processes, but the participant-observer may have inside information that gives insight regarding what is happening in the group. A group that has been experiencing serious conflict may view the consultant-observer as a hatchet person for an executive. On the other hand, a participant-observer may be seen as biased rather than objective, thereby undermining his or her effectiveness as an adviser to the group.

GLOSSARY

Consultant-Observer

An outsider who observes and evaluates a group

In general, observers seek to answer two questions: How well is this group performing? and How can it improve? However, *many* elements contribute to a group's performance. Observers cannot look at everything at once or they will become overwhelmed. They plan their observation strategy in advance. Table A.1 lists questions you can use as a general guide for observing. Don't try to answer all the questions; instead, use the list to screen out elements that seem to be working well so you can concentrate your observation on those that can be improved.

Both participant- and consultant-observers should follow several guidelines when they are giving feedback to a group:

1. *Stress the positive* and point out what the group or the leader is doing well.

2. *Do not overwhelm the group* by telling the members each and every thing you think should be improved. Instead, emphasize one or two things that most need improvement.

3. *Avoid arguing* when you present your observations and advice. Leave the group members free to decide whether and how your advice will be used.

4. *Do not interrupt the whole meeting* to give advice to the group's leader during a meeting. Instead, whisper or write your suggestions.

5. *Speak clearly and concisely* when you are giving feedback. Do not ramble or belabor your points. Consider the following remarks by Larry, who observed that group members were switching to new topics without completing the original one:

   One of the problems I see is that you are having trouble staying on track with your discussion! In the past five minutes, you have talked about a pedestrian overpass at Grand and National, why money was spent on artificial turf instead of library books, how you can handle a landlord who won't repair plumbing, and several other topics. Your discussion would be more efficient if you helped each other focus on the original question: How can pedestrian/car accidents be eliminated on National Avenue?

   In this example of giving feedback, Larry states the problem he has observed, gives a few (rather than 10 or 20) examples to clarify what he means, and provides a suggestion that makes the whole group responsible for solving the problem. He doesn't ramble endlessly about the problem or blame individual members.

6. *Prepare members to use special procedures* by explaining the procedure or giving them a handout that outlines the key steps. (Feel free to use the figures in this book, as long as you give credit to the source.)

7. *Make individual critical comments in private* to the appropriate person so that he or she will not feel attacked or publicly humiliated.

Now that you have an idea of what observers look for and how they present their findings, here are a variety of instruments to help you gather information about your group.

Observation Instruments and Techniques

The following techniques and instruments may be used by group members as part of a self-evaluation of the group or by observers. They can be used as is or adapted to suit particular situations and groups.

TABLE A.1   **Questions to Guide Your Observations**

GROUP GOALS
- Are there clear and accepted group goals?
- How well does the group understand its charge?
- Does the group know and accept limits on its area of freedom?
- Do members know what output they are supposed to produce?

SETTING
- Does the physical environment (seating arrangements, privacy, attractiveness) facilitate group discussions?

COMMUNICATION SKILLS AND INTERACTION PATTERNS
- How clearly do members express their ideas and opinions?
- Do members complete one topic before they switch to another?
- Is verbal participation balanced equally among all members?
- Is the pattern of interaction all-channel or unduly restricted?

COMMUNICATION CLIMATE AND NORMS
- Does the group climate seem supportive and cooperative or defensive and competitive?
- What attitudes do the members exhibit toward themselves and each other?
- Do any hidden agenda items seem to interfere with group progress?
- Do any norms seem to interfere with group progress or cohesiveness?

LEADERSHIP AND MEMBER ROLES
- What style of leadership is the designated leader providing?
- Is the leadership appropriate for the group's needs?
- Are the roles performed by members appropriate both for their skills and the needs of the group?
- Are there any needed functions not being provided by anyone?

DECISION-MAKING AND PROBLEM-SOLVING PROCEDURES
- Are members adequately prepared for meetings?
- Does the group use an agenda? How well is it followed? Does it serve the group?
- Is anyone providing periodic internal summaries so members can keep track of major points of discussion?
- Are decisions, assignments, and proposals being recorded?
- How are decisions being made?
- Has the group defined and analyzed the problem before developing solutions?
- Do members understand and agree on criteria in making decisions?
- How creative is the group in generating potential solutions?
- Do members defer judgment until all solutions have been listed and understood?
- Are information and ideas being evaluated critically or accepted at face value?
- Do you see any tendency toward groupthink?
- Has the group made adequate plans to implement decisions?
- Are special procedures (brainstorming, focus groups, etc.) being used as needed?
- Could procedural changes benefit the group?

FIGURE A.1   Verbal Interaction Diagram

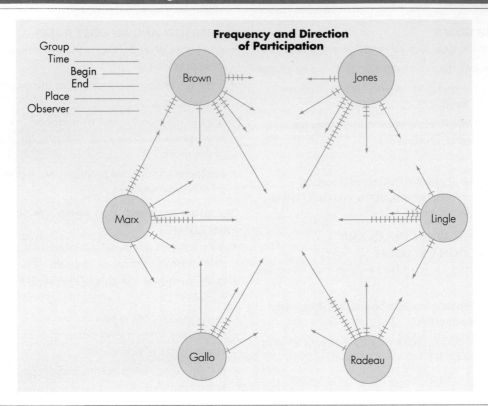

**Frequency and Direction
of Participation**

Group _____
Time _____
Begin _____
End _____
Place _____
Observer _____

VERBAL INTERACTION ANALYSIS

A **verbal interaction analysis** shows who talks to whom, how often each member speaks, and whether the group participation is balanced or dominated by one or more individuals. A model interaction diagram is shown in Figure A.1. The names of all participants are located around the circle in the same order in which they sit during the discussion. Whenever a person speaks, an arrow is drawn from that person's position toward the individual to whom the remark was addressed. Subsequent remarks in the same direction are indicated by the short cross marks on the base of the arrow. (For example, Gallo addressed three remarks to Brown in the model diagram.) The longer arrow pointing toward the center indicates remarks made to the group as a whole.

An interaction diagram can look messy or confusing. For easier interpretation, display the numbers and percentages in a chart (see Figure A.2). From the frequency of participation to the group as a whole and to specific members, who might you guess is the leader of this group? Do you consider the participation balanced or not? Does anyone appear to dominate the discussion?

GLOSSARY

**Verbal
Interaction
Analysis**

*A technique to
discover who talks
to whom*

FIGURE A.2   How to Display Data from a Verbal Interaction Diagram

Group ___CURRICULUM COMMITTEE___   Place ___CRAIG HALL___

Observer ___SMITH___   Date ___9-5-2002___

Beginning time ___9:00 a.m.___   Ending Time ___10:30 a.m.___

TO:

FROM:	Brown	Jones	Lingle	Radeau	Gallo	Marx	Group	Total
Brown	–	5	2	4	2	5	5	23 / 16.1
Jones	3	–	3	4	4	3	13	30 / 21
Lingle	2	2	–	3	2	4	12	25 / 17.5
Radeau	3	3	4	–	0	2	12	24 / 16.8
Gallo	3	3	2	0	–	0	6	14 / 9.8
Marx	8	2	2	3	2	–	10	27 / 18.9
Total number	19	15	13	14	10	14	58	143
Total percent	13.3	10.5	9.1	9.8	7	9.8	40.6	100

CONTENT ANALYSIS PROCEDURES

Content analysis procedures examine the *type* of remarks being made by specific members. In Figure A.3, specific task, maintenance, and self-centered behaviors are listed along the left margin and the participants' names across the top. Each time a member speaks, the observer places a mark in the appropriate box according to the type of remark made. The tally marks are converted to percentages, as shown in Figure A.4. Who is probably the task leader of this group? Who is the maintenance leader? Are any individuals acting in self-centered ways?

Any category system can be used as the basis for a content analysis diagram. For example, you may want to focus on the defensive and supportive behaviors described in Chapter 7. In that case, you would record all the individual defensive and supportive communication categories (i.e., control, superiority, provisionalism, empathy, etc.) along the left side.

GLOSSARY

Content Analysis Procedures

Techniques to help analyze the types of remarks being made

FIGURE A.3   Content Analysis of Task, Maintenance, and Self-Centered Behaviors

Group _____   Place _____   Observer _____

Date _____   Beginning time _____   Ending Time _____

Participants' Names

	Behavioral Functions						
Task-Oriented	1. Initiating and orienting						
	2. Information giving						
	3. Information seeking						
	4. Opinion giving						
	5. Opinion seeking						
	6. Clarifying and elaborating						
	7. Evaluating						
	8. Summarizing						
	9. Coordinating						
	10. Consensus testing						
	11. Recording						
	12. Suggesting procedure						
Maintenance	13. Gatekeeping						
	14. Supporting						
	15. Harmonizing						
	16. Tension relieving						
	17. Dramatizing						
	18. Norming						
Self-Centered	19. Withdrawing						
	20. Blocking						
	21. Status and recognition seeking						

FIGURE A.4   How to Display Data from Content Analysis of Member Behaviors

Group _EXECUTIVE COMMITTEE_   Place _CU LOBBY_

Observer _ANDY_   Date _8-28-96_

Beginning time _4:30 p.m._   Ending Time _6:30 p.m._

	Behavioral Functions	Mary	John	Edna	Dave	Jodi	Total number percent
Task-Oriented	1. Initiating and orienting	5	3				8 / 5.7
	2. Information giving	6	5		2	3	16 / 11.4
	3. Information seeking			3			3 / 2.1
	4. Opinion giving	8	8	4	2	1	23 / 16.4
	5. Opinion seeking			2			2 / 1.4
	6. Clarifying and elaborating			3			3 / 2.1
	7. Evaluating	2	4			1	7 / 5
	8. Summarizing	2					2 / 1.4
	9. Coordinating	8					8 / 5.7
	10. Consensus testing				3		3 / 2.1
	11. Recording			5			5 / 3.6
	12. Suggesting procedure	3		6			9 / 6.4
Maintenance	13. Gatekeeping			1	5		6 / 4.3
	14. Supporting	2		2	6		10 / 7.1
	15. Harmonizing				3	2	5 / 3.6
	16. Tension relieving					6	6 / 4.3
	17. Dramatizing		5			3	8 / 5.7
	18. Norming				4		4 / 2.9
Self-Centered	19. Withdrawing		1				1 / .7
	20. Blocking	2	5				7 / 5
	21. Status and recognition seeking		4				4 / 2.9
	Total number / percent	38 / 27.1	35 / 25	26 / 18.6	25 / 17.9	16 / 11.4	140 / 100

FIGURE A.5	All-Purpose Discussion Rating Scale

Date _____   Group _____

Time _____   Observer _____

Group Characteristic	5 Excellent	4 Good	3 Average	2 Fair	1 Poor
Organization of discussion					
Equality of opportunity to speak					
Cooperative group orientation					
Listening to understand					
Evaluation of ideas					
Comments:					

Other types of content analyses can be performed. For example, you might want to trace the development of any fantasy chains in the group, the progression of an idea from its original introduction by one member through all its modifications by the rest of the group, the types of conflicts, or the types of arguments members use to support their ideas. It is easier if you tape-record (with permission, of course) the group's interaction first.

RATING SCALES

Rating scales are questionnaires that ask members or observers to assess any aspect of a group, such as group climate, cohesiveness, efficiency, satisfaction, freedom to express disagreement, and organization of discussion. For example, the question "How well did the committee chair keep the discussion organized?" asks you to rate the leader's ability to conduct a systematic discussion. Scale questions may be closed-ended, in which the responses are already provided for you (such as *very well, adequately,* and *very poorly*), or open-ended, in which you are free to respond any way you choose. The following figures provide a number of examples of rating scales. Figure A.5 is a general scale to evaluate any group discussion, and Figure A.6 is a scale adapted from one developed by Patton and

GLOSSARY

Rating Scales

Questions (scales) to help evaluate specific aspects of a group

FIGURE A.6	Problem-Solving Process Rating Scale

Instructions: Indicate the degree to which the group accomplished each identified behavior. Use the following scale for your evaluations:

	Poor	Fair	Average	Good	Excellent
	1	2	3	4	5

Circle the appropriate number in front of each item.

1 2 3 4 5   1. The concern of each member was identified regarding the problem the group attempted to solve.

1 2 3 4 5   2. This concern was identified *before* the problem was analyzed.

1 2 3 4 5   3. In problem analysis, the present condition was carefully compared with the specific condition desired.

1 2 3 4 5   4. The goal was carefully defined and agreed to by all members.

1 2 3 4 5   5. Valid (and relevant) information was secured when needed.

1 2 3 4 5   6. Possible solutions were listed and clarified before they were evaluated.

1 2 3 4 5   7. Criteria for evaluating proposed solutions were clearly identified and accepted by the group.

1 2 3 4 5   8. Predictions were made regarding the probable effectiveness of each proposed solution, using the available information and criteria.

1 2 3 4 5   9. Consensus was achieved on the most desirable solution.

1 2 3 4 5   10. A detailed plan to implement the solution was developed.

1 2 3 4 5   11. The problem-solving process was systematic and orderly.

Giffin to identify deficiencies in problem-solving procedures. Figure A.7 is the Seashore Index of Group Cohesiveness, which measures cohesiveness of a work group.[1] We encourage you to modify these scales or create your own.

FIGURE A.7   Seashore Index of Group Cohesiveness

Check one response for each question.

1. Do you feel that you are really a part of your work group?

_____ Really a part of my work group

_____ Included in most ways

_____ Included in some ways, but not in others

_____ Don't feel I really belong

_____ Don't work with any one group of people

_____ Not ascertained

2. If you had a chance to do the same kind of work for the same pay in another work group, how would you feel about moving?

_____ Would want very much to move

_____ Would rather move than stay where I am

_____ Would make no difference to me

_____ Would want very much to stay where I am

_____ Not ascertained

3. How does your group compare with other similar groups on each of the following points?

	Better than Most	About the Same as Most	Not as Good as Most	Not Ascertained
a. The way the members get along together	_____	_____	_____	_____
b. The way the members stick together	_____	_____	_____	_____
c. The way the members help each other on the job	_____	_____	_____	_____

SOURCE: From Stanley Seashore; *Group Cohesiveness in the Industrial Work Group* (Ann Arbor: Institute for Social Research, University of Michigan, 1954).

FIGURE A.8   **Postmeeting Reaction Form**

1. How do you feel about today's discussion?

   Excellent ___ Good ___ All right ___ So-so ___ Bad ___

2. What were the strong points of the discussion?

3. What were the weaknesses?

4. What changes would you suggest for future meetings?

(You need not sign your name.)

POSTMEETING REACTION FORMS

Postmeeting reaction (PMR) forms are questionnaires designed to get feedback from members about a particular meeting. PMR forms may focus on a particular aspect (such as leadership) or deal with several broad aspects (such as how effective members believe the meetings are). The leader, a member, or an observer distributes the PMR forms; members complete them anonymously, the results are tallied, and the findings are reported to the group as soon as possible. The findings provide a basis for the group to discuss how to improve its communication and effectiveness. Basil, the group leader in our introductory example, could have used PMR forms himself to get feedback from the other members about how the group's discussions could be improved.

PMR forms are tailored to fit the purposes and needs of the group. Questions may concern substantive items, interpersonal relationships, matters of procedure, or a mixture of all three. Two different examples of PMR forms are shown in Figures A.8 and A.9.

Evaluating Individual Participants

In addition to evaluating general group processes, it is often useful to evaluate behaviors of individual participants. An observer or the members themselves may complete the following forms. Figure A.10 is a simple rating form that focuses on some of the most important aspects of participation. A more detailed form is shown in Figure A.11. Figure A.12 is a scale to evaluate leadership and A.13 is a leader's self-rating scale.

FIGURE A.9   Postmeeting Reaction Form

Instruction: Circle the number that best indicates your reactions to the following questions about the discussion in which you participated:

1. *Adequacy of Communication.* To what extent do you feel members were understanding each others' statements and positions?

0	1	2	3	4	5	6	7	8	9	10

Talked past each other;   Communicated directly with
misunderstanding   each other; understanding well

2. *Opportunity to Speak.* To what extent did you feel free to speak?

0	1	2	3	4	5	6	7	8	9	10

Never had a chance to speak   Had all the opportunity to talk I wanted

3. *Climate of Acceptance.* How well did members support each other, show acceptance of individuals?

0	1	2	3	4	5	6	7	8	9	10

Highly critical and punishing   Supportive and receptive

4. *Interpersonal Relations.* How pleasant and concerned were members with interpersonal relations?

0	1	2	3	4	5	6	7	8	9	10

Quarrelsome, status differences emphasized   Pleasant, empathic, concerned with persons

5. *Leadership.* How adequate was the leader (or leadership) of the group?

0	1	2	3	4	5	6	7	8	9	10

Too weak ( ) or dominating ( )   Shared, group-centered, and sufficient

6. *Satisfaction with Role.* How satisfied are you with your personal participation in the discussion?

0	1	2	3	4	5	6	7	8	9	10

Very dissatisfied   Very satisfied

7. *Quality of Product.* How satisfied are you with the discussions, solutions, or learnings that came out of this discussion?

0	1	2	3	4	5	6	7	8	9	10

Very displeased   Very satisfied

8. *Overall.* How do you rate the discussion as a whole apart from any specific aspect of it?

0	1	2	3	4	5	6	7	8	9	10

Awful; waste of time   Superb; time well spent

FIGURE A.10   Participating Rating Scale

Date _____

_____   Observer _____
(Name of participant)

1. Contributions to the *content of the discussion?* (well prepared, supplied information, adequate reasoning, etc.)

5	4	3	2	1

Outstanding in quality   Fair share   Few or none
and quantity

2. Contributions to *efficient group procedures?* (agenda planning, relevant comments, summaries, keeping on track)

5	4	3	2	1

Always relevant,   Relevant, no   Sidetracked,
aided organization   aid in order   confused group

3. Degree of *cooperating?* (listening to understand, responsible, agreeable, group-centered, open-minded)

5	4	3	2	1

Very responsible   Self-centered
and constructive

4. *Speaking?* (clear, to group, one point at a time, concise)

5	4	3	2	1

Brief, clear,   Vague, indirect,
to group   wordy

5. *Value* to the group? (overall rating)

5	4	3	2	1

Most valuable   Least valuable

Suggestions:

FIGURE A.11   Participating Rating Scale

Participant's name _____

Instructions: Circle the number that best reflects your evaluation of the discussant's participation on each scale.

Superior   Poor

1	2	3	4	5	1. Was prepared and informed.
1	2	3	4	5	2. Contributions were brief and clear.
1	2	3	4	5	3. Comments relevant and well timed.
1	2	3	4	5	4. Spoke distinctly and audibly to all.
1	2	3	4	5	5. Contributions made readily and voluntarily.
1	2	3	4	5	6. Frequency of participation (if poor, too low [ ] or high [ ]).
1	2	3	4	5	7. Nonverbal responses were clear and constant.
1	2	3	4	5	8. Listened to understand and follow discussion.
1	2	3	4	5	9. Open-minded.
1	2	3	4	5	10. Cooperative and constructive.
1	2	3	4	5	11. Helped keep discussion organized, following outline.
1	2	3	4	5	12. Contributed to evaluation of information and ideas.
1	2	3	4	5	13. Respectful and tactful with others.
1	2	3	4	5	14. Encouraged others to participate.
1	2	3	4	5	15. Overall rating in relation to other discussants.

Comments   Evaluator _____

FIGURE A.12   Barnlund-Haiman Leadership Rating Scale

Instructions: This rating scale may be used to evaluate leadership in groups with or without official leaders. In the latter case (the leaderless group), use part A of each item only. When evaluating the actions of an official leader, use parts A and B of each item on the scale.

Influence in Procedure

Initiating Discussion

A. 3	2	1	0	1	2	3
Group needed more help in getting started			Group got right amount of help		Group needed less help in getting started	

B. The quality of the introductory remarks was:

Excellent	Good	Adequate	Fair	Poor

Organizing Group Thinking

A. 3	2	1	0	1	2	3
Group needed more direction in thinking			Group got right amount of help		Group needed less direction in thinking	

B. If and when attempts were made to organize group thinking, they were:

Excellent	Good	Adequate	Fair	Poor

Clarifying Communication

A. 3	2	1	0	1	2	3
Group needed more help in clarifying communication			Group got right amount of help		Group needed less help in clarifying communication	

B. If and when attempts were made to clarify communication, they were:

Excellent	Good	Adequate	Fair	Poor

Summarizing and Verbalizing Agreements

A. 3	2	1	0	1	2	3
Group needed more help in summarizing and verbalizing agreements			Group got right amount of help		Group needed less help in summarizing and verbalizing agreements	

B. If and when attempts were made to summarize and verbalize, they were:

Excellent	Good	Adequate	Fair	Poor

Resolving Conflict

A. 3	2	1	0	1	2	3
Group needed more help in resolving conflict			Group got right amount of help		Group needed less help in resolving conflict	

B. If and when attempts were made to resolve conflict, they were:

Excellent	Good	Adequate	Fair	Poor

(continues)

SOURCE: From D. C. Barnlund and F. S. Haiman, *The Dynamics of Discussion* (Houghton-Mifflin, 1960), pp. 401–4. Used by permission of Robert Goldsmith, M.D., executor of Barnlund estate.

FIGURE A.12   *Concluded*

Influence in Creative and Critical Thinking

Stimulating Critical Thinking

A. 3   2   1   0   1   2   3

Group needed more stimulation in creative thinking	Group got right amount of help	Group needed less stimulation in creative thinking

B. If and when attempts were made to stimulate ideas, they were:

Excellent	Good	Adequate	Fair	Poor

Encouraging Criticism

A. 3   2   1   0   1   2   3

Group needed more encouragement to be critical	Group got right amount of help	Group needed less encouragement to be critical

B. If and when attempts were made to encourage criticism, they were:

Excellent	Good	Adequate	Fair	Poor

Balancing Abstract and Concrete Thought

A. 3   2   1   0   1   2   3

Group needed to be more concrete	Group achieved proper balance	Group needed to be more abstract

B. If and when attempts were made to balance abstract and concrete thought, they were:

Excellent	Good	Adequate	Fair	Poor

Influence in Interpersonal Relations

Climate-Making

A. 3   2   1   0   1   2   3

Group needed more help in securing a permissive atmosphere	Group got right amount of help	Group needed less help in securing a permissive atmosphere

B. If and when attempts were made to establish a permissive atmosphere, they were:

Excellent	Good	Adequate	Fair	Poor

Regulating Participation

A. 3   2   1   0   1   2   3

Group needed more regulation of participation	Group got right amount of help	Group needed less regulation of participation

B. If and when attempts were made to regulate participation, they were:

Excellent	Good	Adequate	Fair	Poor

Overall Leadership

A. 3   2   1   0   1   2   3

Group needed more control	Group got right amount of control	Group needed less control

B. If and when attempts were made to control the group, they were:

Excellent	Good	Adequate	Fair	Poor

FIGURE A.13   Leader Self-Rating Scale

Instructions: Rate yourself on each item by putting a check mark in the "Yes" or "No" column. Your score is five times the number of items marked "Yes." Rating: *excellent,* 90 or higher; *good,* 80–85; *fair,* 70–75; *inadequate,* 65 or lower.

	Yes	No
1. I prepared all needed facilities.	___	___
2. I started the meeting promptly and ended on time.	___	___
3. I established an atmosphere of permissiveness and informality. I was open and responsive to all ideas.	___	___
4. I clearly oriented the group to its purpose and area of freedom.	___	___
5. I encouraged all members to participate and maintained equal opportunity for all to speak.	___	___
6. I used a plan for leading the group in an organized consideration of all major phases of the problem.	___	___
7. I listened actively and (if needed) encouraged all members to do so.	___	___
8. I saw to it that the problem was discussed thoroughly before solutions were considered.	___	___
9. I integrated related ideas or suggestions and urged the group to arrive at consensus on a solution.	___	___
10. My questions were clear and brief.	___	___
11. I saw to it that unclear statements were paraphrased or otherwise clarified.	___	___
12. I prompted open discussion of substantive conflicts.	___	___
13. I maintained order and organization, promptly pointing out tangents, making transitions, and keeping track of the passage of time.	___	___
14. I saw to it that the meeting produced definite assignments or plans for action, and that any subsequent meeting was arranged.	___	___
15. All important information, ideas, and decisions were promptly and accurately recorded.	___	___
16. I actively encouraged creative thinking.	___	___
17. I encouraged thorough evaluation of information and all ideas for solutions.	___	___
18. I was able to remain neutral during constructive arguments and otherwise encourage teamwork.	___	___
19. I suggested or urged establishment of needed norms and standards.	___	___
20. I encouraged members to discuss how they felt about the group process and resolve any blocks to progress.	___	___

RESOURCES FOR REVIEW AND DISCUSSION

SUMMARY

- A consultant-observer is an outsider brought in to observe a group; such observers may be more objective than participant-observers.

- Participant- and consultant-observers cannot look at everything at once, so they concentrate on those elements a group needs to improve most.

- When they give feedback, they focus on a few elements rather than risk overwhelming the group.

- Observers and group members themselves can use a variety of methods to gather information, including verbal interaction analyses, content analyses, and a variety of rating scales.

Chapter 1

1. Information for the following story about the El Cajon Book Club was taken from Marla Abramson, "The After-School Bunch," *Book,* May/June 2001, pp. 85–87.

2. Ellen Neuborne, "Companies Save, but Workers Pay," *USA Today,* February 25, 1997, pp. 1B–2B

3. Neuborne, "Companies Save," p. 1B.

4. Daniel McGinn, "Mired in Meetings," *Newsweek,* October 16, 2000, pp. 52–54.

5. Lawrence R. Frey, "The Call of the Field: Studying Communication in Natural Groups," in *Group Communication in Context,* ed. Lawrence R. Frey (Hillsdale, NJ: Lawrence Erlbaum Associates, 1994), pp. ix–xiv.

6. Charles C. DuBois, "Portrait of the Ideal MBA," *The Penn Stater,* September/October 1992, p. 131.

7. Joann Keyton, "Relational Communication in Groups," in *Handbook of Group Communication Theory & Research,* ed. Lawrence R. Frey (Thousand Oaks, CA: Sage, 1999), p. 192.

8. Information about Saturn is compiled from the following articles: William B. Cook, "Ringing in Saturn," *U.S. News & World Report,* October 22, 1990, pp. 51–54; S.C. Gwynne, "The Right Stuff," *Time,* October 29, 1990, pp. 74–77; James B. Treece, "Here Comes GM's Saturn," *Business Week,* April 9, 1990, pp. 56–62; and Douglas Williams, "Shop Floor Democracy," *Automotive Industries,* June 1989, pp. 48–49.

9. This line of research began in 1928 and continues to the present. For a concise summary of the research up to 1980, see Marvin E. Shaw, *Group Dynamics,* 3rd ed. (New York: McGraw-Hill, 1981), pp. 57–64.

10. Herm W. Smith, "Group versus Individual Problem Solving and Type of Problem Solved," *Small Group Behavior* 20 (1989), pp. 357–74.

11. Janis Andersen, Jon Nussbaum, Loretta Pecchioni, and Jo Anna Grant, "Interaction Skills in Instructional Settings," in *Teaching Communication,* 2nd ed., eds. Anita Vangelisti, John A. Daly, and Gustav W. Friedrich (Mahwah, NJ: LEA, 1999), pp. 359–74.

12. Robert G. Powell and Dana Caseau, *Classroom Communication and Diversity: Enhancing Instructional Practice* (Mahwah, NJ: LEA, 2004), pp. 193–94.

13. Dennis S. Gouran and Randy Y. Hirokawa, "Counteractive Functions of Communication in Effective Group Decision Making," in *Communication and Group Decision Making,* eds. Randy Y. Hirokawa and Marshall Scott Poole (Beverly Hills, CA: Sage, 1986), pp. 81–90.

14. Ann Margaret Trautlein, "The Rock, Egg, and Chicken: Metaphorical Perspectives on the Concept of a Group," in *Small Group Communication: Theory and Practice,* 7th ed., eds. Robert S. Cathcart, Larry A. Samovar, and Linda D. Henman (Madison, WI: Brown & Benchmark, 1996), pp. 33–39.

15. Shaw, *Group Dynamics,* p. 8.

16. Paul V. Crosby, ed., *Interaction in Small Groups* (New York: Macmillan, 1975), p. 7.

17. Randy Y. Hirokawa, Robert S. Cathcart, Larry A. Samovar, and Linda D. Henman, "Part IV: Group Processes," in *Small Group Communication: Theory and Practice,* 8th ed., eds. Randy Y. Hirokawa, Robert S. Cathcart, Larry A. Samovar, and Linda D. Henman (Los Angeles, CA: Roxbury, 2003), p. 83.

18. Sandra Ketrow, "Nonverbal Aspects of Group Communication," in *Handbook of Group Communication Theory & Research,* ed. Lawrence R. Frey (Thousand Oaks, CA: Sage, 1999), pp. 251–87.

19. John F. Cragan and David W. Wright, *Communication in Small Groups: Theory, Process, Skills,* 5th ed. (Belmont, CA: Wadsworth, 1999), pp. 20–21.

20. William C. Schutz, *FIRO: A Three-Dimensional Theory of Interpersonal Behavior* (New York: Rinehart, 1958).

21. Thomas J. Socha, "Communication in Family Units," in *Handbook of Group Communication Theory & Research,* ed. Lawrence R. Frey (Thousand Oaks, CA: Sage, 1999), pp. 475–92.

22. Carolyn M. Anderson and Matthew M. Martin, "The Effects of Communication Motives, Interaction Involvement, and Loneliness on Satisfaction: A Model of Small Groups," *Small Group Research* 26 (February 1995), pp. 118–37.

23. Kevin Wright, "Perceptions of On-Line Support Providers: An Examination of Perceived Homophily, Course Credibility, Communication and Social Support Within On-Line Support Groups," *Communication Quarterly* 48 (Winter 2000), pp. 44–59.

24. Susan A. Wheelan and Alan R. List, "Cohort Group Effectiveness and the Educational Achievement of Adult Undergraduate Students," *Small Group Research* 31 (December 2000), pp. 724–38.

25. Joseph M. Putti and Wong K. Choeng, "Singapore's Positive Experience with Quality Circles," *National Productivity Review* 9 (Spring 1990), pp. 193–200.

26. Henry P. Sims, Jr., and James W. Dean, Jr., "Beyond Quality Circles: Self-Managing Teams," *Personnel Journal* (1985), pp. 25–32.

27. Suggestions synthesized from Neil Clark, *Teambuilding: A Practical Guide for Trainers* (New York: McGraw-Hill, 1994); Glenn M. Parker, *Team Players and Teamwork* (San Francisco: Jossey-Bass, 1991); and Glenn H. Varney, *Building Productive Teams: An Action Guide and Resource Book* (San Francisco: Jossey-Bass, 1989).

28. Sharon L. Murrell, "The Impact of Communicating through Computers," unpublished doctoral dissertation, State University of New York at Stony Brook, 1983.

29. *The Random House Dictionary of the English Language,* 2nd ed. unabridged (New York: Random House, 1987), p. 665.

30. See Rob Anderson and Veronica Ross, *Questions of Communication: A Practical Introduction to Theory,* 2nd ed. (Boston: Bedford/St. Martin's, 1998), chap. 10.

Chapter 2

1. Dawn Steel (Producer) and Jon Turtetaub (Director), *Cool Runnings* [Film]. Distributed by Walt Disney Pictures (1993) and available on video.

2. Stephen W. Littlejohn, *Theories of Human Communication,* 7th ed. (Belmont, CA: Wadsworth/Thomson Learning, 2002).

3. Daniel Katz and Robert Kahn, *The Social Psychology of Organizations,* 2nd ed. (New York: Wiley, 1978).

4. Benjamin J. Broome and Luann Fulbright, "A Multistage Influence Model of Barriers to Small Group Problem Solving: A Participant-Generated Agenda for Small Group Research," *Small Group Research* 26 (February 1995), pp. 25–55.

5. Linda Putnam and Cynthia Stohl, "Bona Fide Groups: An Alternative Perspective for Communication and Small Group Decision Making," in *Communication and Group Decision Making,* 2nd ed., eds. Randy Hirokawa and Marshall Poole (Thousand Oaks, CA: Sage, 1996), pp. 147–78.

6. Broome and Fulbright, "A Multistage Influence Model."

7. Randy Y. Hirokawa and Joann Keyton, "Perceived Facilitators and Inhibitors of Effectiveness in Organizational Work Teams," *Management Communication Quarterly* 8 (May 1995), pp. 424–46.

8. Deborah G. Ancona and David F. Caldwell, "Bridging the Boundary: External Activity and Performance in Organizational Teams," *Administrative Science Quarterly* 37 (December 1992), pp. 634–65.

9. Cynthia Stohl and Kasey Walker, "A Bona Fide Perspective for the Future of Groups," in *New Directions in Group Communication,* ed. Lawrence R. Frey (Thousand Oaks, CA: Sage, 2002), pp. 237–52.

10. Ibid.

11. Ronald Brownstein, "Tapping Talent, Not Just Names," *Los Angeles Times,* July 4, 2004, pp. A1, A21.

12. Beth Bonniwell Haslett and John R. Oglive, "Feedback Processes in Task Groups," in *Small Group Communication: Theory and Practice,* 8th ed., eds. Randy Hirokawa, Robert Cathcart, Larry Samovar, and Linda Henman (Los Angeles: Roxbury, 2003), pp. 97–108.

13. Ibid.

14. Ibid.

15. Ibid.

16. Abran J. Salazar, "Understanding the Synergistic Effects of Communication in the Small Group: Making the Most of Group Member Abilities," *Small Group Research* 26 (May 1995), pp. 169–99.

17. Jeremy Rose, "Communication Challenges and Role Functions of Performing Groups," *Small Group Research* 25 (August 1994), pp. 411–32.

Chapter 3

1. Richard West and Lynn H. Turner, *Introducing Communication Theory: Analysis and Application,* 2nd ed. (New York: McGraw-Hill, 2004).

2. Julia T. Wood, *Communication Theories in Action: An Introduction,* 3rd ed. (Belmont, CA: Thomson Wadsworth, 2004).

3. Ibid.

4. Martin Fackler, "Homeward Bound: Carefully Worded Letter to China Earns Release of Crew Members," *San Francisco Chronicle,* April 12, 2001, pp. A1, A17.

5. Frank E. X. Dance, "A Helical Model of Communication," in *Foundations of Communication Theory,* eds. Kenneth K. Sereno

and C. David Mortensen (New York: Harper & Row, 1970), pp. 103–07.

6. Paul Watzlaweick, Janet H. Beavin, and Don D. Jackson, *The Pragmatics of Human Communication* (New York: Norton, 1967).

7. Kittie W. Watson, "Listener Preferences: The Paradox of Small-Group Interactions," in *Small Group Communication: Theory and Practice,* 7th ed., eds. Robert S. Cathcart, Larry A. Samovar, and Linda Henman (Madison, WI: Brown & Benchmark, 1996), pp. 268–82.

8. Dan B. Curtis, Jerry L. Windsor, and R. D. Stephens, "National Preferences in Business and Communication Education," *Communication Education* 38 (1989), pp. 6–14.

9. John Gastil, "Identifying Obstacles to Small Group Democracy," *Small Group Research* 24 (February 1993), pp. 5–27.

10. Curt Bechler and Scott D. Johnson, "Leadership and Listening: A Study of Members' Perceptions," *Small Group Research* 26 (February 1995), pp. 77–85.

11. Lyman K. Steil, Larry L. Barker, and Kittie W. Watson, *Effective Listening: Key to Your Success* (Reading, MA: Addison-Wesley, 1983), pp. 21–22.

12. Kenneth N. Leone Cissna and Evelyn Sieburg, "Patterns of Intentional Confirmation and Disconfirmation," in *Bridges, Not Walls,* 4th ed., ed. John Stewart (New York: Random House, 1986), pp. 231–39.

13. Watson, "Listener Preferences," pp. 271–75.

14. Ibid., p. 270.

15. George R. Bach and Peter Wyden, *The Intimate Enemy* (New York: Avon, 1968).

16. David M. Berg, "A Descriptive Analysis of the Distribution and Duration of Themes Discussed by Task-Oriented Small Groups," *Speech Monographs* 34 (1967), pp. 172–75.

Chapter 4

1. Richard West and Lynn H. Turner, *Introducing Communication Theory: Analysis and Application,* 2nd ed. (New York: McGraw-Hill, 2004).

2. Joseph A. DeVito, *The Communication Handbook: A Dictionary* (New York: Harper & Row, 1986).

3. Wendy Leeds-Hurwitz, *Communication in Everyday Life: A Social Interpretation,* 3rd ed. (Norwood, NJ: Ablex, 1992).

4. Marshall S. Poole, David R. Siebold, and Robert D. McPhee, "Group Decision Making as a Structurational Process," *Quarterly Journal of Speech* 71 (1985), pp. 74–102; and Marshall S. Poole, "Group Communication and the Structuring Process," in *Small Group Communication: A Reader,* 6th ed., ed. Robert S. Cathcart and Larry A. Samovar (Dubuque, IA: Wm. C. Brown, 1992), pp. 147–57.

5. Meredith May, "Talkin' off the Hizzle with Homeys," *The San Francisco Chronicle,* April 29, 2001, pp. A1, A17.

6. Ibid. p. A17. (You can purchase the *Berkeley High Slang Dictionary* for $5 by contacting Rick Ayres at *rickilene@igc.org*.)

7. Dale G. Leathers, "Process Disruption and Measurement: Small Group Communication," *Quarterly Journal of Speech* 55 (1969), pp. 288–98.

8. This example is a modification of a case where a Fresno, California, high school student was suspended from school for using "nigga" to greet a friend on school grounds.

9. John Stewart and Carol Logan, *Together: Communicating Interpersonally,* 5th ed. (New York: McGraw-Hill, 1998).

10. Ibid.

11. Ray L. Birdwhistell, lecture at Nebraska Psychiatric Institute, Omaha, Nebraska, May 11, 1972.

12. Sandra Ketrow, "Nonverbal Aspects of Group Communication," in *The Handbook of Group Communication Theory & Research,* ed. Lawrence R. Frey (Thousand Oaks, CA: Sage, 1999), pp. 251–87.

13. Ibid.

14. Robert Freeman, *The Beatles: A Private View* (New York: Barnes & Noble, 1990).

15. Ibid., p. 46.

16. Edward T. Hall, *The Silent Language* (Garden City, NY: Doubleday, 1959).

17. Ketrow, "Nonverbal Aspects of Group Communication."

18. Ibid.

19. Judee K. Burgoon, Don W. Stacks, and Steven A. Burch, "The Role of Interpersonal Rewards and Violations of Distancing Expectations in Achieving Influence in Small Groups," *Communication: Journal of the Association of the Pacific* 11 (1982), pp. 114–28.

20. Ketrow, "Nonverbal Aspects of Group Communication."

21. P. Eckman, P. Ellsworth, and W. V. Friesen, *Emotion in the Human Face: Guidelines for Research and an Integration of Findings* (New York: Pergamon, 1971).

22. A. E. Scheffler, "Quasi-Courtship Behavior in Psychotherapy," *Psychiatry* 28 (1965), pp. 245–56.

23. Edward A. Mabry, "Developmental Aspects of Nonverbal Behavior in Small Group Settings," *Small Group Behavior* 20 (1989), pp. 190–202.

24. Martin Remland, "Developing Leadership Skills in Nonverbal Communication: A Situational Perspective," *Journal of Business Communication* 3 (1981), pp. 17–29.

25. Judee K. Burgoon and Thomas Saine, *The Unknown Dialogue: An Introduction to Nonverbal Communication* (Boston: Houghton Mifflin, 1978).

26. Joel D. Davitz and Lois Davitz, "Nonverbal Vocal Communication of Feelings," *Journal of Communication* 11 (1961), pp. 81–86.

27. Ketrow, "Nonverbal Aspects of Group Communication."

28. Donald Klopf, *Intercultural Encounters: The Fundamentals of Intercultural Communication* (Englewood, CO: Morion, 1987), p. 177.

29. R. G. Harper, A. N. Weins, and J. D. Matarazzo, *Nonverbal Communication: The State of the Art* (New York: Wiley, 1978).

30. Hall, *The Silent Language,* pp. 175–76.

31. Ketrow, "Nonverbal Aspects of Group Communication."

32. Ibid.

33. Craig R. Scott, "New Communication Technologies and Teams," in *Small Group Communication: Theory and Practice,* 8th ed., eds. Randy Hirokawa, Robert Cathcart, Larry Samovar, and Linda Henman (Los Angeles: Roxbury, 2003), pp. 134–47.

34. Jennifer Zaino, "Employee Collaboration on the Upswing," *InformationWeek.com* (February 11, 2002). Retrieved June 28, 2004, from www.Informationweek.com/story/IW200202027S0008.

35. Tyrone Adams and Norman Clark. *The Internet: Effective Online Communication* (Fort Worth, TX: Harcourt, 2001), pp. 112–19.

36. Ibid.

37. S. R. Hiltz and M. Turoff, "Virtual Meetings: Computer Conferencing and Distributed Group Support," in *Computer Augmented Teamwork: A Guided Tour,* eds. R. P. Bostrom, R. T. Watson, and S. T. Kinney (New York: Van Nostrand Reinhold, 1992), pp. 67–85.

38. Everett M. Rogers, *Communication Technology: The New Media in Society* (New York: Free Press, 1986).

39. Compiled from Larry L. Barker, Kathy J. Wahlers, Kittie W. Watson, and Robert J. Kibler, *Groups in Process: An Introduction to Small Group Communication,* 3rd ed. (Englewood Cliffs, NJ: Prentice Hall, 1987), p. 208, and Robert J. Johansen, J. Vallee, and K. Spangler, *Electronic Meetings: Technical Alternatives and Social Choices* (Reading, MA: Addison-Wesley, 1979), pp. 113–15.

40. Ketrow, "Nonverbal Aspects of Group Communication."

Chapter 5

1. Sunwolf, "Getting to 'GroupAha!' Provoking Creative Processes in Task Groups," in *The Handbook of Group Communication Theory and Research,* ed. Lawrence R. Frey (Thousand Oaks, CA: Sage, 1999), p. 205.

2. Susan Jarboe, "Group Communication and Creativity Processes," in *The Handbook of Group Communication Theory & Research,* ed. Lawrence (Thousand Oaks, CA: Sage, 1999), p. 336.

3. David F. Caldwell and Charles A. O'Reilly, III, "The Determinants of Team-Based Innovations in Organizations: The Role of Social Influence," *Small Group Research* 34 (August 2003), pp. 497–517.

4. Paul G. Bain, Leon Mann, and Andrew Pirola-Merlo, "The Innovation Imperative: The Relationship Between Team Climate, Innovation, and Performance in Research and Development Teams," *Small Group Research* 32 (February 2001), pp. 55–73.

5. Bernard A. Nijstad and Paul B. Paulus, "Group Creativity: Common Themes and Future Directions," in *Group Creativity: Innovation Through Collaboration,* eds. Paul B. Paulus and Bernard A. Nijstad (New York: Oxford University Press, 2003), pp. 326–39.

6. John J. Sosik, Bruce J. Avolio, and Surinder S. Kahai, "Inspiring Group Creativity: Comparing Anonymous and Identified Electronic Brainstorming," *Small Group Research* 29 (1998), pp. 3–31.

7. Nijstad and Paulus, "Group Creativity," p. 330.

8. Jarboe, "Group Communication and Creativity Processes," pp. 336–41.

9. Nijstad and Paulus, "Group Creativity," pp. 326–32.

10. Alex Osborn, *Applied Imagination,* rev. ed. (New York: Charles Scribner's Sons, 1957).

11. M. Basadur and R. Thompson, "Usefulness of the Ideation Principle of Extended Effort in Real World Professional and Managerial Problem Solving," *Journal of Creative Behavior* 20 (1982), pp. 23–34.

12. R. Brent Gallupe, Alan R. Dennis, William H. Cooper, Joseph S. Valacich, Lame M. Bastianum, and Jay F. Nunamaker, Jr., "Electronic Brainstorming and Group Size," *Academy of Management Journal* 35 (June 1992), pp. 350–70. See also Joseph S. Valacich, Alan R. Dennis, and T. Connolly, "Idea Generation in Computer-Based Groups: A New Ending to an Old Story," *Organizational Behavior and Human Decision Processes* 57 (1994), pp. 448–68.

13. Russell L. Ackoff and Elsa Vergara, "Creativity in Problem Solving and Planning," in *Handbook for Creative and Innovative Managers,* ed. Robert L. Kuhn (New York: McGraw-Hill, 1988), pp. 77–90.

14. Accessed June 14, 2004, www.ideafinder.com/history/inventions//story015.htm.

15. Del Jones, "GE Leader Recalls 'Eureka' Moment: Being No. 1 Was Limiting Opportunity," *The Cincinnati Enquirer,* April 8, 2001, pp. D1–2.

16. See Tony Buzan with Barry Buzan, *The Mind Map® Book* (New York: Plume, 1996), for a detailed description of the process with examples and information about the theoretical underpinnings of mind mapping.

17. Sunwolf, "Getting to 'GroupAha!,'" p. 209.

18. R. L. Firestein, "Effects of Creative Problem-Solving Training on Communication Behaviors in Small Groups," *Small Group Research* 21 (1990), pp. 507–21.

19. For a clear review of these issues, see Dale E. Brashers, Mark Adkins, and Renee A. Meyers, "Argumentation and Computer-Mediated Group Decision-Making," in *Group Communication in Context,* ed. Lawrence R. Frey (Hillsdale, NJ: Lawrence Erlbaum Associates, 1994), pp. 263–82.

20. Columbia Accident Investigation website, "Columbia Accident Investigation Board Press Briefing," August 26, 2003, accessed June 5, 2004, www.caib.us/events/press_briefings/20030826/transcript.html.

21. Marcia Dunn, "NASA Chiefs: Managers Must Embrace Change," Yahoo! News, accessed April 14, 2004, http://story.news.yahoo.com/news.

22. Dennis S. Gouran, Randy Y. Hirokawa, and Amy E. Martz, "A Critical Analysis of Factors Related to Decisional Processes Involved in the *Challenger* Disaster," *Central States Speech Journal* 37 (1986), pp. 119–35.

23. Brashers et al., "Argumentation and Computer-Mediated Group Decision-Making."

24. Richard Huseman, Glenn Ware, and Charles Gruner, "Critical Thinking, Reflective Thinking, and the Ability to Organize Ideas: A Multivariate Approach," *Journal of the American Forensic Association* 9 (1972), pp. 261–65.

25. M. Neil Browne and Stuart M. Keeley, *Asking the Right Questions: A Guide to Critical Thinking,* 3rd ed. (Englewood Cliffs, NJ: Prentice Hall, 1992), pp. 3–5.

26. Ibid., pp. 3–7.

27. Brashers et al., "Argumentation and Computer-Mediated Group Decision-Making," pp. 263–82.

28. Gouran et al., "A Critical Analysis of Factors Related to Decisional Processes Involved in the *Challenger* Disaster," p. 130.

29. Mark F. Stasson and Scott D. Bradshaw, "Explanations of Individual-Group Performance Differences: What Sort of 'Bonus' Can Be Gained Through Group Interaction?" *Small Group Research* 26 (May 1995), pp. 296–308.

30. For a more detailed description of and source for these GSS tools and their potential impact on group critical thinking, see Brashers et al., "Argumentation and Computer-Mediated Group Decision-Making."

Chapter 6

1. Jay Hall, "Decisions, Decisions, Decisions," *Psychology Today,* November 1971, pp. 51–54, 86–87; Jay Hall and W. H. Watson, "The Effects of a Normative Intervention on Decision-Making Performance," *Human Relations* 23 (1970), pp. 299–317; Irving L. Janis, *Groupthink: Psychological Studies of Policy Decisions and Fiascoes,* 2nd ed. (Boston: Houghton Mifflin, 1982); Randy Y. Hirokawa, "Consensus Group Decision-Making, Quality of Decision and Group Satisfaction: An Attempt to Sort Fact from Fiction," *Central States Speech Journal* 33 (1982), pp. 407–15; Lester Coch and J. R. P. French, Jr., "Overcoming Resistance to Change," *Human Relations* 1 (1948), pp. 512–32; and Myron W. Block and L. R. Hoffman, "The Effects of Valence of Solutions and Group Cohesiveness on Members' Commitment to Group Decisions," in *The Group Problem-Solving Process,* ed. L. Richard Hoffman (New York: Prager, 1979), p. 121.

2. Kathleen M. Propp, "In Search of the Assembly Bonus Effect: Continued Exploration of Communication's Role in Group Memory," *Human Communication Research* 29, no. 4 (2003), pp. 600–06.

3. Hirokawa, "Consensus Group Decision-Making," pp. 407–15; Hirokawa, "Why Informed Groups Make Faulty Decisions: An Investigation of Possible Interaction-Based Explanations," *Small Group Behavior* 18 (1987), pp. 3–29; and Hirokawa, "Discussion Procedures and Decision-Making Performance: A Test of the Functional Perspective," *Human Communication Research* 12 (1985), pp. 203–24.

4. Carl E. Larson and Frank M. J. LaFasto, *TeamWork: What Must Go Right, What Can Go Wrong* (Newbury Park, CA: Sage, 1989), pp. 27–38.

5. John E. Dewey, *How We Think* (Boston: D.C. Heath, 1910).

6. This research is synthesized in Dennis S. Gouran and Randy Y. Hirokawa, "Effective Decision Making and Problem Solving in Groups," in *Small Group Communication: Theory and Practice,* 8th ed., eds. Randy Y. Hirokawa, Robert S. Cathcart, Larry A. Samovar, and Linda D. Henman (Los Angeles: Roxbury Publishing Co., 2003), pp. 27–38.

7. Lucia Savadori, Lun M. Van Swol, and Janet A. Sniezek, "Information Sampling and Confidence Within Groups and Judge Advisor Systems," *Communication Research* 28 (2001), pp. 737–71; Michael G. Cruz and David Dryden Henningsen, "The Presence of Norms in the Absence of Groups?" *Human Communication Research* 26 (2000), pp. 104–24.

8. Susan Jarboe, "Procedures for Enhancing Group Decision Making," in *Communication and Group Decision Making,* 2nd ed., eds. Randy Y. Hirokawa and Marshall Scott Poole (Thousand Oaks, CA: Sage, 1996), pp. 345–83.

9. Marshall S. Poole, "Decision Development in Small Groups II: A Study of Multiple Sequences in Decision Making," *Communication Monographs* 50 (1983), pp. 224–25, and "Decision Development in Small Groups III: A Multiple Sequence Model of Group Decision Development," *Communication Monographs* 50 (1983), pp. 321–41.

10. Randy Y. Hirokawa, "Group Communication and Decision-Making Performance: A Continued Test of the Functional Perspective," paper presented at the annual convention of the Speech Communication Association (Boston, 1987);

Randy Y. Hirokawa and Kathryn M. Rost, "Effective Group Decision Making in Organizations: Field Test of the Vigilant Interaction Theory," paper presented at the annual convention of the Speech Communication Association (Atlanta, 1991).

11. Elizabeth E. Graham, Michael J. Papa, and Mary B. McPherson, "An Applied Test of the Functional Communication Perspective of Small Group Decision Making," *Southern Communication Journal* 62 (Summer 1997), pp. 269–79.

12. Among these studies were John K. Brilhart and Lurene M. Jochem, "Effects of Different Patterns on Outcomes of Problem-Solving Discussion," *Journal of Applied Psychology* 48 (1964), pp. 175–79; Ovid L. Bayless, "An Alternative Model for Problem Solving Discussion," *Journal of Communication* 17 (1967), pp. 188–97; Carl E. Larson, "Forms of Analysis and Small Group Problem Solving," *Speech Monographs* 36 (1969), pp. 452–55; and Hirokawa, "Discussion Procedures and Decision-Making Performance."

13. Benjamin J. Broome and Luann Fulbright, "A Multistage Influence Model of Barriers to Group Problem Solving: A Participant-Generated Agenda for Small Group Research," *Small Group Research* 26 (February 1995), pp. 25–55.

14. Joseph A. Bonito, "An Information-Processing Approach to Participation in Small Groups," *Communication Research* 28 (June 2001), pp. 275–303; Michael G. Cruz, Franklin J. Boster, and Jose I. Rodriquez, "The Impact of Group Size and Proportion of Shared Information on the Exchange and Integration of Information in Groups," *Communication Research* 27 (June 1997), pp. 291–313.

15. Michael E. Mayer, Kevin T. Sonoda, and William B. Gudykunst, "The Effect of Time Pressures and Type of Information on Decision Quality," *Southern Communication Journal* 62 (Summer 1997), pp. 280–92.

16. For example, see Sidney J. Parnes, "Effects of Extended Effort in Creative Problem Solving," *Journal of Educational Psychology* 52 (1961), pp. 117–22.

17. Graham, Papa, and McPherson, "An Applied Test of the Functional Communication Perspective of Small Group Decision Making."

18. For a more detailed description of these support systems, see Joseph E. McGrath and Andrea B. Hollingshead, *Groups Interacting with Technology* (Thousand Oaks, CA: Sage, 1994).

19. Leonard M. Jessup and Joseph S. Valacich, eds., *Group Support Systems: New Perspectives* (New York: Macmillan, 1993).

20. S. Opper and H. Fresko-Weiss, *Technology for Teams: Enhancing Productivity in Networked Organizations* (New York: Van Nostrand Reinhold, 1992).

21. Andrea B. Hollingshead, Joseph E. McGrath, and Kathleen M. O'Connor, "Group Task Performance and Communication Technology: A Longitudinal Study of Computer-Mediated versus Face-to-Face Work Groups," *Small Group Research* 24 (August 1993), pp. 307–33.

22. Izak Benbasat and Lai-Huat Lim, "The Effects of Group, Task, Context, and Technology Variables on the Usefulness of Group Support Systems: A Meta-Analysis of Experimental Studies," *Small Group Research* 24 (November 1993), pp. 430–62.

23. Poppy McLeod, "New Communication Technologies for Group Decision Making: Toward an Integrative Framework," in *Communication and Group Decision Making*, 2nd ed., eds. Randy Y. Hirokawa and Marshall Scott Poole (Thousand Oaks, CA: Sage, 1996), pp. 426–61.

24. Robert F. Bales, *Interaction Process Analysis* (Reading, MA: Addison-Wesley, 1950); Donald G. Ellis and B. Aubrey Fisher, *Small Group Decision Making: Communication and the Group Process*, 4th ed. (New York: McGraw-Hill, 1994); and Poole, "Decision Development in Small Groups II."

25. Ellis and Fisher, *Small Group Decision Making*, pp. 144–57.

26. Poole, "Decision Development in Small Groups II."

27. David R. Siebold, "Making Meetings More Successful: Plans, Formats, and Procedures for Group Problem Solving," in *Small Group Communication: A Reader*, 5th ed., eds. Robert S. Cathcart and Larry A. Samovar (Dubuque, IA: Wm. C. Brown, 1988), pp. 219–20.

Chapter 7

1. Robert F. Bales, "The Equilibrium Problem in Small Groups," in *Working Papers in the Theory of Action*, eds. Talcott Parsons, Robert F. Bales, and Edward A. Shils (New York: Free Press, 1953), pp. 111–61.

2. The terms *primary* and *secondary* tension were first used by Ernest G. Bormann; elaboration of the concepts may be found in Bormann, *Discussion and Group Methods: Theory and Practice*, 2nd ed. (New York: Harper & Row, 1975), pp. 181–90.

3. Donald G. Ellis and B. Aubrey Fisher, *Small Group Decision Making: Communication and the Group Process*, 4th ed. (New York: McGraw-Hill, 1994), p. 38.

4. Bormann, *Discussion and Group Methods*.

5. Ellis and Fisher, *Small Group Decision Making*, p. 38.

6. Katherine E. Finkelstein, "Tempers Seem to Be Shorter in Many Jury Rooms," *The New York Times*, (August 3, 2001). Retrieved July 8, 2004, from www.nytimes.com/2001/08/03/nyregion/03JURY.htm?ex=1089604800&en=9dlfl46719a4ab93&ei=5070&ex=997841696&.

7. Joseph B. Walther and Judee K. Burgoon, "Relational Communication in Computer-Mediated Interaction," *Human Communication Research* 19 (1992), pp. 50–88.

8. Connie Gersick, "Time and Transition in Work Teams," in *Small Group Communication: Theory & Practice*, 8th ed., eds. Randy Hirokawa, Robert Cathcart, Larry Samovar, and Linda Henman (Los Angeles: Roxbury, 2003), pp. 59–75.

9. Carolyn M. Anderson, Bruce L. Riddle, and Mathew M. Martin, "Socialization Processes in Groups," in *Handbook of Group Communication Theory & Research*, ed. Lawrence R. Frey (Thousand Oaks, CA: Sage, 1999), pp. 139–63.

10. Ibid., p. 142.

11. Ibid.

12. Ibid.

13. Joann Keyton, *Group Communication* (Mountain View, CA: Mayfield, 1999), p. 115.

14. Anderson et al., p. 147.

15. Ibid., p. 148.

16. Ibid., p. 149.

17. Stewart Sigman, "The Applicability of the Concept of Recruitment to the Communication Study of a Nursing Home: An Ethnographic Case Study," *International Journal of Aging and Human Development* 22 (1985–86), pp. 215–33. See also Melanie Booth-Butterfield, Stephen Booth-Butterfield, and Jolene Koester, "The Function of Uncertainty Reduction in Alleviating Primary Tension in Small Groups," *Communication Research Reports* 5 (1988), pp. 146–53.

18. Anderson et al., p. 151

19. K.E.W. Morrison, "Information Usefulness and Acquisition During Organizational Encounter," *Management Communication Quarterly* 9 (1995), pp. 131–55.

20. Anderson et al., p. 152.

21. Ibid., p. 164.

22. Joann Keyton, "Group Termination: Completing the Study of Group Development," *Small Group Research* 24 (1993), pp. 84–100.

23. Stephanie Zimmerman, "Social Cognition and Evaluations of Health Care Team Communication Effectiveness," *Western Journal of Communication* 58 (Spring 1994), pp. 116–41.

24. Craig R. Scott, "New Communication Technologies and Teams," in *Small Group Communication: Theory & Practice,* 8th ed., eds. Randy Hirokawa, Robert Cathcart, Larry Samovar, and Linda Henman (Los Angeles: Roxbury, 2003), pp. 134–47.

25. Michael K. Kramer, Communication in a Community Theatre Group: Managing Multiple Group Roles," *Communication Studies* 53 (2002), pp. 151–70.

26. Ibid.

27. Susan B. Shimanoff, "Coordinating Group Interaction via Communication Rules," in *Small Group Communication: A Reader,* 6th ed., eds. Robert Cathcart and Larry Samovar (Dubuque, IA: Wm. C. Brown, 1992), p. 255.

28. Daniel Feldman, "Development and Enforcement of Group Norms," *Academy of Management Review* 9 (1984), pp. 47–53.

29. Stanley Schacter, "Deviation, Rejection, and Communication," *Journal of Abnormal and Social Psychology* 46 (1951), pp. 190–207, and Harold Leavitt, *Managerial Psychology,* 2nd ed. (Chicago: University of Chicago Press, 1964), pp. 270–74.

30. Ronald R. Sims, "Linking Groupthink to Unethical Behavior in Organizations," *Journal of Business Ethics* 11 (September 1992), pp. 651–62.

31. Katherine W. Hawkins and Bryant P. Fillion, "Perceived Communication Skill Needs for Work Groups," *Communication Research Reports* 16 (Spring 1999), pp. 167–74.

32. Joseph P. Folger and Marshall S. Poole, *Working Through Conflict: A Communication Perspective* (Glenview, IL: Scott, Foresman, 1984), p. 84.

33. Hawkins and Fillion, "Perceived Communication Skill Needs for Work Groups," pp. 167–74.

34. Carl E. Larson and Frank M. J. LaFasto, *TeamWork: What Must Go Right, What Can Go Wrong* (Newbury Park, CA: Sage, 1989).

35. M. E. Johnson and J. G. Fortman, "Internal Structure of the Gross Cohesiveness Scale," *Small Group Behavior* 19 (February 1988), pp. 187–96.

36. C. N. Greene, "Cohesion and Productivity in Work Groups," *Small Group Behavior* 21 (February 1989), pp. 221–25.

37. Brian Mullen, Tara Anthony, Eduardo Salas, and James E. Driskell, "Group Cohesiveness and Quality of Decision Making: An Integration of Tests of the Groupthink Hypothesis," *Small Group Research* 25 (May 1995), pp. 189–204.

38. Claus W. Langfred, "Is Group Cohesiveness a Double-Edged Sword? An Investigation on the Effects of Cohesiveness on Performance," *Small Group Research* 29 (1996), pp. 124–43.

39. Jack R. Gibb, "Defensive Communication," *Journal of Communication* 11 (1961), pp. 141–48.

Chapter 8

1. G. M. Parker, *Team Players and Teamwork: The New Competitive Business Strategy* (San Francisco: Jossey-Bass, 1990), and R. A. Eisenstat, "Fairfield Systems Group," in *Groups That Work and Those That Don't,* ed. J. R. Hackman (San Francisco: Jossey-Bass, 1990), pp. 171–81.

2. Robert Freed Bales, *Personality and Interpersonal Behavior* (New York: Holt, Rinehart & Winston, 1970).

3. Carolyn M. Anderson and Matthew M. Martin, "Communication Motives (State vs. Trait?) and Task Group Outcomes," *Communication Research Reports* 19 (Summer 2002), pp. 269–82.

4. Ibid., p. 193.

5. Dirk Scheerhorn and Patricia Geist, "Social Dynamics in Groups," in *Managing Group Life,* eds. Lawrence R. Frey and J. Kevin Barge (Boston: Houghton Mifflin Co., 1997), pp. 80–103.

6. Carolyn M. Anderson and Matthew M. Martin, "The Effects of Communication Motives, Interaction Involvement, and Loneliness on Satisfaction: A Model of Small Groups," *Small Group Research* 26 (February 1995), pp. 118–37.

7. William F. Owen, "Metaphor Analysis of Cohesiveness in Small Discussion Groups," *Small Group Behavior* 16 (1985), pp. 415–26.

8. David A. Kolb, *Experiential Learning: Experience as the Source of Learning and Development* (Englewood Cliffs, NJ: Prentice Hall, 1984).

9. Synthesized from Isabel Briggs Myers, *Introduction to Type: A Description of the Theory and Application of the Myers-Briggs Type Indicator* (Palo Alto, CA:

Consulting Psychologists Press, 1987); Otto Kroeger and Janet A. Thuesen, *Type Talk: The 16 Personality Types That Determine How We Live, Love, and Work* (New York: Dell Publishing, 1988); Otto Kroeger with Janet A. Thuesen, *Type Talk at Work: How the 16 Personality Types Determine Your Success on the Job* (New York: Dell Publishing, 1992); and Paul D. Tieger and Barbara Barron-Tieger, *Nurture by Nature: Understand Your Child's Personality Type—And Become a Better Parent* (Boston: Little, Brown and Company, 1997), pp. 5–62.

10. The following information about culture is synthesized from a number of sources, including Edward T. Hall, *Beyond Culture* (New York: Anchor Press, 1977); Geert Hofstede, *Culture's Consequences: International Differences in Work-Related Values* (Beverly Hills, CA: Sage Publications, 1980); William B. Gudykunst and Stella Ting-Toomey, *Culture and Interpersonal Communication* (Newbury Park, CA: Sage Publications, 1988); Myron Lustig and Jolene Koester, *Interpersonal Competence: Interpersonal Communication Across Cultures* (New York: HarperCollins College Publishers, 1993); and Myron W. Lustig and Laura L. Casotta, "Comparing Group Communication Across Culture: Leadership, Conformity, and Discussion Procedures," in *Small Group Communication: A Reader,* 6th ed., eds. Robert S. Cathcart and Larry A. Samovar (Dubuque, IA: Wm. C. Brown Publishers, 1992), pp. 393–404.

11. Larry A. Samovar and Richard E. Porter, *Communication Between Cultures,* 4th ed. (Belmont, CA: Wadsworth, 2001), pp. 52–88.

12. Min-Sun Kim and William F. Sharkey, "Independent and Interdependent Construals of Self: Explaining Cultural Patterns of Interpersonal Communication in Multicultural Organizational Settings," *Communication Quarterly* 43 (Winter 1995), pp. 20–38.

13. Judith N. Martin and Thomas K. Nakayama, *Experiencing Intercultural Communication: An Introduction* (Mountain View, CA: Mayfield Publishing Company, 2001), pp. 166–67.

14. Nina M. Reich and Julia T. Wood, "Sex, Gender and Communication in Small Groups," in *Small Group Communication: Theory and Practice,* 8th ed., eds. Randy Y. Hirokawa, Robert S. Cathcart, Larry A. Samovar, and Linda D. Henman (Los Angeles: Roxbury Publishing Co., 2003), pp. 218–29.

15. Andrew J. Flanagin, Vanessa Tiyaamornwong, Joan O'Connor, and David R. Seibold, "Computer-Mediated Group Work: The Interaction of Member Sex and Anonymity," *Communication Research* 29 (February 2002), pp. 66–93.

16. This information is synthesized from Michael L. Hecht, Mary Jane Collier, and Sidney A. Ribeau, *African American Communication: Ethnic Identity and Cultural Interpretation,* vol. 2, Language and Language Behaviors series (Newbury Park, CA: Sage Publications, 1993), especially Chap. 3, pp. 82–113, and Anita K. Foeman and Gary Pressley, "Ethnic Culture and Corporate Culture: Using Black Styles in Organizations," *Communication Quarterly* 35 (Fall 1987), pp. 293–307.

17. Rebecca Leonard and Don C. Locke, "Communication Stereotypes: Is Interracial Communication Possible?" *Journal of Black Studies* 23 (March 1993), pp. 332–43.

18. Mark P. Orbe, "Remember, It's Always Whites' Ball: Descriptions of African American Male Communication," *Communication Quarterly* 35 (Fall 1987), pp. 293–307.

19. C. Kirchmeyer and A. Cohen, "Multicultural Groups: Their Performance and Reactions with Constructive Conflict," *Group & Organization Management* 17 (1992), pp. 153–70, and C. Kirchmeyer, "Multicultural Task Groups: An Account of the Low Contribution Level of Minorities," *Small Group Research* 24 (February 1993), pp. 127–48.

20. This information is taken primarily from Rick Hicks and Kathy Hicks, *Boomers, Xers, and Other Strangers: Understanding the Generational Differences that Divide Us* (Wheaton, IL: Tyndale House Publishers, 1999), especially pp. 229–353. Other sources of information include Morris E. Massey, *The People Puzzle: Understanding Yourself and Others* (Reston, VA: Reston Publishing Co., 1979), and Don Tapscott, *Growing Up Digital: The Rise of the Net Generation* (New York: McGraw-Hill, 1998).

21. Warren E. Watson, Kumar Kamalesh, and Larry K. Michaelson, "Cultural Diversity's Impact on Interaction Process and Performance: Comparing Homogeneous and Diverse Task Groups," *Academy of Management Journal* 36 (1993), pp. 590–602, and Leisa D. Sargent and Christina Sue-Chan, "Does Diversity Affect Group Efficacy? The Intervening Role of Cohesion and Task Interdependence," *Small Group Research* 32 (August 2001), pp. 426–50.

22. Ernest G. Bormann, "Symbolic Convergence Theory and Communication in Group Decision

Making," in *Communication and Group Decision Making,* 2nd ed., eds. Randy Y. Hirokawa and M. Scott Poole (Thousand Oaks, CA: Sage Publications, 1996), pp. 81–113.

23. Catherine Cobb Morocco, "Development and Function of Group Metaphor," *Journal for the Theory of Social Behavior* 9 (1979), pp. 15–27.

24. Bormann, "Symbolic Convergence," pp. 229–30.

25. Complete information on constructing a SYMLOG diagram, along with an abbreviated explanation of SYMLOG theory, may be found in a workbook, R. F. Bales, *SYMLOG Case Study Kit* (New York: The Free Press, 1980). An even more simplified explanation of SYMLOG theory and method for constructing a diagram may be found in Joann Keyton, "Coding Communication in Decision-Making Groups," in *Managing Group Life: Communicating in Decision-Making Groups* (Boston: Houghton Mifflin Co., 1997), pp. 236–69. For readers who are interested in details of both the theory and methodology, we refer them to R. F. Bales and Stephen P. Cohen, *SYMLOG: A System for the Multiple-Level Observation of Groups* (New York: Free Press, 1979).

26. Richard V. Polley, SYMLOG computer software, Lewis and Clark University, Portland, OR.

Chapter 9

1. Joyce L. Hocker and William W. Wilmot, *Interpersonal Conflict,* 3rd ed. (Dubuque, IA: Wm. C. Brown, 1991), p. 12.

2. Ana Zornoza, Pilar Ripoll, and José M. Peiró, "Conflict Management in Groups that Work in Two Different Communication Contexts: Face-to-Face and Computer-Mediated Communication," *Small Group Research* 33 (October 2002), pp. 481–508.

3. Irving L. Janis, *Groupthink: Psychological Studies of Policy Decisions and Fiascoes,* 2nd ed. (Boston: Houghton-Mifflin, 1983), pp. 14–47.

4. D. Cole, "Meetings that Make Sense," *Psychology Today* (May 1989), pp. 14–15.

5. Brian Mullen, Tara Anthony, Eduardo Salas, and James E. Driskell, "Group Cohesiveness and Quality of Decision Making: An Integration of the Groupthink Hypothesis," *Small Group Research* 25 (May 1994), pp. 189–204.

6. Irving L. Janis and Leon Mann, *Decision Making: A Psychological Analysis of Conflict, Choice, and Commitment* (New York: Free Press, 1977).

7. Lucia Savadori, Lyn M. Van Swol, and Janet A. Sniezek, "Information Sampling and Confidence Within Groups and Judge Advisor Systems," *Communication Research* 28 (December 2001), pp. 737–71; Michael G. Cruz and David D. Henningsen, "The Presence of Norms in the Absence of Groups?" *Human Communication Research* 26 (January 2000), pp. 104–24; Mark Schiettekatte and Alain Van Niel, "Effects of Partially Shared Information and Awareness of Unshared Information on Information Sampling," *Small Group Research* 25 (May 1994), pp. 189–204.

8. Janis and Mann, *Decision Making.*

9. Charles R. Franz and K. Gregory Jin, "The Structure of Group Conflict in a Collaborative Work Group During Information Systems Development," *Journal of Applied Communication Research* 23 (1995), pp. 108–27.

10. Markus Brauer, Charles M. Judd, and Vincent Jacquelin, "The Communication of Social Stereotypes: The Effects of Group Discussion and Information Distribution on Stereotypic Appraisals," *Journal of Personality and Social Psychology* 81, no. 3 (2001), pp. 463–75.

11. R. Spears and M. Leah, "Panacea or Panopticon? The Hidden Power in Computer-Mediated Communication," *Communication Research* 21 (1994), pp. 427–59.

12. Kenneth Thomas, "Conflict and Conflict Management," in *Handbook of Industrial and Organizational Psychology,* ed. Marvin Dunnette (Chicago: Rand McNally, 1976), pp. 890–934.

13. Hal Witteman, "Analyzing Interpersonal Conflict: Nature of Awareness, Type of Initiating Event, Situational Perceptions, and Management Styles," *Western Journal of Communication* 56 (Summer 1992), pp. 248–80.

14. Victor D. Wall and Linda L. Nolan, "Small Group Conflict: A Look at Equity, Satisfaction, and Styles of Conflict Management," *Small Group Behavior* 18 (1987), pp. 188–211.

15. Renee Meyers and Dale Brashers, "Influence Processes in Group Interaction," *The Handbook of Group Communication Theory and Research,* ed. Lawrence Frey (Thousand Oaks, CA: Sage, 1999), pp. 288–312.

16. Victor D. Wall, Gloria J. Galanes, and Susan B. Love, "Small Task-Oriented Groups: Conflict, Conflict Management, Satisfaction, and Decision Quality," *Small Group Behavior* 18 (1987), pp. 31–55.

17. Tim Kuhn and Marshall Scott Poole, "Do Conflict Management Styles Affect Group Decision Making?" *Human Communication Research* 26 (October 2000), pp. 558–90.

18. Min-Sun Kim and Truman Leung, "A Multicultural View of Conflict Management Styles: Review and Critical Synthesis," *Communication Yearbook 23,* ed. Michael E. Roloff (Thousand Oaks, CA: Sage, 2000), pp. 227–69.

19. Arie W. Kruglanski and Donna M. Webster, "Group Members' Reactions to Opinion Deviates and Conformists at Varying Degrees of Proximity to Decision Deadline and of Environmental Noise," *Journal of Personality and Social Psychology* 61 (1991), pp. 212–26.

20. Rick Garlick and Paul A. Mongeau, "Argument Quality and Group Member Status as Determinants of Attitudinal Minority Influence," *Western Journal of Communication* 57 (Summer 1993), pp. 289–308.

21. Lisa J. Gebhart and Renee A. Meyers, "Subgroup Influence in Decision-Making Groups: Examining Consistency from a Communication Perspective," *Small Group Research* 26 (May 1995), pp. 147–68.

22. Dale Brashers and Renee Meyers, "Tag-team Argument and Group Decision Making: A Preliminary Investigation," *Spheres of Argument: Proceedings of the Sixth Speech Communication Association/American Forensics Association Conference on Argumentation,* ed. Bruce Gronbeck (Annandale, VA: Speech Communication Association, 1989), pp. 542–50.

23. Gebhart and Meyers, "Subgroup Influence."

24. James B. Thomas, Reuben R. McDaniel, Jr., and Michael J. Dooris, "Strategic Issue Analysis: NGT and Decision Analysis for Resolving Strategic Issues," *Journal of Applied Behavioral Science* 25 (May 1989), pp. 189–201.

25. Roger Fisher and William Ury, *Getting to Yes: Negotiating Agreement Without Giving In* (New York: Penguin Books, 1983).

Chapter 10

1. Michael Z. Hackman and Craig E. Johnson, *Leadership: A Communication Perspective,* 2nd ed. (Prospect Heights, IL: Waveland Press, 1996), p. 14.

2. John R. P. French and Bertram Raven, "The Bases of Social Power," in *Group Dynamics: Research and Theory,* 3rd ed., eds. Dorwin Cartwright and Alvin Zander (New York: Harper & Row, 1968), pp. 259–69.

3. Ernest G. Bormann, *Discussion and Group Methods: Theory and Practice,* 2nd ed. (New York: Harper & Row, 1975), pp. 253–69, and John C. Geier, "A Trait Approach to the Study of Leadership in Small Groups," *Journal of Communication* 17 (1967), pp. 316–23.

4. Katherine W. Hawkins, "Effects of Gender and Communication Content on Leadership Emergence in Small Task-Oriented Groups," *Small Group Research* 26 (May 1995), pp. 234–49.

5. Scott D. Johnson and Curt Bechler, "Examining the Relationship Between Listening Effectiveness and Leadership Emergence," *Small Group Research* 29 (August 1998), pp. 452–71.

6. David A. Kenny and Steven J. Zaccaro, "An Estimate of Variance Due to Traits in Leadership," *Journal of Applied Psychology* 68 (1983), pp. 678–85; Robert J. Ellis and Steven F. Cronshaw, "Self-Monitoring and Leader Emergence: A Test of Moderator Effects," *Small Group Research* 23 (February 1992), pp. 113–29; and Steven F. Cronshaw and Robert J. Ellis, "A Process Investigation of Self-Monitoring and Leadership Emergence," *Small Group Research* 22 (September 1991), pp. 403–20.

7. Simon Taggar and Rick Hackett, "Leadership Emergence in Autonomous Work Teams: Antecedents and Outcomes, *Personnel Psychology* 52 (Winter 1999), pp. 899–926.

8. Robert S. Rubin, Lynn K. Bartels, and William H. Bommer, "Are Leaders Smarter or Do They Just Seem That Way? Exploring Perceived Intellectual Competence and Leadership Emergence," *Social Behavior & Personality* 30, no. 2 (2002), pp. 105–18; Simon Taggar and Rick Hackett, "Leadership Emergence in Autonomous Work Teams: Antecedents and Outcomes, *Personnel Psychology* 52 (Winter 1999), pp. 899–926; Robert G. Lord, Christy L. deVader, and George M. Alliger, "A Meta-Analysis of the Relation Between Personality Traits and Leadership Perceptions: An Application of Validity Generalization Procedures," *Journal of Applied Psychology* 71 (August 1986), pp. 402–10.

9. Amy B. Gershenoff and Roseanne J. Foti, "Leader Emergence and Gender Roles in All-Female Groups: A Critical Examination," *Small Group Research* 34 (April 2003), pp. 170–96.

10. Judith A. Kolb, "Are We Still Stereotyping Leadership? A Look at Gender and Other Predictors of Leader Emergence," *Small Group Research* 28 (August 1997), pp. 370–93.

11. Susan B. Shimanoff and Mercilee M. Jenkins, "Leadership and Gender: Challenging Assumptions and Recognizing Resources," in *Small Group Communication: Theory and Practice,* 8th ed., eds. Randy Y. Hirokawa, Robert S. Cathcart, Larry A. Samovar, and Linda Henman (Los Angeles: Roxbury, 2003), pp. 184–98.

12. Ralph M. Stogdill, Carrol L. Shartle, Willis L. Scott, Alvin E. Coons, and William E. Jaynes, *A Predictive Study of Administrative Work Patterns* (Columbus: The Ohio State University, Bureau of Business Research, 1956); Ralph M. Stogdill and Alvin E. Coons, eds., *Leader Behavior: Its Description and Measurement* (Columbus: The Ohio State University, Bureau of Business Research, 1957); and Robert Blake and Jane Mouton, *The Managerial Grid* (Houston: Gulf, 1964).

13. Hackman and Johnson, *Leadership: A Communication Perspective,* 2nd ed.

14. Ibid., p. 27.

15. John Gastil, "A Meta-Analytic Review of the Productivity and Satisfaction of Democratic and Autocratic Leadership," *Small Group Research* 25 (August 1994), pp. 384–410, and John Gastil, *Democracy in Small Groups* (Philadelphia: New Society Publishers, 1993).

16. William C. Schutz, "The Leader as Completer," in *Small Group Communication: A Reader,* 3rd ed., eds. Robert S. Cathcart and Larry A. Samovar (Dubuque, IA: Wm C. Brown, 1979), pp. 454–60.

17. Fred Fiedler, *A Theory of Leadership Effectiveness* (New York: McGraw-Hill, 1967).

18. Paul Hersey and Kenneth H. Blanchard, *Management of Organizational Behavior,* 4th ed. (Englewood Cliffs, NJ: Prentice Hall, 1982).

19. Gastil, "A Meta-Analytic Review," p. 403.

20. J. Kevin Barge, "Leadership as Medium: A Leaderless Group Discussion Model," *Communication Quarterly* 37 (Fall 1989), pp. 237–47.

21. This information is synthesized from Frank LaFasto and Carl Larson, *When Teams Work Best: 6000 Team Members and Leaders Tell What It Takes to Succeed* (Thousand Oaks, CA: Sage, 2001), and Gloria J. Galanes, "In Their Own Words: An Exploratory Study of Bona Fide Group Leaders," *Small Group Research* 34 (December 2003), pp. 741–70.

22. Much of the following information is discussed in detail in John K. Brilhart and Gloria J. Galanes, *Effective Group Discussion,* 8th ed. (Madison, WI: Brown & Benchmark, 1995), pp. 177–202.

23. Katherine W. Hawkins, "Effects of Gender and Communication Content on Leadership Emergence in Small Task-Oriented Groups," *Small Group Research* 26 (May 1995), pp. 234–49.

24. Carl Larson and Frank M. J. LaFasto, *Team Work: What Must Go Right/What Can Go Wrong* (Newbury Park, CA: Sage, 1989), pp. 27–33.

25. Dong L. Jung and John J. Sosik, "Transformational Leadership in Work Groups: The Role of Empowerment, Cohesiveness, and Collective-Efficacy on Perceived Group Performance," *Small Group Research* 33 (June 2002), pp. 313–36.

26. P. H. Andrews and R. T. Herschel, *Organizational Communication: Empowerment in a Technological Society* (Boston: Houghton Mifflin, 1996).

27. Hackman and Johnson, *Leadership: A Communication Perspective.*

28. National Communication Association, "Code of Professional Responsibilities for the Communication Scholar/Teacher," www.natcom. org/policies/Internal/code_of_professional_ethics. htm, accessed June 18, 2004.

Chapter 11

1. Cindy Griffin, *Invitation to Public Speaking* (Belmont, CA: Thomson Wadsworth, 2004), chap. 5.

2. Dan O'Hair, Rob Stewart, and Hannah Rubenstein, *A Speaker's Guidebook: Text and Reference* (Boston: Bedford/St. Martin's, 2004), chap. 6.

3. Ibid., p. 88.

4. Ibid., pp. 96–99.

5. *Spectra,* IX (December 1973), n.p.

6. George Kennedy (trans.), *Aristotle, On Rhetoric* (New York: Oxford, 1991), p. 181.

7. Jane Blankenship, *A Sense of Style* (Belmont, CA: Dickenson, 1968), p. 12.

8. Ibid., p. 41.

9. Karyn Rybacki and Donald Rybacki, *Communication Criticism: Approaches and Genres* (Belmont, CA: Wadsworth, 1991), p. 40.

Appendix

1. Stanley Seashore, *Group Cohesiveness in the Industrial Work Group* (Ann Arbor: University of Michigan Institute for Social Research, 1954).

2. Dean C. Barnlund and Franklyn S. Haiman, *The Dynamics of Discussion* (Boston: Houghton Mifflin, 1960), pp. 401–04.

Chapter 1

Brilhart, John K., and Gloria J. Galanes. *Effective Group Discussion.* 11th ed. New York: McGraw-Hill, 2004.

Keyton, Joann. "Relational Communication in Groups." In *The Handbook of Group Communication Theory & Research,* ed. Lawrence R. Frey. Thousand Oaks, CA: Sage, 1999, pp. 192–224.

Chapter 2

Fisher, Aubrey, and Donald Ellis. *Small Group Decision Making: Communication and the Group Process.* 4th ed. New York: McGraw-Hill, 1994.

Von Bertalanffy, Ludwig. *General Systems Theory: Foundations, Development, Applications.* New York: Braziller, 1968.

Chapter 3

Brilhart, John K., and Gloria J. Galanes. *Effective Group Discussion.* 11th ed. New York: McGraw-Hill, 2004, chaps. 3 and 5.

Cathcart, Robert S.; Larry A. Samovar; and Linda Henman, eds. *Small Group Communication: Theory & Practice.* 7th ed. Madison, WI: Brown & Benchmark, 1996, sections 5 and 6.

Ellis, Donald G., and Aubrey B. Fisher. *Small Group Decision Making,* 4th ed. New York: McGraw-Hill, 1994, chap. 4.

Steil, Lyman K., and Larry Barker. *Effective Listening: Key to Your Success.* Reading, MA: Addison-Wesley, 1983.

Watzlawick, Paul; Janet A. Beavin; and Don D. Jackson. *The Pragmatics of Human Communication.* New York: Norton, 1967.

Chapter 4

Anderson, Peter A. "Nonverbal Communication in the Small Group. " In *Small Group Communication: A Reader.* 6th ed., eds. Robert S. Cathcart and Larry A. Samovar. Dubuque, IA: Wm. C. Brown, 1992, pp. 272–86.

Brilhart, John K., and Gloria J. Galanes. *Effective Group Discussion.* 11th ed. New York: McGraw-Hill, 2004, chaps. 3, 4, and 5.

Burgoon, Judee K. "Spatial Relationships in Small Groups." In *Small Group Communication: Theory & Practice.* 7th ed., eds. Robert S. Cathcart, Larry A. Samovar, and Linda Henman. Madison, WI: Brown & Benchmark, 1996, pp. 241–53.

Ketrow, Sandra. "Nonverbal Aspects of Group Communication." In *The Handbook of Group Communication Theory & Research,* ed. Lawrence R. Frey. Thousand Oaks, CA: Sage, 1999, pp. 251–87.

Chapter 5

Browne, M. Neil, and Stuart M. Keeley. *Asking the Right Questions: A Guide to Critical Thinking.* 5th ed. Englewood Cliffs, NJ: Prentice Hall, 1998.

Buzan, Tony, with Barry Buzan. *The Mind Map® Book.* New York: Plume, 1996.

Jarboe, Susan. "Group Communication and Creativity Processes." And Keyton, Joann. "Relational Communication in Groups." In *The Handbook of Group Communication Theory & Research,* ed. Lawrence R. Frey. Thousand Oaks, CA: Sage, 1999.

Nijstad, Bernard A., and Paul B. Paulus. "Group Creativity: Common Themes and Future Directions." In *Group Creativity: Innovation through Collaboration,* eds. Paul B. Paulus and Bernard A. Nijstad. New York: Oxford University Press, 2003, pp. 326–39.

Sunwolf. "Getting to 'GroupAha!' Provoking Creative Processes in Task Groups." In *The Handbook of Group Communication Theory and Research,* ed. Lawrence R. Frey. Thousand Oaks, CA: Sage, 1999.

Chapter 6

Broome, Benjamin J., and Luann Fulbright. "A Multistage Influence Model of Barriers to Group Problem Solving: A Participant-Generated Agenda for Small Group Research." *Small Group Research* 26 (February 1995), pp. 25–55.

Dewey, John. *How We Think.* Boston: D.C. Heath, 1910.

Gouran, Dennis S., and Randy Y. Hirokawa. "Effective Decision Making and Problem Solving in Groups: A Functional Perspective." In *Small Group Communication: Theory and Practice.* 8th ed., eds. Randy Y. Hirokawa, Robert S. Cathcart, Larry A. Samovar, and Linda D. Henman. Los Angeles: Roxbury Publishing Co., 2003, pp. 27–38.

Larson, Carl E., and Frank M. J. LaFasto. *TeamWork: What Must Go Right, What Can Go Wrong.* Newbury Park, CA: Sage, 1989.

McGrath, Joseph E., and Andrea B. Hollingshead. *Groups Interacting with Technology.* Thousand Oaks, CA: Sage, 1994.

Chapter 7

Anderson, Carolyn N.; Bruce L. Riddle; and Matthew M. Martin. "Socialization Processes in Groups." In *The Handbook of Group Communication Theory &*

Research, ed. Lawrence R. Frey. Thousand Oaks, CA: Sage, 1999, pp. 139–66.

Bormann, Ernest G. *Discussion and Group Methods: Theory and Practice.* 2nd ed. New York: Harper & Row, 1975, chaps. 8 and 9.

Brilhart, John K., and Gloria J. Galanes. *Effective Group Discussion.* 11th ed. New York: McGraw-Hill, 2004, chap. 7.

Ellis, Donald G., and B. Aubrey Fisher. *Small Group Decision Making.* 4th ed. New York: McGraw-Hill, 1994, chaps. 5 and 8.

Chapter 8

Bales, Robert Freed, and Stephen P. Cohen. *SYMLOG: A System for the Multiple-Level Observation of Groups.* New York: Free Press, 1979.

Hecht, Michael L.; Mary Jane Collier; and Sidney A. Ribeau. *African American Communication: Ethnic Identity and Cultural Interpretation,* vol. 2. Language and Language Behaviors series, Newbury Park, CA: Sage Publications, 1993, especially chap. 3.

Hicks, Rick, and Kathy Hicks. *Boomers, Xers, and Other Strangers: Understanding the Generational Differences that Divide Us.* Wheaton, IL: Tyndale House Publishers, 1999.

Kolb, David. *Experiential Learning: Experience as the Source of Learning and Development.* Englewood Cliffs, NJ: Prentice Hall, 1984.

Kroeger, Otto, with Janet A. Thuesen. *Type Talk at Work: How the 16 Personality Types Determine Your Success on the Job.* New York: Dell Publishing, 1992.

Reich, Nina M., and Julia T. Wood. "Sex, Gender and Communication in Small Groups." In *Small Group Communication: Theory and Practice,* 8th ed., eds. Randy Y. Hirokawa, Robert S. Cathcart, Larry A. Samovar, and Linda D. Henman. Los Angeles: Roxbury Publishing Co., 2003, pp. 218–29.

Samovar, Larry A., and Richard E. Porter. *Communication Between Cultures,* 4th ed. Belmont, CA: Wadsworth, 2001, in particular chap. 3, "Cultural Diversity in Perception: Alternative Views of Reality," pp. 52–88.

Tannen, Deborah. *You Just Don't Understand: Women and Men in Conversation.* New York: Ballantine Books, 1990.

Chapter 9

Fisher, Roger, and Scott Brown. *Getting Together: Building a Relationship That Gets to Yes.* Boston: Houghton Mifflin, 1988.

Fisher, Roger, and William Ury. *Getting to Yes: Negotiating Agreement Without Giving In.* New York: Penguin Books, 1983.

Janis, Irving L. *Groupthink: Psychological Studies of Policy Decisions and Fiascoes.* 2nd ed. Boston: Houghton Mifflin, 1983.

Meyers, Renee, and Dale Brashers. "Influence Processes in Group Interaction." In *The Handbook of Group Communication Theory and Research,* ed. Lawrence Frey. Thousand Oaks, CA: Sage, 1999, pp. 288–312.

Thomas, Kenneth W. "Conflict and Conflict Management." In *Handbook of Industrial and Organizational Psychology,* ed. Marvin Dinette. Chicago: Rand McNally, 1976.

Chapter 10

Brilhart, John K., and Gloria J. Galanes. *Effective Group Discussion.* 11th ed. New York, McGraw-Hill, 2004, chaps. 9 and 10.

Galanes, Gloria J. "In Their Own Words: An Exploratory Study of Bona Fide Group Leaders," *Small Group Research* 34 (December 2003), pp. 741–70.

Hirokawa, Randy Y., Robert S. Cathcart, Larry A. Samovar, and Linda D. Henman. *Small Group Communication: Theory and Practice, An Anthology,* 8th ed. Los Angeles: Roxbury, 2003, section 7, pp. 169–213.

LaFasto, Frank, and Carl Larson. *When Teams Work Best: 6000 Team Members and Leaders Tell What It Takes to Succeed.* Thousand Oaks, CA: Sage, 2001, particularly section 4, pp. 97–154.

Robert, Henry M. *Robert's Rules of Order Revised.* Glenview, IL: Scott, Foresman, 1981.

Tropman, John E. *Making Meetings Work: Achieving High Quality Group Decisions,* Thousand Oaks, CA: Sage, 1996.

Chapter 11

Griffin, Cindy. *Invitation to Public Speaking.* Belmont, CA: Thomson Wadsworth, 2004.

Lucas, Stephen. *The Art of Public Speaking.* New York: McGraw-Hill, 1998.

O'Hair, Dan; Rob Stewart; and Hannah Rubenstein. *A Speaker's Guidebook: Text and Reference.* Boston: Bedford/St. Martin's, 2004.

Rybacki, Karyn, and Donald Rybacki. *Communication Criticism: Approaches and Genres.* Belmont, CA: Wadsworth, 1991.